THE HARBRACE ANTHOLOGY OF POETRY

THIRD EDITION

SENIOR EDITORS

Jon C. Stott, emeritus, University of Alberta
Raymond E. Jones, University of Alberta
Rick Bowers, University of Alberta

CONTRIBUTING EDITORS

William Connor, University of Alberta
Sara Marie Jones, University of Western Ontario
Glennis Stephenson, Sterling University
Bruce Stovel, University of Alberta

NELSON

™

THOMSON LEARNING

Australia • Canada • Mexico • Singapore • Spain • United Kingdom • United States

NELSON

THOMSON LEARNING ™

The Harbrace Anthology of Poetry
Third Edition

by Jon C. Stott, Raymond E. Jones,
and Rick Bowers

Editorial Director and Publisher:
Evelyn Veitch

Acquisitions Editor:
Anne Williams

Marketing Manager:
Cara Yarzab

Developmental Editors:
Shefali Mehta and
Martina van de Velde

Production Editor:
Gil Adamson

Production Coordinators:
Hedy Sellers and Cheri Westra

Copy Editor/Proofreader:
Faith Gildenhuys

Proofreader:
Mary Dickie

Creative Director:
Angela Cluer

Cover and Interior Design:
The Brookview Group Inc.

Cover Image:
The Illuminated Tree by Brian
Kipping. Oil on wood, 8.25 by
8.25". Copyright 1992 Brian
Kipping. Reproduced with
permission of the artist and Bau-Xi
Gallery, Toronto.

Compositor:
Carolyn Sebestyen

Printer:
Transcontinental Printing Inc.

**National Library of Canada
Cataloguing in Publication Data**

Main entry under title:

The Harbrace anthology of poetry

3rd ed.
Includes bibliographical references
and indexes.
ISBN 0-7747-3726-3

1. English poetry. 2. American
poetry. 3. Canadian poetry
(English).* 4. College readers. I.
Stott, Jon C., 1939- . II. Jones,
Raymond E. III. Bowers, Rick.

PN6101.H37 2001   821.008
C2001-930672-5

PREFACE

"We imagine ourselves, we create ourselves, we touch ourselves into being with words, words that are important to us," writes Native North American author Gerald Vizenor. One means by which we imagine or create ourselves is through the reading of literature.

The Harbrace Anthology of Poetry uses three approaches to encourage its readers in this activity. First, it presents significant and representative works from the increasingly widening canon of literature in English. Second, it provides strategies to assist readers in their appreciation of works of literature. Third, by introducing readers to the language of literature, both simple and complex, and by suggesting methods for articulating responses, it provides opportunities to explore literature and to respond to language in its rich and varied forms.

Although no anthology can include all of its readers' favourite works, the editors have attempted to make their selections as varied and diverse as possible. Thus, The Harbrace Anthology of Poetry offers many contemporary poems, by men and women alike, from a variety of cultures and backgrounds, in addition to many of those works that have always formed an integral part of the accepted canon of literature in English. It also includes a large sampling of English-Canadian texts in the belief that Canadian students should have the opportunity to experience the major works of their literary tradition both on their own terms and within the larger context of literature written in English.

Individual works in The Harbrace Anthology of Poetry mirror the diversity of backgrounds and interests of Canadian students as well as reflecting an expanded canon. The poems reveal many of the characteristic themes and artistic techniques of their authors; they also reflect the cultural and social contexts in which they were written. In particular, they embody, as the eighteenth-century poet Alexander Pope observed, "what oft was thought but ne'er so well expressed." Most readers of this anthology will find its works speaking directly to them and addressing their most deeply felt concerns.

The Harbrace Anthology of Poetry presents selections that span eleven hundred years. Poems are presented in chronological order according to the birth dates of their authors. Following a selection, its date of publication is printed in parentheses on the right; when it differs significantly and is known, the date of composition appears in parentheses on the left. Such an organizational pattern, based on chronology rather than on pedagogical or theoretical concerns, invites a broad range of responses to a work, unencumbered by artificial or purely technical groupings based on content or theme. It does, of course, implicitly suggest a historical continuity in literature: that works from a specific period often have technical and thematic similarities; and that earlier works and authors can influence later ones.

The book's Introduction considers the reading of literature both as a personal, necessary lifelong activity and as a discipline. It explores how reading poems allows individuals to understand their own lives and responses to literature in relation to those of other people. It also demonstrates how readers can engage more deeply with a text, experiencing it more fully and relating it more completely to their own lives.

The introduction to the genre focuses directly on the conventions of poetry, using examples presented in *The Harbrace Anthology of Poetry*. Discussions of individual characteristics are intended not to offer explanations or explications, but to indicate ways in which authors have used the various elements of the genre. For the reader, an awareness of these characteristics may assist in engagement with the text and lead to a broader range of responses.

Each group of poems by the same author is prefaced by a brief headnote establishing a biographical and literary context. The headnote may also touch on technique or theme. Explanatory footnotes identify historical, fictional, and mythological personages; literary and artistic works; real and fictional places; and terms not usually found in standard dictionaries. This material provides resources to assist readers in the personal creation of meaning — not to impose a critical viewpoint or to force interpretation in a specific, narrow direction.

Reading literature invites writing about it. The chapter entitled "Writing Essays about Literature" explores some of the challenges that writing about literature poses, without prescribing a recipe or rigid format for writing. It offers constructive suggestions to assist readers and writers in articulating responses — intellectual, aesthetic, or emotional — to poems and other works of literature.

The Glossary offers definitions of key terms, providing for readers both an awareness of essential concepts and a standard vocabulary for use in discussing literature.

ACKNOWLEDGEMENTS

The compilation of this anthology was a co-operative venture of the seven colleagues whose names appear on the title page; however, no book, even one developed by seven people, is ever created in a vacuum. During the planning, compiling, writing, and editing stages of *The Harbrace Anthology of Poetry*, many people offered suggestions and made valuable comments. We wish to acknowledge the contributions and suggestions of reviewers from universities across Canada.

As well, we thank Anne Williams, Martina van de Velde, Shefali Mehta, Gil Adamson, Faith Gildenhuys, and Cindy Howard. These people have made this a better anthology; the responsibility for its limitations is our own.

A Note from the Publisher

Thank you for selecting *The Harbrace Anthology of Poetry*, Third Edition, edited by Jon C. Stott, Raymond E. Jones, and Rick Bowers. The editors and publisher have devoted considerable time and care to the development of this book. We appreciate your recognition of this effort and accomplishment.

A Note to the Reader

We would like to draw your attention to two elements of this text:

1. *Dates at the end of poems:* One or two dates follow each poem in the poetry section. The date on the left is the date of the poem's original composition, and the date on the right is the date of the poem's first publication. Where the date of the poem's creation is unknown or where it is the same as the date of the poem's first publication, the date on the left has been omitted.

2. *Stanza continuation symbol (⟶):* We have introduced a unique feature in the poetry section of this text. Because stanzas often flow onto a new page, it is sometimes difficult for the reader to establish whether a stanza ends at the bottom of the page or continues on the next page. Stanza breaks often have significant implications for the interpretation of poems. To avoid confusion about where stanzas end or continue, we have placed the symbol " ⟶ " below the last line on a page to indicate that a stanza continues on the next page. We hope this will assist your reading of the poetry.

CONTENTS

INTRODUCTION

"Part of the beauty of all literature," commented novelist and short story writer F. Scott Fitzgerald, is that "you discover that your longings are universal longings, that you're not lonely and isolated from anyone. You belong." Sharing experience through the creation and reception of stories, poems, and plays is a very old, basic, and necessary human activity, as necessary to human existence as food, shelter, and clothing. The literary critic Northrop Frye further emphasized the importance of literature, observing that "whenever a society is reduced to the barest primary requirements of food and sex and shelter, the arts, including poetry, stand out sharply in relief as ranking with those primary requirements." The need to bring order, through language and stories, to human experience seems to be fundamental to all societies and cultures.

While some literature may simply entertain or allow escape from everyday lives, the works that ultimately stay with their readers are those that challenge, engage, or make demands. Well-crafted literature invites its readers to laugh, to cry, to wonder, to analyze, to explore, to understand.

Throughout our lives, we seek to understand ourselves, our emotions, our experiences, and our relationships with others. We also attempt to define our connections to larger social and cultural institutions. One way that we can do so is through literature, for works of literature are the records of individual response to the world in which we live.

Because of our own experiences, we are able to understand the self-doubts and uncertainties expressed in T.S. Eliot's "The Love Song of J. Alfred Prufrock," the wonder of first love experienced by Ferdinand and Miranda in William Shakespeare's *The Tempest*, the disillusionment and disappointment of returning to a family home after a prolonged absence in Greg Hollingshead's "The Naked Man," and the anguish of Phyllis Webb's "Treblinka Gas Chamber." The specific experiences may be different from our own, but we recognize similarities in the thoughts and emotions of the characters; examination and reflection may lead to clearer insights into our own lives.

Because works of literature are often demanding, they offer great rewards. Readers come to fuller awareness of themselves and others. They discover both the uniqueness and the universality of human experience; they explore both their own world and worlds they may never otherwise see. Through critical response to literature, readers question a work, examine their relationship to the author, consider the author's role, and develop an appreciation of the work, both on its own terms and as an expression of the author's vision of life. Readers may also explore a work in the context of its times, whether social, historical, or ideological.

Until fairly recently, much of the literature studied in English courses was chosen from a list of works deemed important by a majority of critics and scholars, a list referred to as the canon of English literature. Like most of these

1

critics and scholars, most of the writers were white, male, and British or of British descent. The list usually began with the anonymous creator of the Anglo-Saxon epic "Beowulf" and ended with such earlier twentieth-century writers as T.S. Eliot, W.H. Auden, and Dylan Thomas. Because it included very few works by women, members of ethnic minorities, or writers from the British colonies, however, it could not be said to reflect the diversity of writing in English.

The past 30 years have seen a remarkable change in our society as a whole: the recognition of the equal place of all people in it, regardless of gender or ethnic origin. As a consequence, many literary scholars and critics have vigorously sought to expand the canon so that it speaks to everyone. They have demanded the inclusion of the many voices whose stories, poems, and dramas are worthy of study, both on their own merits and because of the insights they offer into a very large segment of the population of the English-speaking world. Such critics have argued that literature should certainly present universal human concerns but should also help readers understand how gender, cultural background, and social position influence responses to life. The works in this anthology reflect this expanded canon.

Reading and reflecting on works of literature reveal human similarities as well as differences. Aphra Behn's drama *The Rover* makes us aware of the position of women in the male-dominated upper-class English society of the late seventeenth century. Tennessee Williams's *Cat on a Hot Tin Roof* presents intense family conflicts as these take place within the culture of the rural American south in the middle of the twentieth century. The poetry of Oodgeroo Noonuccal (Kath Walker) reveals a modern Australian aboriginal woman examining her people's past and its troubled relationships with both government and newcomers.

Readers who come actively to such works with an open, questioning mind will be able to join with their authors in making explicit the implicit. They will appreciate that an author has used language connotatively, choosing words that, in addition to their dictionary meanings, suggest a range of emotions, ideas, or associations. They will recognize the symbolic nature of actions, characters, and objects. As the German literary critic Wolfgang Iser has commented, literary texts are incomplete; they contain gaps that readers fill in or bridge to create meaning. Readers anticipate, make inferences, draw conclusions; in short, they actively work with the language of a piece of literature to arrive at meaning.

Reading for meaning is a very personal act. It is not simply a matter of paraphrasing or summarizing a story or play, of transforming poetry into prose, or of examining literary technique or metaphorical language. Each reader is unique and will, therefore, respond differently — perhaps slightly, perhaps dramatically — to a work. A Dubliner will no doubt react differently to James Joyce's "Araby" than will a Winnipegger; a man about to retire will react differently to Shakespeare's *The Tempest* than will a young woman who has just left home for first-year college or university; a woman will react differently to Margaret Atwood's "The Resplendent Quetzal" than will a man. People who have read widely in each of these three authors or who have a well-developed knowledge of literature would likely have a different and broader interpretation of these three works than someone who seldom reads. Readers draw on personal experience, knowledge, and awareness of both specific literature and literary techniques to appreciate and interpret a literary work.

There is no one simple process for interpreting literature; different readers develop different approaches, some of which will be more useful for some works than for others. That said, interpretation of a literary work begins with the words of the text themselves. Readers question the choice and arrangement of details and ponder their significance. Such active inquiry may commence on reading the title or during a first reading. Individual interpretation will change with each rereading as readers observe more details, acquire more information about them, and perceive new relationships among them.

Readers bring their own experiences to their interpretation of literature. Basing interpretation on the words of the text, they can compare and contrast their own responses to life with those of authors and characters. Readers who have had intense family conflicts will be able to make inferences about the domestic arguments in Eudora Welty's "Why I Live at the P.O." Reciprocally, interpretation of literature can enrich experiences of life. Younger readers will not have had the experiences of the middle-aged women in Jane Rule's "Inland Passage," but a reading of that story may bring empathy for problems different from theirs. Recalling personal experience while reading a work for the first time can assist in its interpretation.

Readers also bring considerable literary experience to their reading of literature: an understanding of the ways in which authors use language and the general patterns of the major literary genres (poetry, drama, and fiction), awareness of important themes, and, frequently, familiarity with other works by the same writer. For example, knowledge of Shakespeare's use of blank verse, his creation of patterns of imagery, and the structure of his earlier comedies will make a study of *The Tempest* more rewarding. Reflection on the myths surrounding men and women will aid in the interpretation of Adrienne Rich's "Diving into the Wreck." Readers draw on what they already know and on critical literature to expand their interpretation of a literary work.

While readers bring considerable knowledge and experience to a literary work, they must also be conscious of the creative intelligence behind the selection and arrangement of its elements. General techniques and genre characteristics, as well as cultural or other forces at play during the writing, may influence some of the selection and arrangement, but most choices arise from the author's purpose in writing the work. Although readers may not find this purpose apparent on first reading, speculation on purpose, based on attention to details and their sequence, may reveal potentially deeper meanings in a work.

Understanding is enhanced as readers acquire more relevant background information and apply it to the text. Knowledge of the actual people and literary or mythological characters mentioned in the text, of allusions to historical events and episodes in other works, and of geographical or architectural settings will clarify their function in a work. In "Fogbound in Avalon," for example, Annie, the narrator, reads a magazine article about the painter Edvard Munch. Examining that artist's works may reveal a clearer picture of Annie's state of mind.

Literary works often reflect events and conflicts in the lives of their authors; awareness of such personal details can enhance a reader's understanding of how and why authors have written as they have. For example, James Joyce, in "Araby," William Wordsworth, in "Lines Composed a Few Miles Above Tintern Abbey," and Amy Tan, in "Two Kinds," drew on facts from their own lives. What is perhaps most interesting is the way in which an author has taken such raw materials of life and shaped them to meet the needs of the work.

Literary works are also products of the times in which they were written, for nearly all writers have been sensitive to and influenced by the literary, intellectual, political, and social forces around them. Ernest Hemingway's attitude toward the rejection by many of traditional moral and religious values during and after World War I helps to explain the actions of the two waiters and the elderly man in "A Clean, Well-Lighted Place." Familiarity with Margaret Atwood's musings on being a woman writer will enrich interpretations of her poetry and such short stories as "The Resplendent Quetzal."

Finally, readers should remember that just as it is impossible to understand completely another person or even oneself, so there is no such thing as a final, complete, or totally correct interpretation of a work of literature. To successive readings of a work readers bring different frames of mind, other personal experiences, new literary or other factual knowledge, and greater familiarity with the work. Thus, with each reading, fuller, more rewarding, and potentially new interpretations are possible.

To assist readers in the creation of meaning, the introductions to the three genres in this anthology — poetry, drama, and short stories — discuss technical aspects of literary works. Headnotes and footnotes provide information about authors and their works and about names, places, and obscure terms mentioned in the texts. The Glossary defines terms frequently used in discussing literature.

Critical response to literature often involves writing about poems, stories, and dramas. Through writing, readers explore the parts and the whole of a work, examine their previous interpretations and test their validity, evaluate the significance of relationships among parts of a work, and create new meanings. Of course, new interpretations may not be final ones; indeed, they may be modified several times during the writing process. Exploration of apparently contradictory information may provide fresh insights into a work. If, in creating an interpretation, the writer has based the statements on the text, has provided evidence and not ignored contradictory evidence, and has argued logically and clearly, then the interpretation is valid. For those seeking assistance in the writing of interpretive essays, the chapter entitled "Writing Essays about Literature" offers a number of suggestions and guidelines.

What are the rewards of becoming active readers and interpreters? An answer can be found by returning to this introduction's opening discussion of essential human needs. Poems, plays, and short stories are artistic and articulate responses to life that offer emotional, intellectual, and imaginative nourishment to their readers. Anthologies such as this provide exposure to literature that enhances the readers' knowledge of themselves and the world outside of themselves. Such experiences can lead to self-discovery and a lifelong love of reading.

POETRY

INTRODUCTION

DEFINING POETRY

No one can state definitely how poetry began, but we know that it existed as an oral medium long before writing developed. Perhaps it originated in primitive religious rituals; people probably used rhythmical, repetitive chants to placate angry gods, to beseech them for success in the hunt or in battle, or to honour them for food and victories received. Furthermore, the rhythm of these chants probably exercised an almost hypnotic power, arousing the appropriate feelings of awe or fear in those who listened. Even today, poetry continues to arouse and express religious feelings, for it is prominent in the sacred texts and hymns of many religions.

Poetry, however, has served many other purposes. It instilled pride in nations, celebrating in the lofty language of epics the great deeds of their heroes. Poetry also became a major feature of important public ceremonies, such as coronations, inaugurations, and victory celebrations. Poetry was not, of course, limited to official and public events. Primarily in the form of **ballads** and other songs, poetry has entertained and expressed the feelings of ordinary people, the "folk." As well, the development of a tradition of writing poetry, either instead of or in addition to reciting it, allowed poetry to serve even more functions because it was now available whenever anyone wanted to read it, and not only when a bard recited it. Poetry could, among other things, entertain and inform in printed collections, express gratitude in dedications to books, celebrate passion in love letters, and honour the memory of the dead on monuments and tombstones. In short, throughout history, whenever people have wanted to give elevated verbal expression to deeds or ideas, whenever they have wanted to make memorable their thoughts, whenever they have wanted to convey their feelings, they have turned to poetry.

Poetry was once a major form of entertainment, providing stories, jokes, descriptions, and reflections. Novels, movies, and television have now replaced many of its storytelling functions, but poetry is everywhere in the modern world. Parents continue to recite it to their children, who delight in the rollicking metres of nursery rhymes. Teenagers and adults who listen to music often listen to poetry, which exists in the lyrics of many popular songs. They also meet poetry in commercials on television and radio, for advertisers rely on its ability to linger in the memory when they devise slogans to sell products. People still mark special occasions with it, expressing their feelings through greeting-card verse that ranges in mood from the sentimental to the humorously bawdy. Of course, numerous magazines still include poetry, and book publishers prominently display it in their catalogues. What is more, in an age that often demands elaborate spectacles in its public entertainments, poetry readings enjoy remarkable popularity.

Defining poetry, however, is like wrestling with Proteus: just when we think we have pinned it into submission, it changes shape, like the ancient Greek god, and eludes us. Poetry, that is, is so varied in form and content that comprehensive definitions always seem inadequate. Nevertheless, some of the most accomplished poets have tried to identify the essence of their art. Many have emphasized the emotional and intellectual depth of poetry. William Wordsworth said that "poetry is the spontaneous overflow of powerful feelings" and that "poetry is the breath and finer spirit of all knowledge. . . ." Emily Dickinson emphasized emotional response: "If I read a book and it makes my whole body so cold no fire can ever warm me I know that is poetry. If I feel physically as if the top of my head were taken off, I know that is poetry." Percy Bysshe Shelley defined poetry as "the record of the best and happiest moments of the happiest and best minds." Similarly, Matthew Arnold declared: "Poetry is simply the most beautiful, impressive and wisely effective mode of saying things, and hence its importance." Twentieth-century poets have given their own cast to such ideas. Wallace Stevens stressed the metaphysical: "Poetry is a search for the inexplicable." Adrienne Rich has emphasized poetry's power, its ability to condense and communicate significant meaning: "Poetry is above all a concentration of the *power* of language, which is the power of our ultimate relationship to everything in the universe. It is as if forces we can lay claim to in no other way, [sic] become present to us in sensuous form." Robert Frost was more colourful: "Poetry is a way of taking life by the throat." The Canadian poet Irving Layton has described it as a way of bridging the gap between mundane reality and the world of imagination, a process that creates a separate world: "Mercifully, all poetry, in the final analysis, is about poetry itself; creating through its myriad forms a world in which the elements of reality are sundered; are, as it were, preserved for a time in suspension."

Instead of defining poetry through its connections to feelings, ideas, and actions, however, some writers have tried to look at the aesthetic and technical elements of the craft. Edgar Allan Poe called poetry *"the Rhythmical Creation of Beauty."* Samuel Taylor Coleridge avoided both the emphasis on refined feelings or ideas and the insistence on beauty when he stressed verbal craftsmanship in this equation: "poetry = the best words in their best order." Throughout the twentieth century, writers have returned to this concept of craftsmanship in their definitions. Dylan Thomas, for instance, described the task of creating poetry as "constructing a formally watertight compartment of words." Frost defined poetry even more simply as "a performance in words." Wallace Stevens probably went as far as possible in dissociating the poet's task from that described in definitions stressing ethical thought, declaring: "Poetry is poetry, and one's objective as a poet is to achieve poetry precisely as one's objective in music is to achieve music."

The precise nature of the poetic achievement is, as these disparate definitions suggest, very much open to debate. Poetry does not seem to depend upon content: poems may be about beauty or ugliness, refined feelings or base ones, matters of perpetual importance or of transient interest. Neither is any single technical feature, such as rhyme, rhythm, or division into lines with ragged right margins, the determinant: it is possible for a good poem to exhibit none of these features. Probably the best we can do is to describe poetry as a concentrated form of literary expression. Poetry employs evocative, often rhythmical language that describes or comments on ideas and experiences and that evokes feelings about them. In poetry the manner of expression is as important as the matter.

POETRY AND LITERARY READING

Because each word in a poem is charged with meaning and feeling to a degree rarely possible in prose, reading poetry may require patience. One reading is simply not sufficient to allow readers to engage with the text, to sense all of its intellectual, emotional, and aesthetic resources. Literary reading demands rereading. As the general Introduction makes clear, no single reading procedure is adequate in all circumstances. In fact, theorists do not agree on how poems work and how they should be read. Competing theories emphasize different elements of the relationships among poet, reader, and poem. Nevertheless, readers who are aware of the various biographical, historical, and theoretical contexts may find their reading of a poem more meaningful and, therefore, more enjoyable.

Understanding biographical and cultural contexts may at first seem to be a separate area of study, but these contexts can be vital in constructing meaning. Many critics and theorists, that is, insist that poems do not exist in isolation from the poets who wrote them or apart from the societies in which the poets lived. Personal feelings and experiences shape what poets write and how they write. In turn, their feelings and experiences, if not directly shaped by cultural situations, have often been influenced by the social and moral assumptions of their societies. No one argues that readers must know everything about a poet's life to enjoy a poem. Many critics do suggest, however, that an understanding of a poet's life and artistic ideas may provide information that will help readers to understand the mind and verbal habits of the poet and thus better to construct meaning when reading poetry. The poet's gender and attitudes to gender, for example, may be crucial. The American poet Adrienne Rich says, "I had been taught that poetry should be 'universal,' which meant, of course, nonfemale." In her own poems, therefore, she seeks to express her feelings as a female whose views and experiences may be distinct from those previously celebrated as universal.

Similarly, some critics claim that an understanding of cultural history is sometimes essential. First, literary conventions and habits of expression change from generation to generation; understanding these may help in the understanding of works written during an earlier period. Second, what people of any age write reflects their connection to the dominant culture of their time. Literature may thus openly express attitudes officially sanctioned by a given society. This is the belief of Thomas Carlyle, who saw poetry as a mirror of the spirit of an age: "The history of a nation's poetry is the essence of its history, political, scientific, religious." Of course, as Marxist and other theorists concerned with class and economic factors note, poetry may also seek, often covertly, to subvert the dominant culture. In developing meaning, the contemporary reader may thus require an understanding of the sometimes latent assumptions within a poem.

Many other theorists downplay the significance of such contexts. For some of these, poetry is an artifact, like a Greek vase, that exists separate from the reader and must be understood on its own terms. For others, poetry is more of a tool kit or an Erector set that the reader plays with, constructing and reconstructing meaning. One group argues for the realization of a final meaning inherent in the work; the other argues that no single meaning can be inherent in the work and, instead, stresses the process of reading rather than the results. The more traditional theorists point out that the word *poetry* comes from a Greek root meaning "thing made" and that a poet is a "maker." They see poems as carefully constructed, unified artifacts, and they argue that the reader needs to note the contribution of all of the parts of a work to discover its inherent meaning. For example, some of these theorists argue that a poem's basic structure is a set of binary oppositions, such as life and death or virtue and sin, and that meaning comes when the poem "privileges," or gives approval to, one set of these oppositions. They believe that the reader's task in understanding a poem is to locate the structure of binary oppositions. Those who look at poetry more as the tool kit that the reader uses take differing approaches. Some have extended this notion of binary oppositions, arguing that every literary work actually contains not only oppositions but also contradictions and that, therefore, no poem can have a determinate meaning. They contend that a work "deconstructs" itself, saying two contradictory things at once. Finally, another group of theorists concentrates on the reader's involvement with poems, arguing that the work itself contains no meaning: a poem is simply a series of squiggles on the page until the reader engages with the text and actively creates meaning from it. The reader not only "decodes" individual words — deciding, for example, that the letters *d-o-g* refer to a particular kind of animal — but also, because of previous personal and literary experiences, associates particular ideas and attitudes with each word decoded: when faced with the word *dog*, some readers will envisage a slavering attack beast, whereas others will envisage a friendly lapdog. Although many poems use what Wolfgang Iser calls "response-inviting structures," devices that encourage readers to read in particular ways, these devices cannot possibly limit readers to one single response. Because each person's experiences and associations are different, each will read a given poem differently.

Although the competition between rival theories may suggest to some readers that a poem means anything a given reader thinks it means, all theories imply that literary understanding begins with close attention to words. Many theories stress that poetry is a playful use of language, even in poems about serious matters, and that a playful attitude in reading, an attitude that brings all of a person's associations and experiences to bear on each word, makes it easier to discover or construct meaning.

In truth, few readers are concerned about competing theories when first reading a poem; instead, most readers ordinarily want to construct at least a provisional meaning as soon as possible. Such readers may find some guidelines useful as the basis for beginning a significant reading of a work.

Because poetry is an art that depends upon achieving the maximum effect from each word, readers need to understand both the **denotations**, or dictionary meanings, of words and the **connotations**, or implications, of these words. Some words, that is, carry extra meaning: they have negative or positive associations that may influence interpretation. We may think positively about an adult who is *childlike*, but negatively about one who is *childish*. We may also have different attitudes about speakers who use colloquial language and speakers who consistently use elaborate, formal language. Sensitivity to words and their nuances is an important step in meaningful reading.

Traditionally, readers have also found useful a number of basic questions about the content and form of a poem. The first questions focus on the speaker in the poem: Who is the speaker? To whom is he or she speaking? What are the circumstances? These questions may not be very important in a poem like Tennyson's "The Eagle," but they are crucial considerations in dramatic monologues such as Browning's "The Bishop Orders His Tomb at Saint Praxed's Church," in which an understanding of the speaker's character and the context in which he or she is speaking is necessary to make the poem meaningful. Another question concerns the arrangement of content: How is the poem organized to develop its ideas? The order in which details are presented can influence our attitudes toward them and our understanding of the development of major ideas within the poem. In Browning's "My Last Duchess," the duke's description of the fate of his last wife precedes his discussion of arrangements for a new bride, making him seem especially arrogant, cynical, and brutal. In Sonnet 73, Shakespeare emphasizes both the narrator's age and the brevity of time by arranging images that imply death: he creates a sequence that moves from larger to smaller measures of time, from a season, to a day, to the moment when a fire is dying out.

Readers may also find it useful to ask questions about the technical elements of a poem: How do techniques or elements such as rhythm, sound devices, images, and diction influence our understanding? The purpose of examining techniques is not to catalogue them but to understand their role in shaping our ideas and feelings within the poem as a whole. For example, readers who notice the difference in rhythm in the first and final sections of Marvell's "To His Coy Mistress" can determine how it influences their understanding of the narrator's attitudes toward traditional ideals of courtship and his own growing sense of urgency. Finally, readers often find it useful to consider literary contexts: How does this poem compare to other poems, especially those with similar forms, those from the same period, and those about similar subjects? An understanding of conventions of form or subject matter and of literary "schools" or literary periods enables readers to place the work in a literary and historical context that can be helpful in understanding the poem. Shakespeare's Sonnet 130, "My mistress' eyes are nothing like the sun," for instance, is far more meaningful to readers who understand something of the Petrarchan tradition of love sonnets and have read some English love sonnets by such poets as Wyatt, Surrey, and Constable.

FIGURATIVE LANGUAGE (1): IMAGERY, SIMILE, METAPHOR, CONCEIT

Poetry is a sensual medium. Sound, discussed later, and imagery, the subject of this section, appeal to the senses, stimulating an imaginative body of impressions, feelings, and ideas. These may be new, or they may be familiar, but the sensory appeals of poetry give them an immediacy that directly involves readers.

At its most basic level, **imagery** is language that creates images, or pictures, in the imagination. Some poems, like "The Red Wheelbarrow," by William Carlos Williams, rely almost exclusively on verbal pictures. Most poems, however, use imagery to develop statements about feelings and ideas. The opening section of Wordsworth's "Lines Composed a Few Miles above Tintern Abbey" creates a picture of the scene, describing such things as "These hedge-rows, hardly hedge-rows, little lines / Of sportive wood run wild...." In this way, the narrator impresses on readers the power the setting holds over him as a scene of "beauteous forms." Although the roots of the word suggest a visual element, imagery is not exclusively visual; it frequently makes appeals to touch, taste, and sound. In the final stanza of "To Autumn," for example, Keats describes the "music" of autumn, with such sound images as "Then in a wailful choir the small gnats mourn / Among the river sallows...." In "Dover Beach," Arnold uses sound imagery to convey "The eternal note of sadness": he describes "the grating roar / Of pebbles" flung back and forth by the waves.

Images, like all appeals to the senses, can evoke emotional reactions. Because they can give concrete form to ideas by forcing readers to understand one idea in terms of another, they also can be a medium of intellectual discourse. This linking of objects or ideas is the basis of most figurative language, language that goes beyond the literal denotation of the words by imaginatively extending their meanings.

The most common figures of speech are similes and metaphors. Both tend to give concrete form to abstract ideas or to make the unfamiliar clearer and more forceful by linking it to something familiar. **Simile** expresses similarity between things and always uses such linking terms as *like, as, than,* or *as if.* Keats, in "On First Looking into Chapman's Homer," conveys the magnitude of his feelings of discovery with a simile that connects his reactions upon reading a book to a rarer but more public experience: "Then felt I like some watcher of the skies / When a new planet swims into his ken." In the opening simile of T.S. Eliot's "The Love Song of J. Alfred Prufrock," the narrator provides a clue to his own emotional numbness by saying that "the evening is spread out against the sky / Like a patient etherised upon a table." P.K. Page does much the same thing when she describes the secretaries in "The Stenographers" as being "taut as net curtains / stretched upon frames." **Metaphor** compares by equating things. In Shakespeare's Sonnet 73, the metaphor in which the boughs become "Bare ruin'd choirs" creates a sense of collapse and destruction because it implicitly equates the trees in late autumn and abandoned, ruined churches. In "The Flea," John Donne's narrator uses metaphor as part of his strategy of seduction, aggrandizing the flea: "This flea is you and I, and this / Our marriage bed, and marriage temple is."

Not every comparison is as brief as those just discussed. More elaborate and extended comparisons, whether similes or metaphors, are called **conceits.** The **Petrarchan conceit,** developed by those who followed the example of the Italian Petrarch, the poet who popularized the sonnet form, uses rather conventional extended comparisons, as in Wyatt's "My galley...," which compares the lover to a ship at sea, or Surrey's "Love that doth reign...," which personifies love as a military leader. More original and startling comparisons are called **metaphysical conceits** because they were developed by the so-called **metaphysical poets** of the seventeenth century, who linked physical with metaphysical or spiritual elements in their images. John Donne's "A Valediction: Forbidding Mourning" contains the most famous of these, his comparison of separated lovers to "stiff twin compasses."

FIGURATIVE LANGUAGE (2): PERSONIFICATION, APOSTROPHE, METONYMY, SYNECDOCHE, SYMBOL, MOTIF

Other figurative devices also link ideas. **Personification** gives human qualities to abstractions or to things that do not possess them. Thus, William Wordsworth, in "The world is too much with us," suggests the sensuousness of nature through personification: "This Sea that bares her bosom to the moon." In one of his odes, John Keats personifies an object, an ancient Greek urn, as a "Sylvan historian," suggesting that it can tell much about life. Personification often develops through **apostrophe**, a direct address to a thing or abstraction, as in Shelley's "O wild West Wind, thou breath of Autumn's being" or Donne's "Death be not proud." Apostrophe is not always part of personification because the device also includes direct addresses to an absent or dead person, as in Wordsworth's "Milton! thou shouldst be living at this hour." In either case, it gives immediacy and concreteness to people, events, and ideas.

Two other linking devices are frequently used to condense complex experiences into images. **Metonymy**, or "substitute naming," uses an associated idea to name something. In "London, 1802," for example, Wordsworth talks of "altar, sword, and pen," instead of the clergy, soldiers, and authors, in order to suggest concretely both the people and the function of those people. A related device is **synecdoche**, in which a part stands for the whole, or the whole stands for the part. It is most evident in such expressions as "All hands on deck!" in which *hands* stands for *sailors*, and in the prayer for "daily bread," in which *bread* stands for all food. In Eliot's "Prufrock," synecdoche, evident in the naming of a part instead of the whole crab or lobster, suggests the narrator's lack of a fully developed identity: "I should have been a pair of ragged claws / Scuttling across the floors of silent seas." Synecdoche is most shockingly apparent, however, in the vision of death in Marvell's "To His Coy Mistress," which reduces the woman's morality to sexual organs: "... then worms shall try / That long preserved virginity, / And your quaint honour turn to dust."

The linking device that many readers find most difficult to grasp is **symbolism**. *Symbol* comes from the Greek "to throw together." A symbol throws together objects, people, or actions and a meaning that is not necessarily inherent in them. Symbols fall into two major categories, conventional symbols and contextual symbols. **Conventional symbols** are those that traditionally carry a particular meaning. Sometimes, the symbol is conventional only within a given culture. A cross, for example, means something quite different to Christians in North America than to Buddhists in China. The rose, to cite another example, traditionally suggests love or beauty in Western culture. Such conventional symbols may be the basis of relatively simple ideas: "Gather ye rose-buds while ye may," the opening line of Herrick's "To the Virgins, To Make Much of Time," develops the *carpe diem* ("seize the day") idea of living for the moment because, like the rose, youth and beauty fade. They may also develop more complex and even ambiguous ideas, as in William Blake's "The Sick Rose," in which the rose suggests ideas of love but leaves open to speculation the exact nature of that love and of the worm that destroys it. Not all conventional symbols are limited to a specific culture. Some seem to be universal, having appeared so frequently and for such a long time in the literatures of various cultures that their meanings seem to be natural. These are known as **archetypes**. One such archetype is the description of the sun's movement from sunrise to sunset to symbolize aging in human beings. This archetype appears in such different works as Herrick's "To the Virgins, To Make Much of Time," where it reinforces the idea that youth must live for the moment, and Earle Birney's "Bushed," where it suggests the rapidly approaching death of the trapper.

Readers acquire understanding of conventional symbols by familiarity with a large number of works using them. In Frost's "Stopping by Woods on a Snowy Evening," for example, repetition of the last line, "And miles to go before I sleep," puts such additional stress on both *miles* and *sleep* that these words imply more than they literally say. Readers familiar with other poems that use either a journey or sleep as a symbol can see this poem as using the conventional archetypal symbol of a journey toward death, an additional implication that co-exists with its surface meaning of a journey on a winter's night.

Contextual symbols, however, become symbolic only within the context of a given work; they may not have the same symbolic meaning, or even any symbolic meaning, in a different work. For example, the tiger symbolizes, among other things, fierceness and destructiveness in Blake's "The Tyger," but it symbolizes the repressed dreams of a conventional woman in Adrienne Rich's "Aunt Jennifer's Tigers." Sometimes the accumulation of details creates a contextual symbol, as it does in Shelley's "Ozymandias," in which the ruined statue of the pharaoh gradually becomes a general symbol of mutability and the vanity of human desires. Such contextual symbols are not always obvious: during an initial reading, they may seem to be simply a part of the concrete description or narrative movement of the poem. This is why rereading is important. With each rereading, a poem becomes more familiar, and its details, patterns, and emphases — the elements that create contextual symbols — become more apparent.

With each rereading, as well, the links to other poems and the connecting links within the poem itself become more apparent. Any poem using an archetype, for example, is using an element that occurs in many works. Understanding the archetype in one poem thus helps in understanding others. Archetypes and symbols are not the only recurring elements, of course. Images, characters, objects, settings, situations, or themes may recur in many works; these recurring elements are called **motifs**. The *carpe diem* theme, for example, is a thematic motif, whether or not it is expressed by the archetype of the setting sun. Elements can also be repeated to link the parts of an individual work. For example, Margaret Atwood's "Progressive Insanities of a Pioneer" contains several references to water and to terms associated with measurement and enclosure. Such recurring elements within an individual work, whether recurring words, phrases, images, situations, or themes, are also sometimes called motifs, although they are more generally called **leitmotifs**. Readers who note such recurring devices will be able to respond more completely to the poem, to link together its various parts, to connect the poem to other works and to situations outside the poem itself, and to construct more meaning.

IRONY, PARADOX, OXYMORON, ZEUGMA

Simile, metaphor, symbol, and other devices of figurative language discussed above link images to feelings and ideas, but they do not always forge their links in the way that we may at first expect. Sometimes another device, irony, twists the connections. **Irony** is a discrepancy between appearance and reality, expectation and result, or surface meaning and implied meaning. Traditionally, critics have described three major kinds of irony: dramatic irony, situational irony, and verbal irony. Dramatic irony, a device found more frequently in drama and fiction than in poetry, is the discrepancy between what a character says or does and what the reader knows to be the truth of the situation. Situational irony, which is also inherent in dramatic irony, presents a situation in which the result is the reverse of what a character or speaker expected. Verbal irony reverses the denotation of words so that a given statement actually means the opposite of what it says literally, as when we call "graceful" someone who has just tripped.

Whatever its form, irony is a device that is often integral to the **theme**, the central idea developed by a poem. In "Ozymandias," for example, both verbal irony, the boast that Ozymandias makes about his greatness, and situational irony, the image of a shattered statue upon whose base the boastful words are carved, reverse the pharaoh's intention: instead of celebrating glorious, lasting achievements, both the words and the statue make a moving statement about mutability and the impermanence of human achievement. Similarly, in Margaret Atwood's "Progressive Insanities of a Pioneer," the language of measurement and geometry, normally a sign of logic and control, reverses itself to reveal the mad egocentricity of the pioneer. Unable to recognize nature for what it is, he tries to impose his vision on it and stands "a point / on a sheet of green paper / proclaiming himself the centre." His failure of vision eventually leads to his defeat by the very forces he sought to dominate. Irony can also be a powerful device for political comment and protest. Wilfred Owen deliberately uses the juxtaposition of the title phrase in "*Dulce et Decorum Est*" and the scene of a soldier dying in a gas attack to reverse the wartime propaganda that called it glorious for the young to die for their country.

Two other devices found frequently in poetry depend upon an unusual link of expression and idea. **Paradox** is a statement that seems contradictory on the surface but contains a truth on deeper examination. Among the most famous of paradoxes is Wordsworth's statement that "The Child is father of the Man," a claim that is biologically absurd but psychologically profound: the statement concisely expresses the idea that the experiences of childhood shape adult lives. Paradox often serves to convey complex spiritual and psychological truths, as in Donne's Holy Sonnet XIV ("Batter my heart"), which concludes with a notable and shocking set of paradoxes about the narrator's relationship with God:

> Take me to you, imprison me, for I
> Except you enthral me, never shall be free,
> Nor ever chaste, except you ravish me.

A related device is **oxymoron**, a word whose Greek roots imply "sharp stupidity" or "wise foolishness." Oxymoron contains a contradiction: it links opposites in the surface expression in order to defamiliarize or make unusual the connections we expect. Thus, Milton describes hell as having "darkness visible."

Although found less frequently than paradox and oxymoron, another notable device also twists connections for comical or critical effect. **Zeugma** grammatically links a term to two words, but the linkage is logically appropriate in a different way for each word. One of the most famous examples is in Pope's *The Rape of the Lock*: "Or stain her Honour, or her new Brocade." With its first object, "Honour," the verb "stain" indicates the ruin of a woman's virtue; with its second, "Brocade," it merely points to the soiling of a gown. By linking these two incompatible meanings in one sentence, Pope succinctly and wittily implies that women in high society do not discriminate between realms of morality and fashion, that both are equally trivial, or equally important, to them. Zeugma does not, however, have to be a comic device. In "The Devil's Language," for example, Marilyn Dumont speaks of the mother who "fed you bannock and tea / and syllables." By linking food and language, zeugma here stresses that language is part of nurture and that it thus has both cultural and emotional significance.

LINE LENGTH, METRE, AND RHYTHM

Two things immediately distinguish poetry from prose: the look upon the page and the sound when read aloud. The distinctive look of most poetry comes from its organization into lines. In most English poems written before the twentieth century, the line lengths were dependent upon **metre**. English, with its stressed syllables (indicated by ´) and unstressed syllables (indicated by ˘), naturally creates rhythm, the flow of rising and falling sounds, but poetry organizes rhythm, as prose and common speech do not. Metre, a word derived from the Greek "to measure," measures the organization of repeated stressed and unstressed syllables, giving names to the rhythmic patterns within a poem.

At various times and in various places, different systems of measurement have been used. French poetry, for example, counts only syllables. The same is true of the Japanese haiku, a form sometimes adopted by writers in English: it contains three lines of five, seven, and five syllables, respectively. Anglo-Saxon, or Old English, poetry, on the other hand, is accentual: it measures only the stresses in a given line and does not count the unstressed syllables. Furthermore, it organizes the stresses by placing two in each half, or hemistich, of a line, by having three stresses share an **alliterative** sound, and by separating each half with a **caesura**, or pause. A few poets have tried to use this form with modern English. In "Anglosaxon Street," for example, Earle Birney graphically indicates the hemistiches by using a wide space for each caesura:

Dáwndrízzle ended   dámpness stéams from

blótching brick and   blánk plásterwaste

The most common system for measuring poetry in modern English, however, considers both the **accents** and the number of syllables in a line. The base of the system is the **foot**, a unit consisting of one or more syllables, usually with one stressed. Repetition of the pattern of stressed and unstressed syllables found within a given foot creates a regular **rhythm**, and each of the various regular rhythms has a name based on the pattern within the foot and the number of feet composing the line. Table 1 lists the names and shows the patterns of the metrical feet. The dominant rhythm in a poem will probably be one of the first four patterns: the others are normally variations within a regular rhythm. Table 2 names the various line lengths according to the number of feet in each. A process called **scansion** indicates graphically the metre of a poem. This process requires the marking of all stressed and unstressed syllables and the clear division of feet from each other by means of a vertical line. Scansion graphically shows, for example, that the opening line of Shakespeare's Sonnet 73 is iambic pentameter, a pattern formed from five iambic feet:

Thăt tíme | ŏf yéar | thŏu máyst | ĭn mĕ | bĕhóld

Table 1 The Metrical Feet

Noun	Adjective	Pattern	Example
iamb	iambic	˘ ´	remote
trochee	trochaic	´ ˘	joker
anapest	anapestic	˘ ˘ ´	interrupt
dactyl	dactylic	´ ˘ ˘	heavenly
spondee	spondaic	´ ´	heartbreak
pyrrhic	pyrrhic	˘ ˘	in the
amphibrach	amphibrachic	˘ ´ ˘	soprano
amphimacer (or cretic)	amphimacric	´ ˘ ´	first and last

Table 2 Line Lengths

Number of Feet in Line	Name of Line Length
1	monometer
2	dimeter
3	trimeter
4	tetrameter
5	pentameter
6	hexameter
7	heptameter
8	octameter

Rhythmic Variation

Poets do not always write according to strict metre. They frequently intro-
duce variations within their lines not only to avoid the potential monotony of
a regular metre but also to emphasize particular words or ideas. For example,
in the last line of Sonnet 73, Shakespeare substitutes a spondee for the iamb
in the final foot:

> Tŏ lóve | thăt wéll | whĭch thóu | mŭst léave | ére lóng

This substitution creates three stressed syllables in a row. Generally, a sequence
of stressed syllables slows the movement of a line, whereas a sequence of unac-
cented syllables quickens the flow. Here, the rhythmic flow slows down,
emphasizing these last words, which summarize the idea of the brief time
remaining to the narrator.

While it is common to vary rhythm within lines by using metrical feet that
deviate from the dominant pattern and by adding extra feet or extra syllables
to a line, poets can affect the flow of their lines in other ways. One is by judi-
cious use of the caesura, or pause (indicated in scansion by two vertical lines).
Because the most emphatic positions in any unit of expression (line, phrase,
sentence, paragraph) are first, at the end, and second, at the beginning, the
caesura creates emphasis by increasing the number of these positions. In
Tennyson's "Ulysses," for example, the caesura effectively halts the flow of
the lines to emphasize tedium:

> Hŏw dúll | ĭt ís | tŏ páuse, ‖ tŏ máke | ăn énd.

> Tŏ rúst | unbúrn|ĭsh'd, ‖ nŏt | tŏ shíne | ĭn úse!

In the first line, "pause" immediately precedes a pause, and "end" comes at
the end of the line, the meaning of both words thus being effectively reinforced
by their position. In the second line, the caesura comes in the middle of a
foot, disrupting the regular flow and creating an oral counterpoint to it. Strictly
speaking, that is, metre expresses the division into feet according to the stresses

of syllables, and this line is a perfectly regular iambic line. Dramatic reading of it, however, provides a different sense of how the line flows. If we consider the caesura as creating a pause that divides this line into two units, we would scan this line for reading by marking it as consisting of an iamb, amphibrach, amphimacer, and iamb:

To rŭst | ŭnbúrnish'd, ‖ nót tŏ shíne | ĭn úse!

The dramatic, interpretive rhythm exists simultaneously with the regular metre. The interpretive rhythm insists on a pause, accentuating the contrast between the sedentary state and the active one that follows; the conventional metre pulls the reader forward in expectation of completing the iambic pattern. Interpretive rhythm could also make the contrast between the two parts of the line even more emphatic: when "not to shine" is read as an anapest, the two unaccented syllables quicken the pace, indicating joy, and place an even more meaningful and emphatic stress on *shine*.

In the lines just quoted, Tennyson uses **end-stopped lines**, lines that ter-minate with a natural pause. Such lines are usually indicated by punctuation, which reinforces this pause. Poets often vary the flow of their lines by using run-on lines, or **enjambment** (from the French for "striding over"). Tennyson uses enjambment throughout "Ulysses":

Ĭ cán | nŏt rést | frŏm tráv | ĕl; ‖ Í | wĭll drínk

Lífe tŏ | thĕ lées.

Because of the caesura in the middle of a foot in the first line and the shift to trochee in the first foot of the second line, the key words I, *drink*, *Life*, and *lees* are all accented and are all visually, grammatically, or by strict measure in positions of emphasis, at the beginning or end of a unit. The enjambment, however, creates a variation in the rhythmic flow, linking the last part of the first line to the first part of the second line: although the iambic pentameter pattern is completed with *drink*, the reader cannot pause at the end of the line because the idea is incomplete; instead, the reader must continue until the completion of the idea in the middle of the second line.

Beyond Scansion: Free Verse And Shaped Verse

Not every poem displays a dominant rhythm that can be scanned like those in the preceding examples. Some poems are written in **free verse** or *vers libre*, terms popularized by Ezra Pound, among others. Pound compared the con-ventional patterns of regularly repeated metrical feet to the monotonous beat of a metronome. He argued that the lines of a poem should be free from the conventional system, that, instead, lines should follow the more natural pat-terns evident in spoken language and music. (Incidentally, free verse should not be confused with **blank verse**, a form popular in Elizabethan England, which usually means an unrhymed line of iambic pentameter.) Other writers, however, may organize lines by meaning. In "The Country North of Belleville," for example, Al Purdy intensifies the irony of defeat by placing each stage of the farmers' recognition of futility in a separate line:

> without grandeur or self deception in
>   noble struggle
> of being a fool —

Margaret Atwood is even subtler in her description of the man standing in a field in "Progressive Insanities of a Pioneer":

> with no walls, no borders
> anywhere; the sky no height
> above him, totally un-
> enclosed

She divides the lines to place words suggesting measurement and logical calculation in emphatic positions. Furthermore, she breaks up the word "unenclosed" to emphasize the ironic discrepancy between the pioneer's perception that he is "enclosed," which leads him to shout insanely that he wants out, and the reader's understanding that nothing actually encloses him.

Line length may also graphically reflect meaning. George Herbert's "The Altar" arranges lines to form a picture that represents the central idea of the poem. Lines in such shaped verse convey meaning, but they must be seen on the page to be fully appreciated. Much the same is true of concrete poetry, a form popular in the 1960s and early 1970s. In some concrete poems, however, the lines forming the picture may be letters or other typographical elements that can have no meaning on their own. Meaning exists entirely in the picture as a whole.

RHYME AND STANZA FORM

Many poems, especially those written before the twentieth century, link lines by more than subject matter and rhythm: they use **rhyme**, the repetition of accented vowels and all syllables following the accented vowel. **Single rhymes**, or **masculine rhymes**, repeat only the last syllable of words: *know, go; delight, fight*. **Double rhymes**, also called **feminine rhymes** or **trochaic rhymes**, repeat identical sounds in both an accented syllable and the following unaccented syllable: *kissing, missing; seasons, reasons*. **Triple rhymes**, or **dactylic rhymes**, also occur: *tenderly, slenderly; scornfully, mournfully*. Rhymes most frequently occur as **end rhymes**, in which the rhyming words are at the end of lines. **Internal rhymes** operate within lines, as in this example from "The Rime of the Ancient Mariner": "And every *day*, for food or *play*."

All the examples so far have been **exact rhymes** or **true rhymes**. In some cases, poets use **near rhyme** (also known as **slant**, **off**, **imperfect**, or **oblique** rhyme), a rhyme that approximates rather than exactly repeats a sound: *bridge, hedge; still, wheel; tucker, supper*. Slant rhyme usually depends on similarity of the final consonant, but it can include such imperfect rhymes as *flew* and *boot*, which rhyme the vowel but not the consonant. Another form is **eye rhyme**, or **sight rhyme,** in which words spelled similarly but pronounced differently are treated as rhymes. In some cases, as with Shakespeare's rhyming of *proved* and *loved,* the words may have been pronounced similarly at the time the poem was written. In other cases, such as Coleridge's rhyming of *prow* and *blow* in "The Rime of the Ancient Mariner," the rhymes are purely visual.

Rhyme can be a mnemonic device, something that helps poets, listeners, and readers to remember a work; it is also an important structural device that helps to group lines into meaningful sections. The normal grouping of lines is called the **stanza.** Table 3 provides the general names for stanzas according to the number of lines they contain. Stanzas are infinitely variable, but a number of poetic forms specify the precise number of lines the stanza can contain and the pattern of rhymes, known as the rhyme scheme, that those lines must follow.

Table 3 Names of Stanzas and Line Groupings

Number of Lines	Name
2	couplet
3	tercet (triplet when all three lines rhyme together)
4	quatrain
5	quintet
6	sestet
7	septet
8	octave

Table 4 names and describes the most notable of these fixed forms. We describe rhyme schemes by using a separate letter for each end rhyme. Thus, we indicate a stanza in which the first and fourth lines and the second and third lines rhyme by the formula *a b b a.* Sometimes, however, we must resort to a more complex description because line lengths vary. In these cases, we describe a stanza by indicating its predominant rhythm and by noting with each letter of the rhyme scheme the number of feet in that line. Consider the opening stanza of "Sir Patrick Spens," which we could describe as predominantly iambic with a rhyme scheme of 4a, 3b, 4c, 3b:

The king | sits in | Dumfer | ling toune,　　　　　*a* (4 feet)

Drinking | the blude- | reid wine:　　　　　*b* (3 feet)

"Ŏ whar | will I gét | guid | sailŏr,　　　　　*c* (4 feet)

To sail | this schip | of mine?"　　　　　*b* (3 feet)

This pattern is known as ballad measure; many other patterns also have names, and knowing these can simplify the description.

Stanzas depend upon a few basic patterns in their rhymes. **Couplets** are pairs of rhyming lines: *a a b b*. Heroic couplets are in iambic pentameter. If the idea expressed by the couplet is completed within the compass of the two lines, the couplet is a **closed couplet**. **Triplets** or **tercets** consist of three lines, rhymed or unrhymed. A **quatrain** is any group of four lines, rhymed or unrhymed; it is the most common form in English poetry. A **sestet** is a unit of six lines, whereas an **octave** is one of eight lines.

These last three — the quatrain, the sestet, and the octave — are important terms in describing one of the most pervasive and highly controlled of poetic forms, the **sonnet**. The **Italian** or **Petrarchan sonnet** is a fourteen-line iambic pentameter form usually rhyming *abba abba cdecde* (but the last six lines have many variations in rhyme scheme). The Italian sonnet develops an idea in the octave, and then uses a **volta**, or turn (often signalled by such words as "yet" or "but"), before concluding that idea in the sestet. The **English** or **Shakespearean sonnet** is an iambic pentameter poem rhyming *abab cdcd efef gg*. It consists of three quatrains and a heroic couplet. Its turn of thought occurs in the couplet and must be more compressed and concentrated than that in an Italian sonnet. A Spenserian sonnet is similar, except that it rhymes *abab bcbc cdcd ee*. A fourth variation is the **Miltonic sonnet**. It follows the Italian form, but it does not pause after the octave.

Table 4 Notable Fixed and Complex Forms

Number of Lines in Poem or Stanza	Name and Description
3	TERZA RIMA: tercets of iambic pentameter with linked rhymes (*aba bcb cdc...*)
4	COMMON MEASURE: a quatrain in iambic metre, with the first and third lines having four iambic feet and the second and fourth having three iambic feet (*abcb*)
	BALLAD STANZA: similar to common measure but the four lines can be in any metre, with four metrical feet in the first and third and three in the second and fourth lines (*abcb*)
6	ITALIAN SESTET: six lines of iambic pentameter (*abcabc*)
	SICILIAN SESTET: six lines of iambic pentameter (*ababab*)
	HEROIC SESTET: six lines of iambic pentameter (*ababcc*)
7	RIME ROYAL: seven lines of iambic pentameter (*ababbcc*)
8	OTTAVA RIMA: eight lines of iambic pentameter (*abababcc*)
	ITALIAN OCTAVE: eight lines of iambic pentameter (*abbaabba*)
	SICILIAN OCTAVE: eight lines of iambic pentameter (*ababab ab*)
9	SPENSERIAN STANZA: nine lines rhyming *ababbcbcc* with the first eight in iambic pentameter and the last in iambic hexameter (which is called an Alexandrine)

(continued)

Table 4 Notable Fixed and Complex Forms *(continued)*

Number of Lines in Poem or Stanza	Name and Description
10	ENGLISH (KEATSIAN) ODE: Three ten-line iambic pentameter stanzas, each with the same rhyme scheme (*ababcdecde*)
14	SONNET: fourteen iambic pentameter lines ENGLISH (SHAKESPEAREAN) SONNET: (*abab cdcd efef gg*) SPENSERIAN SONNET (*abab bcbc cdcd ee*) PETRARCHAN (ITALIAN) SONNET (*abba abba cde cde or abba abba cdcdcd*)
19	VILLANELLE: nineteen lines of any length, divided into five tercets and one quatrain; built on two rhymes and two refrains (shown by superscripts ^{R1} and ^{R2}, both of which end with the *a* rhyme ($a^{R1}ba^{R2}aba^{R1}aba^{R2}aba^{R1}aba^{R2}aba^{R1}a^{R2}$)

Some stanzaic forms can be very complicated, requiring the poet to possess exceptional skill in order both to meet the technical requirements of the form and to produce a work that is moving or interesting. For example, Dylan Thomas's "Do Not Go Gentle into That Good Night" and Theodore Roethke's "The Waking" are built on a medieval French form called the **villanelle**: this nineteen-line form requires five tercets and one quatrain, contains only two rhymes, and uses two refrains that must appear in a specified order.

Line length, rhythm, rhyme, and stanzaic form contribute to the development of thought and feeling. Whether the work is in free verse or follows a restrictive form like that of the villanelle, these elements emphasize certain words and create links between words and groups of lines. Readers who note these emphases are not only better able to appreciate the craft of the poet, but they are better able to understand the textures of a poem's ideas and to feel its emotional shadings.

SOUND AND SOUND DEVICES

The rhythmic flow of a line of poetry is not entirely a matter of rhythm patterns, caesurae, and run-on lines; the choice of words, their very sounds, can make a line flow more swiftly or slowly. In "An Essay on Criticism," a work not included in this anthology, Alexander Pope argued that "the sound must seem an echo to the sense," and illustrated how word choice and placement can make a strict iambic rhythm seem ponderously slow or light and quick:

> When Ajax strives some rock's vast weight to throw,
> The line too labors, and the words move slow;
> Not so, when swift Camilla scours the plain,
> Flies o'er th' unbending corn and skims along the main.

In the first of these lines, Pope slows the reading of the line by using a number of monosyllabic words and cacophony, harsh or unpleasant-sounding language, produced here by a sequence of consonants that are relatively difficult to pronounce together. In the third and fourth lines, he quickens the pace with a careful placement of polysyllabic words and the use of euphony, or pleasant-sounding language with pleasing combinations of vowels and consonants.

Several other sound devices affect a poem's pace and meaning; sometimes these are instrumental in conveying the tone, which is the speaker's attitude toward the subject and the audience (both the audience implied by the context, as in a dramatic monologue, and the audience actually reading or listening to the poem). One of the most notable of these is **alliteration**, the repetition of initial consonants. In Donne's Holy Sonnet XIV, for example, the *b* sound is repeated when the speaker pleads that God "bend / Your force, to break, blow, burn, and make me new." Alliteration tends to emphasize words, giving them extra force and linking them as a unit. Here, the *b* sound emphasizes the violence of the action Donne requests of God and suggests that it will require all of God's force to save the speaker. Alliteration, therefore, suggests both the difficulty of the task and the intensity of the speaker's desire for renewal. It can, of course, be used for gentler effects, as in Christina Rossetti's "Song": "When I am dead, my dearest, / Sing no sad songs for me." In this case, the heaviness of the *d* sounds in the first line suggests the sadness normally associated with death, but the softness of the *s* sounds in the second line lightens the mood to indicate the speaker's contrary feeling. Furthermore, the alliteration surrounds the word *no*, a word that in scansion receives an accent, or heavy beat, creating a contrast that emphasizes the word and its idea even more.

Repetition of sound is also central to assonance and consonance. **Assonance** is the repetition of vowel sounds, as in the *i* sound of "swift Camilla" and "skims" in Pope's lines quoted above. **Consonance** is the repetition of consonant sounds within or at the end of words, as with the repeated *l* sounds in the last line of Archibald Lampman's "Winter Evening": "Glittering and still shall come the awful night."

One other important device is **onomatopoeia**, or imitative harmony, in which a word imitates or echoes a sound, as in "clip clop" to suggest the movement of horses, or as in the word *break* in Donne's alliterative "break, blow, bend" quoted above, or as in this famous example from a long poem that does not appear in this anthology, Tennyson's *The Princess* (1847): "The moan of doves in immemorial elms, / And murmuring of innumerable bees." Here *moan* and *murmur* imitate natural sounds, and alliteration of the *m* heightens and extends the effect throughout both lines.

Although it has been necessary to examine them separately, sound devices most frequently work together. In the final line of Shakespeare's Sonnet 73, "To love that well which thou must leave ere long," discussed earlier to show meaningful variation in metre, alliteration links *love*, *leave*, and *long*, emphasizing these three important words. Moreover, the two major terms, *love* and *leave*, are further linked and intensified by internal slant rhyme. Finally, consonance links *love* and *well*, uniting these words into a single concept. Readers who notice such uses of sound gain a greater appreciation of the resources and technical demands of the craft of poetry, but they also gain something personally enriching. Sensitivity to sound enables readers to respond more fully to the nuances of language and, thus, to be more open to both emotional stimulation and intellectual meaning in their reading.

POETRY AND PLEASURE

The preceding sections have explored only the major technical elements that make poetry such a complex literary form. Poems can use these techniques in inexhaustible combinations. Poems, however, are much more than compilations of techniques, and reading poetry is more than cataloguing techniques. Poems express the deepest feelings, the most moving thoughts, the heartiest laughter, the most scathing denunciations that people throughout the ages have felt. Poems are expressions of unique personalities and bear the marks of originating in particular social, cultural, and historical contexts, but poems are open to all readers who take the time to open themselves to them, who listen to the rhythms and the sounds, who imaginatively perceive the imagery. The more readers discover about a poem, its context, and literature and poetry in general, the more they can extend their appreciation and enjoyment of poetry. The key to such appreciation and enjoyment, however, is to forget that a poem is a work of "serious literature" that must be studied. Readers need to approach the poem in the same way they approach music, plays, short stories, and novels; they should, that is, be willing to be entertained, be open to new sensations and ideas, be ready to be teased and puzzled, be eager to enter into the imaginative life of the poem. This willingness allows readers to experience an array of emotions and ideas they may not otherwise have. Reading poetry in this way can thus become an act of self-revelation that makes readers more deeply aware of their own humanity. Such reading does not, however, lock us into ourselves. Because poetry originates in another's mind and voice and because it touches on nearly universal experiences and feelings, such reading can connect us to other human beings. It can also make the moments of reading moments of pleasure. That, in itself, is a worthwhile reason for reading poetry.

Anonymous Medieval Lyrics and Ballads

Medieval lyrics and ballads may be remnants of the popular entertainment of the twelfth to fifteenth centuries. In the case of the lyrics, it is unlikely that the polished poems recorded in manuscripts are unaltered compositions of the common people. Their history is not clear, but lyrics probably began among the common people as songs. The conventions of this folk poetry probably influenced the art of the minstrels and educated poets, whose compositions have been preserved. In any case, from its beginnings as oral poetry to its later manifestation as written compositions, the medieval lyric remained relatively unaltered in form and content. Its very conventionality in constantly returning to such themes as the joy of spring, the sorrow of lost love, the inevitability of death, and the sacrifice of Christ suggests that these lyrics represent direct expression of ideas that the medieval world considered to be of compelling universal importance.

Many ballads also originated in the medieval period, but they were not recorded until the eighteenth century, being preserved for centuries almost entirely through oral performances. Unlike the lyrics, which express feelings, these anonymous songs concentrate on events. Ballads are not, however, fully developed narratives. Usually, that is, they focus on a climactic episode, often involving murder, tragic death, or supernatural phenomena. Events leading to the climax typically function as a series of condensed scenes, and the events that link them are omitted or swiftly passed over. The narrator seldom offers interpretations or judgements, allowing the story to advance through a spare recitation of events and a heavy reliance on dialogue. Because they are set to music, ballads have a simple stanzaic structure and rhythm: they usually consist of quatrains in which each line has four stresses or in which lines of four stresses and three stresses alternate. They also commonly employ refrains, or repeated phrases, some of which contain nonsense phrases. As a kind of common man's romance, ballads offer evidence of the intense passions, the fears, and the heroism that have entertained and inspired people for hundreds of years and that continue to do so in some contemporary songs.

Anonymous Lyrics

Western Wind

Western wind, when will thou blow,
    The small rain down can rain?
Christ, if my love were in my arms
    And I in my bed again!

Sumer is icumen in (The Cuckoo Song)

Sumer is icumen in,
   Lhude[1] sing cuccu;
Groweth sed and bloweth[2] med[3]
   And springth the wode[4] nu.[5]
5   Sing cuccu!
Awe[6] bleteth after lamb,
   Lhouth[7] after calve cu[8]
Bulluc sterteth,[9] bucke verteth[10]
   Murie[11] sing cuccu.
10   Cuccu, Cuccu,
   Wel singes thu, cuccu,
   Ne swik[12] thu[13] never nu.

    Sing cuccu nu! Sing cuccu!
    Sing cuccu! Sing cuccu nu!

I sing of a maiden

I sing of a maiden
   That is makeles,[1]
King of all kinges
   To[2] her sone sche ches.[3]
5 He cam also stille[4]
   There[5] his moder was
As dew in Aprille
   That falleth on the grass.
He cam also stille
10   To his moderes bour,[6]
As dew in Aprille
   That falleth on the flour.
He cam also stille
   There his moder lay,
15 As dew in Aprill
   That falleth on the spray.

        →

1 loud. 2 blows, or blooms, into flower. 3 meadow. 4 wood. 5 now. 6 ewe. 7 loweth. 8 cow.
9 the bullock starts, or leaps. 10 farteth; eating fresh green grass causes flatulence. 11 merry, merrily.
12 nor cease. 13 thou.
1 both matchless (incomparable) and mateless. 2 as, for. 3 chose. 4 as quietly or gently. 5 where.
6 bower; boudoir.

Moder and maiden
   Was never non but sche
Well may swich a lady
20   Godes[7] moder be.

Anonymous Popular Ballads

Sir Patrick Spens

The king sits in Dumferling toune,[1]
   Drinking the blude-reid wine:[2]
"O whar will I get guid sailor,
   To sail this schip of mine?"

5 Up and spak an eldern knicht,
   Sat at the kings richt kne:
"Sir Patrick Spens is the best sailor
   That sails upon the se."

The king has written a braid[3] letter,
10 And signed it wi' his hand,
And sent it to Sir Patrick Spens,
   Was walking on the sand.

The first line that Sir Patrick red,
   A loud lauch[4] lauched he;
15 The next line that Sir Patrick red,
   The teir blinded his ee.[5]

"O wha is this has don this deid,
   This ill deid don to me,
To send me out this time o' the yeir,
20   To sail upon the se?"

"Mak haste, mak haste, my mirry men all,
   Our guid schip sails the morne."

               ⟶

7 God's.
1 Dunfermline, in eastern Scotland, was a favourite residence of Scottish kings. 2 blood-red. 3 broad.
4 laugh. 5 eye.

"O say na sae,[6] my master deir,
    For I feir a deadlie storme.

25   "Late late yestreen I saw the new moone
    Wi' the auld moone in her arme;
And I feir, I feir, my deir master,
    That we will come to harme."

O our Scots nobles were richt laith[7]
30   To weet[8] their cork-heild schoone;[9]
Bot lang owre[10] a' the play were played,
    Their hats they swam aboone.[11]

O lang, lang may their ladies sit
    Wi' their fans into their hand,
35   Or eir they see Sir Patrick Spens
    Come sailing to the land.

O lang, lang may the ladies stand
    Wi' their gold kems[12] in their hair,
Waiting for their ain[13] deir lords,
40   For they'll see thame na mair.[14]

Haf owre, haf owre[15] to Aberdour,[16]
    It's fiftie fadom[17] deip:
And there lies guid Sir Patrick Spens
    Wi' the Scots lords at his feit.

The Three Ravens

There were three ravens sat on a tree,
    Downe a downe, hay down, hay downe
There were three ravens sat on a tree,
    With a downe
5   There were three ravens sat on a tree,
They were as blacke as they might be.
    With a downe derrie, derrie, derrie, downe, downe.

6 not so. 7 loath. 8 wet. 9 cork-healed shoes. 10 ere; before. 11 above. 12 combs. 13 own.
14 no more. 15 half(way) over. 16 Aberdeen. 17 fathoms.

The one of them said to his mate,
"Where shall we our breakefast take?"

10   "Downe in yonder greene field,
There lies a knight slain under his shield.

"His hounds they lie downe at his feete,
So well they can their master keepe.

"His hawkes they fly so eagerly,
15   There's no fowle dare him come nie."

Downe there comes a fallow[1] doe,
As great with yong as she might goe.

She lift up his bloudy hed,
And kist his wounds that were so red.

20   She got him up upon her backe,
And carried him to earthen lake.

She buried him before the prime,[2]
She was dead herselfe ere even-song[3] time.

God send every gentleman,
25   Such hawkes, such hounds, and such a leman.[4]

Bonny Barbara Allan

It was in and about the Martinmas time,[1]
    When the green leaves were a falling,
That Sir John Graeme, in the West Country,
    Fell in love with Barbara Allan.

---

1 light brown, dun. 2 the first hour after dawn in canonical system. 3 vespers, the sixth of seven canonical hours,
a period of worship in the late afternoon or early evening. 4 mistress, sweetheart, lover.
1 November 11, the feast day of Saint Martin of Tours.

5 He sent his men down through the town
   To the place where she was dwelling:
  "O haste and come to my master dear,
   Gin ye be Barbara Allan."

  O hooly,[2] hooly rose she up,
10   To the place where he was lying,
  And when she drew the curtain by,
   "Young man, I think you're dying."

  "O it's I'm sick, and very, very sick,
   And 't is a' for Barbara Allan."
15 "O the better for me ye 's[3] never be,
   Tho your heart's blood were a spilling.

  "O dinna, ye mind, young man," said she,
   "When ye was in the tavern a drinking,
  That ye made the healths gae round and round,
20   And slighted Barbara Allan?"

  He turned his face unto the wall,
   And death was with him dealing:
  "Adieu, adieu, my dear friends all,
   And be kind to Barbara Allan."

25 And slowly, slowly raise she up,
   And slowly, slowly left him,
  And sighing said, she could not stay,
   Since death of life had reft[4] him.

  She had not gane a mile but twa,
30   When she heard the dead-bell ringing,
  And every jow[5] that the dead-bell geid,[6]
   It cried, Woe to Barbara Allan!

  "O mother, mother, make my bed!
   O make it saft and narrow!
35 Since my love died for me to-day,
   I'll die for him to-morrow."

[Handwritten annotations:]
- Ballads have 4,3,4,3 stresses per stanza
- *even though iamb is not everywhere in sentence main flow hence name
- 4 stresses / 3 " / 4 " / 3 " (lines 29–32)
- She had not gane a mile but twa, → Iambic tetrameter
- When she heard the dead-bell ringing, → trochaic tetrameter
- And every jow that the dead-bell geid, → Iambic tetrameter
- It cried, Woe to Barbara Allan! → trochaic tetrameter
- "O mother, mother, make my bed! → Iambic tetrameter
- O make it saft and narrow! → Iambic tetrameter
- Since my love died for me to-day, → Iambic tetrameter
- I'll die for him to-morrow." → Iambic trimeter

2 cautiously, slowly. 3 ye shall. 4 torn from; robbed. 5 ring or toll. 6 gave or made.

The Renaissance Sonnet

The sonnet originated in thirteenth-century Italy, but the sonnet sequences of Dante (1265–1321) and Petrarch (1304–74) made the form popular throughout Europe during the fifteenth and sixteenth centuries. In every country, the topics and attitudes of the sonnet were quite conventional. The Platonic love themes developed by the Italian masters created a pattern of contemplation, love, and rejection: the Lover begs acceptance of the Lady through various metaphors of agony, disenchantment, and bliss; she, with studied disregard, rebuffs or ignores his advances; such rejection only intensifies his next attempt. Even when it did not speak of unrequited love, however, the sonnet was frequently artificial in its expression. Compare, for example, Constable's "My lady's presence makes the roses red," a conventional celebration of the beloved, with Shakespeare's biting satire of such formulaic comparisons in Sonnet 130 ("My mistress' eyes are nothing like the sun"), which is included among the sonnets printed in the author entry for Shakespeare. The six poems in this section represent various approaches to the love sonnet that dominated the Renaissance. For sonnets on other topics, see the author entries for John Donne and John Milton.

Although the sonnet is rigid in length, it can be remarkably varied in structure and rhyme. Sir Thomas Wyatt, who introduced the sonnet to England through free English translations of Petrarch, preserved the rhyming of the Italian octave (*abba abba*), but he concluded the sestet with the couplet, a device that became characteristic of the English sonnet. His contemporary, Henry Howard, Earl of Surrey, established the division into three quatrains and a couplet (*abab cdcd efef gg*). This structural change altered the Italian conception of the sonnet as a poem divided into two parts: an eight-line exposition of the problem or an observation and a six-line statement of conclusion or resolution. The English sonnet allows greater repetition and development of the problem while forcing a concentrated resolution in the epigrammatic couplet. Furthermore, because English is harder to rhyme than Italian, this structure gave greater freedom by permitting seven instead of the conventional five rhymes. Note, however, that variations in the three-quatrain scheme are possible: Surrey's "Love that doth reign," for example, contains only six rhymes. Edmund Spenser made a further adaptation, linking quatrains through the couplet created when one quatrain begins with the rhyme with which the previous one ends (*abab bcbc cdcd ee*). Sir Philip Sidney, although he usually followed Wyatt in using the Italian pattern in his octaves and a closing couplet in his sestet, also experimented with alternating rhyme in "Loving in truth" (*abab abab cdcd ee*). The last great poet of the Renaissance, John Milton, followed the true Italian pattern (*abba abba cdecde*), but he intensified the unity of his sonnets by having the octave run into the sestet. After Milton's death, the sonnet lost favour, but it was revived as a powerful lyrical force by the Romantics, notably Wordsworth and Keats (see their author entries).

Sir Thomas Wyatt (1503–1542)

My galley charged with forgetfulness

The lover compareth his state to a ship in perilous storm
tossed on the sea.

My galley charged with forgetfulness, *a*
Through sharp seas, in winter nights, doth pass *b*
'Tween rock and rock; and eke[1] my foe, alas, *b*
That is my lord,[2] steereth with cruelness: *a*
5 And every hour, a thought in readiness, *a*
As though that death were light in such a case *c*
An endless wind doth tear the sail apace *c*
Of forced sighs and trusty fearfulness; *a*
A rain of tears, a cloud of dark disdain, *D*
10 Have done the wearied cords great hinderance: *e*
Wreathed with error, and with ignorance; *e*
The stars[3] be hid that lead me to this pain; *D*
    Drown'd is reason that should be my comfort, *f*
    And I remain, despairing of the port. *f*

(1520–30?)   (1557)

Henry Howard, Earl of Surrey (1517–1547)

Love that doth reign

Love that doth reign and live within my thought, *a*
And built his seat within my captive breast, *b*
Clad in the arms wherein with me he fought, *a*
Oft in my face he doth his banner rest. *b*
5 But she that taught me love and suffer pain, *C*
My doubtful hope and eke[1] my hot desire *D C*
With shamefast[2] look to shadow and refrain, *C*

1 also. 2 i.e., Cupid. 3 i.e., the lady's eyes.
1 also. 2 shamefaced.

Her smiling grace converteth straight to ire.
And coward love then to the heart apace
10 Taketh his flight, where he doth lurk and plain[3]
His purpose lost, and dare not show his face.
For my lord's guilt thus faultless bide I pain;
Yet from my lord shall not my foot remove.
Sweet is the death that taketh end by love.

(1542?)   (1557)

Edmund Spenser (1552–1599)

One day I wrote her name upon the strand

One day I wrote her name upon the strand;[1]
But came the waves, and washed it away:
Agayne, I wrote it with a second hand;
But came the tyde, and made my paynes his pray.
5 Vayne man, sayd she, that doest in vaine assay
A mortall thing so to immortalize;
For I my selve shall lyke to this decay,
And eke[2] my name bee wyped out lykewize.
Not so, quod I; let baser things devize
10 To dy in dust, but you shall live by fame:
My verse your vertues rare shall eternize,
And in the hevens wryte your glorious name.
    Where, when as death shall all the world subdew,
    Our love shall live, and later life renew.

(1595)

Sir Philip Sidney (1554–1586)

Who will in fairest book of nature know

Who will in fairest book of nature know,
How virtue may best lodged in beauty be,

—→

3 complain.
1 beach. 2 also .

Let him but learn of love to read in thee
Stella, those fair lines which true Beauty show.
5   There shall he find all vices' overthrow;
Not by rude force, but sweetest sovereignty
Of reason, from whose light, the night birds fly;
That inward sun in thine eyes shineth so.
And not content to be perfection's heir
10   Thyself, dost strive all minds that way to move,
Who mark in thee what is in thee most fair.
So while thy beauty drives my heart to love,
As fast thy virtue bends that love to good:
"But ah," desire still cries, "give me some food."

(1581–83?)   (1591)

Henry Constable (1562–1613)

My lady's presence makes the roses red

My lady's presence makes the roses red
Because to see her lips they blush for shame.
The lilies leaves for envy pale became,
And her white hands in them this envy bred.
5   The marigold the leaves abroad doth spread
Because the sun's and her power is the same.
The violet of purple colour came,
Dyed in the blood she made my heart to shed.
In brief, all flowers from her their virtue take;
10   From her sweet breath their sweet smells do proceed;
The living heat which her eyebeams doth make
Warmeth the ground and quickeneth the seed.
    The rain wherewith she watereth the flowers
    Falls from mine eyes which she dissolves in showers.

(1594)

Michael Drayton (1563–1631)

Since there's no help, come let us kiss and part

Since there's no help, come let us kiss and part,
Nay, I have done: you get no more of me,
And I am glad, yea glad with all my heart,
That thus so cleanly I myself can free;
5　Shake hands forever, cancel all our vows,
And when we meet at any time again,
Be it not seen in either of our brows
That we one jot of former love retain.
Now at the last gasp of love's latest breath,
10　When his pulse failing, passion speechless lies,
When faith is kneeling by his bed of death,
and innocence is closing up his eyes,
　　Now if thou would'st, when all have given him over,
　　From death to life, thou might'st him yet recover.

(1619)

Sir Walter Ralegh (c. 1552–1618)

Ralegh is perhaps best known for his colonization of Virginia and for populariz-
ing the use of tobacco in England. He was also friend and patron to Edmund
Spenser. Notoriously proud, ambitious, and ostentatious, he commanded
extremes of loyalty and hatred through the power of his public personality.
Though he was a favourite of Queen Elizabeth in the 1580s, Ralegh spent most
of the final fifteen years of his life imprisoned in the Tower by James I. While in
the Tower, Ralegh wrote the bulk of his voluminous *History of the World.* But he
was a poet as well as a man of action and confirmed sceptic. His is a hard-minded
poetic vision that rejects easy idealizations. Released from prison in 1616 to
lead the ill-fated Guiana expedition in search of gold for the English treasury,
Ralegh was tried on charges of reopening hostilities with Spain and beheaded.

The Nymph's Reply [1]

If all the world and love were young,
And truth in every shepherd's tongue,
These pretty pleasures might me move
To live with thee and be thy love.

1 reply to Christopher Marlowe's "The Passionate Shepherd to His Love" (see page 38).

5   But time drives flocks from field to fold,
When rivers rage and rocks grow cold;
And Philomel[2] becometh dumb;
The rest complains of cares to come.

The flowers do fade, and wanton fields
10   To wayward winter reckoning yields:
A honey tongue, a heart of gall,
Is fancy's spring, but sorrow's fall.

Thy gowns, thy shoes, thy beds of roses,
Thy cap, thy kirtle, and thy posies,
15   Soon break, soon wither, soon forgotten,—
In folly ripe, in reason rotten.

Thy belt of straw and ivy buds,
Thy coral clasps and amber studs,—
All those in me no means can move
20   To come to thee and be thy love.

But could youth last, and love still breed;
Had joys no date, nor age no need;
Then those delights my mind might move
To live with thee and be thy love.

(1600)

Christopher Marlowe (1564–1593)

Born the son of a Canterbury shoemaker, Christopher Marlowe received the M.A. degree from Cambridge in 1587. Best known as a dramatic poet using blank verse, he demonstrated technical virtuosity in translating such classics as Ovid's *Amores* and the first book of Lucan's *Pharsalia*. His unfinished erotic narrative *Hero and Leander* is written in ironic and smooth rhyming couplets. Thus, the short pastoral verse entitled "The Passionate Shepherd to His Love" seems somewhat uncharacteristic. And yet, since at least the seventeenth century, it has been celebrated, and linked with Sir Walter Ralegh's sceptical "answer."

    Marlowe's mercurial career saw him gain prominence very early with the introduction of his "mighty line": the blank verse metre of *Tamburlaine* (1587), which was to become the poetic medium of Shakespearean and Renaissance drama, as well as the measure of Milton's *Paradise Lost*. Surrey had used

---

2 nightingale (mythological).

unrhymed decasyllables in translating the *Aeneid* some 35 years before, but his verse was meant to be stately and Latinate. It was Marlowe who made the measure distinctly English by demonstrating its directness, versatility, and power.

The Passionate Shepherd to His Love

Come live with me, and be my love;
And we will all the pleasures prove[1]
That hills and valleys, dales and fields,
Woods, or steepy mountain yields.

5 And we will sit upon the rocks,
Seeing the shepherds feed their flocks
By shallow rivers, to whose falls
Melodious birds sing madrigals.

And I will make thee beds of roses,
10 And a thousand fragrant posies;
A cap of flowers, and a kirtle[2]
Embroidered all with leaves of myrtle;

A gown made of the finest wool
Which from our pretty lambs we pull;
15 Fair-lined slippers for the cold,
With buckles of the purest gold;

A belt of straw and ivy-buds,
With coral clasps and amber-studs:
And if these pleasures may thee move,
20 Come live with me, and be my love.

The shepherd-swains shall dance and sing
For thy delight each May-morning;
If these delights thy mind may move,
Then live with me, and be my love.

(1599)

1 try. 2 a skirt or loose gown.

William Shakespeare (1564–1616)

Shakespeare was born in Stratford-upon-Avon, probably a day or two previous to his christening on April 26, 1564. It is traditional that his birthday be celebrated on April 23, which is the feast day of St. George, England's patron saint. Much of Shakespeare's adult life was spent in London as an actor and playwright with the Globe Theatre.

Although celebrated as the foremost dramatist in the language, Shakespeare is also a sonneteer. His 154 sonnets were published in 1609 but were noted previously by Francis Meres, who in 1598 made mention of Shakespeare's "sugared sonnets among his private friends." The sonnets, however, are far from sugary. They are profound moral and aesthetic contemplations that adapt metaphors from the theatrical world and from the world of human emotions. Investigators have been fascinated by the biographical possibilities of Shakespeare's sonnets, but they are primarily metaphorical contemplations that probe the complexities of love, death, fame, and mutability.

Sonnets

18

Shall I compare thee to a summer's day?
Thou art more lovely and more temperate:
Rough winds do shake the darling buds of May,
And summer's lease hath all too short a date:
5   Sometime too hot the eye of heaven shines,
And often is his gold complexion dimm'd;
And every fair from fair sometime declines
By chance or nature's changing course untrimm'd;
But thy eternal summer shall not fade
10 Nor lose possession of that fair thou ow'st;[1]
Nor shall Death brag thou wander'st in his shade,
When in eternal lines to time thou grow'st:
    So long as men can breathe or eyes can see,
    So long lives this and this gives life to thee.

(1609)

1 ownest.

55

Not marble, nor the gilded monuments
Of princes, shall outlive this powerful rime;
But you shall shine more bright in these contents
Than unswept stone besmear'd with sluttish time.
5   When wasteful war shall statues overturn,
And broils root out the work of masonry,
Nor Mars his sword nor war's quick fire shall burn
The living record of your memory.
'Gainst death and all-oblivious enmity
10 Shall you pace forth: your praise shall still find room
Even in the eyes of all posterity
That wear this world out to the ending doom.
    So, till the judgement that yourself arise,[1]
    You live in this, and dwell in lovers' eyes.

(1609)

73

That time of year thou mayst in me behold
When yellow leaves, or none, or few, do hang
Upon those boughs which shake against the cold,
Bare ruin'd choirs where late the sweet birds sang.
5   In me thou see'st the twilight of such day
As after sunset fadeth in the west;
Which by and by black night doth take away,
Death's second self, that seals up all in rest.
In me thou see'st the glowing of such fire
10 That on the ashes of his youth doth lie,
As the death-bed whereon it must expire,
Consumed with that which it was nourish'd by.
    This thou perceiv'st, which makes thy love more strong,
    To love that well which thou must leave ere long.

(1609)

---

1 i.e., "So until you arise from the dead on Judgement Day."

116

Let me not to the marriage of true minds
Admit impediments. Love is not love
Which alters when it alteration finds,
Or bends with the remover to remove:
5   O, no! it is an ever-fixed mark,
That looks on tempests and is never shaken;
It is the star to every wandering bark,[1]
Whose worth's unknown, although his height be taken.
Love's not Time's fool,[2] though rosy lips and cheeks
10   Within his bending sickle's compass come;
Love alters not with his brief hours and weeks,
But bears it out even to the edge of doom.
    If this be error and upon me proved,
    I never writ, nor no man ever loved.

(1609)

130

My mistress' eyes are nothing like the sun;
Coral is far more red than her lips' red:
If snow be white, why then her breasts are dun;
If hairs be wires, black wires grow on her head.
5   I have seen roses damask'd,[1] red and white,
But no such roses see I in her cheeks;
And in some perfumes is there more delight
Than in the breath that from my mistress reeks.
I love to hear her speak, yet well I know
10   That music hath a far more pleasing sound:
I grant I never saw a goddess go;
My mistress, when she walks, treads on the ground:
    And yet, by heaven, I think my love as rare
    As any she belied[2] with false compare.

(1609)

1 sailing ship. 2 i.e., victim.
1 mingled, variegated. 2 misrepresented.

John Donne (1572–1631)

John Donne was a talented young man hopeful of worldly advancement. Appointed private secretary to Sir Thomas Egerton in 1598, Donne ruined hope of further preferment in that household when his secret marriage to Sir Thomas's seventeen-year-old niece became public. But Donne's gifts of learning, intelligence, and social grace would not let him fade away from the public eye. On the encouragement of King James himself, Donne took holy orders and was appointed Dean of St. Paul's Cathedral, London, in 1621.

Next to nothing of Donne's literary output was published during his own lifetime. (The first edition of his collected poems appeared in 1633.) His brilliance as a "metaphysical" poet is a virtual rediscovery by twentieth-century criticism, and he is now recognized as one of the greatest English love poets. Donne's forceful exposition and bold metaphorical style also made him one of the greatest preachers of the seventeenth century, as well as a significant religious poet. He seemed singularly adept at uniting passion and intellect. And the two periods of "Jack Donne," lyrical poet, and "Doctor Donne," learned divine, into which Donne himself separated his life might not seem all that irreconcilable in light of the powerful rhetoric and deep meditational technique common to both.

Song

Go, and catch a falling star,
    Get with child a mandrake root,
Tell me where all past years are,
    Or who cleft the Devil's foot,
5 Teach me to hear Mermaids singing,
Or to keep off envy's stinging,
        And find
        What wind
Serves to advance an honest mind.

10 If thou be'st born to strange sights,
    Things invisible to see,
Ride ten thousand days and nights,
    Till age snow white hairs on thee,
Thou, when thou return'st, wilt tell me
15 All strange wonders that befell thee,

———→

And swear
No where
Lives a woman true, and fair.

If thou find'st one, let me know,
20   Such a Pilgrimage were sweet;
Yet do not, I would not go,
     Though at next door we might meet,
Though she were true, when you met her,
And last, till you write your letter,
25   Yet she
        Will be
False, ere I come, to two, or three.

(1633)

The Bait[1]

Come live with me, and be my love,
And we will some new pleasures prove[2]
Of golden sands, and crystal brooks,
With silken lines, and silver hooks.

5   There will the river whispering run
Warm'd by thy eyes, more than the Sun.
And there th' enamour'd fish will stay,
Begging themselves they may betray.

When thou wilt swim in that live bath,
10 Each fish, which every channel hath,
Will amorously to thee swim,
Gladder to catch thee, than thou him.

If thou, to be so seen, be'st loth,
By Sun, or Moon, thou dark'nest both,
15 And if myself have leave to see,
I need not their light, having thee.

---

1 reply to Marlowe's "The Passionate Shepherd to His Love" (see page 38). 2. try.

Let others freeze with angling reeds,
And cut their legs, with shells and weeds,
Or treacherously poor fish beset,
20   With strangling snare, or windowy net:

Let coarse bold hands, from slimy nest
The bedded fish in banks out-wrest,
Or curious traitors, sleeve-silk flies
Bewitch poor fishes' wand'ring eyes.

25   For thee, thou need'st no such deceit,
For thou thyself art thine own bait;
That fish, that is not catch'd thereby,
Alas, is wiser far than I.

(1633)

A Valediction: Forbidding Mourning

As virtuous men pass mildly away,
    And whisper to their souls, to go,
Whilst some of their sad friends do say,
    The breath goes now, and some say, no:

5   So let us melt, and make no noise,
    No tear-floods, nor sigh-tempests move,
'Twere profanation of our joys
    To tell the laity our love.

Moving of th' earth brings harms and fears,
10   Men reckon what it did and meant,
But trepidation of the spheres,[1]
    Though greater far, is innocent.

Dull sublunary lovers' love
    (Whose soul is sense) cannot admit
15   Absence, because it doth remove
    Those things which elemented it.

1 in pre-Copernican cosmology, the shaking of the nine concentric spheres around the earth.

But we by a love, so much refin'd,
    That ourselves know not what it is,
Inter-assured of the mind,
20   Care less eyes, lips, and hands to miss.

Our two souls therefore, which are one,
    Though I must go, endure not yet
A breach, but an expansion,
    Like gold to aery thinness beat.

25 If they be two, they are two so
    As stiff twin compasses are two,
Thy soul the fixed foot, makes no show
    To move, but doth, if th' other do.

And though it in the centre sit,
30   Yet when the other far doth roam,
It leans, and hearkens after it,
    And grows erect, as that comes home.
Such wilt thou be to me, who must
    Like th' other foot, obliquely run;
35 Thy firmness draws my circle just,
    And makes me end, where I begun.

                              (1633)

The Canonization

For God's sake hold your tongue, and let me love;
    Or chide my palsy, or my gout,
My five grey hairs, or ruin'd fortune flout;
    With wealth your state, your mind with arts improve,
5   Take you a course, get you a place,
      Observe his Honour, or his Grace,
Or the King's real, or his stamped face
    Contemplate; what you will, approve,
    So you will let me love.
10 Alas, alas, who's injur'd by my love?
    What merchant's ships have my sighs drown'd?

                              ⟶

Who says my tears have overflow'd his ground?
  When did my colds a forward spring remove?
    When did the heats which my veins fill
15   Add one more to the plaguy bill?[1]
Soldiers find wars, and lawyers find out still
  Litigious men, which quarrels move,
  Though she and I do love.

Call us what you will, we are made such by love;
20   Call her one, me another fly,
We're tapers too, and at our own cost die,
  And we in us find the Eagle and the Dove.
    The Phœnix riddle hath more wit
    By us; we two being one, are it.
25 So to one neutral thing both sexes fit,
  We die and rise the same, and prove
  Mysterious by this love.

We can die by it, if not live by love,
  And if unfit for tombs and hearse
30 Our legend be, it will be fit for verse;
  And if no piece of Chronicle we prove,
    We'll build in sonnets pretty rooms;
    As well a well-wrought urn becomes
The greatest ashes, as half-acre tombs,
35   And by these hymns, all shall approve
    Us canonized for Love:

And thus invoke us; You whom reverend love
  Made one another's hermitage;
You, to whom love was peace, that now is rage;
40 Who did the whole world's soul contract, and drove
    Into the glasses of your eyes
    (So made such mirrors, and such spies,
That they did all to you epitomize,)
    Countries, Towns, Courts: beg from above
45   A pattern of your love!

                                        (1633)

---

1 i.e., add one more name to the weekly list (bill) of plague victims.

The Flea

Mark but this flea, and mark in this,
How little that which thou deny'st me is;
It suck'd me first, and now sucks thee,
And in this flea, our two bloods mingled be;
5   Thou know'st that this cannot be said
A sin, nor shame, nor loss of maidenhead,
 Yet this enjoys before it woo,
  And pamper'd swells with one blood made of two,
  And this, alas, is more than we would do.

10   Oh stay, three lives in one flea spare,
Where we almost, yea more than married are.
This flea is you and I, and this
Our marriage bed, and marriage temple is;
Though parents grudge, and you, we're met,
15   And cloistered in these living walls of jet.
 Though use make you apt to kill me,
  Let not to that, self murder added be,
  And sacrilege, three sins in killing three.

Cruel and sudden, hast thou since
20   Purpled thy nail, in blood of innocence?
Wherein could this flea guilty be,
Except in that drop which it suck'd from thee?
Yet thou triumph'st, and say'st that thou
Find'st not thyself, nor me, the weaker now;
25   'Tis true, then learn how false, fears be;
 Just so much honour, when thou yield'st to me,
  Will waste, as this flea's death took life from thee.

(1633)

Holy Sonnet X

Death be not proud, though some have called thee
Mighty and dreadful, for, thou art not so,
For, those, whom thou think'st, thou dost overthrow,
Die not, poor death, nor yet canst thou kill me.
5   From rest and sleep, which but thy pictures be,
Much pleasure, then from thee, much more must flow,
And soonest our best men with thee do go,
Rest of their bones, and soul's delivery.
Thou art slave to Fate, Chance, kings, and desperate men,
10   And dost with poison, war, and sickness dwell,
And poppy, or charms can make us sleep as well,
And better than thy stroke; why swell'st thou then?
One short sleep past, we wake eternally,
And death shall be no more; death, thou shalt die.

(1633)

Holy Sonnet XIV

Batter my heart, three-person'd God; for, you
As yet but knock, breathe, shine, and seek to mend;
That I may rise, and stand, o'erthrow me, and bend
Your force, to break, blow, burn and make me new.
5   I, like an usurp'd town, to another due,
Labour to admit you, but Oh, to no end,
Reason your viceroy in me, me should defend,
But is captiv'd, and proves weak or untrue.
Yet dearly I love you, and would be loved fain,
10   But am betroth'd unto your enemy:
Divorce me, untie, or break that knot again,
Take me to you, imprison me, for I
Except you enthral me, never shall be free,
Nor ever chaste, except you ravish me.

(1633)

Ben Jonson (1572–1637)

Scholar, poet, playwright, classicist, and controversialist — Jonson's career con-solidates the emergence of professional letters in the English Renaissance. He was the first English poet to publish his own works, in 1616, and his first play, *Every Man in His Humour* (1598), included actor William Shakespeare in the cast. Master of the English plain style, Jonson, whose output was voluminous and various, held pride of place at the Mermaid Tavern where he presided over a club of aspiring poets known as the "sons of Ben."

Jonson was also a man of action who, while a soldier in Flanders, killed an enemy champion in hand-to-hand combat — a biographical fact that he gloried in relating to his host, William Drummond of Hawthornden. Argumentative, satirical, and pugnacious, Jonson was a professional writer who took his business seriously enough to insist on its critical appreciation in both the public playhouse and the private masquing house where he also triumphed as author. With stage architect Inigo Jones (a detested rival), Jonson prepared many lavish ceremonial masques for the court of James I, and he was still a significant cultural spokes-person in the reign of Charles I.

Song: To Celia

Drink to me only with thine eyes,
   And I will pledge with mine;
Or leave a kiss within the cup,
   And I'll not look for wine.
5   The thirst that from the soul doth rise,
   Doth ask a drink divine;
But might I of Jove's nectar sup,
   I would not change for thine.

I sent thee late a rosy wreath,
10   Not so much honouring thee,
As giving it a hope that there
   It could not withered be.
But thou thereon didst only breathe,
   And sent'st it back to me;
15   Since when it grows, and smells, I swear,
   Not of itself, but thee.

(1616)

On My First Son

Farewell, thou child of my right hand, and joy;
My sin was too much hope of thee, lov'd boy:
Seven years thou wert lent to me, and I thee pay,
Exacted by thy fate, on the just day.
O, could I lose all father,[1] now! for why,
Will man lament the state he should envy?
To have so soon scaped world's, and flesh's rage,
And, if no other misery, yet age!
Rest in soft peace, and ask'd, say here doth lie
BEN JONSON his best piece of poetry:
For whose sake henceforth all his vows be such,
As what he loves may never like too much.

(1603?)   (1616)

Robert Herrick   (1591–1674)

Herrick was a clergyman from London who found himself at the age of 38 posted to the tiny vicarage of Dean Prior, Devonshire. There he performed the social and religious rituals for a largely illiterate population, all the while recording his own witty poetic observations on his flock. But his observations are never condescending. His rural themes are consistently simple, often playful, but seldom trivial: beauty, love, art, natural splendour, religious devotion. And his speaking voice or persona—somewhat risqué for a bachelor country parson—no doubt occasioned the final couplet in the first part of his collection: "To his book's end this last line he'd have placed: / Jocund his Muse was, but his life was chaste."

Expelled from his vicarage in 1647 as a Royalist sympathizer, Herrick went back to London where he published his verses in a single volume, *Hesperides* (1648), comprising over fourteen hundred sacred and secular lyrics. After the Puritan interregnum, Herrick was reinstated under Charles II and lived out the end of his long life in Dean Prior.

1 i.e., give up all gentle, fatherly thoughts.

To the Virgins, To Make Much of Time

Gather ye rose-buds while ye may,
    Old time is still a flying,
And this same flower that smiles to-day,
    To-morrow will be dying.

5   The glorious lamp of Heaven, the sun,
    The higher he's a getting,
The sooner will his race be run,
    And neerer he's to setting.

That age is best which is the first,
10   When youth and blood are warmer;
But being spent, the worse, and worst
    Times still succeed the former.

Then be not coy, but use your time,
    And while ye may, go marry;
15   For having lost but once your prime,
    You may for ever tarry.

(1648)

Upon Julia's Clothes

Whenas in silks my Julia goes,
Then, then, me thinks, how sweetly flows
That liquefaction of her clothes.

Next, when I cast mine eyes and see
5   That brave vibration, each way free,
O how that glittering taketh me!

(1648)

George Herbert (1593–1633)

George Herbert was born into an ancient and respected Welsh family. His brother Edward was the philosopher-statesman Lord Herbert of Cherbury, and another brother, Sir Henry, was Master of the Revels in England, whose job it was to censor and approve public entertainment during the Stuart reign. George was more private, if (it seems) no less ambitious. A scholar and ecclesiastic, he attained the position of Public Orator at Cambridge University but never received the place at court that he must surely have coveted. Instead, in 1629 he accepted a minor church living at Bemerton near Salisbury, where he lived out the rest of his short life in good works, holy contemplation, and poetic composition.

Herbert's poetry is sharply expressed, richly imaginative, and concrete. Here, a poem's shape expresses meaning, souls have voices, love speaks. Consistently devotional, his verse has an artistic originality and cleverness that mark it as among the most exalted of the "metaphysical" mode.

The Altar

A broken ALTAR, Lord, thy servant rears,
Made of a heart, and cemented with tears:
Whose parts are as thy hand did frame;
No workman's tool hath touch'd the same.
A   HEART   alone
Is   such   a   stone,
As   nothing   but
Thy power doth cut.
Wherefore each part
Of my hard heart
Meets in this frame,
To praise thy name:
That, if I chance to hold my peace,
These stones to praise thee may not cease.
O   let   thy   blessed   SACRIFICE   be   mine,
And   sanctify   this   ALTAR   to   be   thine.

(1633)

Easter Wings

LORD, who createdst man in wealth and store,[1]
Though foolishly he lost the same,
Decaying more and more,
Till he became
Most poor:

With Thee
O let me rise
As larks, harmoniously,
And sing this day Thy victories:
Then shall the fall further the flight in me.

My tender age in sorrow did begin:
And still with sicknesses and shame
Thou didst so punish sin,
That I became
Most thin.

With Thee
Let me combine,
And feel this day Thy victory,
For, if I imp[2] my wing on Thine,
Affliction shall advance the flight in me.

(1633)

John Milton (1608–1674)

Milton was born into a middle-class London family. Prodigiously intellectual, he received a thorough education at St. Paul's School, London, and in Christ's College, Cambridge. Later, he travelled on the Continent where he met the aged and broken Galileo. Milton, too, would later survey the heavens, but as a blind poet with a self-proclaimed mandate to "justify the ways of God to men" (*Paradise Lost* I.26).

---

1 abundance. 2 to graft a feather on a falcon's wing or tail, either to repair a deficiency or to improve its power of flight.

Milton was also a public figure who held the position of Latin Secretary to Oliver Cromwell during the Puritan interregnum. His journalism on topical matters such as divorce, church government, and censorship, in addition to diplomatic and political matters, was prolific. He lived out his final days after the restoration of Charles II in humble circumstances. But it was during this time that Milton gained his immortal reputation as a poet. His poetry is celebrated for its profound spiritual and metaphorical sense of inquiry. Considered by many as the highest achievement in English non-dramatic verse, his epic *Paradise Lost* stands as testament to his genius.

Lycidas [1]

In this Monody the Author bewails a learned Friend,[2] unfortunately drowned in his passage from Chester on the Irish Sea, 1637; and, by occasion, foretells the ruin of our corrupted Clergy, then in their height.

Yet once more, O ye laurels, and once more,
Ye myrtles brown, with ivy never sere,[3]
I come to pluck your berries harsh and crude,
And with forced fingers rude
5 Shatter your leaves before the mellowing year.
Bitter constraint and sad occasion dear
Compels me to disturb your season due;
For Lycidas is dead, dead ere his prime,
Young Lycidas, and hath not left his peer.
10 Who would not sing for Lycidas? he knew
Himself to sing, and build the lofty rhyme.
He must not float upon his watery bier
Unwept, and welter to the parching wind,
Without the meed[4] of some melodious tear.
15 Begin, then, Sisters of the sacred well[5]
That from beneath the seat of Jove doth spring;
Begin, and somewhat loudly sweep the string.
Hence with denial vain and coy excuse:
So may some gentle Muse
20 With lucky words favour my destined urn,
And as he passes turn,
And bid fair peace to be my sable shroud!

———→

1 traditional pastoral name for a shepherd. 2 Edward King, a fellow student of Milton's acquaintance at Cambridge. 3 laurels, myrtles, ivy: evergreens associated with poetic inspiration and honour. 4 reward. 5 i.e., the nine sister Muses responsible for the flow of poetic inspiration.

For we were nursed upon the self-same hill,
Fed the same flock, by fountain, shade, and rill;
25   Together both, ere the high lawns appeared
Under the opening eyelids of the morn,
We drove a-field, and both together heard
What time the grey-fly winds her sultry horn,
Battening our flocks with the fresh dews of night,
30   Oft till the star that rose at evening bright
Toward heaven's descent had sloped his westering wheel.
Meanwhile the rural ditties were not mute;
Tempered to the oaten flute,
Rough Satyrs danced, and Fauns with cloven heel
35   From the glad sound would not be absent long;
And old Damœtas[6] loved to hear our song.

      But O! the heavy change, now thou art gone,
Now thou art gone and never must return!
Thee, Shepherd, thee the woods and desert caves,
40   With wild thyme and the gadding vine o'ergrown,
And all their echoes, mourn.
The willows, and the hazel copses green,
Shall now no more be seen
Fanning their joyous leaves to thy soft lays.
45   As killing as the canker to the rose,
Or taint-worm to the weanling herds that graze,
Or frost to flowers, that their gay wardrobe wear,
When first the white-thorn blows;
Such, Lycidas, thy loss to shepherd's ear.
50   Where were ye, Nymphs,[7] when the remorseless deep
Closed o'er the head of your loved Lycidas?
For neither were ye playing on the steep
Where your old bards, the famous Druids,[8] lie,
Nor on the shaggy top of Mona high,
55   Nor yet where Deva spreads her wizard stream.[9]
Ay me! I fondly dream
"Had ye been there," — for what could that have done?
What could the Muse herself that Orpheus[10] bore,
The Muse herself, for her enchanting son,
60   Whom universal nature did lament,

                  ⟶

6 traditional pastoral name which perhaps refers to a specific Cambridge don known to both Milton and King. 7 female nature spirits. 8 priestly class in ancient Britain. 9 Mona: isle of Anglesey; Deva: the river Dee in Cheshire that empties into the Irish Sea. 10 archetypal poet born of the muse Calliope.

When, by the rout that made the hideous roar,
His gory visage down the stream was sent,
Down the swift Hebrus to the Lesbian shore?[11]
    Alas! what boots[12] it with uncessant care
65 To tend the homely, slighted, shepherd's trade,
And strictly meditate the thankless Muse?
Were it not better done, as others use,
To sport with Amaryllis in the shade,
Or with the tangles of Neæra's hair?[13]
70 Fame is the spur that the clear spirit doth raise
(That last infirmity of noble mind)
To scorn delights and live laborious days;
But the fair guerdon[14] when we hope to find,
And think to burst out into sudden blaze,
75 Comes the blind Fury with the abhorred shears,[15]
And slits the thin-spun life. "But not the praise,"
Phœbus[16] replied, and touched my trembling ears:
    "Fame is no plant that grows on mortal soil,
Nor in the glistering foil
80 Set off to the world, nor in broad rumour lies
But lives and spreads aloft by those pure eyes
And perfect witness of all-judging Jove;
As he pronounces lastly on each deed,
Of so much fame in heaven expect thy meed."
85   O fountain Arethuse, and thou honoured flood,
Smooth-sliding Mincius, crowned with vocal reeds,[17]
That strain I heard was of a higher mood.
But now my oat[18] proceeds,
And listens to the Herald of the Sea,[19]
90 That came in Neptune's plea.
He asked the waves, and asked the felon winds,
What hard mishap hath doomed this gentle swain?
And questioned every gust of rugged wings
That blows from off each beaked promontory.
95 They knew not of his story;
And sage Hippotades[20] their answer brings,
That not a blast was from his dungeon strayed:

→

11 decapitated by angered and overzealous celebrants, Orpheus's head floated down the river Hebrus to
the isle of Lesbos. 12 profits. 13 Amaryllis, Neæra: pastoral names for pretty shepherdesses. 14 reward.
15 i.e., Atropos, the Fate who finally cuts off the thread of life. 16 i.e., Phoebus Apollo, god of poetry.
17 Arethuse, a spring; Mincius, a river: Italian locations associated respectively with the great pastoral
poets Theocritus and Virgil. 18 i.e., "oaten flute" (line 33). 19 Triton is Neptune's "herald of the sea."
20 god of winds.

The air was calm, and on the level brine
Sleek Panope[21] with all her sisters played.
100 It was that fatal and perfidious bark,
Built in the eclipse, and rigged with curses dark,
That sunk so low that sacred head of thine.
    Next, Camus,[22] reverend sire, went footing slow,
His mantle hairy, and his bonnet sedge,
105 Inwrought with figures dim, and on the edge
Like to that sanguine flower inscribed with woe.
    "Ah! who hath reft," quoth he, "my dearest pledge?"
Last came, and last did go,
The Pilot of the Galilean Lake;[23]
110 Two massy keys he bore of metals twain
(The golden opes, the iron shuts amain).
He shook his mitred locks, and stern bespake:—
"How well could I have spared for thee, young swain,
Enow of such as, for their bellies' sake,
115 Creep, and intrude, and climb into the fold!
Of other care they little reckoning make
Than how to scramble at the shearers' feast,
And shove away the worthy bidden guest.
Blind mouths! that scarce themselves know how to hold
120 A sheep-hook, or have learnt aught else the least
That to the faithful herdman's art belongs!
What recks it them? What need they? They are sped;
And, when they list, their lean and flashy songs
Grate on their scrannel[24] pipes of wretched straw;
125 The hungry sheep look up, and are not fed,
But, swoln with wind and the rank mist they draw,
Rot inwardly, and foul contagion spread;
Besides what the grim wolf with privy paw
Daily devours apace, and nothing said.
130 But that two-handed engine at the door
Stands ready to smite once, and smite no more."
    Return, Alpheus;[25] the dread voice is past
That shrunk thy streams; return Sicilian Muse,
And call the vales, and bid them hither cast
135 Their bells and flowerets of a thousand hues.
Ye valleys low, where the mild whispers use

→

21 sea nymph: one of 50 sisters who were daughters of Nereus. 22 god of the river Cam, upon which
Cambridge University is situated. 23 i.e., St. Peter. 24 thin, meagre. 25 Arcadian river, symbol for gentle
pastoral verse.

Of shades, and wanton winds, and gushing brooks,
On whose fresh lap the swart star[26] sparely looks,
Throw hither all your quaint enamelled eyes,
140 That on the green turf suck the honeyed showers,
And purple all the ground with vernal flowers.
Bring the rathe[27] primrose that forsaken dies,
The tufted crow-toe, and pale jessamine,
The white pink, and the pansy freaked[28] with jet,
145 The glowing violet,
The musk-rose, and the well-attired woodbine,
With cowslips wan that hang the pensive head,
And every flower that sad embroidery wears;
Bid amaranthus[29] all his beauty shed,
150 And daffadillies fill their cups with tears,
To strew the laureate hearse where Lycid lies.
For so, to interpose a little ease,
Let our frail thoughts dally with false surmise,
Ay me! whilst thee the shores and sounding seas
155 Wash far away, where'er thy bones are hurled;
Whether beyond the stormy Hebrides,[30]
Where thou perhaps under the whelming tide
Visit'st the bottom of the monstrous world;
Or whether thou, to our moist vows denied,
160 Sleep'st by the fable of Bellerus[31] old,
Where the great Vision of the guarded mount
Looks toward Namancos and Bayona's hold.[32]
Look homeward, Angel, now, and melt with ruth:
And, O ye dolphins, waft the hapless youth.
165   Weep no more, woeful shepherds, weep no more,
For Lycidas, your sorrow, is not dead,
Sunk though he be beneath the watery floor.
So sinks the day-star[33] in the ocean bed,
And yet anon repairs his drooping head,
170 And tricks his beams, and with new-spangled ore
Flames in the forehead of the morning sky:
So Lycidas sunk low, but mounted high,
Through the dear might of Him that walked the waves,
Where, other groves and other streams along,

———→

26 Sirius, the Dog Star of late summer. 27 early. 28 freckled. 29 imaginary flower that is always in bloom.
30 islands off the coast of Scotland that mark the northern boundary of the Irish Sea. 31 imaginary giant
supposed to be buried at Land's End, Cornwall. 32 Namancos, Bayona: locations on the coast of Spain,
imagined as visible from St. Michael's Mount, Cornwall. 33 i.e., the sun.

175 With nectar pure his oozy locks he laves,
And hears the unexpressive nuptial song,
In the blest kingdoms meek of joy and love.
There entertain him all the Saints above,
In solemn troops, and sweet societies,
180 That sing, and singing in their glory move,
And wipe the tears for ever from his eyes.
Now, Lycidas, the shepherds weep no more;
Henceforth thou art the Genius [34] of the shore,
In thy large recompense, and shalt be good
185 To all that wander in that perilous flood.

    Thus sang the uncouth swain to the oaks and rills,
While the still morn went out with sandals grey:
He touched the tender stops of various quills,
With eager thought warbling his Doric lay: [35]
190 And now the sun had stretched out all the hills,
And now was dropt into the western bay.
At last he rose, and twitched his mantle blue:
To-morrow to fresh woods, and pastures new.

                            (1638)

How soon hath Time

How soon hath Time, the subtle thief of youth,
    Stol'n on his wing my three-and-twentieth year!
    My hasting days fly on with full career,
    But my late spring no bud or blossom shew'th.
5 Perhaps my semblance might deceive the truth
    That I to manhood am arrived so near;
    And inward ripeness doth much less appear,
    That some more timely-happy spirits endu'th. [1]
Yet, be it less or more, or soon or slow,
10   It shall be still in strictest measure even
    To that same lot, however mean or high,
Toward which Time leads me, and the will of Heaven,
    All is, if I have grace to use it so,
    As ever in my great Task-Master's eye.

(1631–32)   (1645)

34 i.e., protective local deity. 35 i.e., simple song.
1 endoweth.

When I consider how my light is spent

When I consider how my light is spent
  Ere half my days in this dark world and wide,
  And that one talent which is death to hide
  Lodged with me useless, though my soul more bent
5 To serve therewith my Maker, and present
  My true account, lest He returning chide,
  "Doth God exact day-labour, light denied?"
  I fondly ask. But Patience, to prevent
That murmur, soon replies, "God doth not need
10 Either man's work or his own gifts. Who best
  Bear his mild yoke, they serve him best. His state
Is kingly: thousands at his bidding speed,
  And post o'er land and ocean without rest;
  They also serve who only stand and wait."

(1652?)   (1673)

On the Late Massacre in Piedmont[1]

Avenge, O Lord, thy slaughtered saints, whose bones
  Lie scattered on the Alpine mountains cold;
  Even them who kept thy truth so pure of old,
  When all our fathers worshiped stocks and stones,
5 Forget not: in thy book record their groans
  Who were thy sheep, and in their ancient fold
  Slain by the bloody Piemontese, that rolled
  Mother with infant down the rocks. Their moans
The vales redoubled to the hills, and they
10 To heaven. Their martyred blood and ashes sow
  O'er all the Italian fields, where still doth sway
The triple Tyrant;[2] that from these may grow
  A hundredfold, who, having learnt thy way,
  Early may fly the Babylonian woe.[3]

(1655)   (1673)

1 the Piedmont region of northwestern Italy, bounded by France and Switzerland. On April 24, 1655, Italian troops massacred the Protestant Piedmontese for their dissenting views. 2 i.e., the pope, identified by his triple crown. 3 apocalyptic destruction; see Revelation 18.

Anne Bradstreet (c. 1612–1672)

Born in Northampton, England, Anne Bradstreet, unlike most young women of her day, read widely in classical and English poetry. When she was eighteen years old, she came to Massachusetts with her family and husband. While taking care of the family's frequent moves and raising eight children, she wrote a great deal of poetry and is recognized as one of the first important American poets. Although she wrote many long, complex works on theological subjects, she is best remembered for those poems that sensitively communicate her feelings and observations about her home and family.

To my Dear and loving Husband

If ever two were one, then surely we.
If ever man were lov'd by wife, then thee;
If ever wife was happy in a man,
Compare with me ye women if you can.
5   I prize thy love more than whole Mines of gold,
Or all the riches that the East doth hold.
My love is such that Rivers cannot quench,
Nor ought but love from thee, give recompence.
Thy love is such I can no way repay,
10 The heavens reward thee manifold I pray.
Then while we live, in love lets so persever,[1]
That when we live no more, we may live ever.

(1678)

Upon the burning of our house, July 10, 1666

In silent night when rest I took,
For sorrow neer I did not look,
I waken'd was with thundring nois
And Piteous shreiks of dreadfull voice.
5   That fearfull sound of fire and fire,
Let no man know is my Desire.

---

1 persevere.

I, starting up, the light did spye,
And to my God my heart did cry
To strengthen me in my Distresse
And not to leave me succourlesse.[1]
Then coming out beheld a space,
The flame consume my dwelling place.

And, when I could no longer look,
I blest his Name that gave and took,
That layd my goods now in the dust:
Yea so it was, and so 'twas just.
It was his own: it was not mine;
Far be it that I should repine.

He might of All justly bereft,
But yet sufficient for us left.
When by the Ruines oft I past,
My sorrowing eyes aside did cast,
And here and there the places spye
Where oft I sate, and long did lye.

Here stood that Trunk, and there that chest;
There lay that store I counted best:
My pleasant things in ashes lye,
And them behold no more shall I.
Under thy roof no guest shall sitt,
Nor at thy Table eat a bitt.

No pleasant tale shall e'er be told,
Nor things recounted done of old.
No Candle e'er shall shine in Thee,
Nor bridegroom's voice e'er heard shall bee.
In silence ever shalt thou lye;
Adeiu, Adeiu; All's vanity.

Then streight I gin my heart to chide,
And did thy wealth on earth abide?
Didst fix thy hope on mouldring dust,
The arm of flesh didst make thy trust?
Raise up thy thoughts above the skye
That dunghill mists away may flie.

1 without help.

Thou hast an house on high erect
Fram'd by that mighty Architect,
45   With glory richly furnished,
Stands permanent tho' this bee fled.
It's purchaséd, and paid for too
By him who hath enough to doe.

A Prise so vast as is unknown,
50   Yet, by his Gift, is made thine own.
Ther's wealth enough, I need no more;
Farewell my Pelf,[2] farewell my Store.
The world no longer let me Love,
My hope and Treasure lyes Above.

(1678)

Andrew Marvell (1621–1678)

Andrew Marvell was the son of a Yorkshire clergyman. He obtained his B.A. at Trinity College, Cambridge, and proceeded to travel widely on the Continent. Adept at learning, he absorbed French, Italian, Dutch, and Spanish — languages important for an Englishman bent on a career in public service and diplomacy. He was appointed assistant to Cromwell's Latin secretary, John Milton, in 1658, and was later elected M.P. for Hull. It seems Marvell brought some influence to bear upon securing the release and safety of Milton at the Restoration. Throughout his career in public life, Marvell was prudent, honest, and committedly faithful to Puritan politics during and after the time of Cromwell's administration.

But he was also a poet. His verses are smooth and urbane with a metaphysical quality of irony and control that reinvests conventional images with freshness. Although overshadowed in reputation by Milton, Marvell creates lucid images of nature and time with wit and precision. None of his poems was published in his own lifetime.

2 property, earthly possessions.

To His Coy Mistress

Had we but world enough, and time,
This coyness, lady, were no crime.
We would sit down, and think which way
To walk, and pass our long love's day.
5   Thou by the Indian Ganges' side
Should'st rubies find: I by the tide
Of Humber[1] would complain. I would
Love you ten years before the flood,
And you should, if you please, refuse
10 Till the conversion of the Jews:[2]
My vegetable[3] love should grow
Vaster than empires, and more slow;
An hundred years should go to praise
Thine eyes, and on thy forehead gaze;
15 Two hundred to adore each breast,
But thirty thousand to the rest;
An age at least to every part,
And the last age should show your heart.
For, lady, you deserve this state,
20 Nor would I love at lower rate.
    But at my back I always hear
Time's winged chariot hurrying near,
And yonder all before us lie
Deserts of vast eternity.
25 Thy beauty shall no more be found,
Nor, in thy marble vault, shall sound
My echoing song: then worms shall try
That long preserved virginity,
And your quaint[4] honour turn to dust,
30 And into ashes all my lust:
The grave's a fine and private place,
But none, I think, do there embrace.
    Now therefore, while the youthful hue
Sits on thy skin like morning dew,
35 And while thy willing soul transpires
At every pore with instant fires,

⟶

1 a river flowing through Hull, Marvell's home town. 2 an event expected at the end of time. 3 following Aristotle, Renaissance scientists saw humans as possessing three qualities: the rational, the sensitive, and the vegetative; the vegetative provided only life and growth. 4. fastidious, prim, with a vulgar pun on the female sexual organ.

Now let us sport us while we may,
And now, like amorous birds of prey
Rather at once our time devour,
40   Than languish in his slow-chapped[5] power.
Let us roll all our strength and all
Our sweetness up into one ball,
And tear our pleasures with rough strife,
Thorough[6] the iron gates of life;
45   Thus, though we cannot make our sun
Stand still, yet we will make him run.

(1650–58?)   (1681)

The Garden

How vainly men themselves amaze,[1]
To win the palm, the oak, or bays,[2]
And their incessant labours see
Crowned from some single herb, or tree,
5   Whose short and narrow-verged shade
Does prudently their toils upbraid,
While all the flowers, and trees, do close
To weave the garlands of repose!

     Fair Quiet, have I found thee here,
10   And Innocence, thy sister dear?
Mistaken long, I sought you then
In busy companies of men.
Your sacred plants, if here below,
Only among the plants will grow;
15   Society is all but rude
To this delicious solitude.

     No white nor red was ever seen
So amorous as this lovely green.
Fond lovers, cruel as their flame,
20   Cut in these trees their mistress' name:

⟶

---

5 i.e., slow-jawed, slow-chewing. 6 through.
1 bewilder, perplex. 2 classical trophies for military, civic, or poetic achievement.

Little, alas! they know or heed,
How far these beauties her exceed!
Fair trees! where'er your barks I wound,
No name shall but your own be found.

25   When we have run our passion's heat,
Love hither makes his best retreat.
The gods, who mortal beauty chase,
Still in a tree did end their race;
Apollo hunted Daphne so,
30   Only that she might laurel grow;
And Pan did after Syrinx speed,
Not as a nymph, but for a reed.[3]

What wond'rous life is this I lead!
Ripe apples drop about my head;
35   The luscious clusters of the vine
Upon my mouth do crush their wine;
The nectarine, and curious peach,
Into my hands themselves do reach;
Stumbling on melons, as I pass,
40   Insnared with flowers, I fall on grass.

Meanwhile the mind, from pleasure less,
Withdraws into its happiness; —
The mind, that ocean where each kind
Does straight its own resemblance find;[4]—
45   Yet it creates, transcending these,
Far other worlds, and other seas,
Annihilating all that's made
To a green thought in a green shade.

Here at the fountain's sliding foot,
50   Or at some fruit-tree's mossy root,
Casting the body's vest aside,
My soul into the boughs does glide:
There, like a bird, it sits and sings,
Then whets and combs its silver wings,

——→

3 Marvell here alters the motivation of the gods in Ovid's *Metamorphoses*, in which the nymphs Daphne and Syrinx elude pursuit by the lustful gods Apollo and Pan by turning themselves into a laurel tree and a reed, respectively. 4 the sea was supposed to contain creatures corresponding to all those on land.

55   And, till prepared for longer flight,
     Waves in its plumes the various light.

     Such was that happy garden-state,
     While man there walked without a mate:
     After a place so pure and sweet,
60   What other help could yet be meet!
     But 'twas beyond a mortal's share
     To wander solitary there:
     Two paradises 'twere in one,
     To live in paradise alone.

65   How well the skilful gardener drew
     Of flowers, and herbs, this dial[2] new,
     Where, from above, the milder sun
     Does through a fragrant zodiac run,
     And, as it works, the industrious bee
70   Computes its time as well as we!
     How could such sweet and wholesome hours
     Be reckoned but with herbs and flowers?

     (1650–58?)   (1681)

Alexander Pope   (1688–1744)

Pope dominated English poetry during the first half of the eighteenth century. His greatest poems were satires, public statements that had the power to change the course of public events. Like most poets of his own and the previous age, Pope wrote primarily in heroic couplets (i.e., closed iambic pentameter couplets); unlike others, however, Pope lived on his earnings as a poet. He had to, since he faced two devastating handicaps. He was born into a Roman Catholic family, which meant that he was forbidden by law from attending university, holding public office, or even living in London. Even worse, when he was a boy he contracted tuberculosis of the spine, which stunted his growth (he was never more than about four-foot-eight in height), made his body crooked, and gave him almost constant pain during his adult life. Fortunately, however, he had kindly and well-to-do parents, who raised him just outside London and saw that he had a thorough education in classical literature. Pope's poetic career falls into three distinct phases. His early poems, up to about 1713, were witty and playful satires; The Rape of the Lock, first published in 1712, is the gem of these early poems and still his best-known work. During a middle

2 sundial.

period, from roughly 1713 to 1726, he devoted himself to translating Homer's two great epics, the *Iliad* (completed in 1720) and the *Odyssey* (completed in 1726), and to producing an edition of Shakespeare's plays (1725). These projects gave him financial security, and from 1727 onward Pope again wrote his own poetry, but now of a much more sober nature: satires, including the autobiographical *Epistle to Dr. Arbuthnot* (1735) and *The Dunciad* (1728–43), a mock-epic celebrating the triumph of duncedom in contemporary Britain; moral essays in verse upon such topics as the proper use of riches; and his philosophical poem *An Essay on Man*, published anonymously in 1733–34.

The Rape of the Lock;
An Heroi-Comical Poem[1]

Nolueram, Belinda, tuos violare capillos,
Sed juvat hoc precibus me tribuisse tuis.
                                    — Martial[2]

TO
Mrs.[3] *ARABELLA FERMOR.*

Madam,
It will be in vain to deny that I have some Regard for this Piece, since I Dedicate it to You. Yet You may bear me Witness, it was intended only to divert a few young Ladies, who have good Sense and good Humour enough, to laugh not only at their Sex's little unguarded Follies, but at their own. But as it was communicated with the Air of a Secret, it soon found its Way into the World. An imperfect Copy having been offer'd to a Bookseller, You had the Good-Nature for my Sake to consent to the Publication of one more correct: This I was forc'd to before I had executed half my Design, for the *Machinery* was entirely wanting to compleat it.[4]

---

1 Pope's title alludes to the poem's origin. A quarrel had developed between two prominent Roman Catholic families when Robert, Lord Petre, cut off a lock from the head of Arabella Fermor, a celebrated beauty known as "Belle." John Caryll, Pope's friend, urged Pope to write a poem that would restore good feelings. Pope's subtitle alludes to the poem's genre: it is a mock-epic, and the well-known features of epic poems are comically transformed. The combat of heroic warriors becomes the drawing-room war between the sexes; the rape of Helen becomes that of a lock of hair; the arming of the hero for combat becomes the heroine's dressing and beautification for a social engagement, and so on. 2 Pope's epigraph is slightly altered from the Roman satirist Martial: "I did not wish, Belinda, to profane your locks, but it pleases me to have granted this to your prayers." 3 "Mrs." was used for ladies, whether married or single. 4 in its original (1712) form, the poem consisted of two cantos of 334 lines; as Pope explains, he expanded the poem to five cantos in 1714 by adding the "machinery" (the supernatural agents found in epic poems).

The *Machinery*, Madam, is a Term invented by the Criticks, to signify that Part which the Deities, Angels, or Dæmons, are made to act in a Poem: For the ancient Poets are in one respect like many modern Ladies; Let an Action be never so trivial in it self, they always make it appear of the utmost Importance. These Machines I determin'd to raise on a very new and odd Foundation, the *Rosicrucian* [5] Doctrine of Spirits.

I know how disagreeable it is to make use of hard Words before a Lady; but 'tis so much the Concern of a Poet to have his Works understood, and particularly by your Sex, that You must give me leave to explain two or three difficult Terms.

The *Rosicrucians* are a People I must bring You acquainted with. The best Account I know of them is in a French Book call'd *Le Comte de Gabalis*, which both in its Title and Size is so like a *Novel*, that many of the Fair Sex have read it for one by Mistake.[6] According to these Gentlemen, the four Elements [7] are inhabited by Spirits, which they call *Sylphs, Gnomes, Nymphs*, and *Salamanders*. The *Gnomes*, or Dæmons of Earth, delight in Mischief; but the *Sylphs*, whose Habitation is in the Air, are the best-condition'd Creatures imaginable. For they say, any Mortals may enjoy the most intimate Familiarities with these gentle Spirits, upon a Condition very easie to all true *Adepts*, an inviolate Preservation of Chastity.

As to the following Canto's, all the Passages of them are as Fabulous, as the Vision at the Beginning, or the Transformation at the End; (except the Loss of your Hair, which I always mention with Reverence.) The Human Persons are as Fictitious as the Airy ones; and the Character of *Belinda*, as it is now manag'd, resembles You in nothing but in Beauty.

If this Poem had as many Graces as there are in Your Person, or in Your Mind, yet I could never hope it should pass thro' the World half so Uncensured as You have done. But let its Fortune be what it will, mine is happy enough, to have given me this Occasion of assuring You that I am, with the truest Esteem,

Madam,
Your Most Obedient
Humble Servant.
A. POPE

---

5 eccentric occult religion that originated in Germany early in the seventeenth century. 6 in fact, *Le Comte de Gabalis* (1670), written by the Abbé de Montfaucon de Villars, is a facetious and largely fictitious summary of Rosicrucianism that had been published as a novel when translated into English in 1680. 7 air, earth, water, and fire, according to traditional science.

CANTO I.

What dire Offence from am'rous Causes springs,
What mighty Contests rise from trivial Things,[8]
I sing — This Verse to *Caryll*, Muse! is due;
This, ev'n *Belinda* may vouchsafe to view:
Slight is the Subject, but not so the Praise,
If She inspire, and He approve my Lays.
　　Say what strange Motive, Goddess! cou'd compel
A well-bred *Lord* t'assault a gentle *Belle*?[9]
Oh say what stranger Cause, yet unexplor'd,
Cou'd make a gentle *Belle* reject a *Lord*?
In Tasks so bold, can Little Men engage,
And in soft Bosoms dwells such mighty Rage?
　　Sol thro' white Curtains shot a tim'rous Ray,
And Op'd those Eyes that must eclipse the Day;
Now Lapdogs give themselves the rowzing Shake,
And sleepless Lovers, just at Twelve, awake:
Thrice rung the Bell, the Slipper knock'd the Ground,[10]
And the press'd Watch return'd a silver Sound.[11]
Belinda still her downy Pillow prest,
Her Guardian *Sylph* prolong'd the balmy Rest.
'Twas he had summon'd to her silent Bed
The Morning-Dream that hover'd o'er her Head.[12]
A Youth more glitt'ring than a *Birth-night Beau*,[13]
(That ev'n in Slumber caus'd her Cheek to glow)
Seem'd to her Ear his winning Lips to lay,
And thus in Whispers said, or seem'd to say.
　　Fairest of Mortals, thou distinguish'd Care
Of thousand bright Inhabitants of Air!
If e'er one Vision touch'd thy infant Thought,
Of all the Nurse and all the Priest have taught,[14]
Of airy Elves by Moonlight Shadows seen,
The silver Token,[15] and the circled Green,[16]

5

10

15

20

25

30

———▶

8 like Homer, Virgil, and Milton, Pope begins his poem with a concise statement of its theme, immediately
followed by an invocation of the Muse. 9 again, like Virgil and Milton, before plunging into the action of
his poem Pope asks questions about the causes of all that will follow. 10 ladies summoned their maids by
ringing a hand-bell or by knocking on the floor with a high-heeled shoe. 11 England was famous for its
"repeater" watches; when the stem was pressed, the watch chimed the most recent hour and quarter-hour.
12 epic heroes often receive warnings about coming events from the gods in dreams; cf. Eve's dream in *Paradise
Lost* V.28–93. 13 courtier splendidly dressed for the royal birthday. 14 the traditional promulgators of super-
stitions. 15 fairies were believed to skim off the cream from jugs of milk left standing overnight, leaving a coin
as payment. 16 "fairy rings" (withered circles in grass) were thought to be caused by fairies dancing.

Or Virgins visited by Angel-Pow'rs,[17]
With Golden Crowns and Wreaths of heav'nly Flow'rs,
35 Hear and believe! thy own Importance know,
Nor bound thy narrow Views to Things below.
Some secret Truths from Learned Pride conceal'd,
To Maids alone and Children are reveal'd:
What tho' no Credit doubting Wits may give?
40 The Fair and Innocent shall still believe.
Know then, unnumber'd Spirits round thee fly,
The light *Militia* of the lower Sky;
These, tho' unseen, are ever on the Wing,
Hang o'er the *Box*,[18] and hover round the *Ring*.[19]
45 Think what an Equipage[20] thou hast in Air,
And view with scorn *Two Pages* and a *Chair*.[21]
As now your own, our Beings were of old,
And once inclos'd in Woman's beauteous Mold;
Thence, by a soft Transition, we repair
50 From earthly Vehicles[22] to these of Air.
Think not, when Woman's transient Breath is fled,
That all her Vanities at once are dead:
Succeeding Vanities she still regards,
And tho' she plays no more, o'erlooks the Cards.
55 Her Joy in gilded Chariots, when alive,
And Love of *Ombre*,[23] after Death survive.
For when the Fair in all their Pride expire,
To their first Elements[24] their Souls retire:
The Sprights[25] of fiery Termagants[26] in Flame
60 Mount up, and take a *Salamander's*[27] Name.
Soft yielding Minds to Water glide away,
And sip with *Nymphs*, their Elemental Tea.
The graver Prude sinks downward to a *Gnome*,
In search of Mischief still on Earth to roam.
65 The light Coquettes in *Sylphs* aloft repair,
And sport and flutter in the Fields of Air.

———→

17 many saints were virgins to whom angels appeared in mystic visions (St. Theresa of Avila, for instance).
18 the theatre box, where the elite among playgoers sat. 19 a fashionable circular drive in Hyde Park.
20 carriage with horses and footmen. 21 sedan-chair, in which passengers were carried. 22 meaning both
carriages and bodies (the body is the vehicle of the soul). 23 popular card game (see note 73). 24 tradi-
tionally, the four elements of all matter (earth, air, fire, water) had their counterparts in the four "humours"
or fluids of the human body (black bile, yellow bile, blood, phlegm); one of these humours was supposed to
dominate each person, determining his or her temperament. 25 spirits. 26 shrews. 27 salamanders were
believed able to live in fire.

Know farther yet; Whoever fair and chaste
Rejects Mankind, is by some *Sylph* embrac'd:
For Spirits, freed from mortal Laws, with ease
70 Assume what Sexes and what Shapes they please.[28]
What guards the Purity of melting Maids,
In Courtly Balls, and Midnight Masquerades,[29]
Safe from the treach'rous Friend, the daring Spark,[30]
The Glance by Day, the Whisper in the Dark;
75 When kind Occasion prompts their warm Desires,
When Musick softens, and when Dancing fires?
'Tis but their *Sylph*, the wise Celestials know,
Tho' *Honour* is the Word with Men below.

Some Nymphs there are, too conscious of their Face,
80 For Life predestin'd to the *Gnomes'* Embrace.
These swell their Prospects and exalt their Pride,
When Offers are disdain'd, and Love deny'd.
Then gay Ideas crowd the vacant Brain;
While Peers and Dukes, and all their sweeping Train,
85 And Garters, Stars, and Coronets[31] appear,
And in soft Sounds, *Your Grace*[32] salutes their Ear.
'Tis these that early taint the Female Soul,
Instruct the Eyes of young *Coquettes* to roll,
Teach Infant-Cheeks a bidden Blush to know,
90 And little Hearts to flutter at a *Beau*.

Oft when the World imagine Women stray,
The *Sylphs* thro' mystick Mazes guide their Way,
Thro' all the giddy Circle they pursue,
And old Impertinence expel by new.
95 What tender Maid but must a Victim fall
To one Man's Treat,[33] but for another's Ball?
When *Florio* speaks, what Virgin could withstand,
If gentle *Damon* did not squeeze her Hand?
With varying Vanities, from ev'ry Part,
100 They shift the moving Toyshop of their Heart;
Where Wigs with Wigs, with Sword-knots[34] Sword-knots strive,
Beaus banish Beaus, and Coaches Coaches drive.
This erring Mortals Levity may call,
Oh blind to Truth! the *Sylphs* contrive it all.

—————→

28 as Milton had explained in *Paradise Lost* I.423–31. 29 masked balls. 30 fop or beau. 31 garters, stars, and coronets are all insignia of noble rank. 32 the courtesy title used to address a duke or duchess. 33 feast, entertainment. 34 ribbons tied to the hilt of a sword.

105   Of these am I, who thy Protection claim,
A watchful Sprite, and *Ariel* is my Name.
Late, as I rang'd the Crystal Wilds of Air,
In the clear Mirror of thy ruling *Star*
I saw, alas! some dread Event impend,
110   Ere to the Main this Morning Sun descend.
But Heav'n reveals not what, or how, or where:
Warn'd by thy *Sylph*, oh Pious Maid beware!
This to disclose is all thy Guardian can.
Beware of all, but most beware of Man!
115   He said; when *Shock*,[35] who thought she slept too long,
Leapt up, and wak'd his Mistress with his Tongue.
'Twas then *Belinda*! if Report say true,
Thy Eyes first open'd on a *Billet-doux*;[36]
Wounds, *Charms*, and *Ardors*, were no sooner read,
120   But all the Vision vanish'd from thy Head.
       And now, unveil'd, the *Toilet*[37] stands display'd,
Each Silver Vase in mystic Order laid.
First, rob'd in White, the Nymph intent adores
With Head uncover'd, the *Cosmetic* Pow'rs.
125   A heavn'ly Image in the Glass appears,
To that she bends, to that her Eyes she rears;
Th'inferior Priestess,[38] at her Altar's side,
Trembling, begins the sacred Rites of Pride.
Unnumber'd Treasures ope at once, and here
130   The various Off'rings of the World appear;
From each she nicely[39] culls with curious[40] Toil,
And decks the Goddess with the glitt'ring Spoil.
This Casket *India*'s glowing Gems unlocks,
And all *Arabia* breathes from yonder Box.
135   The Tortoise here and Elephant unite,
Transform'd to *Combs*, the speckled and the white.
Here Files of Pins extend their shining Rows,
Puffs, Powders, Patches, Bibles, Billet-doux.
Now awful[41] Beauty puts on all its Arms;
140   The Fair each moment rises in her Charms,
Repairs her Smiles, awakens ev'ry Grace,
And calls forth all the Wonders of her Face;

                      ——→

35 Belinda's lap dog. 36 love letter. 37 dressing table. 38 Belinda's maid Betty. 39 fastidiously.
40 careful. 41 awe-inspiring.

Sees by Degrees a purer Blush arise,
And keener Lightnings quicken in her Eyes.
145 The busy *Sylphs* surround their darling Care;
These set the Head, and those divide the Hair,
Some fold the Sleeve, whilst others plait the Gown;
And *Betty*'s prais'd for Labours not her own.

CANTO II.

Not with more Glories, in th' Etherial Plain,
The Sun first rises o'er the purpled Main,
Than issuing forth, the Rival of his Beams
Lanch'd on the Bosom of the Silver *Thames*.[42]
5 Fair Nymphs, and well-drest Youths around her shone,
But ev'ry Eye was fix'd on her alone.
On her white Breast a sparkling *Cross* she wore,
Which *Jews* might kiss, and Infidels adore.[43]
Her lively Looks a sprightly Mind disclose,
10 Quick as her Eyes, and as unfix'd as those:
Favours to none, to all she Smiles extends,
Oft she rejects, but never once offends.
Bright as the Sun, her Eyes the Gazers strike,
And, like the Sun, they shine on all alike.
15 Yet graceful Ease, and Sweetness void of Pride,
Might hide her Faults, if *Belles* had Faults to hide:
If to her share some Female Errors fall,
Look on her Face, and you'll forget 'em all.
This Nymph, to the Destruction of Mankind,
20 Nourish'd two Locks, which graceful hung behind
In equal Curls, and well conspir'd to deck
With shining Ringlets the smooth Iv'ry Neck.
Love in these Labyrinths his Slaves detains,
And mighty Hearts are held in slender Chains.
25 With hairy Sprindges[44] we the Birds betray,
Slight Lines of Hair surprize the Finny Prey,
Fair Tresses Man's Imperial Race insnare,
And Beauty draws us with a single Hair.
Th' Adventrous *Baron* the bright Locks admir'd,
30 He saw, he wish'd, and to the Prize aspir'd:

———→

42 Belinda travels by boat up the Thames from London to Hampton Court Palace, the royal palace some
ten kilometres upstream. 43 kissing or adoration of the cross marked conversion to Christianity.
44 snares, traps; pronounced *sprin-jez*.

Resolv'd to win, he meditates the way,
By Force to ravish, or by Fraud betray;
For when Success a Lover's Toil attends,
Few ask, if Fraud or Force attain'd his Ends.
35   For this, ere *Phœbus*[45] rose, he had implor'd
Propitious Heav'n, and ev'ry Pow'r ador'd,
But chiefly *Love* — to *Love* an Altar built,
Of twelve vast *French* Romances,[46] neatly gilt.
There lay three Garters, half a Pair of Gloves;
40   And all the Trophies of his former Loves.
With tender *Billet-doux* he lights the Pyre,
And breathes three am'rous Sighs to raise the Fire.
Then prostrate falls, and begs with ardent Eyes
Soon to obtain, and long possess the Prize:
45   The Pow'rs gave Ear, and granted half his Pray'r,
The rest, the Winds dispers'd in empty Air.[47]
        But now secure[48] the painted Vessel glides,
The Sun-beams trembling on the floating Tydes,
While melting Musick steals upon the Sky,
50   And soften'd Sounds along the Waters die.
Smooth flow the Waves, the Zephyrs[49] gently play,
Belinda smil'd, and all the World was gay.
All but the *Sylph* — With careful Thoughts opprest,
Th'impending Woe sate heavy on his Breast.
55   He summons strait his Denizens of Air;
The lucid Squadrons round the Sails repair:[50]
Soft o'er the Shrouds[51] Aerial Whispers breathe,
That seem'd but *Zephyrs* to the Train beneath.
Some to the Sun their Insect-Wings unfold,
60   Waft on the Breeze, or sink in Clouds of Gold.
Transparent Forms, too fine for mortal Sight,
Their fluid Bodies half dissolv'd in Light.
Loose to the Wind their airy Garments flew,
Thin glitt'ring Textures of the filmy Dew;
65   Dipt in the richest Tincture of the Skies,
Where Light disports in ever-mingling Dies,
While ev'ry Beam new transient Colours flings,
Colours that change whene'er they wave their Wings.

$\longrightarrow$

45 the sun. 46 notoriously long and idealized love stories, written by seventeenth-century French aristocrats
and set in ancient Greece and Rome. 47 in epics, the gods frequently grant only half of a character's prayer,
with the other half being abandoned to the winds. 48 free from care. 49 gentle breezes. 50 gather.
51 ropes.

Amid the Circle, on the gilded Mast,
70   Superior by the Head,[52] was *Ariel* plac'd;
His Purple Pinions opening to the Sun,
He rais'd his Azure Wand, and thus begun.
        Ye *Sylphs* and *Sylphids*,[53] to your Chief give Ear,
Fays, Fairies, Genii, Elves, and *Dæmons* hear![54]
75   Ye know the Spheres and various Tasks assign'd,
By Laws Eternal, to th' Aerial Kind.
Some in the Fields of purest *aether*[55] play,
And bask and whiten in the Blaze of Day.
Some guide the Course of wandring Orbs on high,
80   Or roll the Planets thro' the boundless Sky.
Some less refin'd, beneath the Moon's pale Light
Pursue the Stars that shoot athwart the Night,
Or suck the Mists in grosser Air below,
Or dip their Pinions in the painted Bow,
85   Or brew fierce Tempests on the wintry Main,
Or o'er the Glebe[56] distill the kindly Rain.
Others on Earth o'er human Race preside,
Watch all their Ways, and all their Actions guide:
Of these the Chief the Care of Nations own,
90   And guard with Arms Divine the *British Throne*.
        Our humbler Province is to tend the Fair,
Not a less pleasing, tho' less glorious Care.
To save the Powder from too rude a Gale,
Nor let th' imprison'd Essences[57] exhale,
95   To draw fresh Colours from the vernal[58] Flow'rs,
To steal from Rainbows ere they drop in Show'rs
A brighter Wash;[59] to curl their waving Hairs,
Assist their Blushes, and inspire their Airs;
Nay oft, in Dreams, Invention we bestow,
100   To change a *Flounce*, or add a *Furbelo*.[60]
        This Day, black Omens threat the brightest Fair
That e'er deserv'd a watchful Spirit's Care;
Some dire Disaster, or by Force, or Slight,[61]
But what, or where, the Fates have wrapt in Night.

⟶

52 epic heroes are usually taller than their followers. 53 female sylphs. 54 the epic hero normally rallies his forces for action by a stirring speech that begins by addressing each of the ranks present in turn. 55 the air above the moon was considered pure and was known as the aether. 56 farmland. 57 perfumes. 58 spring. 59 lotion, rinse. 60 ruffle. 61 sleight, trick.

105   Whether the Nymph shall break *Diana's*[62] Law,
      Or some frail *China* Jar receive a Flaw,
      Or stain her Honour, or her new Brocade,
      Forget her Pray'rs, or miss a Masquerade,
      Or lose her Heart, or Necklace, at a Ball;
110   Or whether Heav'n has doom'd that *Shock* must fall.
      Haste then ye Spirits! to your Charge repair;
      The flutt'ring Fan be *Zephyretta's* Care;
      The Drops[63] to thee, *Brillante*, we consign;
      And, *Momentilla*, let the Watch be thine;
115   Do thou, *Crispissa*, tend her fav'rite Lock;
      Ariel himself shall be the Guard of *Shock*.
         To Fifty chosen *Sylphs*, of special Note,
      We trust th'important Charge, the *Petticoat*:
      Oft have we known that sev'nfold Fence to fail,
120   Tho' stiff with Hoops, and arm'd with Ribs of Whale.
      Form a strong Line about the Silver Bound,
      And guard the wide Circumference around.
         Whatever Spirit, careless of his Charge,
      His Post neglects, or leaves the Fair at large,
125   Shall feel sharp Vengeance soon o'ertake his Sins,
      Be stopt in *Vials*, or transfixt with *Pins*;
      Or plung'd in Lakes of bitter *Washes* lie,
      Or wedg'd whole Ages in a *Bodkin's*[64] Eye:
      Gums and *Pomatums*[65] shall his Flight restrain,
130   While clog'd he beats his silken Wings in vain;
      Or Alom-*Stypticks*[66] with contracting Power
      Shrink his thin Essence like a rivell'd[67] Flower.
      Or as *Ixion*[68] fix'd, the Wretch shall feel
      The giddy Motion of the whirling Mill,[69]
135   In Fumes of burning Chocolate shall glow,
      And tremble at the Sea that froaths below!
         He spoke; the Spirits from the Sails descend;
      Some, Orb in Orb, around the Nymph extend,
      Some thrid the mazy Ringlets of her Hair,
140   Some hang upon the Pendants of her Ear;
      With beating Hearts the dire Event they wait,
      Anxious, and trembling for the Birth of Fate.

---

62 Diana was the Roman goddess of the hunt and the protector of chastity. 63 diamond earrings. 64 needle's. 65 ointments. 66 astringents to stop bleeding. 67 shrivelled, wrinkled. 68 in Greek mythology, Ixion was a king whose punishment for his attempt to seduce the goddess Hera was to be bound in hell to a perpetually turning wheel. 69 for beating chocolate.

CANTO III.

Close by those Meads for ever crown'd with Flow'rs,
Where *Thames* with Pride surveys his rising Tow'rs,
There stands a Structure of Majestick Frame,[70]
Which from the neighb'ring *Hampton* takes it Name.
5   Here *Britain's* Statesmen oft the Fall foredoom
Of Foreign Tyrants, and of Nymphs at home;
Here Thou, Great *Anna!*[71] whom three Realms obey,
Dost sometimes Counsel take — and sometimes *Tea*.
Hither the Heroes and the Nymphs resort,
10   To taste awhile the Pleasures of a Court;
In various Talk th' instructive hours they past,
Who gave the *Ball*, or paid the *Visit* last:
One speaks the Glory of the *British Queen*,
And one describes a charming *Indian Screen*;
15   A third interprets Motions, Looks, and Eyes;
At ev'ry Word a Reputation dies.
Snuff, or the *Fan*, supply each Pause of Chat,
With singing, laughing, ogling, and all that.
Mean while declining from the Noon of Day,
20   The Sun obliquely shoots his burning Ray;
The hungry Judges soon the Sentence sign,
And Wretches hang that Jury-men may Dine;
The Merchant from th'*Exchange*[72] returns in Peace,
And the long Labours of the *Toilette* cease —
25   *Belinda* now, whom Thirst of Fame invites,
Burns to encounter two adventrous Knights,
At *Ombre*[73] singly to decide their Doom;
And swells her Breast with Conquests yet to come.
Strait the three Bands prepare in Arms to join,
30   Each Band the number of the Sacred Nine.
Soon as she spreads her Hand, th' Aerial Guard
Descend, and sit on each important Card:
First *Ariel* perch'd upon a *Matadore*,[74]
Then each, according to the Rank they bore;

———→

70 Hampton Court Palace, largest of the royal palaces. 71 Queen Anne, ruler of England, Scotland, and Ireland. 72 the Royal Exchange in London's financial district, where merchants, bankers, and stockbrokers met to do business. 73 Belinda's card game mimics the epic games at which warriors relax and at the same time celebrate their heroic code; see Homer's *Iliad*, Book XXIII. Ombre (pronounced *om-ber*, from the Spanish *hombre*, meaning man) is played by three persons with 40 cards, the eights, nines, and tens being removed from the deck. Nine cards are dealt to each player, and nine tricks are played, with the highest card winning each. One player, called the "Ombre," undertakes to win more tricks than either of the other two and chooses which suit will be trumps. 74 one of the three cards of highest value; they are, in order, the ace of spades, the two of the trump suit (when, as here, a black suit is trumps), the ace of clubs.

35   For *Sylphs*, yet mindful of their ancient Race,
Are, as when Women, wondrous fond of Place.[75]
     Behold, four *Kings* in Majesty rever'd,
With hoary Whiskers and a forky Beard;
And four fair *Queens* whose hands sustain a Flow'r,
40   Th' expressive Emblem of their softer Pow'r;
Four *Knaves* in Garbs succinct,[76] a trusty Band,
Caps on their heads, and Halberds[77] in their hand;
And Particolour'd Troops, a shining Train,
Draw forth to Combat on the Velvet Plain.
45   The skilful Nymph reviews her Force with Care;
Let Spades be Trumps! she said, and Trumps they were.[78]
     Now move to War her Sable *Matadores*,
In Show like Leaders of the swarthy *Moors*.
Spadillio[79] first, unconquerable Lord!
50   Led off two captive Trumps, and swept the Board.
As many more *Manillio*[80] forc'd to yield,
And march'd a Victor from the verdant Field.
Him *Basto*[81] follow'd, but his Fate more hard
Gain'd but one Trump and one *Plebeian* Card.
55   With his broad Sabre next, a Chief in Years,
The hoary Majesty of *Spades* appears;
Puts forth one manly Leg, to sight reveal'd;
The rest of his many-colour'd Robe conceal'd.
The Rebel-*Knave*, who dares his Prince engage,
60   Proves the just Victim of his Royal Rage.
Ev'n mighty *Pam*[82] that Kings and Queens o'erthrew,
And mow'd down Armies in the Fights of *Lu*,
Sad Chance of War! now, destitute of Aid,
Falls undistinguish'd by the Victor *Spade*!
65   Thus far both Armies to *Belinda* yield;
Now to the *Baron* Fate inclines the Field.
His warlike *Amazon*[83] her Host invades,
Th' Imperial Consort of the Crown of *Spades*.
The *Club*'s black Tyrant first her Victim dy'd,
70   Spite of his haughty Mien, and barb'rous Pride:
What boots the Regal Circle on his Head,
His Giant Limbs in State unwieldy spread?

→

75 rank. 76 girded up. 77 battle-axes attached to long spears. 78 cf. Genesis 1:3: "And God said, Let there be light; and there was light." 79 the ace of spades. 80 the two of spades. 81 the ace of clubs. 82 the knave of clubs, highest card in the game of Loo, or Lu. 83 the queen of spades.

That long behind he trails his pompous Robe,
And of all Monarchs only grasps the Globe?
75   The *Baron* now his *Diamonds* pours apace;
Th' embroider'd *King* who shows but half his Face,
And his refulgent[84] *Queen*, with Pow'rs combin'd,
Of broken Troops an easie Conquest find.
Clubs, Diamonds, Hearts, in wild Disorder seen,
80 With Throngs promiscuous strow the level Green.
Thus when dispers'd a routed Army runs,
Of *Asia*'s Troops, and *Africk*'s Sable Sons,
With like Confusion different Nations fly,
Of various Habit and of various Dye,
85 The pierc'd Battalions dis-united fall,
In Heaps on Heaps; one Fate o'erwhelms them all.
     The *Knave* of *Diamonds* tries his wily Arts,
And wins (oh shameful Chance!) the *Queen* of *Hearts*.
At this, the Blood the Virgin's Cheek forsook,
90 A livid Paleness spreads o'er all her Look;
She sees, and trembles at th' approaching Ill,
Just in the Jaws of Ruin, and *Codille*.[85]
And now, (as oft in some distemper'd State)
On one nice[86] *Trick* depends the gen'ral Fate.
95 An *Ace* of Hearts steps forth: The *King* unseen
Lurk'd in her Hand, and mourn'd his captive *Queen*.
He springs to Vengeance with an eager pace,
And falls like Thunder on the prostrate *Ace*.[87]
The Nymph exulting fills with Shouts the Sky,
100 The Walls, the Woods, and long Canals reply.
     Oh thoughtless Mortals! ever blind to Fate,
Too soon dejected, and too soon elate!
Sudden these Honours shall be snatch'd away,
And curs'd for ever this Victorious Day.
105 For lo! the Board with Cups and Spoons is crown'd,
The Berries crackle, and the Mill[88] turns round.
On shining Altars of *Japan*[89] they raise
The silver Lamp; the fiery Spirits[90] blaze.

—→

84 shining, glorious. 85 if the Ombre failed to win more tricks than one of the other players, he or she was said to be given "codille" (from the Spanish for elbow). 86 precise. 87 when a black suit is trumps, the king, queen, and knave of a red suit outrank the ace; Belinda thus wins the trick and the game. 88 the coffee mill, which grinds coffee beans (the "Berries"). 89 japanned or lacquered tables. 90 in spirit-lamps.

From silver Spouts the grateful [91] Liquors glide,
110 While *China*'s Earth [92] receives the smoking Tyde.
At once they gratify their Scent and Taste,
And frequent Cups prolong the rich Repast.
Strait hover round the Fair her Airy Band;
Some, as she sip'd the fuming Liquor fann'd,
115 Some, o'er her Lap their careful Plumes display'd,
Trembling, and conscious of the rich Brocade.
Coffee, (which makes the Politician wise,
And see thro' all things with his half-shut Eyes)
Sent up in Vapours to the *Baron*'s Brain
120 New Stratagems, the radiant Lock to gain.
Ah cease rash Youth! desist ere 'tis too late,
Fear the just Gods, and think of *Scylla*'s [93] Fate!
Chang'd to a Bird, and sent to flit in Air,
She dearly pays for *Nisus*' injur'd Hair!
125   But when to Mischief Mortals bend their Will,
How soon they find fit Instruments of Ill!
Just then, *Clarissa* drew with tempting Grace
A two-edg'd Weapon from her shining Case;
So Ladies in Romance assist their Knight,
130 Present the Spear, and arm him for the Fight.
He takes the Gift with rev'rence, and extends
The little Engine on his Fingers' Ends,
This just behind *Belinda*'s Neck he spread,
As o'er the fragrant Steams she bends her Head:
135 Swift to the Lock a thousand Sprights repair,
A thousand Wings, by turns, blow back the Hair,
And thrice they twitch'd the Diamond in her Ear,
Thrice she look'd back, and thrice the Foe drew near.
Just in that instant, anxious *Ariel* sought
140 The close Recesses of the Virgin's Thought;
As on the Nosegay [94] in her Breast reclin'd,
He watch'd th' Ideas rising in her Mind,
Sudden he view'd, in spite of all her Art,
An Earthly Lover lurking at her Heart.
145 Amaz'd, confus'd, he found his Pow'r expir'd,
Resign'd to Fate, and with a Sigh retir'd.

⟶

91 pleasing. 92 cups of china, i.e., fine earthenware. 93 according to legend, Scylla was the daughter of
King Nisus, whose life and kingdom depended on a purple hair growing on his head. Scylla fell in love with
King Minos, who was besieging her father's kingdom, and plucked out the hair and took it to Minos; he
rejected it with horror, and she was turned into a sea bird. 94 corsage of flowers.

The Peer now spreads the glitt'ring *Forfex*[95] wide,
T'inclose the Lock; now joins it, to divide.
Ev'n then, before the fatal Engine clos'd,
150 A wretched *Sylph* too fondly interpos'd;
Fate urg'd the Sheers, and cut the *Sylph* in twain,
(But Airy Substance soon unites again)[96]
The meeting Points the sacred Hair dissever
From the fair Head, for ever and for ever!
155   Then flash'd the living Lightning from her Eyes,
And Screams of Horror rend th' affrighted Skies.
Not louder Shrieks to pitying Heav'n are cast,
When Husbands or when Lap-dogs breathe their last,
Or when rich *China* Vessels, fal'n from high,
160 In glittring Dust and painted Fragments lie!
      Let Wreaths of Triumph now my Temples twine,
(The Victor cry'd) the glorious Prize is mine!
While Fish in Streams, or Birds delight in Air,
Or in a Coach and Six the *British* Fair,
165 As long as *Atalantis*[97] shall be read,
Or the small Pillow grace a Lady's Bed,
While *Visits* shall be paid on solemn Days,
When numerous Wax-lights in bright Order blaze,
While Nymphs take Treats, or Assignations give,
170 So long my Honour, Name, and Praise shall live!
      What Time wou'd spare, from Steel receives its date,
And Monuments, like Men, submit to Fate!
Steel cou'd the Labour of the Gods[98] destroy,
And strike to Dust th' Imperial Tow'rs of *Troy*;
175 Steel cou'd the Works of mortal Pride confound,
And hew Triumphal Arches to the Ground.
What Wonder then, fair Nymph! thy Hairs shou'd feel
The conqu'ring Force of unresisted Steel?

CANTO IV.

But anxious Cares the pensive Nymph opprest,
And secret Passions labour'd in her Breast.

→

---

95 the Latin word for scissors. 96 just as Milton's Satan does when pierced by Michael's sword (*Paradise Lost* VI.330–31). 97 *The New Atalantis* (1709), by Delarivier Manley, a popular novel consisting largely of thinly veiled accounts of scandals in high life. 98 Troy was believed to have been built by two gods, Apollo and Poseidon.

Not youthful Kings in Battel seiz'd alive,
Not scornful Virgins who their Charms survive,
5   Not ardent Lovers robb'd of all their Bliss,
Not ancient Ladies when refus'd a Kiss,
Not Tyrants fierce that unrepenting die,
Not *Cynthia* when her *Manteau's*[99] pinn'd awry,
E'er felt such Rage, Resentment and Despair,
10   As Thou, sad Virgin! for thy ravish'd Hair.

    For, that sad moment, when the *Sylphs* withdrew,
And *Ariel* weeping from *Belinda* flew,
Umbriel,[100] a dusky melancholy Spright,
As ever sully'd the fair face of Light,
15   Down to the Central Earth, his proper Scene,[101]
Repair'd to search the gloomy Cave of *Spleen*.[102]

    Swift on his sooty Pinions flitts the *Gnome*,
And in a Vapour[103] reach'd the dismal Dome.
No cheerful Breeze this sullen Region knows,
20   The dreadful *East*[104] is all the Wind that blows.
Here, in a Grotto, sheltred close from Air,
And screen'd in Shades from Day's detested Glare,
She sighs for ever on her pensive Bed,
Pain at her Side, and *Megrim*[105] at her Head.

25   Two Handmaids wait the Throne: Alike in Place,
But diff'ring far in Figure and in Face.
Here stood *Ill-nature* like an *ancient* Maid,
Her wrinked Form in *Black* and *White* array'd;
With store of Pray'rs, for Mornings, Nights, and Noons,
30   Her Hand is fill'd; her Bosom with Lampoons.

    There *Affectation* with a sickly Mien
Shows in her Cheek the Roses of Eighteen,
Practis'd to Lisp, and hang the Head aside,
Faints into Airs, and languishes with Pride;
35   On the rich Quilt sinks with becoming Woe,
Wrapt in a Gown, for Sickness, and for Show.[106]

————▶

99 loose robe or cloak. 100 a Gnome (see I.63–64); his name is from the Latin word *umbra*, meaning shadow. 101 Umbriel's journey to the cave of Spleen imitates the epic hero's visit to the underworld in search of knowledge unavailable on earth; see Homer's *Odyssey*, Book XI, and Virgil's *Aeneid*, Book VI. 102 the spleen, thought to be the seat of the emotions in traditional medicine, became the name of a fashionable psychosomatic ailment of the rich and leisured; it consisted of ill temper, depression, and hypochondria. 103 suitably, since the disease known as "the spleen" was also called "the vapours" (see lines 39 and 59 of this canto). 104 the east wind was considered unhealthy; it was thought to provoke the spleen. 105 migraine headache. 106 ladies often received formal visits in bed.

The Fair-ones feel such Maladies as these,
When each new Night-Dress gives a new Disease.
 A constant *Vapour* o'er the Palace flies;
40 Strange Phantoms rising as the Mists arise;
Dreadful, as Hermit's Dreams in haunted Shades,
Or bright as Visions of expiring Maids.
Now glaring Fiends, and Snakes on rolling Spires,[107]
Pale Spectres, gaping Tombs and Purple Fires:
45 Now Lakes of liquid Gold, *Elysian*[108] Scenes,
And Crystal Domes, and Angels in Machines.[109]
 Unnumber'd Throngs on ev'ry side are seen
Of Bodies chang'd to various Forms by *Spleen*.[110]
Here living *Teapots* stand, one Arm held out,
50 One bent; the Handle this, and that the Spout:
A Pipkin[111] there like *Homer's Tripod*[112] walks;
Here sighs a Jar, and there a Goose-pye talks;
Men prove with Child, as powr'ful Fancy works,
And Maids turn'd Bottels, call aloud for Corks.
55 Safe past the *Gnome* thro' this fantastick Band,
A Branch of healing *Spleenwort*[113] in his hand.
Then thus addrest the Pow'r — Hail wayward Queen!
Who rule the Sex to Fifty from Fifteen,
Parents of Vapours and of Female Wit,
60 Who give th' *Hysteric* or *Poetic* Fit,
On various Tempers act by various ways,
Make some take Physick,[114] others scribble Plays;
Who cause the Proud their Visits to delay,
And send the Godly in a Pett, to pray.
65 A Nymph there is, that all thy Pow'r disdains,
And thousands more in equal Mirth maintains.
But oh! if e'er thy *Gnome* could spoil a Grace,
Or raise a Pimple on a beauteous Face,
Like Citron-Waters[115] Matrons' Cheeks inflame,
70 Or change Complexions at a losing Game;
If e'er with airy Horns[116] I planted Heads,
Or rumpled Petticoats, or tumbled Beds,

$\longrightarrow$

107 spirals. 108 Elysium in Greek mythology was the abode of the blessed after death, and so a place of
ideal happiness. 109 stage machinery. 110 one symptom of the spleen was suffering from hallucinations.
111 small earthen pot. 112 in the *Iliad* (XVIII.439 ff.), Homer tells how Hephaistos made walking tripods
(three-legged stools). 113 just as Aeneas carries a golden bough to guarantee safe passage through the under-
world in the *Aeneid*, Umbriel carries a branch of spleenwort, a fern believed to protect one against the
spleen. 114 medicine. 115 brandy flavoured with lemon peel. 116 the traditional emblem of the cuckold.

Or caus'd Suspicion when no Soul was rude,
Or discompos'd the Head-dress of a Prude,
75 Or e'er to costive[117] Lap-Dog gave Disease,
Which not the Tears of brightest Eyes could ease:
Hear me, and touch *Belinda* with Chagrin;
That single Act gives half the World the Spleen.
    The Goddess with a discontented Air
80 Seems to reject him, tho' she grants his Pray'r.
A wondrous Bag with both her Hands she binds,
Like that where once *Ulysses* held the Winds;[118]
There she collects the Force of Female Lungs,
Sighs, Sobs, and Passions, and the War of Tongues.
85 A Vial next she fills with fainting Fears,
Soft Sorrows, melting Griefs, and flowing Tears.
The *Gnome* rejoicing bears her Gifts away,
Spreads his black Wings, and slowly mounts to Day.
    Sunk in *Thalestris'*[119] Arms the Nymph he found,
90 Her Eyes dejected and her Hair unbound.
Full o'er their Heads the swelling Bag he rent,
And all the Furies issued at the Vent.
Belinda burns with more than mortal Ire,
And fierce *Thalestris* fans the rising Fire.
95 O wretched Maid! she spread her Hands, and cry'd,
(While *Hampton's* Ecchos, wretched Maid! reply'd)
Was it for this you took such constant Care
The *Bodkin*,[120] *Comb*, and *Essence* to prepare;
For this your Locks in Paper-Durance[121] bound,
100 For this with tort'ring Irons wreath'd around?
For this with Fillets[122] strain'd your tender Head,
And bravely bore the double Loads of Lead?[123]
Gods! shall the Ravisher display your Hair,
While the Fops envy, and the Ladies Stare!
105 *Honour* forbid! at whose unrival'd Shrine
Ease, Pleasure, Virtue, All, our Sex resign.
Methinks already I your Tears survey,
Already hear the horrid things they say,

⟶

117 constipated. 118 Aeolus, god of winds, gave Odysseus, or Ulysses, a bag containing all the winds that could prevent him from returning home; Odysseus's men opened the bag when he was asleep and the ensuing storms drove them far away (*Odyssey* X.19 ff.). 119 the name of a legendary warrior-queen of the Amazons. 120 needle used as a hairpin. 121 inflated epic diction for curling papers, the papers that were wrapped around curling irons (the "tort'ring" of line 100) to prepare the elaborate coiffures worn by women. 122 headbands. 123 the elaborate upright coiffures of ladies were arranged upon a wooden frame; strips of pliant lead attached to the frame kept the curls in place.

Already see you a degraded Toast,[124]
110 And all your Honour in a Whisper lost!
How shall I, then, your helpless Fame defend?
'Twill then be Infamy to seem your Friend!
And shall this Prize, th' inestimable Prize,
Expos'd thro' Crystal to the gazing Eyes,
115 And heighten'd by the Diamond's circling Rays,
On that Rapacious Hand for ever blaze?
Sooner shall Grass in *Hide*-Park *Circus*[125] grow,
And Wits take Lodgings in the Sound of *Bow*;[126]
Sooner let Earth, Air, Sea, to *Chaos* fall,
120 Men, Monkies, Lap-dogs, Parrots, perish all!
  She said; then raging to *Sir Plume*[127] repairs,
And bids her *Beau* demand the precious Hairs:
(*Sir Plume*, of *Amber Snuff-box* justly vain,
And the nice Conduct of a *clouded*[128] *Cane*)
125 With earnest Eyes, and round unthinking Face,
He first the Snuff-box open'd, then the Case,
And thus broke out — "My Lord, why, what the Devil?
"Z — ds![129] damn the Lock! 'fore Gad, you must be civil!
"Plague on't! 'tis past a Jest — nay prithee, Pox!
130 "Give her the Hair" — he spoke, and rapp'd his Box.
  It grieves me much (reply'd the Peer again)
Who speaks so well shou'd ever speak in vain.
But by this Lock, this sacred Lock I swear,
(Which never more shall join its parted Hair,
135 Which never more its Honours[130] shall renew,
Clipt from the lovely Head where late it grew)
That while my Nostrils draw the vital Air,
This Hand, which won it, shall for ever wear.
He spoke, and speaking, in proud Triumph spread
140 The long-contended Honours of her Head.
  But *Umbriel*, hateful *Gnome*! forbears not so;
He breaks the Vial whence the Sorrows flow.
Then see! the *Nymph* in beauteous Grief appears,
Her Eyes half-languishing, half-drown'd in Tears;

→

124 woman whose health is often drunk by men. 125 the Ring (see I.44), where carriages kept the grass from growing. 126 within the sound of St. Mary-le-Bow in Cheapside, the unfashionable commercial quarter of London. 127 Sir George Browne, Arabella's kinsman, who chiefly fomented the quarrel. 128 mottled. 129 Zounds, a corrupted version of "God's wounds" — an oath expressing indignation. 130 beauties, graces (as well as honours); see also line 140 of this canto.

145 On her heav'd Bosom hung her drooping Head,
    Which, with a Sigh, she rais'd; and thus she said.
        For ever curs'd be this detested Day,[131]
    Which snatch'd my best, my fav'rite Curl away!
    Happy! ah ten times happy, had I been,
150 If *Hampton-Court* these Eyes had never seen!
    Yet am not I the first mistaken Maid,
    By Love of *Courts* to num'rous Ills betray'd.
    Oh had I rather un-admir'd remain'd
    In some lone Isle, or distant *Northern* Land;
155 Where the gilt *Chariot* never marks the Way,
    Where none learn *Ombre*, none e'er taste *Bohea*![132]
    There kept my Charms conceal'd from mortal Eye,
    Like Roses that in Desarts bloom and die.
    What mov'd my Mind with youthful Lords to rome?
160 O had I stay'd, and said my Pray'rs at home!
    'Twas this, the Morning *Omens* seem'd to tell;
    Thrice from my trembling hand the *Patch-box* fell;
    The tott'ring *China* shook without a Wind,
    Nay, *Poll* sate mute, and *Shock* was most Unkind!
165 A *Sylph* too warn'd me of the Threats of Fate,
    In mystic Visions, now believ'd too late!
    See the poor Remnants of these slighted Hairs!
    My hands shall rend what ev'n thy Rapine spares:
    These, in two sable Ringlets taught to break,
170 Once gave new Beauties to the snowie Neck.
    The Sister-Lock now sits uncouth, alone,
    And in its Fellow's Fate foresees its own;
    Uncurl'd it hangs, the fatal Sheers demands;
    And tempts once more thy sacrilegious Hands.
175 Oh hadst thou, Cruel! been content to seize
    Hairs less in sight, or any Hairs but these!

CANTO V.

She said: the pitying Audience melt in Tears,
But *Fate* and *Jove* had stopp'd the *Baron*'s Ears.
In Vain *Thalestris* with Reproach assails,
For who can move when fair *Belinda* fails?

———→

131 imitation of Achilles's lament for Patroclus in the *Iliad* (XVIII.107 ff.). 132 costly kind of tea.

5   Not half so fixt the *Trojan* cou'd remain,
While *Anna* begg'd and *Dido* rag'd in vain.[133]
Then grave *Clarissa* graceful wav'd her Fan;
Silence ensu'd, and thus the Nymph began.[134]
    Say, why are Beauties prais'd and honour'd most,
10 The wise Man's Passion, and the vain Man's Toast?
Why deck'd with all that Land and Sea afford,
Why Angels call'd, and Angel-like ador'd?
Why round our Coaches crowd the white-glov'd Beaus,
Why bows the Side-box[135] from its inmost Rows?
15 How vain are all these Glories, all our Pains,
Unless good Sense preserve what Beauty gains:
That Men may say, when we the Front-box grace,
Behold the first in Virtue, as in Face!
Oh! if to dance all Night, and dress all Day,
20 Charm'd the Small-pox,[136] or chas'd old Age away;
Who would not scorn what Huswife's Cares produce,
Or who would learn one earthly Thing of Use?
To patch, nay ogle, might become a Saint,
Nor could it sure be such a Sin to paint.
25 But since, alas! frail Beauty must decay,
Curl'd or uncurl'd, since Locks will turn to grey,
Since painted, or not painted, all shall fade,
And she who scorns a Man, must die a Maid;
What then remains, but well our Pow'r to use,
30 And keep good Humour still whate'er we lose?
And trust me, Dear! good Humour can prevail,
When Airs, and Flights, and Screams, and Scolding fail.
Beauties in vain their pretty Eyes may roll;
Charms strike the Sight, but Merit wins the Soul.
35   So spoke the Dame, but no Applause ensu'd;
Belinda frown'd, *Thalestris* call'd her Prude.
To Arms, to Arms! the fierce Virago[137] cries,
And swift as Lightning to the Combate flies.

$\longrightarrow$

133 Aeneas, burdened with his divine mission of founding a new Troy, left Carthage and Queen Dido, despite her furious reproaches and the prayers of her sister Anna (*Aeneid* IV.296–449). 134 when Pope published his collected early poetry in 1717, he added Clarissa's speech to the five-canto *Rape* of 1714 in order, as he explained, "to open the moral of the poem, in a parody of the speech of Sarpedon to Glaucus in Homer"; Sarpedon's speech is an appeal to his comrade to earn in battle the honour they both enjoy as leaders (*Iliad* XII.371–96). 135 gentlemen preferred the side boxes at the theatre, ladies the front boxes facing the stage (see line 17 of this canto). 136 before vaccination, smallpox was common and deadly; the Lord Petre of this poem died of smallpox in 1713. 137 man-like woman, female warrior.

All side in Parties, and begin th' Attack;
40   Fans clap, Silks russle, and tough Whalebones crack;
Heroes' and Heroins' Shouts confus'dly rise,
And base, and treble Voices strike the Skies.
No common Weapons in their Hands are found,
Like Gods they fight, nor dread a mortal Wound.
45   So when bold *Homer* makes the Gods engage,[138]
And heavn'ly Breasts with human Passions rage;
'Gainst *Pallas*,[139] *Mars*; *Latona*,[140] *Hermes* arms;
And all *Olympus* rings with loud Alarms.
Jove's Thunder roars, Heav'n trembles all around;
50   Blue *Neptune* storms, the bellowing Deeps resound;
Earth shakes her nodding Tow'rs, the Ground gives way;
And the pale Ghosts start at the Flash of Day!
      Triumphant *Umbriel* on a Sconce's[141] Height
Clapt his glad Wings, and sate to view the Fight:
55   Propt on their Bodkin Spears, the Sprights survey
The growing Combat, or assist the Fray.
      While thro' the Press enrag'd *Thalestris* flies,
And scatters Deaths around from both her Eyes,
A *Beau* and *Witling*[142] perish'd in the Throng,
60   One dy'd in *Metaphor*, and one in *Song*.
O cruel Nymph! a living Death I bear,
Cry'd *Dapperwit*,[143] and sunk beside his Chair.
A mournful Glance Sir *Fopling* upwards cast,
Those Eyes are made so killing — was his last:
65   Thus on *Meander*'s[144] flow'ry Margin lies
Th' expiring Swan, and as he sings he dies.[145]
      When bold Sir *Plume* had drawn *Clarissa* down,
Chloe stept in, and kill'd him with a Frown;
She smil'd to see the doughty Hero slain,
70   But at her Smile, the Beau reviv'd again.
      Now *Jove* suspends his golden Scales in Air,[146]
Weighs the Men's Wits against the Lady's Hair;
The doubtful Beam long nods from side to side;
At length the Wits mount up, the Hairs subside.

                        —————→

---

138 see the *Iliad* XX.91 ff. 139 Pallas Athena, the Greek goddess of war (also the goddess of wisdom).
140 the mother of the Greek deities Apollo and Artemis. 141 candlestick attached to the wall. 142 tiny
wit. 143 like "Sir Fopling" in the next line, a type-name for a fop and would-be wit in Restoration comic
plays. 144 celebrated winding river in Asia Minor. 145 swans were believed to sing beautifully only as they
died. 146 epic convention when a decisive battle is about to take place; see the *Iliad* VIII.87 ff. and the
Aeneid XII.725 ff.

75   See fierce *Belinda* on the *Baron* flies,
With more than usual Lightning in her Eyes;
Nor fear'd the Chief th'unequal Fight to try,
Who sought no more than on his Foe to die.
But this bold Lord, with manly Strength indu'd,
80   She with one Finger and a Thumb subdu'd:
Just where the Breath of Life his Nostrils drew,
A Charge of *Snuff* the wily Virgin threw;
The *Gnomes* direct, to ev'ry Atome just,
The pungent Grains of titillating Dust.
85   Sudden, with starting Tears each Eye o'erflows,
And the high Dome re-ecchoes to his Nose.
    Now meet thy Fate, incens'd *Belinda* cry'd,
And drew a deadly *Bodkin* from her Side.
(The same,[147] his ancient Personage to deck,
90   Her great great Grandsire wore about his Neck
In three *Seal-Rings*; which after, melted down,
Form'd a vast *Buckle* for his Widow's Gown:
Her infant Grandame's *Whistle* next it grew,
The *Bells* she gingled,[148] and the *Whistle* blew;
95   Then in a *Bodkin* grac'd her Mother's Hairs,
Which long she wore, and now *Belinda* wears.)
    Boast not my Fall (he cry'd) insulting Foe!
Thou by some other shalt be laid as low.
Nor think, to die dejects my lofty Mind;
100   All that I dread, is leaving you behind!
Rather than so, ah let me still survive,
And burn in *Cupid*'s Flames, — but burn alive.
    Restore the Lock! she cries; and all around
Restore the Lock! the vaulted Roofs rebound.
105   Not fierce *Othello* in so loud a Strain
Roar'd for the Handkerchief that caus'd his Pain.
But see how oft Ambitious Aims are cross'd,
And Chiefs contend 'till all the Prize is lost!
The Lock, obtain'd with Guilt, and kept with Pain,
110   In ev'ry place is sought, but sought in vain:
With such a Prize no Mortal must be blest,
So Heav'n decrees! with Heav'n who can contest?

                                                    ⟶

147 what follows is a parody of epic descriptions of a hero's armour and its descent through the generations in his family. 148 jingled.

Some thought it mounted to the Lunar Sphere,
Since all things lost on Earth, are treasur'd there.[149]
115   There Heroes' Wits are kept in pondrous Vases,
And Beaus' in *Snuff-boxes* and *Tweezer-Cases.*
There broken Vows, and Death-bed Alms are found,
And Lovers' Hearts with Ends of Riband[150] bound;
The Courtier's Promises, and Sick Man's Pray'rs,
120   The Smiles of Harlots, and the Tears of Heirs,
Cages for Gnats, and Chains to Yoak a Flea;
Dry'd Butterflies, and Tomes of Casuistry.[151]
But trust the Muse — she saw it upward rise,
Tho' mark'd by none but quick Poetic Eyes:
125   (So *Rome*'s great Founder to the Heav'ns withdrew,
To *Proculus* alone confess'd in view.)[152]
A sudden Star, it shot thro' liquid[153] Air,
And drew behind a radiant *Trail of Hair.*
Not *Berenice*'s[154] Locks first rose so bright,
130   The Heav'ns bespangling with dishevel'd Light.
The *Sylphs* behold it kindling as it flies,
And pleas'd pursue its Progress thro' the Skies.
This the *Beau-monde*[155] shall from the *Mall*[156] survey,
And hail with Musick its propitious Ray.
135   This, the blest Lover shall for *Venus* take,
And send up Vows from *Rosamonda*'s Lake.[157]
This *Partridge*[158] soon shall view in cloudless Skies,
When next he looks thro' *Galileo*'s Eyes;[159]
And hence th' Egregious Wizard shall foredoom
140   The Fate of *Louis*, and the Fall of *Rome.*
Then cease, bright Nymph! to mourn thy ravish'd Hair
Which adds new Glory to the shining Sphere!

————➔

149 in a striking episode in *Orlando Furioso* (1532), the chivalric epic by the Italian poet Ariosto, the hero's lost wits are found on the moon, where all things that are lost on earth may be found. 150 ribbon.
151 casuistry, the branch of theology that studies the application of general ethical rules to particular cases, had become a synonym for hair-splitting rationalization. 152 Romulus, the founder and first king of Rome, disappeared from earth in the midst of a storm; the senator Proculus affirmed that Romulus had ascended to the heavens. 153 clear, transparent. 154 Berenice, wife of King Ptolemy III of ancient Egypt, vowed to sacrifice her hair to the gods if her husband returned safe from battle; upon his return, she placed her hair in the temple of Aphrodite, but the next day it had disappeared and was believed to have become a constellation. 155 fashionable world. 156 Pall Mall, a walk laid out by Charles II in St. James's Park. 157 pond in St. James's Park considered to be the haunt of unhappy lovers; it was named after Rosamund Clifford (died 1177), known as "Fair Rosamond," mistress of Henry II, who was, according to legend, made to drink poison by his queen. 158 quack astrologer of the time, who predicted every year that the pope and King Louis XIV of France would fall from power that year (see line 140). 159 i.e., telescope; Galileo constructed the first telescope in 1609.

Not all the Tresses that fair Head can boast
Shall draw such Envy as the Lock you lost.
145   For, after all the Murders of your Eye,
When, after Millions slain, your self shall die;
When those fair Suns shall sett, as sett they must,
And all those Tresses shall be laid in Dust;
This Lock, the Muse shall consecrate to Fame,
150   And mid'st the Stars inscribe *Belinda*'s Name!

(1714)

Thomas Gray (1716–1771)

Thomas Gray, a shy scholar, wrote very few poems—but among them is one of the best-known and most-loved poems in the language, his *Elegy Written in a Country Church-Yard* (or, as it is usually called, Gray's *Elegy*). Gray spent his entire adult life as a scholar at Cambridge University; he was known as one of the most learned men in Europe, and helped create scholarly interest in Welsh, Old Norse, and medieval English poetry. Gray published his *Elegy* in 1751. His shyness led him to turn down the position of Poet Laureate when he was offered it in 1757; although named Professor of Modern History at Cambridge, he was unable to deliver a single lecture. Nevertheless, as soon as his *Elegy* was published, he became recognized as the greatest lyric poet of the age. His contemporary Samuel Johnson memorably sums up the poem's appeal: "The *Church-Yard* abounds with images which find a mirror in every mind, and with sentiments to which every bosom returns an echo."

Elegy Written in a Country Church-Yard

The Curfew tolls the knell of parting day,
The lowing herd wind slowly o'er the lea,[1]
The plowman homeward plods his weary way,
And leaves the world to darkness and to me.

5   Now fades the glimmering landscape on the sight,
And all the air a solemn stillness holds,
Save where the beetle wheels his droning flight,
And drowsy tinklings lull the distant folds;

1 open field, grassland.

Save that from yonder ivy-mantled tow'r
10   The mopeing owl does to the moon complain
Of such, as wand'ring near her secret bow'r,
Molest her ancient solitary reign.

Beneath those rugged elms, that yew-tree's shade,
Where heaves the turf in many a mould'ring heap,
15   Each in his narrow cell for ever laid,
The rude[2] Forefathers of the hamlet sleep.

The breezy call of incense-breathing Morn,
The swallow twitt'ring from the straw-built shed,
The cock's shrill clarion, or the echoing horn,
20   No more shall rouse them from their lowly bed.

For them no more the blazing hearth shall burn,
Or busy housewife ply her evening care:
No children run to lisp their sire's return,
Or climb his knees the envied kiss to share.

25   Oft did the harvest to their sickle yield,
Their furrow oft the stubborn glebe[3] has broke;
How jocund did they drive their team afield!
How bow'd the woods beneath their sturdy stroke!

Let not Ambition mock their useful toil,
30   Their homely joys, and destiny obscure;
Nor Grandeur hear with a disdainful smile,
The short and simple annals of the poor.

The boast of heraldry, the pomp of pow'r,
And all that beauty, all that wealth e'er gave,
35   Awaits alike th' inevitable hour.
The paths of glory lead but to the grave.

Nor you, ye Proud, impute to These the fault,
If Mem'ry o'er their Tomb no Trophies raise,
Where thro' the long-drawn isle[4] and fretted vault
40   The pealing anthem swells the note of praise.

2 uneducated. 3 soil. 4 aisle.

Can storied urn or animated bust
Back to its mansion call the fleeting breath?
Can Honour's voice provoke the silent dust,
Or Flatt'ry sooth the dull cold ear of Death?

45   Perhaps in this neglected spot is laid
Some heart once pregnant with celestial fire,
Hands, that the rod of empire might have sway'd,
Or wak'd to extasy the living lyre.

But Knowledge to their eyes her ample page
50   Rich with the spoils of time did ne'er unroll;
Chill Penury repress'd their noble rage,[5]
And froze the genial[6] current of the soul.

Full many a gem of purest ray serene,
The dark unfathom'd caves of ocean bear:
55   Full many a flower is born to blush unseen,
And waste its sweetness on the desert air.

Some village-Hampden,[7] that with dauntless breast
The little Tyrant of his fields withstood;
Some mute inglorious Milton here may rest,
60   Some Cromwell guiltless of his country's blood.

Th' applause of list'ning senates to command,
The threats of pain and ruin to despise,
To scatter plenty o'er a smiling land,
And read their hist'ry in a nation's eyes

65   Their lot forbad: nor circumscrib'd alone
Their growing virtues, but their crimes confin'd;
Forbad to wade through slaughter to a throne,
And shut the gates of mercy on mankind,

The struggling pangs of conscious truth to hide,
70   To quench the blushes of ingenuous shame,
Or heap the shrine of Luxury and Pride
With incense kindled at the Muse's flame.

5 rapture, ardour. 6 creative. 7 John Hampden (1594–1643), member of Parliament who defended the
rights of the people against Charles I and became a leader of the Puritan cause in the Civil War.

Far from the madding[8] crowd's ignoble strife,
Their sober wishes never learn'd to stray;
75 Along the cool sequester'd vale of life
They kept the noiseless tenor of their way.

Yet ev'n these bones from insult to protect
Some frail memorial still erected nigh,
With uncouth rhimes and shapeless sculpture deck'd,
80 Implores the passing tribute of a sigh.

Their name, their years, spelt by th' unletter'd muse,
The place of fame and elegy supply:
And many a holy text around she strews,
That teach the rustic moralist to die.

85 For who to dumb Forgetfulness a prey,
This pleasing anxious being e'er resign'd,
Left the warm precincts of the chearful day,
Nor cast one longing ling'ring look behind?

On some fond breast the parting soul relies,
90 Some pious drops the closing eye requires;
Ev'n from the tomb the voice of Nature cries,
Ev'n in our Ashes live their wonted Fires.

For thee, who mindful of th' unhonour'd Dead
Dost in these lines their artless tale relate;
95 If chance,[9] by lonely contemplation led,
Some kindred Spirit shall inquire thy fate,

Haply some hoary-headed Swain[10] may say,
"Oft have we seen him at the peep of dawn
Brushing with hasty steps the dews away
100 To meet the sun upon the upland lawn.

"There at the foot of yonder nodding beech
That wreathes its old fantastic roots so high,
His listless length at noontide wou'd he stretch,
And pore upon the brook that babbles by.

8 frenzied, maddened. 9 by chance. 10 shepherd.

105 "Hard by yon wood, now smiling as in scorn,
Mutt'ring his wayward fancies he wou'd rove,
Now drooping, woeful wan, like one forlorn,
Or craz'd with care, or cross'd in hopeless love.

"One morn I miss'd him on the custom'd hill,
110 Along the heath and near his fav'rite tree;
Another came; nor yet beside the rill,
Nor up the lawn, nor at the wood was he;

"The next with dirges due in sad array
Slow thro' the church-way path we saw him borne.
115 Approach and read (for thou can'st read) the lay,
Grav'd on the stone beneath yon aged thorn."

The EPITAPH.

HERE rests his head upon the lap of Earth
A Youth to Fortune and to Fame unknown,
Fair Science [11] frown'd not on his humble birth,
120 And Melancholy mark'd him for her own.

Large was his bounty, and his soul sincere,
Heav'n did a recompence as largely send:
He gave to Mis'ry all he had, a tear,
He gain'd from Heav'n ('twas all he wish'd) a friend.

125 No farther seek his merits to disclose,
Or draw his frailties from their dread abode,
(There they alike in trembling hope repose)
The bosom of his Father and his God.

(1751)

William Blake (1757–1827)

Born in London, William Blake studied art at the Royal Academy as a boy before serving an apprenticeship to an engraver. His first collection of poems, *Poetic Sketches* (1783), indicated his departure from the neoclassical conventions that had dominated the eighteenth century. However, *Songs of Innocence and Experience* (1794), illustrated by his own hand-painted engravings, marked the

11 learning.

first flowering of his genius. Lyrics revealing the influence of Elizabethan and seventeenth-century English poetry, they present "two contrasting states of the human mind." Many are companion poems, using the lives and views of children to symbolize innocence and experience. During the 1790s, Blake was influenced by radical political, religious, and philosophical currents prevalent in England and wrote in his poems about tyranny and oppression, the power of "God & his Priest & King," as they affected the lives of common people, especially children. He celebrated the visionary powers of the imagination in a series of "Prophetic Books" written after the publication of the *Songs*. Complex and often obscure, they develop a philosophy in which human life is seen as progressing from the initial innocence of childhood, to the complexity and pain of experience, and finally to a higher, more fulfilled innocence. Relatively ignored during his lifetime and in the 50 years after his death, Blake's works have been studied seriously during the twentieth century, and he is now recognized as one of the greatest Romantic poets.

The Lamb

    Little Lamb who made thee
    Dost thou know who made thee
Gave thee life & bid thee feed,
By the stream & o'er the mead;[1]
5 Gave thee clothing of delight,
Softest clothing wooly bright;
Gave thee such a tender voice,
Making all the vales rejoice!
    Little Lamb who made thee
10   Dost thou know who made thee

    Little Lamb I'll tell thee,
    Little Lamb I'll tell thee!
He is called by thy name,
For he calls himself a Lamb:
15 He is meek & he is mild,
He became a little child:
I a child & thou a lamb,
We are called by his name.
    Little Lamb God bless thee.
20   Little Lamb God bless thee.

(1789)

1 meadow.

The Little Black Boy

My mother bore me in the southern wild,
And I am black, but O! my soul is white;
White as an angel is the English child:
But I am black as if bereav'd[1] of light.

5   My mother taught me underneath a tree
And sitting down before the heat of day,
She took me on her lap and kissed me,
And pointing to the east began to say.

Look on the rising sun: there God does live
10 And gives his light, and gives his heat away.
And flowers and trees and beasts and men receive
Comfort in morning joy in the noon day.

And we are put on earth a little space,
That we may learn to bear the beams of love,
15 And these black bodies and this sun-burnt face
Is but a cloud, and like a shady grove.

For when our souls have learn'd the heat to bear
The cloud will vanish we shall hear his voice.
Saying: come out from the grove my love & care,
20 And round my golden tent like lambs rejoice.

Thus did my mother say and kissed me,
And thus I say to little English boy.
When I from black and he from white cloud free,
And round the tent of God like lambs we joy:

25 I'll shade him from the heat till he can bear,
To lean in joy upon our fathers knee.
And then I'll stand and stroke his silver hair,
And be like him and he will then love me.

(1789)

1 deprived.

The Chimney Sweeper

When my mother died I was very young,
And my father sold me while yet my tongue,
Could scarcely cry weep weep weep weep.
So your chimneys I sweep & in soot I sleep.

5   There's little Tom Dacre, who cried when his head
That curl'd like a lambs back, was shav'd, so I said.
Hush Tom never mind it, for when your head's bare,
You know that the soot cannot spoil your white hair.

And so he was quiet, & that very night,
10   As Tom was a sleeping he had such a sight,
That thousands of sweepers, Dick, Joe, Ned & Jack,
Were all of them lock'd up in coffins of black,

And by came an Angel who had a bright key,
And he open'd the coffins & set them all free.
15   Then down a green plain leaping laughing they run
And wash in a river and shine in the Sun.

Then naked & white, all their bags left behind,
They rise upon clouds, and sport in the wind.
And the Angel told Tom if he'd be a good boy,
20   He'd have God for his father & never want joy.

And so Tom awoke and we rose in the dark
And got with our bags & our brushes to work.
Tho' the morning was cold, Tom was happy & warm,
So if all do their duty, they need not fear harm.

(1789)

Holy Thursday [1]

Twas on a Holy Thursday their innocent faces clean
The children walking two & two in red & blue & green
Grey headed beadles walkd before with wands as white as snow
Till into the high dome of Pauls [2] they like Thames waters flow

---

1 in the Anglican tradition, the Thursday 40 days after Easter, when Christ is said to have ascended to heaven.
2 St. Paul's Cathedral, London.

5   O what a multitude they seemd these flowers of London town
Seated in companies they sit with radiance all their own
The hum of multitudes was there but multitudes of lambs
Thousands of little boys & girls raising their innocent hands

Now like a mighty wind they raise to heaven the voice of song
10   Or like harmonious thunderings the seats of heaven among
Beneath them sit the aged men wise guardians of the poor
Then cherish pity, lest you drive an angel from your door

(1789)

Nurse's[1] Song

When the voices of children are heard on the green
And laughing is heard on the hill,
My heart is at rest within my breast
And every thing else is still

5   Then come home my children, the sun is gone down
And the dews of night arise
Come come leave off play, and let us away
Till the morning appears in the skies

No no let us play, for it is yet day
10   And we cannot go to sleep
Besides in the sky, the little birds fly
And the hills are all covered with sheep

Well well go & play till the light fades away
And then go home to bed
15   The little ones leaped & shouted & laugh'd
And all the hills ecchoed

(c. 1784)   (1789)

1 woman hired to care for a young child.

The Tyger

Tyger Tyger, burning bright,
In the forests of the night;
What immortal hand or eye,
Could frame thy fearful symmetry?

5   In what distant deeps or skies!
Burnt the fire of thine eyes?
On what wings dare he aspire?
What the hand, dare seize the fire?

And what shoulder, & what art,
10   Could twist the sinews of thy heart?
And when thy heart began to beat,
What dread hand? & what dread feet?

What the hammer? what the chain?
In what furnace was thy brain?
15   What the anvil? what dread grasp,
Dare its deadly terrors clasp?

When the stars threw down their spears
And water'd heaven with their tears;
Did he smile his work to see?
20   Did he who made the Lamb make thee?

Tyger Tyger, burning bright,
In the forests of the night;
What immortal hand or eye,
Dare frame thy fearful symmetry?

(1790–92)   (1794)

The Chimney Sweeper

A little black thing among the snow:
Crying weep, weep, in notes of woe!
Where are thy father & mother? say?
They are both gone up to the church to pray.

5 Because I was happy upon the heath,[1]
   And smil'd among the winters snow:
   They clothed me in the clothes of death,
   And taught me to sing the notes of woe.

   And because I am happy, & dance & sing,
10 They think they have done me no injury:
   And are gone to praise God & his Priest & King
   Who make up a heaven of our misery.

   (1790–92)   (1794)

Holy Thursday

   Is this a holy thing to see,
   In a rich and fruitful land,
   Babes reducd to misery,
   Fed with cold and usurous hand?

5 Is that trembling cry a song?
   Can it be a song of joy?
   And so many children poor?
   It is a land of poverty!

   And their sun does never shine.
10 And their fields are bleak & bare.
   And their ways are fill'd with thorns.
   It is eternal winter there.

   For where-e'er the sun does shine,
   And where-e'er the rain does fall:
15 Babe can never hunger there,
   Nor poverty the mind appall.

                                                                (1794)

1 open countryside containing scrubby vegetation.

Nurse's Song

When the voices of children are heard on the green
And whisprings are in the dale:
The days of my youth rise fresh in my mind,
My face turns green and pale.

5   Then come home my children, the sun is gone down
And the dews of night arise
Your spring & your day are wasted in play
And your winter and night in disguise.

(1794)

The Sick Rose

O Rose thou art sick.
The invisible worm,
That flies in the night
In the howling storm:

5   Has found out thy bed
Of crimson joy:
And his dark secret love
Docs thy life destroy.

(1794)

London

I wander thro' each charter'd[1] street,
Near where the charter'd Thames does flow.
And mark in every face I meet
Marks of weakness, marks of woe.

5   In every cry of every Man,
In every Infants cry of fear,
In every voice; in every ban,
The mind-forg'd manacles I hear

1 protected as private property.

How the Chimney-sweepers cry
10   Every blackning Church appalls,
And the hapless Soldiers sigh
Runs in blood down Palace walls

But most thro' midnight streets I hear
How the youthful Harlots curse
15   Blasts the new-born Infants tear
And blights with plagues the Marriage hearse.

(1794)

William Wordsworth (1770–1850)

Born in Cockermouth, near the English Lake District, William Wordsworth attended Cambridge University and then travelled widely in Europe, spending a year in France during the Revolution. There he fathered an illegitimate child, Caroline, referred to indirectly in his sonnet "It is a beauteous evening." In 1798, with his friend Samuel Taylor Coleridge, he published *Lyrical Ballads*, a collection in which, as Coleridge stated, Wordsworth gave "the charm of novelty to things of everyday." In the Preface to the 1800 edition, written in response to criticism of the first edition, Wordsworth explained the theory underlying his poems. Reacting in part against the dominant poetic tastes and conventions of the eighteenth century, he stated that the poems were created from "emotion recollected in tranquillity," an idea illustrated in "Lines Composed a Few Miles above Tintern Abbey," and later in "I wandered lonely as a cloud." As seen in "Michael," he chose as his subjects "incidents and situations of common life," presented in "language really used by men." In 1802, influenced in part by his reading of John Milton, who is addressed in "London, 1802," Wordsworth wrote a number of sonnets considered by many critics to be the finest to have appeared since the seventeenth century. Wordsworth's reputation increased steadily during his lifetime, and, in 1843, he was appointed Poet Laureate. He is now recognized not only as one of the greatest of the Romantics and a major English poet, but as one who, in his portrayal of common people and nature, radically altered the course of English poetry in the nineteenth century.

Lines

COMPOSED A FEW MILES ABOVE TINTERN ABBEY,[1] ON REVISITING THE BANKS
OF THE WYE DURING A TOUR. JULY 13, 1798

Five years have past; five summers, with the length
Of five long winters! and again I hear
These waters, rolling from their mountain-springs
With a soft inland murmur. — Once again
5 Do I behold these steep and lofty cliffs,
That on a wild secluded scene impress
Thoughts of more deep seclusion; and connect
The landscape with the quiet of the sky.
The day is come when I again repose
10 Here, under this dark sycamore, and view
These plots of cottage-ground, these orchard-tufts,
Which at this season, with their unripe fruits,
Are clad in one green hue, and lose themselves
'Mid groves and copses. Once again I see
15 These hedge-rows, hardly hedge-rows, little lines
Of sportive wood run wild: these pastoral farms,
Green to the very door; and wreaths of smoke
Sent up, in silence, from among the trees!
With some uncertain notice, as might seem
20 Of vagrant dwellers in the houseless woods,
Or of some Hermit's cave, where by his fire
The Hermit sits alone.
                              These beauteous forms,
Through a long absence, have not been to me
As is a landscape to a blind man's eye:
25 But oft, in lonely rooms, and 'mid the din
Of towns and cities, I have owed to them
In hours of weariness, sensations sweet,
Felt in the blood, and felt along the heart;
And passing even into my purer mind,
30 With tranquil restoration: — feelings too
Of unremembered pleasure: such, perhaps,
As have no slight or trivial influence
On that best portion of a good man's life,
His little, nameless, unremembered, acts

— — →

1 ruined Cistercian abbey located on the Wye River, Wales.

35 Of kindness and of love. Nor less, I trust,
To them I may have owed another gift,
Of aspect more sublime; that blessed mood,
In which the burthen of the mystery,
In which the heavy and the weary weight
40 Of all this unintelligible world,
Is lightened: — that serene and blessed mood,
In which the affections gently lead us on, —
Until the breath of this corporeal frame
And even the motion of our human blood
45 Almost suspended, we are laid asleep
In body, and become a living soul:
While with an eye made quiet by the power
Of harmony, and the deep power of joy,
We see into the life of things.
       If this
50 Be but a vain belief, yet, oh! how oft —
In darkness and amid the many shapes
Of joyless daylight; when the fretful stir
Unprofitable, and the fever of the world,
Have hung upon the beatings of my heart —
55 How oft, in spirit, have I turned to thee,
O sylvan Wye! thou wanderer thro' the woods,
How often has my spirit turned to thee!
  And now, with gleams of half-extinguished thought,
With many recognitions dim and faint,
60 And somewhat of a sad perplexity,
The picture of the mind revives again:
While here I stand, not only with the sense
Of present pleasure, but with pleasing thoughts
That in this moment there is life and <u>food</u>
65 For future years. And so I dare to hope,
Though changed, no doubt, from what I was when first
I came among these hills; when like a roe
I bounded o'er the mountains, by the sides
Of the deep rivers, and the lonely streams,
70 Wherever nature led: more like a man
Flying from something that he dreads than one
Who sought the thing he loved. For nature then

[handwritten margin note, lines 44–48] By using our, we there is an inclosure gesture which & brings everyone there

[handwritten margin note, lines 58–61] experience of the natural scene

[handwritten margin note, line 64] think of word

     ⟶

as a baby he would not enjoy them as much

(The coarser pleasures of my boyish days,
And their glad animal movements all gone by)

75   To me was all in all. — I cannot paint
What then I was. The sounding cataract
Haunted me like a passion: the tall rock,
The mountain, and the deep and gloomy wood,
Their colours and their forms, were then to me

80   An appetite; a feeling and a love,
That had no need of a remoter charm,
By thought supplied, nor any interest
Unborrowed from the eye. — That time is past,
And all its aching joys are now no more,

85   And all its dizzy raptures. Not for this
Faint I, nor mourn nor murmur; other gifts
Have followed; for such loss, I would believe,
Abundant recompense. For I have learned
To look on nature, not as in the hour

90   Of thoughtless youth; but hearing oftentimes
The still, sad music of humanity,
Nor harsh nor grating, though of ample power
To chasten and subdue. And I have felt
A presence that disturbs me with the joy

95   Of elevated thoughts; a sense sublime
Of something far more deeply interfused,
Whose dwelling is the light of setting suns,
And the round ocean and the living air,
And the blue sky, and in the mind of man:

100 A motion and a spirit, that impels
All thinking things, all objects of all thought,
And rolls through all things. Therefore am I still
A lover of the meadows and the woods,
And mountains; and of all that we behold

105 From this green earth; of all the mighty world
Of eye, and ear, — both what they half create,
And what perceive; well pleased to recognise
In nature and the language of the sense
The anchor of my purest thoughts, the nurse,

110 The guide, the guardian of my heart, and soul
Of all my moral being.

——————→

recognizes his limits and as a poet and as a man of the word of experience

paradox, idealizing merging of natural & however claim that their was a lose but P we were never fully connected before ours fall out.

hence pleasures of his boyhood are more now that he can reflect them

He now finds in nature experience of sublime, an adult experience

mind is able to conceive that regardless of how vast, the mind is still the

purest thoughts are about nature

Nor perchance,
If I were not thus taught, should I the more
Suffer my genial spirits to decay:
For thou art with me here upon the banks
115 Of this fair river; thou my dearest Friend,[2]
My dear, dear Friend; and in thy voice I catch
The language of my former heart, and read
My former pleasures in the shooting lights
Of thy wild eyes. Oh! yet a little while
120 May I behold in thee what I was once,
My dear, dear Sister! and this prayer I make,
Knowing that Nature never did betray
The heart that loved her; 'tis her privilege,
Through all the years of this our life, to lead
125 From joy to joy: for she can so inform
The mind that is within us, so impress
With quietness and beauty, and so feed
With lofty thoughts, that neither evil tongues,
Rash judgments, nor the sneers of selfish men,
130 Nor greetings where no kindness is, nor all
The dreary intercourse of daily life,
Shall e'er prevail against us, or disturb
Our cheerful faith, that all which we behold
Is full of blessings. Therefore let the moon
135 Shine on thee in thy solitary walk;
And let the misty mountain-winds be free
To blow against thee: and, in after years,
When these wild ecstasies shall be matured
Into a sober pleasure; when thy mind
140 Shall be a mansion for all lovely forms,
Thy memory be as a dwelling-place
For all sweet sounds and harmonies; oh! then,
If solitude, or fear, or pain, or grief,
Should be thy portion, with what healing thoughts
145 Of tender joy wilt thou remember me,
And these my exhortations! Nor, perchance —
If I should be where I no more can hear
Thy voice, nor catch from thy wild eyes these gleams
Of past existence — wilt thou then forget
150 That on the banks of this delightful stream

→

she might still look at nature the way he did.

In the face of the world of experience nature can give you the reflect the capacity calm.

Saying that his sister may in fact have the reflective capacity of a poet. Once your pleasures turn to sober ones you might think of me and remember Poetry.

2 Wordsworth's sister, Dorothy.

We stood together; and that I, so long
A worshipper of Nature, hither came
Unwearied in that service: rather say
With warmer love — oh! with far deeper zeal
155   Of holier love. Nor wilt thou then forget
That after many wanderings, many years
Of absence, these steep woods and lofty cliffs,
And this green pastoral landscape, were to me
More dear, both for themselves and for thy sake!

(1798)

[handwritten margin note: Did not loose his love for nature, in fact realized its importance]

Nutting

It seems a day
(I speak of one from many singled out)
One of those heavenly days that cannot die;
When, in the eagerness of boyish hope,
5   I left our cottage-threshold, sallying forth
With a huge wallet[1] o'er my shoulders slung,
A nutting-crook[2] in hand; and turned my steps
Tow'rd some far-distant wood, a Figure quaint,
Tricked out in proud disguise of cast-off weeds
10   Which for that service had been husbanded,
By exhortation of my frugal Dame[3]—
Motley accoutrement, of power to smile
At thorns, and brakes, and brambles, — and in truth
More ragged than need was! O'er pathless rocks,
15   Through beds of matted fern, and tangled thickets,
Forcing my way, I came to one dear nook
Unvisited, where not a broken bough
Drooped with its withered leaves, ungracious sign
Of devastation; but the hazels rose
20   Tall and erect, with tempting clusters hung,
A virgin scene! — A little while I stood,
Breathing with such suppression of the heart
As joy delights in; and with wise restraint

———→

1 a knapsack. 2 a pole with a curved end used to pull down nut-laden branches. 3 Anne Tyson, with whom Wordsworth boarded while attending Hawkshead School in the Lake District.

Voluptuous, fearless of a rival, eyed
25 The banquet; — or beneath the trees I sate
Among the flowers, and with the flowers I played;
A temper known to those who, after long
And weary expectation, have been blest
With sudden happiness beyond all hope.
30 Perhaps it was a bower beneath whose leaves
The violets of five seasons re-appear
And fade, unseen by any human eye;
Where fairy water-breaks do murmur on
For ever; and I saw the sparkling foam,
35 And — with my cheek on one of those green stones
That, fleeced with moss, under the shady trees,
Lay round me, scattered like a flock of sheep —
I heard the murmur and the murmuring sound,
In that sweet mood when pleasure loves to pay
40 Tribute to ease; and, of its joy secure,
The heart luxuriates with indifferent things,
Wasting its kindliness on stocks and stones,
And on the vacant air. Then up I rose,
And dragged to earth both branch and bough, with crash
45 And merciless ravage: and the shady nook
Of hazels, and the green and mossy bower,
Deformed and sullied, patiently gave up
Their quiet being: and unless I now
Confound my present feelings with the past,
50 Ere from the mutilated bower I turned
Exulting, rich beyond the wealth of kings,
I felt a sense of pain when I beheld
The silent trees, and saw the intruding sky. —
Then, dearest Maiden, [4] move along these shades
55 In gentleness of heart; with gentle hand
Touch — for there is a spirit in the woods.

(1798)   (1800)

4 probably his sister, Dorothy.

She dwelt among the untrodden ways

She dwelt among the untrodden ways
    Beside the springs of Dove,[1]
A Maid whom there were none to praise
    And very few to love:

5   A violet by a mossy stone
      Half hidden from the eye!
    — Fair as a star, when only one
      Is shining in the sky.

She lived unknown, and few could know
10   When Lucy ceased to be;
But she is in her grave, and, oh,
    The difference to me!

(1799)   (1800)

It is a beauteous evening, calm and free

It is a beauteous evening, calm and free,
The holy time is quiet as a Nun
Breathless with adoration; the broad sun
Is sinking down in its tranquillity;
5   The gentleness of heaven broods o'er the Sea:
Listen! the mighty Being is awake,
And doth with his eternal motion make
A sound like thunder — everlastingly.
Dear Child![1] dear Girl! that walkest with me here,
10   If thou appear untouched by solemn thought,
Thy nature is not therefore less divine:
Thou liest in Abraham's bosom[2] all the year;
And worshipp'st at the Temple's inner shrine,
God being with thee when we know it not.

(1802)   (1807)

---

1 one of several rivers and streams named Dove is in Wordworth's Lake District, in the northwest of England.
1 Wordsworth's illegitimate daughter, Caroline. 2 heavenly rest, peace. Cf. Luke 16:22–23.

London, 1802

Milton! thou shouldst be living at this hour:
England hath need of thee: she is a fen
Of stagnant waters: altar, sword, and pen,
Fireside, the heroic wealth of hall and bower,
5 Have forfeited their ancient English dower
Of inward happiness. We are selfish men;
Oh! raise us up, return to us again;
And give us manners, virtue, freedom, power.
Thy soul was like a Star, and dwelt apart;
10 Thou hadst a voice whose sound was like the sea:
Pure as the naked heavens, majestic, free,
So didst thou travel on life's common way,
In cheerful godliness; and yet thy heart
The lowliest duties on herself did lay.

(1802)   (1807)

The world is too much with us

The world is too much with us; late and soon,
Getting and spending, we lay waste our powers:
Little we see in Nature that is ours;
We have given our hearts away, a sordid boon!
5 This Sea that bares her bosom to the moon;
The winds that will be howling at all hours,
And are up-gathered now like sleeping flowers;
For this, for everything, we are out of tune;
It moves us not.—Great God! I'd rather be
10 A Pagan suckled in a creed outworn;
So might I, standing on this pleasant lea,
Have glimpses that would make me less forlorn;
Have sight of Proteus[1] rising from the sea;
Or hear old Triton[2] blow his wreathèd horn.

(c. 1802)   (1807)

1 Greek sea deity who had the power of prophecy. 2 Greek sea deity who was half-man and half-fish and
who had the power to calm the ocean.

I wandered lonely as a cloud

I wandered lonely as a cloud
That floats on high o'er vales and hills,
When all at once I saw a crowd,
A host, of golden daffodils;
5   Beside the lake, beneath the trees,
Fluttering and dancing in the breeze.

Continuous as the stars that shine
And twinkle on the milky way,
They stretched in never-ending line
10   Along the margin of a bay:
Ten thousand saw I at a glance,
Tossing their heads in sprightly dance.

The waves beside them danced; but they
Out-did the sparkling waves in glee:
15   A poet could not but be gay,
In such a jocund company:
I gazed — and gazed — but little thought
What wealth the show to me had brought:

For oft, when on my couch I lie
20   In vacant or in pensive mood,
They flash upon that inward eye
Which is the bliss of solitude;
And then my heart with pleasure fills,
And dances with the daffodils.

(1804)   (1807)

Samuel Taylor Coleridge (1772–1834)

Born in the small town of Ottery St. Mary, Devonshire, Samuel Taylor Coleridge grew up in London, an intelligent, but very lonely, unhappy child. He studied at Cambridge, spent a year in the army, and interested himself in radical politics. In 1797, he met William Wordsworth, and a year later the two published *Lyrical Ballads*. Coleridge's contributions were poems written on supernatural or roman-tic subjects, designed to create in the reader what he called "that willing suspen-sion of disbelief for the moment, which constitutes poetic faith." Of these poems, the best known is "The Rime of the Ancient Mariner." Adapting the traditional ballad stanza, which had become popular during the last half of the eighteenth century, he drew on his voluminous reading in folklore and science to create the account of the title figure's symbolic journey of sin, guilt, repentance, and redemp-tion, and the effect its retelling has on the somewhat self-satisfied wedding guest. Also written during this period was "Kubla Khan," which Coleridge said was based on an opium-induced dream. "Frost at Midnight" expresses his intense longing as well as his hope that nature would provide his son with the opportunities and satisfactions that he himself had been denied. Although Coleridge continued to write poetry throughout his life, his most noted later work is *Biographia Literaria* (1817), a combination of autobiography, philosophy, and literary criticism.

Kubla Khan[1]

In Xanadu[2] did Kubla Khan
A stately pleasure-dome decree:
Where Alph, the sacred river, ran
Through caverns measureless to man
5   Down to a sunless sea.
So twice five miles of fertile ground
With walls and towers were girdled round:
And there were gardens bright with sinuous rills,
Where blossomed many an incense-bearing tree;
10   And here were forests ancient as the hills,
Enfolding sunny spots of greenery.

But oh! that deep romantic chasm which slanted
Down the green hill athwart a cedarn cover![3]
A savage place! as holy and enchanted
15   As e'er beneath a waning moon was haunted
By woman wailing for her demon-lover!
And from this chasm, with ceaseless turmoil seething,

———→

1 thirteenth-century emperor of China. He was the grandson of Genghis Khan and a patron of the arts.
2 Shang-tu, a city founded by Kubla Khan, on the site of modern Beijing. 3 covered by cedar trees.

As if this earth in fast thick pants were breathing,
A mighty fountain momently was forced:
20 Amid whose swift half-intermitted burst
Huge fragments vaulted like rebounding hail,
Or chaffy grain beneath the thresher's flail:
And 'mid these dancing rocks at once and ever
It flung up momently the sacred river.
25 Five miles meandering with a mazy motion
Through wood and dale the sacred river ran,
Then reached the caverns measureless to man,
And sank in tumult to a lifeless ocean:
And 'mid this tumult Kubla heard from far
30 Ancestral voices prophesying war!
      The shadow of the dome of pleasure
      Floated midway on the waves
      Where was heard the mingled measure
      From the fountain and the caves.
35 It was a miracle of rare device,
A sunny pleasure-dome with caves of ice!

      A damsel with a dulcimer
      In a vision once I saw:
      It was an Abyssinian maid,
40   And on her dulcimer she played,
      Singing of Mount Abora.[4]
      Could I revive within me
      Her symphony and song,
      To such a deep delight 'twould win me,
45 That with music loud and long,
I would build that dome in air,
That sunny dome! those caves of ice!
And all who heard should see them there,
And all should cry, Beware! Beware!
50 His flashing eyes, his floating hair!
Weave a circle round him thrice,
And close your eyes with holy dread,
For he on honey-dew hath fed,
And drunk the milk of Paradise.

(1797)   (1816)

4 possibly Mt. Amara, in Abyssinia, now Ethiopia.

The Rime of the Ancient Mariner

PART I

It is an ancient Mariner,
And he stoppeth one of three.
"By thy long grey beard and glittering eye,
Now wherefore stopp'st thou me?

An ancient Mariner
meeteth three Gallants
bidden to a wedding feast,
and detaineth one.

5   The Bridegroom's doors are opened wide,
And I am next of kin;
The guests are met, the feast is set:
May'st hear the merry din."

He holds him with his skinny hand,
10 "There was a ship," quoth he.
"Hold off! unhand me, grey-beard loon!"
Eftsoons[1] his hand dropt he.

Does not ease in to the story [handwritten]

He holds him with his glittering eye —
The Wedding-Guest stood still,
15 And listens like a three years' child:
The Mariner hath his will.

mesmerism [handwritten]

The Wedding-Guest is
spellbound by the eye of the
old seafaring man, and
constrained to hear his tale.

The Wedding-Guest sat on a stone:
He cannot choose but hear;
And thus spake on that ancient man,
20 The bright-eyed Mariner.

"The ship was cheered, the harbour cleared,
Merrily did we drop
Below the kirk,[2] below the hill,
Below the lighthouse top.

25 The Sun came up upon the left,
Out of the sea came he!
And he shone bright, and on the right
Went down into the sea.

The Mariner tells how the
ship sailed southward with a
good wind and fair weather,
till it reached the Line.

1 immediately. 2 church.

Higher and higher every day,
30   Till over the mast at noon —"
The Wedding-Guest here beat his breast,
For he heard the loud bassoon.

The bride hath paced into the hall,
Red as a rose is she;
35   Nodding their heads before her goes
The merry minstrelsy.[3]

The Wedding-Guest heareth the bridal music; but the Mariner continueth his tale.

The Wedding-Guest he beat his breast,
Yet he cannot choose but hear;
And thus spake on that ancient man,
40   The bright-eyed Mariner.

"And now the STORM-BLAST came, and he
Was tyrannous and strong:
He struck with his o'ertaking wings,
And chased us south along.

The ship driven by a storm toward the South Pole.

45   With sloping masts and dipping prow,
As who pursued with yell and blow
Still treads the shadow of his foe,
And forward bends his head,
The ship drove fast, loud roared the blast,
50   And southward aye we fled.

And now there came both mist and snow,
And it grew wondrous cold:
And ice, mast-high, came floating by,
As green as emerald.

The land of ice, and of fearful sounds where no living thing was to be seen.

55   And through the drifts the snowy clifts
Did send a dismal sheen:
Nor shapes of men nor beasts we ken —[4]
The ice was all between.

---

3 group of minstrels. 4 know.

The ice was here, the ice was there,
60 The ice was all around:
It cracked and growled, and roared and howled,
Like noises in a swound! [5]

At length did cross an Albatross,
Thorough the fog it came;
65 As if it had been a Christian soul,
We hailed it in God's name.

Till a great sea-bird, called the Albatross, came through the snow-fog, and was received with great joy and hospitality.

It ate the food it ne'er had eat,
And round and round it flew.
The ice did split with a thunder-fit;
70 The helmsman [6] steered us through!

And a good south wind sprung up behind;
The Albatross did follow,
And every day, for food or play,
Came to the mariners' hollo!

And lo! the Albatross proveth a bird of good omen, and followeth the ship as it returned northward through fog and floating ice.

75 In mist or cloud, on mast or shroud,
It perched for vespers [7] nine;
Whiles all the night, through fog-smoke white,
Glimmered the white Moon-shine."

"God save thee, ancient Mariner!
80 From the fiends, that plague thee thus! —
Why look'st thou so?" — "With my cross-bow
I shot the ALBATROSS.

The ancient Mariner inhospitably killeth the pious bird of good omen.

PART II

The Sun now rose upon the right:
Out of the sea came he,
85 Still hid in mist, and on the left
Went down into the sea.

5 swoon. 6 person who steers the ship. 7 evening worship; i.e., the bird remained for nine evenings.

And the good south wind still blew behind,
But no sweet bird did follow,
Nor any day for food or play
90 Came to the mariners' hollo!

And I had done a hellish thing,
And it would work 'em woe:
For all averred, I had killed the bird
That made the breeze to blow.
95 Ah wretch! said they, the bird to slay,
That made the breeze to blow!

His shipmates cry out against the ancient Mariner, for killing the bird of good luck.

*Killed
bird
during
day*

Nor dim nor red, like God's own head,
The glorious Sun uprist:
Then all averred, I had killed the bird
100 That brought the fog and mist.
'Twas right, said they, such birds to slay,
That bring the fog and mist.

But when the fog cleared off, they justify the same, and thus make themselves accomplices in the crime.

The fair breeze blew, the white foam flew,
The furrow followed free;
105 We were the first that ever burst
Into that silent sea.

The fair breeze continues; the ship enters the Pacific Ocean, and sails northward, even till it reaches the Line.

Down dropt the breeze, the sails dropt down,
'Twas sad as sad could be;
And we did speak only to break
110 The silence of the sea!

The ship hath been suddenly becalmed.

All in a hot and copper sky,
The bloody Sun, at noon,
Right up above the mast did stand,
No bigger than the Moon.

115 Day after day, day after day,
We stuck, nor breath nor motion;
As idle as a painted ship
Upon a painted ocean.

Water, water, every where,
And all the boards did shrink;
Water, water, every where,
Nor any drop to drink.

The very deep did rot: O Christ!
That ever this should be!
Yea, slimy things did crawl with legs
Upon the slimy sea.

About, about, in reel and rout
The death-fires danced at night;
The water, like a witch's oils,
Burnt green, and blue and white.

And some in dreams assuréd were
Of the Spirit that plagued us so;
Nine fathom deep he had followed us
From the land of mist and snow.

And every tongue, through utter drought,
Was withered at the root;
We could not speak, no more than if
We had been choked with soot.

Ah! well a-day! what evil looks
Had I from old and young!
Instead of the cross, the Albatross
About my neck was hung.

Part III

There passed a weary time. Each throat
Was parched, and glazed each eye.
A weary time! a weary time!
How glazed each weary eye,
When looking westward, I beheld
A something in the sky.

And the Albatross begins to be avenged.

A Spirit had followed them; one of the invisible inhabitants of this planet, neither departed souls nor angels; concerning whom the learned Jew, Josephus, and the Platonic Constantinopolitan, Michael Psellus, may be consulted. They are very numerous, and there is no climate or element without one or more.

The shipmates, in their sore distress, would fain throw the whole guilt on the ancient Mariner: in sign whereof they hang the dead sea-bird round his neck.

The ancient Mariner beholdeth a sign in the element afar off.

At first it seemed a little speck,
150 And then it seemed a mist;
It moved and moved, and took at last
A certain shape, I wist.

A speck, a mist, a shape, I wist!
And still it neared and neared:
155 As if it dodged a water-sprite,[8]
It plunged and tacked and veered.

With throats unslaked, with black lips baked,   *At its nearer approach, it*
We could nor laugh nor wail: *seemeth him to be a ship;*
Through utter drought all dumb we stood!   *and at a dear ransom he*
160 I bit my arm, I sucked the blood,   *freeth his speech from the*
And cried, A sail! a sail!   *bonds of thirst.*

With throats unslaked, with black lips baked,
Agape they heard me call:
Gramercy![9] they for joy did grin,   *A flash of joy;*
165 And all at once their breath drew in,
As they were drinking all.

See! see! (I cried) she tacks no more!   *And horror follows. For*
Hither to work us weal;   *can it be a ship that comes*
Without a breeze, without a tide,   *onward without wind or tide?*
170 She steadies with upright keel!

The western wave was all a-flame.
The day was well nigh done!
Almost upon the western wave
Rested the broad bright Sun;
175 When that strange shape drove suddenly
Betwixt us and the Sun.

And straight the Sun was flecked with bars,   *It seemeth him but the*
(Heaven's Mother send us grace!)   *skeleton of a ship.*
As if through a dungeon-grate he peered
180 With broad and burning face.

8 spirit living in water. 9 expression of surprise or gratitude, literally, "Great thanks."

Alas! (thought I, and my heart beat loud)
How fast she nears and nears!
Are those *her* sails that glance in the Sun,
Like restless gossameres? [10]

185 Are those *her* ribs through which the Sun
Did peer, as through a grate?
And is that Woman all her crew?
Is that a DEATH? and are there two?
Is DEATH that woman's mate?

And the ribs are seen as bars on the face of the setting Sun. The Spectre-Woman and her Death-mate, and no other on board the skeleton ship.

190 *Her* lips were red, *her* looks were free,
Her locks were yellow as gold:
Her skin was as white as leprosy,
The Night-mare LIFE-IN-DEATH was she,
Who thicks man's blood with cold.

Like vessel, like crew!

Death and Life-in-Death have diced for the ship's crew, and she (the latter) winneth the ancient Mariner.

195 The naked hulk alongside came,
And the twain were casting dice;
'The game is done! I've won! I've won!'
Quoth she, and whistles thrice.

The Sun's rim dips; the stars rush out:
200 At one stride comes the dark;
With far-heard whisper, o'er the sea,
Off shot the spectre-bark. [11]

No twilight within the courts of the Sun.

We listened and looked sideways up!
Fear at my heart, as at a cup,
205 My life-blood seemed to sip!
The stars were dim, and thick the night,
The steersman's face by his lamp gleamed white;
From the sails the dew did drip —
Till clomb above the eastern bar
210 The hornéd Moon,[12] with one bright star
Within the nether tip.

At the rising of the Moon,

One after one, by the star-dogged[13] Moon,
Too quick for groan or sigh,
Each turned his face with a ghastly pang,
215 And cursed me with his eye.

One after another,

10 cobwebs. 11 phantom ship. 12 crescent moon. 13 followed by a star.

Four times fifty living men,
(And I heard nor sigh nor groan)
With heavy thump, a lifeless lump,
They dropped down one by one.

*His shipmates drop down
dead.*

220 The souls did from their bodies fly,—
They fled to bliss or woe!
And every soul, it passed me by,
Like the whizz of my cross-bow!"

*But Life-in-Death begins her
work on the ancient Mariner.*

PART IV

"I fear thee, ancient Mariner!
225 I fear thy skinny hand!
And thou art long, and lank, and brown,
As is the ribbed sea-sand.

*The Wedding-Guest feareth
that a Spirit is talking to him;*

I fear thee and thy glittering eye,
And thy skinny hand, so brown."—
230 "Fear not, fear not, thou Wedding-Guest!
This body dropt not down.

*But the ancient Mariner
assureth him of his bodily life,
and proceedeth to relate his
horrible penance.*

Alone, alone, all, all alone,
Alone on a wide wide sea!
And never a saint took pity on
235 My soul in agony.

The many men, so beautiful!
And they all dead did lie:
And a thousand thousand slimy things
Lived on; and so did I.

*He despiseth the creatures of
the calm,*

240 I looked upon the rotting sea,
And drew my eyes away;
I looked upon the rotting deck,
And there the dead men lay.

*And envieth that they should
live, and so many lie dead.*

I looked to heaven, and tried to pray;
245 But or ever a prayer had gusht,
A wicked whisper came, and made
My heart as dry as dust.

I closed my lids, and kept them close,
And the balls like pulses beat;
250   For the sky and the sea, and the sea and the sky
Lay like a load on my weary eye,
And the dead were at my feet.

The cold sweat melted from their limbs,
Nor rot nor reek did they:
255   The look with which they looked on me
Had never passed away.

*But the curse liveth for him in
the eye of the dead men.*

An orphan's curse would drag to hell
A spirit from on high;
But oh! more horrible than that
260   Is the curse in a dead man's eye!
Seven days, seven nights, I saw that curse,
And yet I could not die.

The moving Moon went up the sky,
And no where did abide:
265   Softly she was going up,
And a star or two beside —

*In his loneliness and fixedness
he yearneth towards the jour-
neying Moon, and the stars
that still sojourn, yet still
move onward; and every
where the blue sky belongs to
them, and is their appointed
rest, and their native country
and their own natural homes,
which they enter unan-
nounced, as lords that are
certainly expected and yet
there is a silent joy at their
arrival.*

Her beams bemocked the sultry main,[14]
Like April hoar-frost spread;
But where the ship's huge shadow lay,
270   The charmèd water burnt alway
A still and awful red.

Beyond the shadow of the ship,
I watched the water-snakes:
They moved in tracks of shining white,
275   And when they reared, the elfish light
Fell off in hoary flakes.

*By the light of the Moon he
beholdeth God's creatures of
the great calm.*

Within the shadow of the ship
I watched their rich attire:
Blue, glossy green, and velvet black,
280   They coiled and swam; and every track
Was a flash of golden fire.

14 sea.

O happy living things! no tongue
Their beauty might declare:
A spring of love gushed from my heart,
285 And I blessed them unaware:
Sure my kind saint took pity on me,
And I blessed them unaware.

Their beauty and their happiness.

He blesseth them in his heart.

The self-same moment I could pray;
And from my neck so free
290 The Albatross fell off, and sank
Like lead into the sea.

The spell begins to break.

PART V

Oh sleep! it is a gentle thing,
Beloved from pole to pole!
To Mary Queen[15] the praise be given!
295 She sent the gentle sleep from Heaven,
That slid into my soul.

The silly buckets on the deck,
That had so long remained,
I dreamt that they were filled with dew;
300 And when I awoke, it rained.

By grace of the holy Mother, the ancient Mariner is refreshed with rain.

My lips were wet, my throat was cold,
My garments all were dank;
Sure I had drunken in my dreams,
And still my body drank.

305 I moved, and could not feel my limbs:
I was so light — almost
I thought that I had died in sleep,
And was a blessèd ghost.

And soon I heard a roaring wind:
310 It did not come anear;
But with its sound it shook the sails,
That were so thin and sere.

He heareth sound and seeth strange sights and commotions in the sky and the element.

15 the Virgin Mary, queen of Heaven.

The upper air burst into life!
And a hundred fire-flags sheen,[16]
315 To and fro they were hurried about!
And to and fro, and in and out,
The wan stars danced between.

And the coming wind did roar more loud,
And the sails did sigh like sedge;
320 And the rain poured down from one black cloud;
The Moon was at its edge.

The thick black cloud was cleft, and still
The Moon was at its side:
Like waters shot from some high crag,
325 The lightning fell with never a jag,
A river steep and wide.

The loud wind never reached the ship,
Yet now the ship moved on!
Beneath the lightning and the Moon
330 The dead men gave a groan.

*The bodies of the ship's crew
are inspired and the ship
moves on;*

They groaned, they stirred, they all uprose,
Nor spake, nor moved their eyes;
It had been strange, even in a dream,
To have seen those dead men rise.

335 The helmsman steered, the ship moved on;
Yet never a breeze up-blew;
The mariners all 'gan work the ropes,
Where they were wont to do;
They raised their limbs like lifeless tools —
340 We were a ghastly crew.

The body of my brother's son
Stood by me, knee to knee:
The body and I pulled at one rope,
But he said nought to me."

16 meteors shone.

345   "I fear thee, ancient Mariner!"
"Be calm, thou Wedding-Guest!
'Twas not those souls that fled in pain,
Which to their corses[17] came again,
But a troop of spirits blest:

350   For when it dawned — they dropped their arms,
And clustered round the mast;
Sweet sounds rose slowly through their mouths,
And from their bodies passed.

Around, around, flew each sweet sound,
355   Then darted to the Sun;
Slowly the sounds came back again,
Now mixed, now one by one.

Sometimes a-dropping from the sky
I heard the sky-lark sing;
360   Sometimes all little birds that are,
How they seemed to fill the sea and air
With their sweet jargoning!

And now 'twas like all instruments,
Now like a lonely flute;
365   And now it is an angel's song,
That makes the heavens be mute.

It ceased; yet still the sails made on
A pleasant noise till noon,
A noise like of a hidden brook
370   In the leafy month of June,
That to the sleeping woods all night
Singeth a quiet tune.

Till noon we quietly sailed on,
Yet never a breeze did breathe:
375   Slowly and smoothly went the ship,
Moved onward from beneath.

But not by the souls of the men, nor by demons of earth or middle air, but by a blessed troop of angelic spirits, sent down by the invocation of the guardian saint.

17 corpses.

Under the keel nine fathom deep,
From the land of mist and snow,
The spirit slid: and it was he
380   That made the ship to go.
The sails at noon left off their tune,
And the ship stood still also.

The Sun, right up above the mast,
Had fixed her to the ocean:
385   But in a minute she 'gan stir,
With a short uneasy motion —
Backwards and forwards half her length
With a short uneasy motion.

Then like a pawing horse let go,
390   She made a sudden bound:
It flung the blood into my head,
And I fell down in a swound.

How long in that same fit I lay,
I have not to declare;
395   But ere my living life returned,
I heard and in my soul discerned
Two voices in the air.

'Is it he?' quoth one, 'Is this the man?
By him who died on cross,[18]
400   With his cruel bow he laid full low
The harmless Albatross.

The spirit who bideth by himself
In the land of mist and snow,
He loved the bird that loved the man
405   Who shot him with his bow.'

The other was a softer voice,
As soft as honey-dew:
Quoth he, 'The man hath penance done,
And penance more will do.'

The lonesome Spirit from the South-Pole carries on the ship as far as the Line, in obedience to the angelic troop, but still requireth vengeance.

The Polar Spirit's fellow-demons, the invisible inhabitants of the element, take part in his wrong; and two of them relate, one to the other, that penance long and heavy for the ancient Mariner hath been accorded to the Polar Spirit, who returneth southward.

18 Christ, who was crucified on a cross.

Part VI

FIRST VOICE

410 'But tell me, tell me! speak again,
Thy soft response renewing —
What makes that ship drive on so fast?
What is the ocean doing?'

SECOND VOICE

'Still as a slave before his lord,
415 The ocean hath no blast;
His great bright eye most silently
Up to the Moon is cast —

If he may know which way to go;
For she guides him smooth or grim.
420 See, brother, see! how graciously
She looketh down on him.'

FIRST VOICE

'But why drives on that ship so fast,
Without or wave or wind?'

SECOND VOICE

'The air is cut away before,
425 And closes from behind.

Fly, brother, fly! more high, more high!
Or we shall be belated:
For slow and slow that ship will go,
When the Mariner's trance is abated.'

430 I woke, and we were sailing on
As in a gentle weather:
'Twas night, calm night, the moon was high;
The dead men stood together.

All stood together on the deck,
435 For a charnel-dungeon[19] fitter:
All fixed on me their stony eyes,
That in the Moon did glitter.

The Mariner hath been cast into a trance; for the angelic power causeth the vessel to drive northward faster than human life could endure.

The supernatural motion is retarded; the Mariner awakes, and his penance begins anew.

19 burial house, or prison in which people are left to die.

The pang, the curse, with which they died,
Had never passed away:
440 I could not draw my eyes from theirs,
Nor turn them up to pray.

And now this spell was snapt: once more
I viewed the ocean green,
And looked far forth, yet little saw
445 Of what had else been seen —

The curse is finally expiated.

Like one that on a lonesome road
Doth walk in fear and dread,
And having once turned round walks on,
And turns no more his head;
450 Because he knows, a frightful fiend
Doth close behind him tread.

But soon there breathed a wind on me,
Nor sound nor motion made:
Its path was not upon the sea,
455 In ripple or in shade.

It raised my hair, it fanned my cheek
Like a meadow-gale of spring —
It mingled strangely with my fears,
Yet it felt like a welcoming.

460 Swiftly, swiftly flew the ship,
Yet she sailed softly too:
Sweetly, sweetly blew the breeze —
On me alone it blew.

Oh! dream of joy! is this indeed
465 The light-house top I see?
Is this the hill? is this the kirk?
Is this mine own countree?

*And the ancient Mariner
beholdeth his native country.*

We drifted o'er the harbour-bar,[20]
And I with sobs did pray —
470 O let me be awake, my God!
Or let me sleep alway.

20 breakwater or sandbar protecting a harbour.

The harbour-bay was clear as glass,
So smoothly it was strewn!
And on the bay the moonlight lay,
475   And the shadow of the Moon.

The rock shone bright, the kirk no less,
That stands above the rock:
The moonlight steeped in silentness
The steady weathercock.

480   And the bay was white with silent light,
Till rising from the same,
Full many shapes, that shadows were,
In crimson colours came.

The angelic spirits leave the dead bodies,

A little distance from the prow
485   Those crimson shadows were:
I turned my eyes upon the deck —
Oh, Christ! what saw I there!

And appear in their own forms of light.

Each corse lay flat, lifeless and flat,
And, by the holy rood! [21]
490   A man all light, a seraph-man, [22]
On every corse there stood.

This seraph-band, each waved his hand:
It was a heavenly sight!
They stood as signals to the land,
495   Each one a lovely light;

This seraph-band, each waved his hand,
No voice did they impart —
No voice; but oh! the silence sank
Like music on my heart.

500   But soon I heard the dash of oars,
I heard the Pilot's [23] cheer;
My head was turned perforce away,
And I saw a boat appear.

21 the cross on which Christ was crucified. 22 fiery angel. 23 person who steers ships into harbour.

The Pilot and the Pilot's boy,
505 I heard them coming fast:
Dear Lord in Heaven! it was a joy
The dead men could not blast.

I saw a third — I heard his voice:
It is the Hermit good!
510 He singeth loud his godly hymns
That he makes in the wood.
He'll shrieve [24] my soul, he'll wash away
The Albatross's blood.

PART VII

This Hermit good lives in that wood   *The Hermit of the Wood,*
515 Which slopes down to the sea.
How loudly his sweet voice he rears!
He loves to talk with marineres
That come from a far countree.

He kneels at morn, and noon, and eve —
520 He hath a cushion plump:
It is the moss that wholly hides
The rotted old oak-stump.

The skiff-boat neared: I heard them talk,
'Why, this is strange, I trow!
525 Where are those lights so many and fair,
That signal made but now?'

'Strange, by my faith!' the Hermit said —   *Approacheth the ship with*
'And they answered not our cheer!   *wonder.*
The planks looked warped! and see those sails,
530 How thin they are and sere!
I never saw aught like to them,
Unless perchance it were

Brown skeletons of leaves that lag
My forest-brook along;
535 When the ivy-tod is heavy with snow,
And the owlet whoops to the wolf below,
That eats the she-wolf's young.'

24 administer spiritual absolution.

'Dear Lord! it hath a fiendish look —
(The Pilot made reply)
540 I am a-feared' —'Push on, push on!'
Said the Hermit cheerily.

The boat came closer to the ship,
But I nor spake nor stirred;
The boat came close beneath the ship,
545 And straight a sound was heard.

Under the water it rumbled on,   *The ship suddenly sinketh.*
Still louder and more dread:
It reached the ship, it split the bay;
The ship went down like lead.

550 Stunned by that loud and dreadful sound,   *The ancient Mariner is saved*
Which sky and ocean smote,   *in the Pilot's boat.*
Like one that hath been seven days drowned
My body lay afloat;
But swift as dreams, myself I found
555 Within the Pilot's boat.

Upon the whirl, where sank the ship,
The boat spun round and round;
And all was still, save that the hill
Was telling of the sound.

560 I moved my lips — the Pilot shrieked
And fell down in a fit;
The holy Hermit raised his eyes,
And prayed where he did sit.

I took the oars: the Pilot's boy,
565 Who now doth crazy go,
Laughed loud and long, and all the while
His eyes went to and fro.
'Ha! ha!' quoth he, 'full plain I see,
The Devil knows how to row.'

570 And now, all in my own countree,
I stood on the firm land!
The Hermit stepped forth from the boat,
And scarcely he could stand.

'O shrieve me, shrieve me, holy man!'
575   The Hermit crossed his brow.
'Say quick,' quoth he, 'I bid thee say —
What manner of man art thou?'

Forthwith this frame of mine was wrenched
With a woful agony,
580   Which forced me to begin my tale;
And then it left me free.

Since then, at an uncertain hour,
That agony returns:
And till my ghastly tale is told,
585   This heart within me burns.

I pass, like night, from land to land;
I have strange power of speech;
That moment that his face I see,
I know the man that must hear me:
590   To him my tale I teach.

What loud uproar bursts from that door!
The wedding-guests are there:
But in the garden-bower the bride
And bride-maids singing are:
595   And hark the little vesper bell,[25]
Which biddeth me to prayer!

O Wedding-Guest! this soul hath been
Alone on a wide wide sea:
So lonely 'twas, that God himself
600   Scarce seeméd there to be.

O sweeter than the marriage-feast,
'Tis sweeter far to me,
To walk together to the kirk
With a goodly company! —

The ancient Mariner earnestly entreateth the Hermit to shrieve him; and the penance of life falls on him.

And ever and anon throughout his future life an agony constraineth him to travel from land to land;

25 bell calling people to evening worship.

605　To walk together to the kirk,
　　　And all together pray,
　　　While each to his great Father bends,
　　　Old men, and babes, and loving friends
　　　And youths and maidens gay!

610　Farewell, farewell! but this I tell
　　　To thee, thou Wedding-Guest!
　　　He prayeth well, who loveth well
　　　Both man and bird and beast.

　　　He prayeth best, who loveth best
615　All things both great and small;
　　　For the dear God who loveth us,
　　　He made and loveth all."

　　　The Mariner, whose eye is bright,
　　　Whose beard with age is hoar,[26]
620　Is gone: and now the Wedding-Guest
　　　Turned from the bridegroom's door.

　　　He went like one that hath been stunned,
　　　And is of sense forlorn:
　　　A sadder and a wiser man,
625　He rose the morrow morn.

And to teach, by his own example, love and reverence to all things that God made and loveth.

(1798)

Frost at Midnight

　　　The Frost performs its secret ministry,
　　　Unhelped by any wind. The owlet's cry
　　　Came loud — and hark, again! loud as before.
　　　The inmates of my cottage, all at rest,
5　　Have left me to that solitude, which suits
　　　Abstruser musings: save that at my side
　　　My cradled infant[1] slumbers peacefully.
　　　'Tis calm indeed! so calm, that it disturbs
　　　And vexes meditation with its strange

———→

26 greyish-white
1 his son Hartley.

10   And extreme silentness. Sea, hill, and wood,
    This populous village! Sea, and hill, and wood,
    With all the numberless goings-on of life,
    Inaudible as dreams! the thin blue flame
    Lies on my low-burnt fire, and quivers not;
15   Only that film, [2] which fluttered on the grate,
    Still flutters there, the sole unquiet thing.
    Methinks, its motion in this hush of nature
    Gives it dim sympathies with me who live,
    Making it a companionable form,
20   Whose puny flaps and freaks the idling Spirit
    By its own moods interprets, everywhere
    Echo or mirror seeking of itself,
    And makes a toy of Thought.

                       But O! how oft,
25   How oft, at school, [3] with most believing mind,
    Presageful, have I gazed upon the bars,
    To watch that fluttering *stranger*! and as oft
    With unclosed lids, already had I dreamt
    Of my sweet birth-place, [4] and the old church-tower,
30   Whose bells, the poor man's only music, rang
    From morn to evening, all the hot Fair-day,
    So sweetly, that they stirred and haunted me
    With a wild pleasure, falling on mine ear
    Most like articulate sounds of things to come!
35   So gazed I, till the soothing things I dreamt,
    Lulled me to sleep, and sleep prolonged my dreams!
    And so I brooded all the following morn,
    Awed by the stern preceptor's[5] face, mine eye
    Fixed with mock study on my swimming book:
40   Save if the door half opened, and I snatched
    A hasty glance, and still my heart leaped up,
    For still I hoped to see the *stranger's* face,
    Townsman, or aunt, or sister more beloved,
    My playmate when we both were clothed alike! [6]

---

2 flake of soot or ash; in his note to the poem, Coleridge wrote, "In all parts of the kingdom these films are called *strangers* and supposed to portend the arrival of some absent friend." 3 the grammar school, Christ's Hospital, London. 4 Ottery St. Mary, Devonshire. 5 Rev. James Boyer, whom Coleridge describes in the first chapter of his *Biographia Litereria* (1817). 6 until they reached a certain age, Coleridge and his sister Ann would have been dressed in infant clothing, which was the same for males and females.

45   Dear Babe, that sleepest cradled by my side,
Whose gentle breathings, heard in this deep calm,
Fill up the interspersed vacancies
And momentary pauses of the thought!
My babe so beautiful! it thrills my heart
50 With tender gladness, thus to look at thee,
And think that thou shalt learn far other lore
And in far other scenes! For I was reared
In the great city, pent 'mid cloisters dim,
And saw nought lovely but the sky and stars.
55 But *thou*, my babe! shalt wander like a breeze
By lakes and sandy shores, beneath the crags
Of ancient mountain, and beneath the clouds,
Which image in their bulk both lakes and shores
And mountain crags: so shalt thou see and hear
60 The lovely shapes and sounds intelligible
Of that eternal language, which thy God
Utters, who from eternity doth teach
Himself in all, and all things in himself.
Great universal Teacher! he shall mould
65 Thy spirit, and by giving make it ask.

      Therefore all seasons shall be sweet to thee,
Whether the summer clothe the general earth
With greenness, or the redbreast sit and sing
Betwixt the tufts of snow on the bare branch
70 Of mossy apple-tree, while the nigh thatch
Smokes in the sun-thaw; whether the eave-drops fall
Heard only in the trances of the blast,
Or if the secret ministry of frost
Shall hang them up in silent icicles,
Quietly shining to the quiet Moon.

(1798)

George Gordon, Lord Byron (1788–1824)

Raised in Aberdeen, Scotland, George Gordon became Lord Byron at age ten, after the death of his uncle. While a student at Cambridge, he became notorious for his flamboyant life. His first major work, *Childe Harold*, cantos I and II (1812), was based in part on his own European travels. An advocate of liberal causes as a member of the House of Lords, he died in Greece while training soldiers for that country's fight for independence. During his life and after, he was regarded as an almost legendary figure: handsome, athletic, proud, talented, but often filled with guilt and remorse. An accomplished craftsman, his works range from the beautiful lyric "She Walks in Beauty," to the long, satirical, and humorous *Don Juan* (1819–24). In "On This Day I Complete My Thirty-Sixth Year," written shortly before his death, Byron portrays himself as a world-weary individual seeking to find meaning in his life through involvement in the political and military struggles of Greece.

She Walks in Beauty

I.

She walks in beauty, like the night
 Of cloudless climes and starry skies;
And all that's best of dark and bright
 Meet in her aspect and her eyes:
5 Thus mellow'd to that tender light
 Which heaven to gaudy day denies.

II.

One shade the more, one ray the less,
 Had half impair'd the nameless grace
Which waves in every raven tress,
10 Or softly lightens o'er her face;
Where thoughts serenely sweet express
 How pure, how dear their dwelling-place.

III.

And on that cheek, and o'er that brow,
 So soft, so calm, yet eloquent,
15 The smiles that win, the tints that glow,
 But tell of days in goodness spent,
A mind at peace with all below,
 A heart whose love is innocent!

(1814)   (1815)

On This Day I Complete My Thirty-Sixth Year

Missolonghi, Jan. 22, 1824.

'Tis time this heart should be unmoved,
　　Since others it hath ceased to move:
Yet, though I cannot be beloved,
　　　Still let me love!

5　My days are in the yellow leaf;
　　The flowers and fruits of love are gone;
The worm, the canker, and the grief
　　　Are mine alone!

The fire that on my bosom preys
10　　Is lone as some volcanic isle;
No torch is kindled at its blaze —
　　　A funeral pile.

The hope, the fear, the jealous care,
　　The exalted portion of the pain
15　And power of love, I cannot share,
　　　But wear the chain.

But 'tis not *thus* — and 'tis not *here* —
　　Such thoughts should shake my soul, nor *now*,
Where glory decks the hero's bier,
20　　　Or binds his brow.

The sword, the banner, and the field,
　　Glory and Greece, around me see!
The Spartan, borne upon his shield,
　　　Was not more free.

25　Awake! (not Greece — she *is* awake!)
　　Awake, my spirit! Think through *whom*
Thy life-blood tracks its parent lake,
　　　And then strike home!

Tread those reviving passions down,
30　　Unworthy manhood! — unto thee
Indifferent should the smile or frown
　　　Of beauty be.

If thou regrett'st thy youth, *why live?*
    The land of honourable death
35 Is here:— up to the field, and give
        Away thy breath!

Seek out — less often sought than found —
    A soldier's grave, for thee the best;
Then look around, and choose thy ground,
40   And take thy rest.

(1824)

Percy Bysshe Shelley (1792–1822)

Born in Field Place, Sussex, Percy Bysshe Shelley lived a stormy life. Expelled from Oxford for writing a pamphlet on atheism, he eloped with sixteen-year-old Harriet Westbrook, whom he later abandoned for Mary Godwin, the daughter of the political radical William Godwin and author of the novel *Frankenstein*. In 1818, he moved permanently to Italy, but never settled in one place. He drowned after his sailboat was swamped in a squall. Frequently condemned during his life for his highly unconventional moral, political, and anti-religious beliefs, Shelley has been praised for his careful craftsmanship as a poet. In "Ozymandias," the words of the pharaoh are juxtaposed with a description of the desert setting and the present condition of the pharaoh's statue to create an implicit satirical comment on the vainglory of tyrants. "Ode to the West Wind" and "To a Skylark" illustrate the various ways in which Shelley used his observations of nature to present his themes. The West Wind becomes a complex symbol representing, among other things, the interrelationship between life and death and the forces of revolution which may create a better world (a new spring) for people. Like John Keats in "Ode to a Nightingale" and Gerard Manley Hopkins in "The Windhover," Shelley, in "To a Skylark," contrasts the freedom of the bird with the limitations of his own life.

Ozymandias [1]

I met a traveller from an antique land
Who said: Two vast and trunkless legs of stone
Stand in the desert. . . Near them, on the sand,
Half sunk, a shattered visage lies, whose frown,

———▶

1 Greek variant of the name of the thirteenth-century B.C. Egyptian pharaoh, Ramses II.

And wrinkled lip, and sneer of cold command,
Tell that its sculptor well those passions read
Which yet survive, stamped on these lifeless things,
The hand that mocked them, and the heart that fed:
And on the pedestal these words appear:
"My name is Ozymandias, king of kings:
Look on my works, ye Mighty, and despair!"
Nothing beside remains. Round the decay
Of that colossal wreck, boundless and bare
The lone and level sands stretch far away.

(1817)   (1818)

Ode to the West Wind

I

O wild West Wind, thou breath of Autumn's being,
Thou, from whose unseen presence the leaves dead
Are driven, like ghosts from an enchanter fleeing,

Yellow, and black, and pale, and hectic red,
Pestilence-stricken multitudes: O thou,
Who chariotest to their dark wintry bed

represents the world as deathly

The wingèd seeds, where they lie cold and low,
Each like a corpse within its grave, until
Thine azure sister of the Spring shall blow

Her clarion o'er the dreaming earth, and fill
(Driving sweet buds like flocks to feed in air)
With living hues and odours plain and hill:

Wild Spirit, which art moving everywhere;
Destroyer and preserver; hear, Oh hear!

II

Thou on whose stream, 'mid the steep sky's commotion,
Loose clouds like earth's decaying leaves are shed,
Shook from the tangled boughs of Heaven and Ocean,

Angels of rain and lightning: there are spread
On the blue surface of thine airy surge,
Like the bright hair uplifted from the head

[handwritten: speaker is flattering the God Westwind]

Of some fierce Mænad,[1] even from the dim verge
Of the horizon to the zenith's height
The locks of the approaching storm. Thou dirge[2]

Of the dying year, to which this closing night
25   Will be the dome of a vast sepulchre,
Vaulted with all thy congregated might

Of vapours, from whose solid atmosphere
Black rain, and fire, and hail will burst: Oh hear!

III

Thou who didst waken from his summer dreams
30   The blue Mediterranean, where he lay,
Lulled by the coil of his crystàlline streams,

Beside a pumice isle in Baiæ's bay,[3]
And saw in sleep old palaces and towers
Quivering within the wave's intenser day,

35   All overgrown with azure moss and flowers
So sweet, the sense faints picturing them! Thou
For whose path the Atlantic's level powers

Cleave themselves into chasms, while far below
The sea-blooms and the oozy woods which wear
40   The sapless foliage of the ocean, know

Thy voice, and suddenly grow gray with fear,
And tremble and despoil themselves: Oh hear!

IV

If I were a dead leaf thou mightest bear;
If I were a swift cloud to fly with thee;
45   A wave to pant beneath thy power, and share

The impulse of thy strength, only less free
Than thou, O uncontrollable! If even
I were as in my boyhood, and could be

The comrade of thy wanderings over Heaven,
50   As then, when to outstrip thy skiey speed
Scarce seemed a vision; I would ne'er have striven

[handwritten: apostrophes one after another. strong]

[handwritten: finally the I shows up. was descriptive now the request is coming]

1 female worshippers of Dionysus, the Greek god of wine. 2 song of mourning. 3 city in southwestern Italy.

As thus with thee in prayer in my sore need.
Oh, lift me as a wave, a leaf, a cloud!
I fall upon the thorns of life! I bleed!

55   A heavy weight of hours has chained and bowed
One too like thee: tameless, and swift, and proud.

V

Make me thy lyre, even as the forest is:
What if my leaves are falling like its own!
The tumult of thy mighty harmonies

60   Will take from both a deep, autumnal tone,
Sweet though in sadness. Be thou, Spirit fierce,
My spirit! be thou me, impetuous one!

Drive my dead thoughts over the universe
Like withered leaves to quicken a new birth!
65   And, by the incantation of this verse,

Scatter, as from an unextinguished hearth
Ashes and sparks, my words among mankind!
Be through my lips to unawakened earth

The trumpet of a prophecy! O, Wind,
70   If Winter comes, can Spring be far behind?

(1819)   (1820)

To a Skylark

Hail to thee, blithe spirit!
    Bird thou never wert,
That from heaven, or near it,
    Pourest thy full heart
5   In profuse strains of unpremeditated art.

Higher still and higher
    From the earth thou springest
Like a cloud of fire;
    The blue deep thou wingest,
10   And singing still dost soar, and soaring ever singest.

In the golden lightning
    Of the sunken sun,
O'er which clouds are brightning,
    Thou dost float and run;
15 Like an unbodied joy whose race is just begun.

The pale purple even
    Melts around thy flight;
Like a star of heaven,
    In the broad daylight
20 Thou art unseen, but yet I hear thy shrill delight,

Keen as are the arrows
    Of that silver sphere,
Whose intense lamp narrows
    In the white dawn clear,
25 Until we hardly see, we feel that it is there.

All the earth and air
    With thy voice is loud,
As, when night is bare,
    From one lonely cloud
30 The moon rains out her beams, and heaven is overflowed.

What thou art we know not;
    What is most like thee?
From rainbow clouds there flow not
    Drops so bright to see,
35 As from thy presence showers a rain of melody.

Like a poet hidden
    In the light of thought,
Singing hymns unbidden,
    Till the world is wrought
40 To sympathy with hopes and fears it heeded not:

Like a high-born maiden
    In a palace-tower,
Soothing her love-laden
    Soul in secret hour
45 With music sweet as love, which overflows her bower:

Like a glow-worm golden
   In a dell of dew,
Scattering unbeholden
   Its aërial hue
50 Among the flowers and grass, which screen it from the view:

Like a rose embowered
   In its own green leaves,
By warm winds deflowered,
   Till the scent it gives
55 Makes faint with too much sweet these heavy-wingèd thieves:

Sound of vernal showers
   On the twinkling grass,
Rain-awakened flowers,
   All that ever was
60 Joyous, and clear, and fresh, thy music doth surpass:

Teach us, sprite or bird,
   What sweet thoughts are thine:
I have never heard
   Praise of love or wine
65 That panted forth a flood of rapture so divine.

Chorus Hymeneal,[1]
   Or triumphal chaunt,
Matched with thine would be all
   But an empty vaunt,
70 A thing wherein we feel there is some hidden want.

What objects are the fountains
   Of thy happy strain?
What fields, or waves, or mountains?
   What shapes of sky or plain?
75 What love of thine own kind? what ignorance of pain?

With thy clear keen joyance
   Languor cannot be:
Shadow of annoyance
   Never came near thee:
80 Thou lovest; but ne'er knew love's sad satiety.

1 marriage hymn.

Waking or asleep,
    Thou of death must deem
Things more true and deep
    Than we mortals dream,
85   Or how could thy notes flow in such a crystal stream?

We look before and after,
    And pine for what is not:
Our sincerest laughter
    With some pain is fraught;
90   Our sweetest songs are those that tell of saddest thought.

Yet if we could scorn
    Hate, and pride, and fear;
If we were things born
    Not to shed a tear,
95   I know not how thy joy we ever should come near.

Better than all measures
    Of delightful sound,
Better than all treasures
    That in books are found,
100   Thy skill to poet were, thou scorner of the ground!

Teach me half the gladness
    That thy brain must know,
Such harmonious madness
    From my lips would flow,
105   The world should listen then, as I am listening now.

(1820)   (1824)

John Keats (1795–1821)

Born in London, John Keats was orphaned at age fourteen. Although he trained as an apothecary-surgeon, he chose to devote his life to the writing of poetry; in his sonnet "On First Looking into Chapman's Homer," he described the inspiration he received on reading the sixteenth-century translation of Homer's *Odyssey*. His talents matured rapidly, and in 1819, at the age of twenty-four, he wrote his greatest works, "La Belle Dame sans Merci," his six famous odes, and several sonnets that, along with those of William Wordsworth, are considered the finest of the Romantic era. In "When I have fears," his rich, concrete imagery reflects his deep appreciation for the physical world and his awareness that his worsening health would probably result in his dying before he had fulfilled his love for his fiancée, Fanny Brawne, and his poetic ambitions. The theme of the destructive power of death appears again in "La Belle Dame sans Merci," in which Keats used the form and imagery of medieval ballads. "Ode to a Nightingale," "Ode on a Grecian Urn," and "To Autumn," three of his best-known poems, reveal Keats's poetic talents at their fullest. The melancholy song of the nightingale, a traditional symbol of suffering transformed into beauty; the burial urn decorated with scenes of life; and the physical splendour of autumn are symbols used to evoke meditations on the nature of art, life and death, and permanence and transience. Imagery that evokes several senses, skilful portrayal of the shifting emotions of the speaker of each poem, the penetrating questions and observations, and the tightly unified stanzas are superb vehicles for Keats's themes. Although he died before his pen had gleaned his "teeming brain," the quality of the works Keats did write marks him as one of the greatest of English poets.

On First Looking into Chapman's Homer

Much have I travell'd in the realms of gold,
  And many goodly states and kingdoms seen;
  Round many western islands have I been
Which bards in fealty to Apollo[1] hold.
5 Oft of one wide expanse had I been told
    That deep-brow'd Homer[2] ruled as his demesne;
    Yet did I never breathe its pure serene
Till I heard Chapman[3] speak out loud and bold:
Then felt I like some watcher of the skies
10   When a new planet swims into his ken;
Or like stout Cortez[4] when with eagle eyes
    He star'd at the Pacific — and all his men
Look'd at each other with a wild surmise —
    Silent, upon a peak in Darien.[5]

(1816)

---

1 Greek god of music and poetry; also the sun. 2 ninth-century B.C. Greek poet, author of the *Iliad* and the *Odyssey*. 3 George Chapman, late-sixteenth-century English translator of Homer. 4 sixteenth-century Spanish conquerer of Mexico whom Keats confused with Balboa, the first European to see the Pacific Ocean. 5 former name of the Isthmus of Panama.

When I have fears

When I have fears that I may cease to be
  Before my pen has glean'd my teeming brain,
Before high-piled books, in charact'ry,[1]
  Hold like rich garners the full-ripen'd grain;
5 When I behold, upon the night's starr'd face,
  Huge cloudy symbols of a high romance,
And think that I may never live to trace
  Their shadows, with the magic hand of chance;
And when I feel, fair creature of an hour!
10 That I shall never look upon thee more,
Never have relish in the faery power
  Of unreflecting love! — then on the shore
Of the wide world I stand alone, and think
Till love and fame to nothingness do sink.

(1818)   (1848)

Ode to a Nightingale

1

My heart aches, and a drowsy numbness pains
  My sense, as though of hemlock[1] I had drunk,
Or emptied some dull opiate to the drains
  One minute past, and Lethe-wards[2] had sunk:
'Tis not through envy of thy happy lot,
  But being too happy in thine happiness, —
    That thou, light-winged Dryad[3] of the trees
    In some melodious plot
Of beechen green, and shadows numberless,
  Singest of summer in full-throated ease.

2

O, for a draught of vintage! that hath been
  Cool'd a long age in the deep-delved earth,

[handwritten annotations: seems to alternate between extreme happiness and sorrow, pain and sorrow. / sounds like the poem = unhappy and drowsy / feels as though it is inhuman to be so happy / nightingale compared / magical thing / effortless song / The nature of intense pleasure will be lost, they do not last forever — the poem is that in the moment*]*

1 printed letters.
1 poison derived from a parsnip-like root, not the common hemlock. 2 toward Lethe, in Greek mythology,
a river in Hades. Drinking its water caused one to forget the past. 3 tree nymph.

[handwritten top margin: wine is emphasized by plosives]

Tasting of Flora [4] and the country green,
    Dance, and Provençal song, [5] and sunburnt mirth!
15 O for a beaker full of the warm South,
    Full of the true, the blushful Hippocrene, [6]
      With beaded bubbles winking at the brim,
        And purple-stained mouth;
    That I might drink, and leave the world unseen,
20   And with thee fade away into the forest dim:

[handwritten right margin: O for some wine maybe I will be in that altered state to produce such beauty like song]
[handwritten: I feel the bubbles popping with plosives]
[handwritten: Involved erotisism with goddess]
[handwritten left margin: breath able to give song]
[handwritten: might retreat from the world or might leave the world]

3

    Fade far away, dissolve, and quite forget
    What thou among the leaves hast never known,
    The weariness, the fever, and the fret
    Here, where men sit and hear each other groan;
25 Where palsy shakes a few, sad, last gray hairs,
    Where youth grows pale, and spectre-thin, and dies;
      Where but to think is to be full of sorrow
        And leaden-eyed despairs,
    Where Beauty cannot keep her lustrous eyes,
30   Or new Love pine at them beyond to-morrow.

[handwritten right margin: links to Dyonisus like madness creativity and vegetation]
[handwritten: retreat from what the world provides]
[handwritten: what makes us human capacity to reflect also = sorrow]
[handwritten: description of what he wants to exist escape, time, age, sorrow]
[handwritten left margin: world of man's social misery]

4

Away! away! for I will fly to thee,
    Not charioted by Bacchus [7] and his pards,
But on the viewless wings of Poesy,
    Though the dull brain perplexes and retards:
35 Already with thee! tender is the night,
    And haply the Queen-Moon is on her throne,
      Cluster'd around by all her starry Fays; [8]
        But here there is no light,
Save what from heaven is with the breezes blown
40   Through verdurous glooms and winding mossy ways.

[handwritten right margin: I am not going to resort to wine to get such beautiful experience, but poesy]
[handwritten: wings bird - nightingale]
[handwritten: with poetic insight comes like a vision shared with Nightingale]

5

I cannot see what flowers are at my feet,
    Nor what soft incense hangs upon the boughs,
But, in embalmed darkness, guess each sweet
    Wherewith the seasonable month endows

[handwritten left margin: making smell physical in a holy beautiful and sensual way]
[handwritten right margin: all of a sudden he is not relying on the vision but on the more tactile senses taste touch]

4 Roman goddess of flowers. 5 in the Middle Ages, Provence, in southern France, was famous for its poets and singers. 6 in Greek mythology, the sacred fountain of the muses of poetry. 7 Roman god of wine, whose chariot was pulled by leopards (pards). 8 fairies.

45 The grass, the thicket, and the fruit-tree wild;
        White hawthorn, and the pastoral eglantine;
            Fast fading violets cover'd up in leaves;
                And mid-May's eldest child,
        The coming musk-rose, full of dewy wine,
50   The murmurous haunt of flies on summer eves.

spring time
wine which is escaped
is the natural wine
of fertility and
creativity

6

Darkling[9] I listen; and, for many a time
    I have been half in love with easeful Death,
Call'd him soft names in many a mused rhyme,
    To take into the air my quiet breath;
55 Now more than ever seems it rich to die,
    To cease upon the midnight with no pain,
        While thou art pouring forth thy soul abroad
            In such an ecstasy!
        Still wouldst thou sing, and I have ears in vain —
60   To thy high requiem[10] become a sod.

7

Thou wast not born for death, immortal Bird!
    No hungry generations tread thee down;
The voice I hear this passing night was heard
    In ancient days by emperor and clown:
65 Perhaps the self-same song that found a path
        Through the sad heart of Ruth,[11] when, sick for home,
            She stood in tears amid the alien corn;
                The same that oft-times hath
        Charm'd magic casements, opening on the foam
70   Of perilous seas, in faery lands forlorn.

8

Forlorn! the very word is like a bell
    To toll me back from thee to my sole self!
Adieu! the fancy cannot cheat so well
    As she is fam'd to do, deceiving elf.

———→

9 in the dark. 10 mass performed for the souls of the dead. 11 in the Old Testament, Ruth was a foreigner
who gleaned corn in the fields of ancient Israel; see Ruth 2:3.

75 Adieu! adieu! thy plaintive anthem fades
        Past the near meadows, over the still stream,
            Up the hill-side; and now 'tis buried deep
                In the next valley-glades:
        Was it a vision, or a waking dream?
80   Fled is that music: — Do I wake or sleep?

(1819)   (1820)

Ode on a Grecian Urn

1

Thou still unravish'd bride of quietness,
    Thou foster-child of silence and slow time,
Sylvan[1] historian, who canst thus express
    A flowery tale more sweetly than our rhyme:
5 What leaf-fring'd legend haunts about thy shape
        Of deities or mortals, or of both,
            In Tempe[2] or the dales of Arcady?[3]
What men or gods are these? What maidens loth?
    What mad pursuit? What struggle to escape?
10   What pipes and timbrels?[4] What wild ecstasy?

2

Heard melodies are sweet, but those unheard
    Are sweeter; therefore, ye soft pipes, play on;
Not to the sensual ear, but, more endear'd,
    Pipe to the spirit ditties of no tone:
15 Fair youth, beneath the trees, thou canst not leave
        Thy song, nor ever can those trees be bare;
            Bold Lover, never, never canst thou kiss,
Though winning near the goal — yet, do not grieve;
    She cannot fade, though thou hast not thy bliss,
20   For ever wilt thou love, and she be fair!

1 belonging to the woods or forests. 2 quiet valley in Greece, noted for its beauty. 3 mountainous area in Greece, symbol of an ideal rural area. 4 tambourine-like musical instrument.

3

Ah, happy, happy boughs! that cannot shed
   Your leaves, nor ever bid the Spring adieu;
And, happy melodist, unwearied,
   For ever piping songs for ever new;
25 More happy love! more happy, happy love!
   For ever warm and still to be enjoy'd,
     For ever panting, and for ever young;
All breathing human passion far above,
   That leaves a heart high-sorrowful and cloy'd,
30   A burning forehead, and a parching tongue.

4

Who are these coming to the sacrifice?
   To what green altar, O mysterious priest,
Lead'st thou that heifer lowing at the skies,
   And all her silken flanks with garlands drest?
35 What little town by river or sea shore,
   Or mountain-built with peaceful citadel,
     Is emptied of this folk, this pious morn?
And, little town, thy streets for evermore
   Will silent be; and not a soul to tell
40   Why thou art desolate, can e'er return.

5

O Attic[5] shape! Fair attitude! with brede[6]
   Of marble men and maidens overwrought,
With forest branches and the trodden weed;
   Thou, silent form, dost tease us out of thought
45 As doth eternity: Cold Pastoral!
   When old age shall this generation waste,
     Thou shalt remain, in midst of other woe
Than ours, a friend to man, to whom thou say'st,
   "Beauty is truth, truth beauty,"— that is all
50   Ye know on earth, and all ye need to know.

(1819)   (1820)

---

5 belonging to or relating to Attica, whose capital was Athens. 6 pattern of interwoven designs.

To Autumn

1

Season of mists and mellow fruitfulness,
    Close bosom-friend of the maturing sun;
Conspiring with him how to load and bless
    With fruit the vines that round the thatch-eves run;
5   To bend with apples the moss'd cottage-trees,
    And fill all fruit with ripeness to the core;
        To swell the gourd, and plump the hazel shells
With a sweet kernel; to set budding more,
    And still more, later flowers for the bees,
10   Until they think warm days will never cease,
        For Summer has o'er-brimm'd their clammy cells.

2

Who hath not seen thee oft amid thy store?
    Sometimes whoever seeks abroad may find
Thee sitting careless on a granary floor,
15   Thy hair soft-lifted by the winnowing wind;
Or on a half-reap'd furrow sound asleep,
    Drows'd with the fume of poppies, while thy hook
        Spares the next swath and all its twined flowers:
And sometimes like a gleaner thou dost keep
20   Steady thy laden head across a brook;
    Or by a cyder-press, with patient look,
        Thou watchest the last oozings hours by hours.

3

Where are the songs of Spring? Ay, where are they?
    Think not of them, thou hast thy music too, —
25 While barred clouds bloom the soft-dying day,
    And touch the stubble-plains with rosy hue;
Then in a wailful choir the small gnats mourn
    Among the river sallows, borne aloft
        Or sinking as the light wind lives or dies;
30 And full-grown lambs loud bleat from hilly bourn;
    Hedge-crickets sing; and now with treble soft
    The red-breast whistles from a garden-croft;
        And gathering swallows twitter in the skies.

(1819)

(1820)

La Belle Dame sans Merci[1]

A BALLAD

I

O what can ail thee, knight-at-arms,
    Alone and palely loitering?
The sedge has wither'd from the lake,
    And no birds sing.

II

5 O what can ail thee, knight-at-arms!
    So haggard and so woe-begone?
The squirrel's granary is full,
    And the harvest's done.

III

I see a lilly on thy brow,
10   With anguish moist and fever dew,
And on thy cheeks a fading rose
    Fast withereth too.

IV

I met a lady in the meads,[2]
    Full beautiful — a faery's child,
15 Her hair was long, her foot was light,
    And her eyes were wild.

V

I made a garland for her head,
    And bracelets too, and fragrant zone;[3]
She look'd at me as she did love,
20   And made sweet moan.

VI

I set her on my pacing steed,
    And nothing else saw all day long,
For sidelong would she bend, and sing
    A faery's song.

---

1 the beautiful lady without pity. 2 meadows. 3 belt.

VII

25　She found me roots of relish sweet,
　　　And honey wild, and manna dew,[4]
　　And sure in language strange she said —
　　　"I love thee true.")

VIII

　　She took me to her elfin grot,[5]
30　　　And there she wept, and sigh'd full sore,
　　And there I shut her wild wild eyes
　　　With kisses four.

IX

　　And there she lulled me asleep,
　　　And there I dream'd — Ah! woe betide!
35　The latest dream I ever dream'd
　　　On the cold hill side.

X

　　I saw pale kings and princes too,
　　　Pale warriors, death-pale were they all;
　　They cried — 'La Belle Dame sans Merci
40　　　Hath thee in thrall!'[6]

XI

　　I saw their starved lips in the gloam,[7]
　　　With horrid warning gaped wide,
　　And I awoke and found me here,
　　　On the cold hill's side.

XII

45　And this is why I sojourn here,
　　　Alone and palely loitering,
　　Though the sedge has wither'd from the lake,
　　　And no birds sing.

　　(1819)　　　　　　　　　　　　　　　　　　　　(1820)

---

4 food that miraculously fell from heaven. 5 grotto: a cave or cavern. 6 in bondage or slavery. 7 twilight.

Elizabeth Barrett Browning   (1806–1861)

Barrett Browning, a self-educated classical scholar and poet, was an invalid for much of her life. At the age of forty she left her notoriously tyrannical father and her home in Wimpole Street, London, and eloped with Robert Browning to Italy, where she lived for the remaining fifteen years of her life. The story of this courtship and her gradual growth toward a belief in and an acceptance of love, transformed into poetry, resulted in the sequence of love poems called the *Sonnets from the Portuguese*, the work for which she is still most popularly known, and which, in its adaptation of the sonnet for the female voice, is still considered one of her most notable achievements. Critical interest now, however, focuses more on *Aurora Leigh* (1857), her verse novel exploring the problems faced by Victorian women generally and the Victorian woman poet in particular. Barrett Browning's extensive body of work reveals a wide thematic range and an innovative use of genre. "Hiram Powers's Greek Slave" contains one of her many protests against injustice with an attack on slavery, whereas "A Musical Instrument" explores the nature of poetic creativity, linking this creativity with pain and isolation. In such works as these, Barrett Browning expands upon the territory traditionally allocated to women poets, replacing the emphasis on love and sensibility with an uncompromising exploration of social and political power.

from Sonnets from the Portuguese [1]

XLIII

How do I love thee? Let me count the ways.
I love thee to the depth and breadth and height
My soul can reach, when feeling out of sight
For the ends of Being and ideal Grace.
5   I love thee to the level of everyday's
Most quiet need, by sun and candle-light.
I love thee freely, as men strive for Right;
I love thee purely, as they turn from Praise.
I love thee with the passion put to use
10   In my old griefs, and with my childhood's faith.
I love thee with a love I seemed to lose
With my lost saints, — I love thee with the breath,
Smiles, tears, of all my life! — and, if God choose,
I shall but love thee better after death.

(1850)

1 the title was an attempt to disguise the personal nature of the sonnets by suggesting that they were translations.

Hiram Powers's Greek Slave [1]

They say Ideal Beauty cannot enter
The house of anguish. On the threshold stands
An alien Image with the shackled hands,
Called the Greek Slave: as if the artist meant her,
5   (That passionless perfection which he lent her,
Shadowed, not darkened, where the sill expands)
To, so, confront man's crimes in different lands,
With man's ideal sense. Pierce to the centre,
Art's fiery finger! — and break up ere long
10 The serfdom of this world! Appeal, fair stone,
From God's pure heights of beauty, against man's wrong!
Catch up in thy divine face, not alone
East griefs but west, — and strike and shame the strong,
By thunders of white silence, overthrown.

(1850)

A Musical Instrument

What was he doing, the great god Pan, [1]
    Down in the reeds by the river?
Spreading ruin and scattering ban,
Splashing and paddling with hoofs of a goat,
5   And breaking the golden lilies afloat
    With the dragon-fly on the river.

He tore out a reed, the great god Pan,
    From the deep cool bed of the river:
The limpid water turbidly ran,
10 And the broken lilies a-dying lay,
And the dragon-fly had fled away,
    Ere he brought it out of the river.

---

1 the American sculptor Hiram Powers (1805–73) first exhibited "The Greek Slave" at the Great
Exhibition in London in 1851; it represents a Greek Christian woman captured by the Turks in the Greek
war of independence (1821–26).
1 half animal and half god, Pan combines the creative and destructive forces. In Ovid's *Metamorphoses*,
he chases the nymph Syrinx, who prays for help and is transformed into reeds. Pan takes these reeds and
produces pipes from them.

High on the shore sat the great god Pan,
   While turbidly flowed the river;
15 And hacked and hewed as a great god can,
With his hard bleak steel at the patient reed,
Till there was not a sign of a leaf indeed
   To prove it fresh from the river.

He cut it short, did the great god Pan,
20   (How tall it stood in the river!)
Then drew the pith, like the heart of a man,
Steadily from the outside ring,
And notched the poor dry empty thing
   In holes, as he sat by the river.

25 "This is the way," laughed the great god Pan,
   (Laughed while he sat by the river,)
"The only way, since gods began
To make sweet music, they could succeed."
Then, dropping his mouth to a hole in the reed,
30   He blew in power by the river.

Sweet, sweet, sweet, O Pan!
   Piercing sweet by the river!
Blinding sweet, O great god Pan!
The sun on the hill forgot to die,
35 And the lilies revived, and the dragon-fly
   Came back to dream on the river.

Yet half a beast is the great god Pan,
   To laugh as he sits by the river,
Making a poet out of a man:
40 The true gods sigh for the cost and pain —
For the reed which grows nevermore again
   As a reed with the reeds in the river.

(1860)

Alfred, Lord Tennyson (1809-1892)

Tennyson, the son of a clergyman, was born in Lincolnshire and educated at Cambridge. Here he joined a group of young intellectuals called the Apostles and formed the friendship with Arthur Hallam that had such an influence upon his work. In May of 1850 Tennyson published *In Memoriam*—the elegy prompted by Hallam's death in 1833—which comprised a cycle of 131 linked poems and which established his reputation. In June of the same year Tennyson married Emily Sellwood, and in November he succeeded Wordsworth as Poet Laureate. His other major works include *The Princess* (1847), an extended narrative, interspersed with lyric, on the question of women's proper sphere, and the *Idylls of the King* (1859-74), a reworking of the Arthurian legends. The languorous, flowing rhythms, which led W.H. Auden to conclude that Tennyson possessed the "finest ear, perhaps, of any English poet," are frequently undercut by sharp dramatic irony. Like Browning, Tennyson is interested in the depiction of varying, sometimes abnormal, psychological states, and often, as in "Ulysses" and "Tithonus," he uses the vehicle of the dramatic monologue to capture these states. And like Arnold, Tennyson repeatedly provides evidence of a divided self; "The Lady of Shalott," probably his best-known and most anthologized work, contains one of the earliest explorations of the dilemma that would continue to trouble him throughout his poetic career: the tension between the artist's desire for aesthetic withdrawal and the recognition of the need for responsible commitment to society.

The Eagle. Fragment

He clasps the crag with crooked hands;
Close to the sun in lonely lands,
Ring'd with the azure world, he stands.

The wrinkled sea beneath him crawls;
5   He watches from his mountain walls,
And like a thunderbolt he falls.

(1851)

The Lady of Shalott

PART I

On either side the river lie
Long fields of barley and of rye,
That clothe the wold and meet the sky;
And thro' the field the road runs by
5   To many-tower'd Camelot;[1]
And up and down the people go,
Gazing where the lilies blow
Round an island there below,
      The island of Shalott.

10   Willows whiten,[2] aspens quiver,
Little breezes dusk and shiver
Thro' the wave that runs for ever
By the island in the river
      Flowing down to Camelot.
15   Four gray walls, and four gray towers,
Overlook a space of flowers,
And the silent isle imbowers
      The Lady of Shalott.

By the margin, willow-veil'd,
20   Slide the heavy barges trail'd
By slow horses; and unhail'd
The shallop flitteth silken-sail'd
      Skimming down to Camelot:
But who hath seen her wave her hand?
25   Or at the casement seen her stand?
Or is she known in all the land,
      The Lady of Shalott?

Only reapers, reaping early
In among the bearded barley,
30   Hear a song that echoes cheerly
From the river winding clearly,
      Down to tower'd Camelot:

———→

1 legendary seat of King Arthur's court. 2 the wind reveals the white underside of the leaves.

And by moon the reaper weary,
Piling sheaves in uplands airy,
35 Listening, whispers, "'Tis the fairy
        Lady of Shalott."

PART II

There she weaves by night and day
A magic web with colours gay.
She has heard a whisper say,
40 A curse is on her if she stay
        To look down to Camelot.
She knows not what the curse may be,
And so she weaveth steadily,
And little other care hath she,
45   The Lady of Shalott.

And moving thro' a mirror clear
That hangs before her all the year,
Shadows of the world appear.
There she sees the highway near
50   Winding down to Camelot:
There the river eddy whirls,
And there the surly village-churls,
And the red cloaks of market girls,
        Pass onward from Shalott.

55 Sometimes a troop of damsels glad,
An abbot on an ambling pad,
Sometimes a curly shepherd-lad,
Or long-hair'd page in crimson clad,
        Goes by to tower'd Camelot;
60 And sometimes thro' the mirror blue
The knights come riding two and two:
She hath no loyal knight and true,
        The Lady of Shalott.

But in her web she still delights
65 To weave the mirror's magic sights,
For often thro' the silent nights
A funeral, with plumes and lights
        And music, went to Camelot:

———→

Or when the moon was overhead,
70 Came two young lovers lately wed;
"I am half sick of shadows," said
      The Lady of Shalott.

PART III

A bow-shot from her bower-eaves,
He rode between the barley-sheaves,
75 The sun came dazzling thro' the leaves,
And flamed upon the brazen greaves
      Of bold Sir Lancelot.
A red-cross knight[3] for ever kneel'd
To a lady in his shield,
80 That sparkled on the yellow field,
      Beside remote Shalott.

The gemmy bridle glitter'd free,
Like to some branch of stars we see
Hung in the golden Galaxy.[4]
85 The bridle bells rang merrily
      As he rode down to Camelot:
And from his blazon'd baldric[5] slung
A mighty silver bugle hung,
And as he rode his armour rung,
90 Beside remote Shalott.

All in the blue unclouded weather
Thick-jewell'd shone the saddle-leather,
The helmet and the helmet-feather
Burn'd like one burning flame together,
95 As he rode down to Camelot.
As often thro' the purple night,
Below the starry clusters bright,
Some bearded meteor, trailing light,
      Moves over still Shalott.

100 His broad clear brow in sunlight glow'd;
On burnished hooves his war-horse trode;

$\longrightarrow$

3 an allusion to the hero in the first book of Spenser's *Faerie Queene*, who shows his Christian devotion by wearing on his chest a red cross. 4 Milky Way. 5 a decorated belt worn over the shoulder and across the chest.

From underneath his helmet flow'd
His coal-black curls as on he rode,
    As he rode down to Camelot.
105 From the bank and from the river
He flash'd into the crystal mirror,
"Tirra lirra," by the river
    Sang Sir Lancelot.

She left the web, she left the loom,
110 She made three paces thro' the room,
She saw the water-lily bloom,
She saw the helmet and the plume,
    She look'd down to Camelot.
Out flew the web and floated wide;
115 The mirror crack'd from side to side;
"The curse is come upon me," cried
    The Lady of Shalott.

PART IV

In the stormy east-wind straining,
The pale yellow woods were waning,
120 The broad stream in his banks complaining,
Heavily the low sky raining
    Over tower'd Camelot;
Down she came and found a boat
Beneath a willow left afloat,
125 And round about the prow she wrote
    The Lady of Shalott.

And down the river's dim expanse
Like some bold seër in a trance,
Seeing all his own mischance —
130 With a glassy countenance
    Did she look to Camelot.
And at the closing of the day
She loosed the chain, and down she lay;
The broad stream bore her far away,
135   The Lady of Shalott.

Lying, robed in snowy white
That loosely flew to left and right —
The leaves upon her falling light —
Thro' the noises of the night
140   She floated down to Camelot:
And as the boat-head wound along
The willowy hills and fields among,
They heard her singing her last song,
      The Lady of Shalott.

145 Heard a carol, mournful, holy,
Chanted loudly, chanted lowly,
Till her blood was frozen slowly,
And her eyes were darken'd wholly,
      Turn'd to tower'd Camelot.
150 For ere she reach'd upon the tide
The first house by the water-side,
Singing in her song she died,
      The Lady of Shalott.

Under tower and balcony,
155 By garden-wall and gallery,
A gleaming shape she floated by,
Dead-pale between the houses high,
      Silent into Camelot.
Out upon the wharfs they came,
160 Knight and burgher, lord and dame,
And round the prow they read her name,
      The Lady of Shalott.

Who is this? and what is here?
And in the lighted palace near
165 Died the sound of royal cheer;
And they cross'd themselves for fear,
      All the knights at Camelot:
But Lancelot mused a little space;
He said, "She has a lovely face;
170 God in his mercy lend her grace,
      The Lady of Shalott."

(1833)   (1842)

Ulysses¹

It little profits that an idle king,
By this still hearth, among these barren crags,
Match'd with an aged wife, I mete and dole
Unequal laws unto a savage race,
5   That hoard, and sleep, and feed, and know not me.
I cannot rest from travel; I will drink
Life to the lees. All times I have enjoy'd
Greatly, have suffer'd greatly, both with those
That loved me, and alone; on shore, and when
10   Thro' scudding drifts the rainy Hyades²
Vext the dim sea. I am become a name;
For always roaming with a hungry heart
Much have I seen and known, — cities of men
And manners, climates, councils, governments,
15   Myself not least, but honor'd of them all, —
And drunk delight of battle with my peers,
Far on the ringing plains of windy Troy.
I am a part of all that I have met;
Yet all experience is an arch wherethro'
20   Gleams that untravell'd world whose margin fades
For ever and for ever when I move.
How dull it is to pause, to make an end.
To rust unburnish'd, not to shine in use!
As tho' to breathe were life! Life piled on life
25   Were all too little, and of one to me
Little remains; but every hour is saved
From that eternal silence, something more,
A bringer of new things; and vile it were
For some three suns to store and hoard myself,
30   And this gray spirit yearning in desire
To follow knowledge like a sinking star,
Beyond the utmost bound of human thought.

1 Ulysses (Greek Odysseus) wandered for ten years following the fall of Troy before returning to his island kingdom of Ithaca and to his wife, Penelope, and son, Telemachus. For Tennyson's sources, see particularly Homer's *Odyssey* XI.100–37 and Dante's *Inferno* XXVI. 2 cluster of stars in the constellation Taurus that are associated with the rainy season.

This is my son, mine own Telemachus,
To whom I leave the sceptre and the isle, —
35 Well-loved of me, discerning to fulfil
This labor, by slow prudence to make mild
A rugged people, and thro' soft degrees
Subdue them to the useful and the good.
Most blameless is he, centred in the sphere
40 Of common duties, decent not to fail
In offices of tenderness, and pay
Meet adoration to my household gods,
When I am gone. He works his work, I mine.

There lies the port; the vessel puffs her sail;
45 There gloom the dark, broad seas. My mariners,
Souls that have toil'd, and wrought, and thought with me, —
That ever with a frolic welcome took
The thunder and the sunshine, and opposed
Free hearts, free foreheads, — you and I are old;
50 Old age hath yet his honor and his toil.
Death closes all; but something ere the end,
Some work of noble note, may yet be done,
Not unbecoming men that strove with Gods.
The lights begin to twinkle from the rocks;
55 The long day wanes; the slow moon climbs; the deep
Moans round with many voices. Come, my friends.
'Tis not too late to seek a newer world.
Push off, and sitting well in order smite
The sounding furrows; for my purpose holds
60 To sail beyond the sunset, and the baths
Of all the western stars, until I die.
It may be that the gulfs will wash us down;
It may be we shall touch the Happy Isles,[3]
And see the great Achilles,[4] whom we knew.
65 Tho' much is taken, much abides; and tho'
We are not now that strength which in old days
Moved earth and heaven, that which we are, we are, —
One equal temper of heroic hearts,
Made weak by time and fate, but strong in will
70 To strive, to seek, to find, and not to yield.

(1833)   (1842)

3 the abode of dead heroes, also known as Elysium. 4 Greek hero who fought at Troy. Homer's *Iliad* revolves
around the wrath of Achilles.

Tithonus[1]

The woods decay, the woods decay and fall,
The vapours weep their burthen to the ground,
Man comes and tills the fields and lies beneath,
And after many a summer dies the swan.
5   Me only cruel immortality
Consumes; I wither slowly in thine arms,
Here at the quiet limit of the world,
A white-hair'd shadow roaming like a dream
The ever-silent spaces of the East,
10   Far-folded mists, and gleaming halls of morn.

      Alas! for this gray shadow, once a man —
So glorious in his beauty and thy choice,
Who madest him thy chosen, that he seem'd
To his great heart none other than a God!
15   I ask'd thee, "Give me immortality."
Then didst thou grant mine asking with a smile,
Like wealthy men who care not how they give.
But thy strong Hours indignant work'd their wills,
And beat me down, and marr'd and wasted me,
20   And tho' they could not end me, left me maim'd
To dwell in presence of immortal youth,
Immortal age beside immortal youth,
And all I was, in ashes. Can thy love,
Thy beauty, make amends, tho' even now,
25   Close over us, the silver star,[2] thy guide,
Shines in those tremulous eyes that fill with tears
To hear me? Let me go; take back thy gift:
Why should a man desire in any way
To vary from the kindly race of men,
30   Or pass beyond the goal of ordinance[3]
Where all should pause, as is most meet for all?

      A soft air fans the cloud apart; there comes
A glimpse of that dark world where I was born.
Once more the old mysterious glimmer steals

⟶

1 Eos, goddess of the dawn, loved the mortal Tithonus and begged Zeus to grant him eternal life; she forgot
to ask also for eternal youth. 2 the morning star. 3 appointed limit.

35 From thy pure brows, and from thy shoulders pure,
    And bosom beating with a heart renew'd.
    Thy cheek begins to redden thro' the gloom,
    Thy sweet eyes brighten slowly close to mine,
    Ere yet they blind the stars, and the wild team[4]
40 Which love thee, yearning for thy yoke, arise,
    And shake the darkness from their loosen'd manes,
    And beat the twilight into flakes of fire.

    Lo! ever thus thou growest beautiful
    In silence, then before thine answer given
45 Departest, and thy tears are on my cheek.

    Why wilt thou ever scare me with thy tears,
    And make me tremble lest a saying learnt,
    In days far-off, on that dark earth, be true?
    "The Gods themselves cannot recall their gifts."

50   Ay me! ay me! with what another heart
    In days far-off, and with what other eyes
    I used to watch — if I be he that watch'd —
    The lucid outline forming round thee; saw
    The dim curls kindle into sunny rings;
55 Changed with thy mystic change, and felt my blood
    Glow with the glow that slowly crimson'd all
    Thy presence and thy portals, while I lay,
    Mouth, forehead, eyelids, growing dewy-warm
    With kisses balmier than half-opening buds
60 Of April, and could hear the lips that kiss'd
    Whispering I knew not what of wild and sweet,
    Like that strange song I heard Apollo sing,
    While Ilion like a mist rose into towers.[5]
    Yet hold me not for ever in thine East:
65 How can my nature longer mix with thine?
    Coldly thy rosy shadows bathe me, cold
    Are all thy lights, and cold my wrinkled feet
    Upon thy glimmering thresholds, when the steam
    Floats up from those dim fields about the homes
70 Of happy men that have the power to die,
    And grassy barrows of the happier dead.
    Release me, and restore me to the ground;

———→

4 horses that draw the chariot of dawn. 5 Troy (Ilion) was supposedly built to the music of Apollo's lyre.

Thou seëst all things, thou wilt see my grave:
Thou wilt renew thy beauty morn by morn;
75   I earth in earth forget these empty courts,
And thee returning on thy silver wheels.

(1833)   (1860)

Robert Browning (1812–1889)

Born in London and educated mostly at home, Browning eloped with Elizabeth Barrett to Italy in 1846 and did not return to live in England until after her death. When his first significant work, *Pauline* (1833), prompted the philosopher and critic J.S. Mill to remark on his "intense and morbid self-consciousness," Browning turned to the objective dramatic mode. He is best known for his development of the dramatic monologue, a form that focuses on a single character whose personality is exposed— often indirectly and ironically— through his or her speech. The culmination of Browning's experiments with this form is *The Ring and the Book* (1869), ten long monologues focusing on a single event, in which he suggests that the only way of knowing "truth" may be through art. His attempt to give this "truth broken into prismatic hues" is represented here by such ironic works as "The Bishop Orders His Tomb at Saint Praxed's Church" (1845) and by the surrealistic psychological study " 'Childe Roland to the Dark Tower Came'." His dramatic monologues, along with his notably "unpoetic" language and his interests in psychology, philosophy, and arcane learning, had a great influence on modern poetic movements and particularly upon the poetry of Ezra Pound and T.S. Eliot.

My Last Duchess

Ferrara[1]

That's my last Duchess painted on the wall,
Looking as if she were alive. I call
That piece a wonder, now: Frà Pandolf's[2] hands
Worked busily a day, and there she stands.
5   Will't please you sit and look at her? I said
"Frà Pandolf" by design, for never read
Strangers like you that pictured countenance,
The depth and passion of its earnest glance,

———→

1 an Italian town. The Duke of Ferrara's first wife died under suspicious circumstances in 1561. Soon after, he began to negotiate for the hand of the niece of the Count of Tyrol.
2 Brother Pandolf, an imaginary painter.

But to myself they turned (since none puts by
10   The curtain I have drawn for you, but I)
And seemed as they would ask me, if they durst,
How such a glance came there; so, not the first
Are you to turn and ask thus. Sir, 'twas not
Her husband's presence only, called that spot
15   Of joy into the Duchess' cheek: perhaps
Frà Pandolf chanced to say 'Her mantle laps
Over my lady's wrist too much,' or 'Paint
Must never hope to reproduce the faint
Half-flush that dies along her throat': such stuff
20   Was courtesy, she thought, and cause enough
For calling up that spot of joy. She had
A heart — how shall I say? — too soon made glad,
Too easily impressed; she liked whate'er
She looked on, and her looks went everywhere.
25   Sir, 'twas all one! My favour at her breast,
The dropping of the daylight in the West,
The bough of cherries some officious fool
Broke in the orchard for her, the white mule
She rode with round the terrace — all and each
30   Would draw from her alike the approving speech,
Or blush, at least. She thanked men, — good! but thanked
Somehow — I know not how — as if she ranked
My gift of a nine-hundred-years-old name
With anybody's gift. Who'd stoop to blame
35   This sort of trifling? Even had you skill
In speech — (which I have not) — to make your will
Quite clear to such an one, and say, "Just this
Or that in you disgusts me; here you miss,
Or there exceed the mark" — and if she let
40   Herself be lessoned so, nor plainly set
Her wits to yours, forsooth, and made excuse,
— E'en then would be some stooping; and I choose
Never to stoop. Oh sir, she smiled, no doubt,
Whene'er I passed her; but who passed without
45   Much the same smile? This grew; I gave commands;
Then all smiles stopped together. There she stands
As if alive. Will't please you rise? We'll meet
The company below, then. I repeat,
The Count your master's known munificence
50   Is ample warrant that no just pretence

→

Of mine for dowry will be disallowed;
Though his fair daughter's self, as I avowed
At starting, is my object. Nay, we'll go
Together down, sir. Notice Neptune, though,
55 Taming a sea-horse, thought a rarity,
Which Claus of Innsbruck³ cast in bronze for me!

(1842)

The Bishop Orders His Tomb at Saint Praxed's Church¹

Rome, 15 —

Vanity, saith the preacher, vanity!²
Draw round my bed: is Anselm keeping back?
Nephews³ — sons of mine . . . ah God, I know not! Well —
She, men would have to be your mother once,
5 Old Gandolf envied me, so fair she was!
What's done is done, and she is dead beside,
Dead long ago, and I am Bishop since,
And as she died so must we die ourselves,
And thence ye may perceive the world's a dream.
10 Life, how and what is it? As here I lie
In this state-chamber, dying by degrees,
Hours and long hours in the dead night, I ask
"Do I live, am I dead?" Peace, peace seems all.
Saint Praxed's ever was the church for peace;
15 And so, about this tomb of mine. I fought
With tooth and nail to save my niche, ye know:
— Old Gandolf cozened me, despite my care;
Shrewd was that snatch from out the corner South
He graced his carrion with, God curse the same!
20 Yet still my niche is not so cramped but thence
One sees the pulpit o' the epistle-side,⁴
And somewhat of the choir, those silent seats,
And up into the airy dome where live
The angels, and a sunbeam's sure to lurk:

———▶

3 imaginary sculptor.
1 Church of Santa Prassede, in Rome. 2 Ecclesiastes 1:2. "Vanity of vanities, saith the Preacher, vanity of vanities." 3 conventional euphemism for illegitimate sons. 4 the right-hand side as one faces the altar.

25 And I shall fill my slab of basalt there,
And 'neath my tabernacle [5] take my rest,
With those nine columns round me, two and two,
The odd one at my feet where Anselm stands:
Peach-blossom marble all, the rare, the ripe
30 As fresh-poured red wine of a mighty pulse.
— Old Gandolf with his paltry onion-stone,[6]
Put me where I may look at him! True peach,
Rosy and flawless: how I earned the prize!
Draw close: that conflagration of my church
35 — What then? So much was saved if aught were missed!
My sons, ye would not be my death? Go dig
The white-grape vineyard where the oil-press stood,
Drop water gently till the surface sink,
And if ye find . . . Ah God, I know not, I! . . .
40 Bedded in store of rotten fig-leaves soft,
And corded up in a tight olive-frail,[7]
Some lump, ah God, of *lapis lazuli*,
Big as a Jew's head cut off at the nape,
Blue as a vein o'er the Madonna's breast . . .
45 Sons, all have I bequeathed you, villas, all,
That brave Frascati[8] villa with its bath,
So, let the blue lump poise between my knees,
Like God the Father's globe on both his hands
Ye worship in the Jesu Church[9] so gay,
50 For Gandolf shall not choose but see and burst!
Swift as a weaver's shuttle fleet our years:
Man goeth to the grave, and where is he?
Did I say basalt for my slab, sons? Black —
'Twas ever antique-black I meant! How else
55 Shall ye contrast my frieze to come beneath?
The bas-relief in bronze ye promised me,
Those Pans and Nymphs ye wot of, and perchance
Some tripod, thyrsus,[10] with a vase or so,
The Saviour at his sermon on the mount,
60 Saint Praxed in a glory,[11] and one Pan
Ready to twitch the Nymph's last garment off,
And Moses with the tables . . . but I know

———→

5 canopy over his tomb. 6 inferior grade of marble. 7 olive basket. 8 fashionable resort town in the mountains. 9 Church of Il Gesu in Rome. 10 classical and pagan ornamentation. The tripod is associated with the priestess of Apollo at Delphi; the thyrsus is the staff carried by Dionysus. 11 with a halo.

Ye mark me not! What do they whisper thee,
Child of my bowels, Anselm? Ah, ye hope
65 To revel down my villas while I gasp
Bricked o'er with beggar's mouldy travertine[12]
Which Gandolf from his tomb-top chuckles at!
Nay, boys, ye love me — all of jasper, then!
'Tis jasper ye stand pledged to, lest I grieve
70 My bath must needs be left behind, alas!
One block, pure green as a pistachio-nut,
There's plenty jasper somewhere in the world —
And have I not Saint Praxed's ear to pray
Horses for ye, and brown Greek manuscripts,
75 And mistresses with great smooth marbly limbs?
— That's if ye carve my epitaph aright,
Choice Latin, picked phrase, Tully's[13] every word,
No gaudy ware like Gandolf's second line —
Tully, my masters? Ulpian[14] serves his need!
80 And then how I shall lie through centuries,
And hear the blessed mutter of the mass,
And see God made and eaten all day long,[15]
And feel the steady candle-flame, and taste
Good strong thick stupefying incense-smoke!
85 For as I lie here, hours of the dead night,
Dying in state and by such slow degrees,
I fold my arms as if they clasped a crook,
And stretch my feet forth straight as stone can point,
And let the bedclothes, for a mortcloth,[16] drop
90 Into great laps and folds of sculptor's-work:
And as yon tapers dwindle, and strange thoughts
Grow, with a certain humming in my ears,
About the life before I lived this life,
And this life too, popes, cardinals and priests,
95 Saint Praxed at his sermon on the mount,[17]
Your tall pale mother with her talking eyes,
And new-found agate urns as fresh as day,
And marble's language, Latin pure, discreet,
— Aha, ELUCESCEBAT[18] quoth our friend?

⟶

12 ordinary limestone. 13 Cicero. 14 the decadent Latin of Ulpianus was far inferior to that of Cicero.
15 reference to doctrine of transubstantiation, the conversion of bread and wine into the body and blood of
Christ which is thought to occur during mass. 16 funeral pall. 17 the Bishop is confusing Praxed with
Christ. 18 "He was illustrious." Phrase in Ulpianus's Latin, which is part of the inscription on Gandolf's
tomb. The Ciceronian form would be *elucebat*.

100 No Tully, said I, Ulpian at the best!
Evil and brief hath been my pilgrimage.
All *lapis*, all, sons! Else I give the Pope
My villas! Will ye ever eat my heart?
Ever your eyes were as a lizard's quick,
105 They glitter like your mother's for my soul,
Or ye would heighten my impoverished frieze,
Piece out its starved design, and fill my vase
With grapes, and add a vizor and a Term,[19]
And to the tripod ye would tie a lynx
110 That in his struggle throws the thyrsus down,
To comfort me on my entablature
Whereon I am to lie till I must ask
"Do I live, am I dead?" There, leave me, there!
For ye have stabbed me with ingratitude
115 To death — ye wish it — God, ye wish it! Stone —
Gritstone,[20] a-crumble! Clammy squares which sweat
As if the corpse they keep were oozing through —
And no more *lapis* to delight the world!
Well go! I bless ye. Fewer tapers there,
120 But in a row: and, going, turn your backs
— Ay, like departing altar-ministrants,
And leave me in my church, the church for peace,
That I may watch at leisure if he leers —
Old Gandolf, at me, from his onion-stone,
125 As still he envied me, so fair she was!

(1845)

"Childe Roland to the Dark Tower Came"[1]

I

My first thought was, he lied in every word,
    That hoary cripple, with malicious eye
    Askance to watch the working of his lie

→

19 a vizor is the eye covering of a helmet; *Term* is an abbreviation of *Terminus*, the Roman god of boundaries, and thus, a common symbol of mortality. A term was also the tapered pedestal on which a bust, such as that of Terminus, would be placed. 20 sandstone.
1 see Edgar's mad song in Shakespeare's *King Lear* 3.4:171–73. "Child Rowland to the dark tower came, / His word was still — Fie, foh, and fum! / I smell the blood of a British man." A childe is a young knight who has not yet proved himself.

On mine, and mouth scarce able to afford
5   Suppression of the glee, that pursed and scored
        Its edge, at one more victim gained thereby.

II

What else should he be set for, with his staff?
        What, save to waylay with his lies, ensnare
        All travellers who might find him posted there,
10   And ask the road? I guessed what skull-like laugh
Would break, what crutch 'gin write my epitaph
        For pastime in the dusty thoroughfare,

III

If at his counsel I should turn aside
        Into that ominous tract which, all agree,
15   Hides the Dark Tower. Yet acquiescingly
I did turn as he pointed: neither pride
Nor hope rekindling at the end descried,
        So much as gladness that some end might be.

IV

For, what with my whole world-wide wandering,
20   What with my search drawn out through years, my hope
        Dwindled into a ghost not fit to cope
With that obstreperous joy success would bring,
I hardly tried now to rebuke the spring
        My heart made, finding failure in its scope.

V

25   As when a sick man very near to death
        Seems dead indeed, and feels begin and end
        The tears and takes the farewell of each friend,
And hears one bid the other go, draw breath
Freelier outside, ("since all is o'er," he saith,
30   "And the blow fallen no grieving can amend";)

VI

While some discuss if near the other graves
        Be room enough for this, and when a day
        Suits best for carrying the corpse away,

→

With care about the banners, scarves and staves:
35   And still the man hears all, and only craves
       He may not shame such tender love and stay.

VII

Thus, I had so long suffered in this quest,
       Heard failure prophesied so oft, been writ
       So many times among "The Band"—to wit,
40   The knights who to the Dark Tower's search addressed
       Their steps—that just to fail as they, seemed best,
       And all the doubt was now—should I be fit?

VIII

So, quiet as despair, I turned from him,
       That hateful cripple, out of his highway
45   Into the path he pointed. All the day
Had been a dreary one at best, and dim
Was settling to its close, yet shot one grim
       Red leer to see the plain catch its estray.[2]

IX

For mark! no sooner was I fairly found
50   Pledged to the plain, after a pace or two,
       Than, pausing to throw backward a last view
O'er the safe road, 'twas gone; grey plain all around:
Nothing but plain to the horizon's bound.
       I might go on; naught else remained to do.

X

55   So, on I went. I think I never saw
       Such starved ignoble nature; nothing throve:
       For flowers—as well expect a cedar grove!
But cockle, spurge,[3] according to their law
Might propagate their kind, with none to awe,
60   You'd think; a burr had been a treasure-trove.

2 someone who has strayed. 3 cockle is any of several weeds that grow in wheat fields; some of the varieties
belong to the spurge family and have an acrid milky juice with purgative properties.

XI

No! penury, inertness and grimace,
    In some strange sort, were the land's portion. "See
    Or shut your eyes," said Nature peevishly,
"It nothing skills: I cannot help my case:
65   'Tis the Last Judgement's fire must cure this place,
    Calcine[4] its clods and set my prisoners free."

XII

If there pushed any ragged thistle-stalk
    Above its mates, the head was chopped; the bents
    Were jealous else. What made those holes and rents
70   In the dock's harsh swarth leaves, bruised as to balk
All hope of greenness? 'tis a brute must walk
    Pashing their life out, with a brute's intents.

XIII

As for the grass, it grew as scant as hair
    In leprosy; thin dry blades pricked the mud
75   Which underneath looked kneaded up with blood.
One stiff blind horse, his every bone a-stare,
Stood stupefied, however he came there:
    Thrust out past service from the devil's stud!

XIV

Alive? he might be dead for aught I know,
80   With that red gaunt and colloped[5] neck a-strain,
    And shut eyes underneath the rusty mane;
Seldom went such grotesqueness with such woe;
I never saw a brute I hated so;
    He must be wicked to deserve such pain.

XV

85   I shut my eyes and turned them on my heart.
    As a man calls for wine before he fights,
    I asked one draught of earlier, happier sights,
Ere fitly I could hope to play my part.
Think first, fight afterwards — the soldier's art:
90   One taste of the old time sets all to rights.

4 pulverize by heat. 5 in folds or ridges.

XVI

Not it! I fancied Cuthbert's reddening face
    Beneath its garniture of curly gold,
    Dear fellow, till I almost felt him fold
An arm in mine to fix me to the place,
95 That way he used. Alas, one night's disgrace!
    Out went my heart's new fire and left it cold.

XVII

Giles then, the soul of honour — there he stands
    Frank as ten years ago when knighted first.
    What honest man should dare (he said) he durst.
100 Good — but the scene shifts — faugh! what hangman-hands
Pin to his breast a parchment? His own bands
    Read it. Poor traitor, spit upon and curst!

XVIII

Better this present than a past like that;
    Back therefore to my darkening path again!
    No sound, no sight as far as eye could strain.
105 Will the night send a howler[6] or a bat?
I asked: when something on the dismal flat
    Came to arrest my thoughts and change their train.

XIX

A sudden little river crossed my path
110   As unexpected as a serpent comes.
    No sluggish tide congenial to the glooms;
This, as it frothed by, might have been a bath
For the fiend's glowing hoof — to see the wrath
    Of its black eddy bespate with flakes and spumes.

XX

115 So petty yet so spiteful! All along,
    Low scrubby alders kneeled down over it;
    Drenched willows flung them headlong in a fit
Of mute despair, a suicidal throng:
The river which had done them all the wrong,
120   Whate'er that was, rolled by, deterred no whit.

6 owl.

XXI

Which, while I forded, — good saints, how I feared
   To set my foot upon a dead man's cheek,
   Each step, or feel the spear I thrust to seek
For hollows, tangled in his hair or beard!
125   — It may have been a water-rat I speared,
   But, ugh! it sounded like a baby's shriek.

XXII

Glad was I when I reached the other bank.
   Now for a better country. Vain presage!
   Who were the strugglers; what war did they wage,
130   Whose savage trample thus could pad the dank
Soil to a plash? Toads in a poisoned tank,
   Or wild cats in a red-hot iron cage —

XXIII

The fight must so have seemed in that fell cirque.
   What penned them there, with all the plain to choose?
135   No foot-print leading to that horrid mews,
None out of it. Mad brewage set to work
Their brains, no doubt, like galley-slaves the Turk
   Pits for his pastime, Christians against Jews.

XXIV

And more than that — a furlong on — why, there!
140   What bad use was that engine for, that wheel,
   Or brake,[7] not wheel — that harrow fit to reel
Men's bodies out like silk? with all the air
Of Tophet's tool,[8] on earth left unaware,
   Or brought to sharpen its rusty teeth of steel.

XXV

145   Then came a bit of stubbed ground, once a wood,
   Next a marsh, it would seem, and now mere earth
   Desperate and done with; (so a fool finds mirth,
Makes a thing and then mars it, till his mood
Changes and off he goes!) within a rood[9]—
150   Bog, clay and rubble, sand and stark black dearth.

7 a machine with teeth used for breaking up flax or hemp to separate the fibre; here used as a device of torture. 8 hell's tool. 9 approximately a quarter of an acre.

XXVI

Now blotches rankling, coloured gay and grim,
  Now patches where some leanness of the soil's
  Broke into moss or substances like boils;
Then came some palsied oak, a cleft in him
155 Like a distorted mouth that splits its rim
  Gaping at death, and dies while it recoils.

XXVII

And just as far as ever from the end!
  Naught in the distance but the evening, naught
  To point my footsteps further! At the thought,
160 A great black bird, Apollyon's bosom-friend,[10]
Sailed past, nor beat his wide wing dragon-penned[11]
  That brushed my cap — perchance the guide I sought.

XXVIII

For, looking up, aware I somehow grew,
  'Spite of the dusk, the plain had given place
165 All round to mountains — with such name to grace
Mere ugly heights and heaps now stolen in view.
How thus they had surprised me, — solve it, you!
  How to get from them was no clearer case.

XXIX

Yet half I seemed to recognize some trick
170 Of mischief happened to me, God knows when —
  In a bad dream perhaps. Here ended, then,
Progress this way. When, in the very nick
Of giving up, one time more, came a click
  As when a trap shuts — you're inside the den!

XXX

175 Burningly it came on me all at once,
  This was the place! those two hills on the right,
  Crouched like two bulls locked horn in horn in fight;
While to the left, a tall scalped mountain . . . Dunce,
Dotard, a-dozing at the very nonce,
180 After a life spent training for the sight!

10 in Revelations 9:11, the devil is called Apollyon, the destroyer. 11 with pinions like a dragon.

XXXI

What in the midst lay but the Tower itself?
    The round squat turret, blind as the fool's heart,
    Built of brown stone, without a counterpart
In the whole world. The tempest's mocking elf
185   Points to the shipman thus the unseen shelf
    He strikes on, only when the timbers start.

XXXII

Not see? because of night perhaps? — why, day
    Came back again for that! before it left,
    The dying sunset kindled through a cleft:
190   The hills, like giants at a hunting, lay,
Chin upon hand, to see the game at bay, —
    "Now stab and end the creature — to the heft!"[12]

XXXIII

Not hear? when noise was everywhere! it tolled
    Increasing like a bell. Names in my ears
195   Of all the lost adventurers my peers, —
How such a one was strong, and such was bold,
And such was fortunate, yet each of old
    Lost, lost! one moment knelled the woe of years.

XXXIV

There they stood, ranged along the hill-sides, met
200   To view the last of me, a living frame
    For one more picture! in a sheet of flame
I saw them and I knew them all. And yet
Dauntless the slug-horn[13] to my lips I set,
    And blew. *"Childe Roland to the Dark Tower came."*

(1855)

12 handle of a dagger. 13 trumpet.

Walt Whitman (1819–1892)

Born on Long Island, New York (referred to by its Native name, Paumanok, in many of his poems), Walt Whitman worked as a labourer, teacher, printer, journalist, and, during the American Civil War, as a nurse. *Leaves of Grass*, first published in 1855 and revised and expanded several times during his life, was the first major collection by an American poet, and influenced such twentieth-century American poets as Hart Crane and Allen Ginsberg. Celebrating the diversity of the United States and the dignity of the common person, the poems were praised by the poet-essayist Ralph Waldo Emerson, but often criticized by reviewers for what they considered obscene passages. Their central figure is a speaker who embodies the diversity and greatness of American life. While many of Whitman's poems have justly been described as massive and formless, others, such as "When Lilacs Last in the Dooryard Bloom'd," in which the death and funeral procession of Abraham Lincoln are the occasion for an elegy examining the interrelationships between life, death, and love, are tightly knit and intricately developed.

When Lilacs Last in the Dooryard Bloom'd

1

When lilacs last in the dooryard bloom'd,
And the great star early droop'd in the western sky in the night,
I mourn'd, and yet shall mourn with ever-returning spring.
Ever-returning spring, trinity sure to me you bring,
5   Lilac blooming perennial and drooping star in the west,
And thought of him[1] I love.

2

O powerful western fallen star!
O shades of night — O moody, tearful night!
O great star disappear'd — O the black murk that hides the star!
10   O cruel hands that hold me powerless — O helpless soul of me!
O harsh surrounding cloud that will not free my soul.

1 Abraham Lincoln, American president assassinated April 14, 1865.

3

In the dooryard fronting an old farm-house near the white-wash'd palings,
Stands the lilac-bush tall-growing with heart-shaped leaves of rich green,
With many a pointed blossom rising delicate, with the perfume strong I love,
15 With every leaf a miracle — and from this bush in the dooryard,
With delicate-color'd blossoms and heart-shaped leaves of rich green,
A sprig with its flower I break.

4

In the swamp in secluded recesses,
A shy and hidden bird is warbling a song.
20 Solitary the thrush,[2]
The hermit withdrawn to himself, avoiding the settlements,
Sings by himself a song.

Song of the bleeding throat,
Death's outlet song of life, (for well dear brother I know,
25 If thou wast not granted to sing thou would'st surely die.)

5

Over the breast of the spring, the land, amid cities,
Amid lanes and through old woods, where lately the violets peep'd from the
        ground, spotting the gray debris,
Amid the grass in the fields each side of the lanes, passing the endless grass,
Passing the yellow-spear'd wheat, every grain from its shroud in the
        dark-brown fields uprisen,
30 Passing the apple-tree blows of white and pink in the orchards,
Carrying a corpse to where it shall rest in the grave,
Night and day journeys a coffin.[3]

6

Coffin that passes through lanes and streets,
Through day and night with the great cloud darkening the land,

⟶

2 thrush, seldom seen, but whose beautiful song is often heard in the spring. 3 Lincoln's coffin was carried
from Washington, D.C., to Springfield, Illinois.

35 With the pomp of the inloop'd flags with the cities draped in black,
With the show of the States themselves as of crape-veil'd women standing,
With processions long and winding and the flambeaus of the night,
With the countless torches lit, with the silent sea of faces and the
      unbared heads,
With the waiting depot, the arriving coffin, and the sombre faces,
40 With dirges through the night, with the thousand voices rising strong
      and solemn,
With all the mournful voices of the dirges pour'd around the coffin,
The dim-lit churches and the shuddering organs — where amid these
      you journey,
With the tolling tolling bells' perpetual clang,
Here, coffin that slowly passes,
45 I give you my sprig of lilac.

7

(Nor for you, for one alone,
Blossoms and branches green to coffins all I bring,
For fresh as the morning, thus would I chant a song for you O sane and
      sacred death.

All over bouquets of roses,
50 O death, I cover you over with roses and early lilies,
But mostly and now the lilac that blooms the first,
Copious I break, I break the sprigs from the bushes,
With loaded arms I come, pouring for you,
For you and the coffins all of you O death.)

8

55 O western orb sailing the heaven,
Now I know what you must have meant as a month since I walk'd,
As I walk'd in silence the transparent shadowy night,
As I saw you had something to tell as you bent to me night after night,
As you droop'd from the sky low down as if to my side, (while the other
      stars all look'd on,)
60 As we wander'd together the solemn night, (for something I know not what

→

kept me from sleep,)
As the night advanced, and I saw on the rim of the west how full you
    were of woe,
As I stood on the rising ground in the breeze in the cool transparent night,
As I watch'd where you pass'd and was lost in the netherward black
    of the night,
As my soul in its trouble dissatisfied sank, as where you sad orb,
65 Concluded, dropt in the night, and was gone.

9

Sing on there in the swamp,
O singer bashful and tender, I hear your notes, I hear your call,
I hear, I come presently, I understand you,
But a moment I linger, for the lustrous star has detain'd me,
70 The star my departing comrade holds and detains me.

10

O how shall I warble myself for the dead one there I loved?
And how shall I deck my song for the large sweet soul that has gone?
And what shall my perfume be for the grave of him I love?

Sea-winds blown from east and west,
75 Blown from the Eastern sea and blown from the Western sea, till there on
    the prairies meeting,
These and with these and the breath of my chant,
I'll perfume the grave of him I love.

11

O what shall I hang on the chamber walls?
And what shall the pictures be that I hang on the walls,
80 To adorn the burial-house of him I love?

Pictures of growing spring and farms and homes,
With the Fourth-month[4] eve at sundown, and the gray smoke lucid
    and bright,

       ⟶

4 Quaker name for April.

With floods of the yellow gold of the gorgeous, indolent, sinking sun,
     burning, expanding the air,
With the fresh sweet herbage under foot, and the pale green leaves of the
     trees prolific,
85 In the distance the flowing glaze, the breast of the river, with a wind-dapple
     here and there,
With ranging hills on the banks, with many a line against the sky, and
     shadows,
And the city at hand with dwellings so dense, and stacks of chimneys,
And all the scenes of life and the workshops, and the workmen homeward
     returning.

12

Lo, body and soul — this land,
90 My own Manhattan with spires, and the sparkling and hurrying tides, and
     the ships,
The varied and ample land, the South and the North in the light,
     Ohio's shores and flashing Missouri,
And ever the far-spreading prairies cover'd with grass and corn.

Lo, the most excellent sun so calm and haughty,
The violet and purple morn with just-felt breezes,
95 The gentle soft-born measureless light,
The miracle spreading bathing all, the fulfill'd noon,
The coming eve delicious, the welcome night and the stars,
Over my cities shining all, enveloping man and land.

13

Sing on, sing on you gray-brown bird,
100 Sing from the swamps, the recesses, pour your chant from the bushes,
Limitless out of the dusk, out of the cedars and pines.

Sing on dearest brother, warble your reedy song,
Loud human song, with voice of uttermost woe.

O liquid and free and tender!
105 O wild and loose to my soul — O wondrous singer!
You only I hear — yet the star holds me, (but will soon depart,)
Yet the lilac with mastering odor holds me.

14

Now while I sat in the day and look'd forth,
In the close of the day with its light and the fields of spring, and the farmers
    preparing their crops,
110   In the large unconscious scenery of my land with its lakes and forests,
In the heavenly aerial beauty, (after the perturb'd winds and the storms,)
Under the arching heavens of the afternoon swift passing, and the voices of
    children and women,
The many-moving sea-tides, and I saw the ships how they sail'd,
And the summer approaching with richness, and the fields all busy
    with labor,
115   And the infinite separate houses, how they all went on, each with its meals
    and minutia of daily usages,
And the streets how their throbbings throbb'd, and the cities pent — lo,
    then and there,
Falling upon them all and among them all, enveloping me with the rest,
Appear'd the cloud, appear'd the long black trail,
And I knew death, its thought, and the sacred knowledge of death.

120   Then with the knowledge of death as walking one side of me,
And the thought of death close-walking the other side of me,
And I in the middle as with companions, and as holding the hands of
    companions,
I fled forth to the hiding receiving night that talks not,
Down to the shores of the water, the path by the swamp in the dimness,
125   To the solemn shadowy cedars and ghostly pines so still.

And the singer so shy to the rest receiv'd me,
The gray-brown bird I know receiv'd us comrades three,
And he sang the carol of death, and a verse for him I love.

From deep secluded recesses,
130   From the fragrant cedars and the ghostly pines so still,
Came the carol of the bird.

And the charm of the carol rapt me,
As I held as if by their hands my comrades in the night,
And the voice of my spirit tallied the song of the bird.

135   *Come lovely and soothing death,*
      Undulate round the world, serenely arriving, arriving,
      In the day, in the night, to all, to each,
      Sooner or later delicate death.

      Prais'd be the fathomless universe,
140   *For life and joy, and for objects and knowledge curious,*
      And for love, sweet love — but praise! praise! praise!
      For the sure-enwinding arms of cool-enfolding death.

      Dark mother always gliding near with soft feet,
      Have none chanted for thee a chant of fullest welcome?
145   *Then I chant it for thee, I glorify thee above all,*
      I bring thee a song that when thou must indeed come, come unfalteringly.

      Approach strong deliveress,
      When it is so, when thou hast taken them I joyously sing the dead,
      Lost in the loving floating ocean of thee,
150   *Laved in the flood of thy bliss O death.*

      From me to thee glad serenades,
      Dances for thee I propose saluting thee, adornments and feastings for thee,
      And the sights of the open landscape and the high-spread sky are fitting,
      And life and the fields, and the huge and thoughtful night.

155   *The night in silence under many a star,*
      The ocean shore and the husky whispering wave whose voice I know,
      And the soul turning to thee O vast and well-veil'd death,
      And the body gratefully nestling close to thee.

      Over the tree-tops I float thee a song,
160   *Over the rising and sinking waves, over the myriad fields and the prairies wide,*
      Over the dense-pack'd cities all and the teeming wharves and ways,
      I float this carol with joy, with joy to thee O death.

15

      To the tally[5] of my soul,
      Loud and strong kept up the gray-brown bird,
165   With pure deliberate notes spreading filling the night.

5 record or account.

Loud in the pines and cedars dim,
Clear in the freshness moist and the swamp-perfume,
And I with my comrades there in the night.

While my sight that was bound in my eyes unclosed,
170   As to long panoramas of visions.

And I saw askant the armies,[6]
I saw as in noiseless dreams hundreds of battle-flags,
Borne through the smoke of the battles and pierc'd with missiles I saw them,
And carried hither and yon through the smoke, and torn and bloody,
175   And at last but a few shreds left on the staffs, (and all in silence,)
And the staffs all splinter'd and broken.

I saw battle-corpses, myriads of them,
And the white skeletons of young men, I saw them,
I saw the debris and debris of all the slain soldiers of the war,
180   But I saw they were not as was thought,
They themselves were fully at rest, they suffer'd not,
The living remain'd and suffer'd, the mother suffer'd,
And the wife and the child and the musing comrade suffer'd,
And the armies that remain'd suffer'd.

16

185   Passing the visions, passing the night,
Passing, unloosing the hold of my comrades' hands,
Passing the song of the hermit bird and the tallying song of my soul,
Victorious song, death's outlet song, yet varying ever altering song,
As low and wailing, yet clear the notes, rising and falling, flooding the night,
190   Sadly sinking and fainting, as warning and warning, and yet again bursting
         with joy,
Covering the earth and filling the spread of the heaven,
As that powerful psalm in the night I heard from recesses,
Passing, I leave thee lilac with heart-shaped leaves,
I leave thee there in the door-yard, blooming, returning with spring.

195   I cease from my song for thee,
From my gaze on thee in the west, fronting the west, communing with thee,
O comrade lustrous with silver face in the night.

6 armies of the American Civil War.

Yet each to keep and all, retrievements out of the night,
The song, the wondrous chant of the gray-brown bird,
200 And the tallying chant, the echo arous'd in my soul,
With the lustrous and drooping star with the countenance full of woe,
With the holders holding my hand nearing the call of the bird,
Comrades mine and I in the midst, and their memory ever to keep, for the
    dead I loved so well,
For the sweetest, wisest soul of all my days and lands — and this for his
    dear sake,
205 Lilac and star and bird twined with the chant of my soul,
There in the fragrant pines and the cedars dusk and dim.

(1865–66)   (1881)

One's-Self I Sing

One's-Self I sing, a simple separate person,
Yet utter the word Democratic, the word En-Masse.[1]

Of physiology from top to toe I sing,
Not physiognomy[2] alone nor brain alone is worthy for the Muse, I say the
    Form complete is worthier far,
5   The Female equally with the Male I sing.

Of Life immense in passion, pulse, and power,
Cheerful, for freest action form'd under the laws divine,
The Modern Man I sing.

(1867)   (1871)

Matthew Arnold (1822–1888)

Arnold, the eldest son of Thomas Arnold, headmaster of Rugby, was educated at Oxford, stayed on as professor of poetry for ten years, and was subsequently appointed an inspector of schools in 1851. He became one of the leading social and literary critics of the age, and such critical works as *Culture and Anarchy* (1869), an investigation into the question of whether the anarchy of individualism should be checked by the authority of culture, are now often considered to be of greater significance than his poetical works. The two genres

1 in a group. 2 facial features.

of poetry and criticism come together in his once-influential theory of critical "touchstones" in "The Study of Poetry" (1888), an attempt to establish standards for distinguishing poetry of "high seriousness." Frequently referred to as the poet of alienation, Arnold is preoccupied with the isolation of the individual and the difficulty of knowing the self. His work is suffused with a sense of frustration, a sharp awareness of the failings of his age, and a poignant nostalgia for a basically illusory earlier age when questions of faith and moral integrity were more easily answered. At the same time, Arnold reveals an unfailing optimistic belief in the efficacy of cultural institutions in bringing about change. The resulting self-division is aptly captured in the haunting lyricism of "Dover Beach." In looking back to a better time and yet still believing in human progress, Arnold is quintessentially Victorian, a man, as he so memorably says in "Stanzas from the Grande Chartreuse" (1855), "Wandering between two worlds, one dead, / The other powerless to be born."

Dover Beach

The sea is calm to-night.
The tide is full, the moon lies fair,
Upon the straits; — on the French coast the light
Gleams and is gone; the cliffs of England stand,
5 Glimmering and vast, out in the tranquil bay.
Come to the window, sweet is the night-air!
Only, from the long line of spray
Where the sea meets the moon-blanch'd land,
Listen! you hear the grating roar
10 Of pebbles which the waves draw back, and fling,
At their return, up the high strand,
Begin, and cease, and then again begin,
With tremulous cadence slow, and bring
The eternal note of sadness in.

15 Sophocles long ago
Heard it on the Ægæan, and it brought
Into his mind the turbid ebb and flow
Of human misery;[1] we
Find also in the sound a thought,
20 Hearing it by this distant northern sea.

1 see Sophocles, *Antigone* 2.583ff.

The Sea of Faith
Was once, too, at the full, and round earth's shore
Lay like the folds of a bright girdle furl'd.
But now I only hear
25   Its melancholy, long, withdrawing roar,
Retreating, to the breath
Of the night-wind, down the vast edges drear
And naked shingles[2] of the world.

Ah, love, let us be true
30   To one another! for the world, which seems
To lie before us like a land of dreams,
So various, so beautiful, so new,
Hath really neither joy, nor love, nor light,
Nor certitude, nor peace, nor help for pain;
35   And we are here as on a darkling plain
Swept with confused alarms of struggle and flight,
Where ignorant armies clash by night.

(1867)

Christina Rossetti (1830–1894)

Rossetti, younger sister of the poet-painter Dante Gabriel Rossetti, was edu-
cated at home and lived with her family in London for most of her life. Like
her mother and sister, she was a devout High Anglican with a great interest in
the Oxford Movement, which attempted to merge Catholic doctrine and ritual
with the Anglican faith. In 1862 she established her reputation as a poet with
the publication of her most famous work, "Goblin Market." Rossetti was the only
woman in the Pre-Raphaelite circle to achieve recognition for her own work, to
be the creative rather than simply the inspirational force, and she is also the only
British woman poet of the nineteenth century to have consistently drawn crit-
ical acclaim right up to the present day. She wrote much religious poetry and
many children's rhymes, as well as numerous ballads and lyrics that reveal a deep
ambivalence toward romantic love and the conventional roles of women; they
have a strong critical subtext rejecting the limitations imposed upon women by
society. Unhappy or frustrated love between men and the women they betray
is often the focus of her frequently melancholy works, and the women she
depicts find their only consolation in resignation, postponement, and the love
of God.

2 pebbled beaches.

Song

When I am dead, my dearest,
    Sing no sad songs for me;
Plant thou no roses at my head,
    Nor shady cypress tree:
5 Be the green grass above me
    With showers and dewdrops wet;
And if thou wilt, remember,
    And if thou wilt, forget.

I shall not see the shadows,
10   I shall not feel the rain;
I shall not hear the nightingale
    Sing on as if in pain:
And dreaming through the twilight
    That doth not rise nor set,
15 Haply I may remember,
    And haply may forget.

(1848)   (1862)

The World

By day she woos me, soft, exceeding fair:
    But all night as the moon so changeth she;
    Loathsome and foul with hideous leprosy,
And subtle serpents gliding in her hair.
5 By day she woos me to the outer air,
    Ripe fruits, sweet flowers, and full satiety:
    But thro' the night a beast she grins at me,
A very monster void of love and prayer.
By day she stands a lie: by night she stands
10   In all the naked horror of the truth,
With pushing horns and clawed and clutching hands.
Is this a friend indeed, that I should sell
    My soul to her, give her my life and youth,
Till my feet, cloven too, take hold on hell!

(1854)   (1862)

Goblin Market

Morning and evening
Maids heard the goblins cry:
"Come buy our orchard fruits,
Come buy, come buy:
5 Apples and quinces,
Lemons and oranges,
Plump unpecked cherries,
Melons and raspberries,
Bloom-down-cheeked peaches,
10 Swart-headed mulberries,
Wild free-born cranberries,
Crab-apples, dewberries,
Pine-apples, blackberries,
Apricots, strawberries;—
15 All ripe together
In summer weather,—
Morns that pass by,
Fair eves that fly;
Come buy, come buy:
20 Our grapes fresh from the vine,
Pomegranates full and fine,
Dates and sharp bullaces,[1]
Rare pears and greengages,
Damsons and bilberries,
25 Taste them and try:
Currants and gooseberries,
Bright-fire-like barberries,[2]
Figs to fill your mouth,
Citrons from the South,
30 Sweet to tongue and sound to eye;
Come buy, come buy."

Evening by evening
Among the brookside rushes,
Laura bowed her head to hear,
35 Lizzie veiled her blushes:
Crouching close together

⟶

1 plums, as are the greengages and damsons mentioned in the following lines. 2 red berries from the berberis, a thorny shrub.

In the cooling weather,
With clasping arms and cautioning lips,
With tingling cheeks and finger tips.
40   "Lie close," Laura said,
Pricking up her golden head:
"We must not look at goblin men,
We must not buy their fruits:
Who knows upon what soil they fed
45   Their hungry thirsty roots?"
"Come buy," call the goblins
Hobbling down the glen.
"Oh," cried Lizzie, "Laura, Laura,
You should not peep at goblin men."
50   Lizzie covered up her eyes,
Covered close lest they should look;
Laura reared her glossy head,
And whispered like the restless brook:
"Look, Lizzie, look, Lizzie,
55   Down the glen tramp little men.
One hauls a basket,
One bears a plate,
One lugs a golden dish
Of many pounds' weight.
60   How fair the vine must grow
Whose grapes are so luscious;
How warm the wind must blow
Through those fruit bushes."
"No," said Lizzie: "No, no, no;
65   Their offers should not charm us,
Their evil gifts would harm us."
She thrust a dimpled finger
In each ear, shut eyes and ran:
Curious Laura chose to linger
70   Wondering at each merchant man.
One had a cat's face,
One whisked a tail,
One tramped at a rat's pace,
One crawled like a snail,
75   One like a wombat[3] prowled obtuse and furry,
One like a ratel[4] tumbled hurry skurry.

———→

3 Australian marsupial like a small bear. 4 nocturnal, carnivorous, burrowing mammal found in India and Africa.

She heard a voice like voice of doves
Cooing all together:
They sounded kind and full of loves
80   In the pleasant weather.

Laura stretched her gleaming neck
Like a rush-imbedded swan,
Like a lily from the beck,[5]
Like a moonlit poplar branch,
85   Like a vessel at the launch
When its last restraint is gone.

Backwards up the mossy glen
Turned and trooped the goblin men,
With their shrill repeated cry,
90   "Come buy, come buy."
When they reached where Laura was
They stood stock still upon the moss,
Leering at each other,
Brother with queer brother;
95   Signalling each other,
Brother with sly brother.
One set his basket down,
One reared his plate;
One began to weave a crown
100   Of tendrils, leaves, and rough nuts brown
(Men sell not such in any town);
One heaved the golden weight
Of dish and fruit to offer her:

"Come buy, come buy," was still their cry.
105   Laura stared but did not stir,
Longed but had no money.
The whisk-tailed merchant bade her taste
In tones as smooth as honey,
The cat-faced purr'd,
110   The rat-paced spoke a word
Of welcome, and the snail-paced even was heard;
One parrot-voiced and jolly
Cried "Pretty Goblin" still for "Pretty Polly";
One whistled like a bird.

5 brook.

115 But sweet-tooth Laura spoke in haste:
"Good Folk, I have no coin;
To take were to purloin:
I have no copper in my purse,
I have no silver either,
120 And all my gold is on the furze
That shakes in windy weather
Above the rusty heather."
"You have much gold upon your head,"
They answered all together:
125 "Buy from us with a golden curl."
She clipped a precious golden lock,
She dropped a tear more rare than pearl,
Then sucked their fruit globes fair or red.
Sweeter than honey from the rock,
130 Stronger than man-rejoicing wine,
Clearer than water flowed that juice;
She never tasted such before,
How should it cloy with length of use?
She sucked and sucked and sucked the more
135 Fruits which that unknown orchard bore;
She sucked until her lips were sore;
Then flung the emptied rinds away
But gathered up one kernel stone,
And knew not was it night or day
140 As she turned home alone.

Lizzie met her at the gate
Full of wise upbraidings:
"Dear, you should not stay so late,
Twilight is not good for maidens;
145 Should not loiter in the glen
In the haunts of goblin men.
Do you not remember Jeanie,
How she met them in the moonlight,
Took their gifts both choice and many,
150 Ate their fruits and wore their flowers
Plucked from bowers
Where summer ripens at all hours?
But ever in the noonlight

→

She pined and pined away;
155 Sought them by night and day,
Found them no more, but dwindled and grew grey;
Then fell with the first snow,
While to this day no grass will grow
Where she lies low:
160 I planted daisies there a year ago
That never blow.
You should not loiter so."
"Nay, hush," said Laura:
"Nay, hush, my sister:
165 I ate and ate my fill,
Yet my mouth waters still:
To-morrow night I will
Buy more;" and kissed her.
"Have done with sorrow;
170 I'll bring you plums to-morrow
Fresh on their mother twigs,
Cherries worth getting;
You cannot think what figs
My teeth have met in,
175 What melons icy-cold
Piled on a dish of gold
Too huge for me to hold,
What peaches with a velvet nap,
Pellucid grapes without one seed:
180 Odorous indeed must be the mead
Whereon they grow, and pure the wave they drink
With lilies at the brink,
And sugar-sweet their sap."

Golden head by golden head,
185 Like two pigeons in one nest
Folded in each other's wings,
They lay down in their curtained bed:
Like two blossoms on one stem,
Like two flakes of new-fall'n snow,
190 Like two wands of ivory
Tipped with gold for awful kings.
Moon and stars gazed in at them,
Wind sang to them lullaby,
Lumbering owls forebore to fly,

[handwritten note: Sleeping together]

→

195 Not a bat flapped to and fro
Round their nest:
Cheek to cheek and breast to breast
Locked together in one nest.

Early in the morning
200 When the first cock crowed his warning,
Neat like bees, as sweet and busy,
Laura rose with Lizzie:
Fetched in honey, milked the cows,
Aired and set to rights the house,
205 Kneaded cakes of whitest wheat,
Cakes for dainty mouths to eat,
Next churned butter, whipped up cream,
Fed their poultry, sat and sewed;
Talked as modest maidens should:
210 Lizzie with an open heart,
Laura in an absent dream,
One content, one sick in part;
One warbling for the mere bright day's delight,
One longing for the night.

215 At length slow evening came:
They went with pitchers to the reedy brook;
Lizzie most placid in her look,
Laura most like a leaping flame.
They drew the gurgling water from its deep.
220 Lizzie plucked purple and rich golden flags,
Then turning homeward said: "The sunset flushes
Those furthest loftiest crags;
Come, Laura, not another maiden lags.
No wilful squirrel wags,
225 The beasts and birds are fast asleep."
But Laura loitered still among the rushes,
And said the bank was steep.

And said the hour was early still,
The dew not fall'n, the wind not chill;
230 Listening ever, but not catching
The customary cry,
"Come buy, come buy,"
With its iterated jingle

———→

Of sugar-baited words:
235 Not for all her watching
Once discerning even one goblin
Racing, whisking, tumbling, hobbling;
Let alone the herds
That used to tramp along the glen,
240 In groups or single,
Of brisk fruit-merchant men.

Till Lizzie urged, "O Laura, come;
I hear the fruit-call, but I dare not look:
You should not loiter longer at this brook:
245 Come with me home.
The stars rise, the moon bends her arc,
Each glow-worm winks her spark,
Let us get home before the night grows dark:
For clouds may gather
250 Though this is summer weather,
Put out the lights and drench us through;
Then if we lost our way what should we do?"

Laura turned cold as stone
To find her sister heard that cry alone,
255 That goblin cry,
"Come buy our fruits, come buy."
Must she then buy no more such dainty fruit?
Must she no more such succous pasture find,
Gone deaf and blind?
260 Her tree of life drooped from the root:
She said not one word in her heart's sore ache:
But peering thro' the dimness, nought discerning,
Trudged home, her pitcher dripping all the way;
So crept to bed, and lay
265 Silent till Lizzie slept;
Then sat up in a passionate yearning,
And gnashed her teeth for baulked desire, and wept
As if her heart would break.

Day after day, night after night,
270 Laura kept watch in vain
In sullen silence of exceeding pain.

$\longrightarrow$

She never caught again the goblin cry,
"Come buy, come buy;"—
She never spied the goblin men
275　Hawking their fruits along the glen:
But when the noon waxed bright
Her hair grew thin and grey;
She dwindled, as the fair full moon doth turn
To swift decay and burn
280　Her fire away.

One day remembering her kernel-stone
She set it by a wall that faced the south;
Dewed it with tears, hoped for a root,
Watched for a waxing shoot,
285　But there came none.
It never saw the sun,
It never felt the trickling moisture run:
While with sunk eyes and faded mouth
She dreamed of melons, as a traveller sees
290　False waves in desert drouth
With shade of leaf-crowned trees,
And burns the thirstier in the sandful breeze.

She no more swept the house,
Tended the fowls or cows,
295　Fetched honey, kneaded cakes of wheat,
Brought water from the brook:
But sat down listless in the chimney-nook
And would not eat.

Tender Lizzie could not bear
300　To watch her sister's cankerous care,
Yet not to share.
She night and morning
Caught the goblins' cry:
"Come buy our orchard fruits,
305　Come buy, come buy:"—
Beside the brook, along the glen,
She heard the tramp of goblin men,
The voice and stir
Poor Laura could not hear;

———→

310 Longed to buy fruit to comfort her,
But feared to pay too dear.
She thought of Jeanie in her grave,
Who should have been a bride;
But who for joys brides hope to have
315 Fell sick and died
In her gay prime,
In earliest winter time,
With the first glazing rime,
With the first snow-fall of crisp winter time.

320 Till Laura dwindling
Seemed knocking at Death's door.
Then Lizzie weighed no more
Better and worse;
But put a silver penny in her purse,
325 Kissed Laura, crossed the heath with clumps of furze
At twilight, halted by the brook:
And for the first time in her life
Began to listen and look.

Laughed every goblin
330 When they spied her peeping:
Came towards her hobbling,
Flying, running, leaping,
Puffing and blowing,
Chuckling, clapping, crowing,
335 Clucking and gobbling,
Mopping and mowing,
Full of airs and graces,
Pulling wry faces,
Demure grimaces,
340 Cat-like and rat-like,
Ratel- and wombat-like,
Snail-paced in a hurry,
Parrot-voiced and whistler,
Helter skelter, hurry skurry,
345 Chattering like magpies,
Fluttering like pigeons,
Gliding like fishes, —

Hugged her and kissed her:
Squeezed and caressed her:
350 Stretched up their dishes,
Panniers,[6] and plates:
"Look at our apples
Russet and dun,
Bob at our cherries,
355 Bite at our peaches,
Citrons and dates,
Grapes for the asking,
Pears red with basking
Out in the sun,
360 Plums on their twigs;
Pluck them and suck them,—
Pomegranates, figs."

"Good folk," said Lizzie,
Mindful of Jeanie:
365 "Give me much and many:"
Held out her apron,
Tossed them her penny.
"Nay, take a seat with us,
Honour and eat with us,"
370 They answered grinning:
"Our feast is but beginning.
Night yet is early,
Warm and dew-pearly,
Wakeful and starry:
375 Such fruits as these
No man can carry;
Half their bloom would fly,
Half their dew would dry,
Half their flavour would pass by.
380 Sit down and feast with us,
Be welcome guest with us,
Cheer you and rest with us."—
"Thank you," said Lizzie: "But one waits
At home alone for me:
385 So without further parleying,
If you will not sell me any

6 baskets.

Of your fruits though much and many,
Give me back my silver penny
I tossed you for a fee." —
390 They began to scratch their pates,
No longer wagging, purring,
But visibly demurring,
Grunting and snarling.
One called her proud,
395 Cross-grained, uncivil;
Their tones waxed loud,
Their looks were evil.
Lashing their tails
They trod and hustled her,
400 Elbowed and jostled her,
Clawed with their nails,
Barking, mewing, hissing, mocking,
Tore her gown and soiled her stocking,
Twitched her hair out by the roots,
405 Stamped upon her tender feet,
Held her hands and squeezed their fruits
Against her mouth to make her eat.

White and golden Lizzie stood,
Like a lily in a flood, —
410 Like a rock of blue-veined stone
Lashed by tides obstreperously, —
Like a beacon left alone
In a hoary roaring sea,
Sending up a golden fire, —
415 Like a fruit-crowned orange-tree
White with blossoms honey-sweet
Sore beset by wasp and bee, —
Like a royal virgin town
Topped with gilded dome and spire
420 Close beleaguered by a fleet
Mad to tug her standard down.

One may lead a horse to water,
Twenty cannot make him drink.
Though the goblins cuffed and caught her,
425 Coaxed and fought her,
Bullied and besought her,

⟶

Scratched her, pinched her black as ink,
Kicked and knocked her,
Mauled and mocked her,
430 Lizzie uttered not a word;
Would not open lip from lip
Lest they should cram a mouthful in:
But laughed in heart to feel the drip
Of juice that syruped all her face,
435 And lodged in dimples of her chin,
And streaked her neck which quaked like curd.
At last the evil people,
Worn out by her resistance,
Flung back her penny, kicked their fruit
440 Along whichever road they took,
Not leaving root or stone or shoot;
Some writhed into the ground,
Some dived into the brook
With ring and ripple,
445 Some scudded on the gale without a sound,
Some vanished in the distance.

In a smart, ache, tingle,
Lizzie went her way;
Knew not was it night or day;
450 Sprang up the bank, tore thro' the furze,
Threaded copse and dingle,
And heard her penny jingle
Bouncing in her purse, —
Its bounce was music to her ear.
455 She ran and ran
As if she feared some goblin man
Dogged her with gibe or curse
Or something worse:
But not one goblin skurried after,
460 Nor was she pricked by fear;
The kind heart made her windy-paced
That urged her home quite out of breath with haste
And inward laughter.

She cried, "Laura," up the garden,
465 "Did you miss me?
Come and kiss me.

→

tried to
force her
to eat

Never mind my bruises,
Hug me, kiss me, suck my juices
Squeezed from goblin fruits for you,
470 Goblin pulp and goblin dew.
Eat me, drink me, love me;
Laura, make much of me;
For your sake I have braved the glen
And had to do with goblin merchant men."

475 Laura started from her chair,
Flung her arms up in the air,
Clutched her hair:
"Lizzie, Lizzie, have you tasted
For my sake the fruit forbidden?
480 Must your light like mine be hidden,
Your young life like mine be wasted,
Undone in mine undoing,
And ruined in my ruin,
Thirsty, cankered, goblin-ridden?"—
485 She clung about her sister,
Kissed and kissed and kissed her:
Tears once again
Refreshed her shrunken eyes,
Dropping like rain
490 After long sultry drouth;
Shaking with anguish fear, and pain,
She kissed and kissed her with a hungry mouth.

Her lips began to scorch,
That juice was wormwood[7] to her tongue,
495 She loathed the feast:
Writhing as one possessed she leaped and sung,
Rent all her robe, and wrung
Her hands in lamentable haste,
And beat her breast.
500 Her locks streamed like the torch
Borne by a racer at full speed,
Or like the mane of horses in their flight,
Or like an eagle when she stems the light
Straight toward the sun,

⟶

7 bitter herb.

505 Or like a caged thing freed,
Or like a flying flag when armies run.

Swift fire spread through her veins, knocked at her heart,
Met the fire smouldering there
And overbore its lesser flame;
510 She gorged on bitterness without a name:
Ah fool, to choose such part
Of soul-consuming care!
Sense failed in the mortal strife:
Like the watch-tower of a town
515 Which an earthquake shatters down,
Like a lightning-stricken mast,
Like a wind-uprooted tree
Spun about,
Like a foam-topped waterspout
520 Cast down headlong in the sea,
She fell at last;
Pleasure past and anguish past,
Is it death or is it life?

Life out of death.
525 That night long Lizzie watched by her,
Counted her pulse's flagging stir,
Felt for her breath,
Held water to her lips, and cooled her face
With tears and fanning leaves.
530 But when the first birds chirped about their eaves,
And early reapers plodded to the place
Of golden sheaves,
And dew-wet grass
Bowed in the morning winds so brisk to pass,
535 And new buds with new day
Opened of cup-like lilies on the stream,
Laura awoke as from a dream,
Laughed in the innocent old way,
Hugged Lizzie but not twice or thrice;
540 Her gleaming locks showed not one thread of grey,
Her breath was sweet as May,
And light danced in her eyes.

Days, weeks, months, years
Afterwards, when both were wives
545 With children of their own;
Their mother-hearts beset with fears,
Their lives bound up in tender lives;
Laura would call the little ones
And tell them of her early prime,
550 Those pleasant days long gone
Of not-returning time:
Would talk about the haunted glen,
The wicked quaint fruit-merchant men,
Their fruits like honey to the throat
555 But poison in the blood
(Men sell not such in any town):
Would tell them how her sister stood
In deadly peril to do her good,
And win the fiery antidote:
560 Then joining hands to little hands
Would bid them cling together, —
"For there is no friend like a sister
In calm or stormy weather;
To cheer one on the tedious way,
565 To fetch one if one goes astray,
To lift one if one totters down,
To strengthen whilst one stands."

(1859)   (1862)

[handwritten note: Lizzie gets antidote and saves Laura]

Emily Dickinson (1830–1886)

Born in Amherst, Massachusetts, where she lived all her life, Emily Dickinson spent her last twenty-five years, those of her greatest poetic creativity, a relative recluse. For several decades after her death she was regarded as a timid hermit. However, recent studies reveal that, while she seldom ventured outside the family home, she read widely in the classics, contemporary philosophy, and particularly the works of major nineteenth-century women poets and novelists. At a time when intellectual activity was considered detrimental to the emotional and physical health of women and their greatest fulfilment was believed to be found in domestic life, Emily Dickinson was a truly radical woman in her attitudes about religion, society, and art. Although she thought, as she said, "New Englandly," her ideas anticipate by nearly a century those of many modern feminists. During her lifetime, only a handful of her more than seventeen hundred poems were published. Today, she is one of the most widely read and studied American writers. None of her poems is long; most are written within a pattern resembling the four-line stanza characteristic of New England hymns, with alternating lines containing 4, 3, 4, and 3 strong beats. Yet within this limitation, Dickinson achieved tremendous variety of poetic effect and complexity of theme. Using dashes to indicate breath pauses, incomplete and inverted syntax, startling images of nature, and homely domestic images, she depicted the individual consciousness questioning itself in relation to other people, society at large, nature, and death.

288

I'm Nobody! Who are you?
Are you — Nobody — Too?
Then there's a pair of us?
Don't tell! they'd advertise — you know!
How dreary — to be — Somebody!
How public — like a Frog —
To tell one's name — the livelong June —
To an admiring Bog!

(c. 1861)   (1891)

303

The Soul selects her own Society —
Then — shuts the Door —
To her divine Majority —
Present no more —

Unmoved — she notes the Chariots — pausing —
At her low Gate —
Unmoved — and Emperor be kneeling
Upon her Mat —

I've known her — from an ample nation —
Choose One —
Then — close the Valves of her attention —
Like Stone —

(c. 1862)   (1890)

328

A Bird came down the Walk —
He did not know I saw —
He bit an Angleworm in halves
And ate the fellow, raw,

5 And then he drank a Dew
From a convenient Grass —
And then hopped sidewise to the Wall
To let a Beetle pass —

He glanced with rapid eyes
10 That hurried all around —
They looked like frightened Beads, I thought —
He stirred his Velvet Head

Like one in danger, Cautious,
I offered him a Crumb
15 And he unrolled his feathers
And rowed him softer home —

Than Oars divide the Ocean,
Too silver for a seam —
Or Butterflies, off Banks of Noon
20 Leap, plashless as they swim.

(c. 1862)   (1891)

465

I heard a Fly buzz — when I died —
The Stillness in the Room
Was like the Stillness in the Air —
Between the Heaves of Storm —

5 The Eyes around — had wrung them dry —
And Breaths were gathering firm

⟶

For that last Onset — when the King
Be witnessed — in the Room —

I willed my Keepsakes — Signed away
10 What portion of me be
Assignable — and then it was
There interposed a Fly —

With Blue — uncertain stumbling Buzz —
Between the light — and me —
15 And then the Windows failed — and then
I could not see to see —

(c. 1862)   (1896)

520

I started Early — Took my Dog —
And visited the Sea —
The Mermaids in the Basement
Came out to look at me —

5 And Frigates[1] — in the Upper Floor
Extended Hempen Hands —
Presuming Me to be a Mouse
Aground — upon the Sands —

But no Man moved Me — till the Tide
10 Went past my simple Shoe —
And past my Apron — and my Belt
And past my Bodice[2] — too —

And made as He would eat me up —
As wholly as a Dew
15 Upon a Dandelion's Sleeve —
And then — I started — too —

1 armed naval vessels.   2 laced garment that fits over a blouse.

And He — He followed — close behind —
I felt His Silver Heel
Upon my Ankle — Then my Shoes
20   Would overflow with Pearl —

Until We met the Solid Town —
No One He seemed to know —
And bowing — with a Mighty look —
At me — The Sea withdrew —

(c. 1862)   (1891)

712

Because I could not stop for Death —
He kindly stopped for me —
The Carriage held but just Ourselves —
And Immortality.

5   We slowly drove — He knew no haste
And I had put away
My labor and my leisure too,
For His Civility —

We passed the School, where Children strove
10   At Recess — in the Ring —
We passed the Fields of Gazing Grain —
We passed the Setting Sun —

Or rather — He passed Us —
The Dews drew quivering and chill —
15   For only Gossamer, my Gown —
My Tippet[1]— only Tulle[2]—

We paused before a House that seemed
A Swelling of the Ground —
The Roof was scarcely visible —
20   The Cornice — in the Ground —

---

1 a covering for the shoulders, like a stole. 2 a fine netting.

Since then —'tis Centuries — and yet
Feels shorter than the Day
I first surmised the Horses' Heads
Were toward Eternity —

(c. 1863)   (1890)

Gerard Manley Hopkins (1844–1889)

Hopkins was born near London and educated at Oxford during a time of violent religious controversy. He converted to Catholicism in 1866, became a Jesuit priest, and spent the remainder of his life serving the order. Hopkins is generally considered one of the most powerful of the religious poets and one of the most daring innovators in poetic technique. Two notions central to his work are what he calls "inscape," the unique quality that distinguishes one thing from every other, and "instress," the response evoked by the perception of inscape. The attempt to capture these elements in his work can be seen in the lyrically powerful "The Windhover." Hopkins was also one of the most effective practitioners of the sonnet during this age, and in the articulation of his struggles with his faith in the "dark" or "terrible" sonnets, including "No worst, there is none," he is typically Victorian.

Pied Beauty[1]

Glory be to God for dappled things —
    For skies of couple-colour as a brinded[2] cow;
       For rose-moles all in stipple[3] upon trout that swim;
Fresh-firecoal chestnut-falls;[4] finches' wings;
5   Landscape plotted and pieced — fold, fallow, and plough;
       And áll trádes, their gear and tackle and trim.

All things counter, original, spare, strange;
    Whatever is fickle, freckled (who knows how?)
      With swift, slow; sweet, sour; adazzle, dim;
10 He fathers-forth whose beauty is past change:
                    Praise him.

(1877)   (1918)

1 having two or more colours; in patches or blotches. 2 streaked. 3 method in painting of applying colour in dots. 4 chestnuts dappling the dark ground like bright coals.

God's Grandeur

The world is charged with the grandeur of God.
   It will flame out, like shining from shook foil;[1]
   It gathers to a greatness, like the ooze of oil
Crushed.[2] Why do men then now not reck his rod?
5 Generations have trod, have trod, have trod;
   And all is seared with trade; bleared, smeared with toil;
   And wears man's smudge and shares man's smell: the soil
Is bare now, nor can foot feel, being shod.

And for all this, nature is never spent;
10 There lives the dearest freshness deep down things;
And though the last lights off the black West went
   Oh, morning, at the brown brink eastward, springs —
Because the Holy Ghost over the bent
   World broods with warm breast and with ah! bright wings.

(1877)   (1917)

The Windhover[1]

TO CHRIST OUR LORD

I caught this morning morning's minion,[2] king-
   dom of daylight's dauphin,[3] dapple-dawn-drawn Falcon, in his riding
   Of the rolling level underneath him steady air, and striding
High there, how he rung upon the rein of a wimpling wing[4]
5 In his ecstasy! then off, off forth on swing,
   As a skate's heel sweeps smooth on a bow-bend: the hurl and gliding
   Rebuffed the big wind. My heart in hiding
Stirred for a bird, — the achieve of, the mastery of the thing!

Brute beauty and valour and act, oh, air, pride, plume, here
10 Buckle![5] AND the fire that breaks from thee then, a billion
Times told lovelier, more dangerous, O my chevalier![6]

---

1 foil leaf or tinsel. 2 like oil crushed out of olives or seeds.
1 small hawk. 2 favourite. 3 name given to the heir to the French throne. 4 in falconry, to ring means to
rise in the air spirally. 5 *buckle* has many possible meanings: fasten, join, enclose, grapple, submit, bend, and
crumple. 6 knight, nobleman, champion.

No wonder of it: shéer plód makes plough down sillion[7]
Shine, and blue-bleak embers, ah my dear,
  Fall, gall themselves, and gash gold-vermilion.

(1877)   (1918)

A.E. Housman   (1859–1936)

Born in Worcestershire and educated at Oxford, Housman failed his final exam-
inations and subsequently worked for ten years as a civil servant before becom-
ing professor of Latin at University College, London. *A Shropshire Lad* (1896),
from which the following selections are taken, initially met with little interest,
but became immensely popular during World War I, probably because of the
recurrent intermingled themes of mutability, pessimism, and patriotism, and the
recurrent theme of doomed youth. Housman's output was limited: he pub-
lished only two small volumes during his lifetime, *A Shropshire Lad* and *Last
Poems* (1922), and another, *More Poems* (1936), appeared after his death.
Housman is important as a link between the Victorian and the modern world,
and he is at his best when he avoids the rather artificial, decadent style that influ-
enced him in his youth and produces the finely crafted, concentrated poems
marked by a vigorous, deceptive simplicity for which he is best known. Revealing
the influence of the classical lyric and the popular ballad, these works skillfully
exploit balance and opposition and frequently close with a pervasive gentle
melancholy undercut by the sudden introduction of irony or bathos.

Loveliest of trees, the cherry now

Loveliest of trees, the cherry now
Is hung with bloom along the bough,
And stands about the woodland ride
Wearing white for Eastertide.

5   Now, of my threescore years and ten,
Twenty will not come again,
And take from seventy springs a score,
It only leaves me fifty more.

7 the ridge between two furrows.

And since to look at things in bloom
10 Fifty springs are little room
About the woodlands I will go
To see the cherry hung with snow.

(1896)

When I was one-and-twenty

When I was one-and-twenty
    I heard a wise man say,
"Give crowns and pounds and guineas
    But not your heart away;
5 Give pearls away and rubies
    But keep your fancy free."
But I was one-and-twenty,
    No use to talk to me.

When I was one-and-twenty
10   I heard him say again,
"The heart out of the bosom
    Was never given in vain;
'Tis paid with sighs a plenty
    And sold for endless rue."
15 And I am two-and-twenty,
    And oh, 'tis true, 'tis true.

(1896)

To an Athlete Dying Young

The time you won your town the race
We chaired you through the market-place;
Man and boy stood cheering by,
And home we brought you shoulder-high.

5 To-day, the road all runners come,
Shoulder-high we bring you home,
And set you at your threshold down,
Townsman of a stiller town.

Smart lad, to slip betimes away
10 From fields where glory does not stay
And early though the laurel[1] grows
It withers quicker than the rose.[2]

Eyes the shady night has shut
Cannot see the record cut,
15 And silence sounds no worse than cheers
After earth has stopped the ears:

Now you will not swell the rout
Of lads that wore their honours out,
Runners whom renown outran
20 And the name died before the man.

So set, before its echoes fade,
The fleet foot on the sill of shade,
And hold to the low lintel up
The still-defended challenge-cup.

25 And round that early-laurelled head
Will flock to gaze the strengthless dead
And find unwithered on its curls
The garland briefer than a girl's.

(1896)

1 symbol of victory, traditionally awarded by the Greeks to the victor in the Pythian Games. 2 symbol of beauty.

Sir Charles G.D. Roberts   (1860–1943)

Credited with creating the first truly Canadian literary form, the realistic animal tale, Charles George Douglas Roberts also played a significant role in the development of Canadian poetry. His first volume, *Orion and Other Poems* (1880), inspired both his cousin, Bliss Carman, and Archibald Lampman, who, together with Duncan Campbell Scott and Roberts, formed the Confederation Poets, a group that consciously sought to create a distinctive Canadian poetry. Born in Douglas, New Brunswick, Roberts worked as an editor and then an English professor, but after 1897 he earned his living by writing prose, living in New York, London, and Europe until his return to Canada in 1925. Paradoxically, his most enduring and universal poems are not the obtrusively moralizing ones in which he deliberately tried to be universal, but the early ones in which he was most regional in subject. These poems show three major influences: his classical training, in the highly organized form and choice of allusions; the English Romantics, especially Wordsworth, in the presentation of sharply detailed landscapes in language that avoids consciously poetic diction; and the Victorian intellectual poets, particularly Matthew Arnold, in the probing for spiritual or philosophical significance. These poems support his claim in "The Poetry of Nature" that "nature-poetry is not mere description of landscape in metrical form, but the expression of one or another of many vital relationships between external nature and 'the deep heart of man.'"

Tantramar[1] Revisited

Summers and summers have come, and gone with the flight of the swallow;
Sunshine and thunder have been, storm, and winter, and frost;
Many and many a sorrow has all but died from remembrance,
Many a dream of joy fall'n in the shadow of pain.
5   Hands of chance and change have marred, or moulded, or broken,
Busy with spirit or flesh, all I most have adored;
Even the bosom of Earth is strewn with heavier shadows, —
Only in these green hills, aslant to the sea, no change!
Here where the road that has climbed from the inland valleys and woodlands,
10   Dips from the hill-tops down, straight to the base of the hills, —
Here, from my vantage-ground, I can see the scattering houses,
Stained with time, set warm in orchards, meadows, and wheat,
Dotting the broad bright slopes outspread to southward and eastward,
Wind-swept all day long, blown by the south-east wind.

---

1 saltwater tidal marshes along the New Brunswick coast of the Bay of Fundy, where Roberts spent his childhood. Minudie (line 25) is across the bay in Nova Scotia.

15 Skirting the sunbright uplands stretches a riband[2] of meadow,
    Shorn of the labouring grass, bulwarked well from the sea,
    Fenced on its seaward border with long clay dikes from the turbid
    Surge and flow of the tides vexing the Westmoreland shores.
    Yonder, toward the left, lie broad the Westmoreland marshes,—
20 Miles on miles they extend, level, and grassy, and dim,
    Clear from the long red sweep of flats to the sky in the distance,
    Save for the outlying heights, green-rampired[3] Cumberland Point;
    Miles on miles outrolled, and the river-channels divide them,—
    Miles on miles of green, barred by the hurtling gusts.

25 Miles on miles beyond the tawny bay is Minudie.
    There are the low blue hills; villages gleam at their feet.
    Nearer a white sail shines across the water, and nearer
    Still are the slim, grey masts of fishing boats dry on the flats.
    Ah, how well I remember those wide red flats, above tide-mark
30 Pale with scurf[4] of the salt, seamed and baked in the sun!
    Well I remember the piles of blocks and ropes, and the net-reels
    Wound with the beaded nets, dripping and dark from the sea!
    Now at this season the nets are unwound; they hang from the rafters
    Over the fresh-stowed hay in upland barns, and the wind
35 Blows all day through the chinks, with the streaks of sunlight, and sways them
    Softly at will; or they lie heaped in the gloom of a loft.

    Now at this season the reels are empty and idle; I see them
    Over the lines of the dikes, over the gossiping grass,
    Now at this season they swing in the long strong wind, thro' the lonesome
40 Golden afternoon, shunned by the foraging gulls.
    Near about sunset the crane will journey homeward above them;
    Round them, under the moon, all the calm night long,
    Winnowing soft grey wings of marsh-owls wander and wander,
    Now to the broad, lit marsh, now to the dusk of the dike.
45 Soon, thro' their dew-wet frames, in the live keen freshness of morning,
    Out of the teeth of the dawn blows back the awakening wind.
    Then, as the blue day mounts, and the low-shot shafts of the sunlight
    Glance from the tide to the shore, gossamers jewelled with dew
    Sparkle and wave, where late sea-spoiling fathoms of drift-net
50 Myriad-meshed, uploomed sombrely over the land.

---

2 ribbon. 3 containing ramparts (protective embankments). 4 scales.

Well I remember it all. The salt, raw scent of the margin;
While, with men at the windlass, groaned each reel, and the net,
Surging in ponderous lengths, uprose and coiled in its station;
Then each man to his home, — well I remember it all!

55   Yet, as I sit and watch, this present peace of the landscape, —
Stranded boats, these reels empty and idle, the hush,
One grey hawk slow-wheeling above yon cluster of haystacks, —
More than the old-time stir this stillness welcomes me home.
Ah, the old-time stir, how once it stung me with rapture, —
60   Old-time sweetness, the winds freighted with honey and salt!
Yet will I stay my steps and not go down to the marshland, —
Muse and recall far off, rather remember than see, —
Lest on too close sight I miss the darling illusion,
Spy at their task even here the hands of chance and change.

(1883)

The Potato Harvest

A high bare field, brown from the plough, and borne
    Aslant from sunset; amber wastes of sky
    Washing the ridge; a clamour of crows that fly
In from the wide flats where the spent tides mourn
5   To yon their rocking roosts in pines wind-torn;
    A line of grey snake-fence that zigzags by
    A pond and cattle; from the homestead nigh
The long deep summonings of the supper horn.

Black on the ridge, against that lonely flush,
10   A cart, and stoop-necked oxen; ranged beside
        Some barrels; and the day-worn harvest-folk,
Here emptying their baskets, jar the hush
    With hollow thunders. Down the dusk hillside
        Lumbers the wain;[1] and day fades out like smoke.

(1886)

1 wagon.

The Winter Fields

Winds here, and sleet, and frost that bites like steel.
　　The low bleak hill rounds under the low sky.
　　Naked of flock and fold the fallows lie,
Thin streaked with meagre drift. The gusts reveal
5　By fits the dim grey snakes of fence, that steal
　　Through the white dusk. The hill-foot poplars sigh,
　　While storm and death with winter trample by,
And the iron fields ring sharp, and blind lights reel.
Yet in the lonely ridges, wrenched with pain,
10　Harsh solitary hillocks, bound and dumb,
Grave glebes[1] close-lipped beneath the scourge and chain,
　　Lurks hid the germ of ecstasy — the sum
Of life that waits on summer, till the rain
　　Whisper in April and the crocus come.

(1890)

The Herring Weir[1]

Back to the green deeps of the outer bay
　　The red and amber currents glide and cringe,
　　Diminishing behind a luminous fringe
Of cream-white surf and wandering wraiths of spray.
5　Stealthily, in the old reluctant way,
　　The red flats are uncovered, mile on mile,
　　To glitter in the sun a golden while.
Far down the flats, a phantom sharply grey,
The herring weir emerges, quick with spoil.
10　Slowly the tide forsakes it. Then draws near,
　　Descending from the farm-house on the height,
A cart, with gaping tubs. The oxen toil
　　Sombrely o'er the level to the weir,
　　And drag a long black trail across the light.

(1893)

1 fields.
1 fence of stakes erected to catch fish.

Archibald Lampman (1861–1899)

Born in 1861 in Morpeth, Canada West (Ontario), Lampman graduated from the University of Toronto in 1882 and spent his working life as a clerk with the Post Office Department, Ottawa. The most accomplished of the Confederation Poets — a group of literary nationalists intent on developing a distinctive Canadian literature — he had a talent for precise observation of nature. Lampman refined his knowledge of nature with walking tours in the country-side and canoe trips into the wilderness with his friend and fellow poet, Duncan Campbell Scott. Not surprisingly, perhaps, his poetry was heavily influenced by the English Romantics, who recorded in poetry their responses to similar excursions. The influence of Keats is especially prominent in Lampman's characteristic device: a detailed description of nature leads to the focus on a solitary observer who begins to "dream," to experience a state of transcendent harmony. It is also evident in his concern for exploiting the musical possibilities of language. Romantic reverie represents only one side of Lampman's poetry, however. He sometimes shows an ambivalence about Canadian nature, presenting it as both beautiful and frightening. In darker poems, he completely replaces the dream of romantic harmony with a vision of modern industrial society as a dehumanizing nightmare.

Heat

From plains that reel to southward, dim,
    The road runs by me white and bare;
Up the steep hill it seems to swim
    Beyond, and melt into the glare.
5   Upward half-way, or it may be
    Nearer the summit, slowly steals
A hay-cart, moving dustily
    With idly clacking wheels.

By his cart's side the wagoner
10   Is slouching slowly at his ease,
Half-hidden in the windless blur
    Of white dust puffing to his knees.
This wagon on the height above,
    From sky to sky on either hand,
15   Is the sole thing that seems to move
    In all the heat-held land.

Beyond me in the fields the sun
　　Soaks in the grass and hath his will;
I count the marguerites one by one;
20　　　Even the buttercups are still.
On the brook yonder not a breath
　　Disturbs the spider or the midge.
The water-bugs draw close beneath
　　The cool gloom of the bridge.

25　Where the far elm-tree shadows flood
　　Dark patches in the burning grass,
The cows, each with her peaceful cud,
　　Lie waiting for the heat to pass.
From somewhere on the slope near by
30　　　Into the pale depth of the noon
A wandering thrush slides leisurely
　　His thin revolving tune.

In intervals of dreams I hear
　　The cricket from the droughty ground;
35　The grasshoppers spin into mine ear
　　A small innumerable sound.
I lift mine eyes sometimes to gaze:
　　The burning sky-line blinds my sight:
The woods far off are blue with haze:
40　　　The hills are drenched in light.

And yet to me not this or that
　　Is always sharp or always sweet;
In the sloped shadow of my hat
　　I lean at rest, and drain the heat;
45　Nay more, I think some blessèd power
　　Hath brought me wandering idly here:
In the full furnace of this hour
　　My thoughts grow keen and clear.

(1888)

In November

With loitering step and quiet eye,
Beneath the low November sky,
I wandered in the woods, and found
A clearing, where the broken ground
5   Was scattered with black stumps and briers,
And the old wreck of forest fires.
It was a bleak and sandy spot,
And, all about, the vacant plot,
Was peopled and inhabited
10 By scores of mulleins[1] long since dead.
A silent and forsaken brood
In that mute opening of the wood,
So shrivelled and so thin they were,
So gray, so haggard, and austere,
15 Not plants at all they seemed to me,
But rather some spare company
Of hermit folk, who long ago,
Wandering in bodies to and fro,
Had chanced upon this lonely way,
20 And rested thus, till death one day
Surprised them at their compline[2] prayer,
And left them standing lifeless there.

There was no sound about the wood
Save the wind's secret stir. I stood
25 Among the mullein-stalks as still
As if myself had grown to be
One of their sombre company,
A body without wish or will.
And as I stood, quite suddenly,
30 Down from a furrow in the sky
The sun shone out a little space
Across that silent sober place,
Over the sand heaps and brown sod,
The mulleins and dead goldenrod,

→

1 tall plants with coarse, woolly leaves and dense spikes of flowers.   2 the last of seven canonical hours; the last service of the day.

35 And passed beyond the thickets gray,
And lit the fallen leaves that lay,
Level and deep within the wood,
A rustling yellow multitude.

All around me the thin light,
40 So sere, so melancholy bright,
Fell like the half-reflected gleam
Or shadow of some former dream;
A moment's golden reverie
Poured out on every plant and tree
45 A semblance of weird joy, or less,
A sort of spectral happiness;
And I, too, standing idly there,
With muffled hands in the chill air,
Felt the warm glow about my feet,
50 And shuddering betwixt cold and heat,
Drew my thoughts closer, like a cloak,
While something in my blood awoke,
A nameless and unnatural cheer,
A pleasure secret and austere.

(1895)

Winter Evening

To-night the very horses springing by
Toss gold from whitened nostrils. In a dream
The streets that narrow to the westward gleam
Like rows of golden palaces; and high
5 From all the crowded chimneys tower and die
A thousand aureoles. Down in the west
The brimming plains beneath the sunset rest,
One burning sea of gold. Soon, soon shall fly
The glorious vision, and the hours shall feel
10 A mightier master; soon from height to height,
With silence and the sharp unpitying stars,
Stern creeping frosts, and winds that touch like steel,
Out of the depth beyond the eastern bars,
Glittering and still shall come the awful night.

(1899)

The City of the End of Things

Beside the pounding cataracts
Of midnight streams unknown to us
'Tis builded in the leafless tracts
And valleys huge of Tartarus.[1]
5   Lurid and lofty and vast it seems;
It hath no rounded name that rings,
But I have heard it called in dreams
The City of the End of Things.

Its roofs and iron towers have grown
10   None knoweth how high within the night,
But in its murky streets far down
A flaming terrible and bright
Shakes all the stalking shadows there,
Across the walls, across the floors,
15   And shifts upon the upper air
From out a thousand furnace doors;
And all the while an awful sound
Keeps roaring on continually,
And crashes in the ceaseless round
20   Of a gigantic harmony.
Through its grim depths re-echoing
And all its weary height of walls,
With measured roar and iron ring,
The inhuman music lifts and falls.
25   Where no thing rests and no man is,
And only fire and night hold sway;
The beat, the thunder and the hiss
Cease not, and change not, night nor day.
And moving at unheard commands,
30   The abysses and vast fires between,
Flit figures that with clanking hands
Obey a hideous routine;
They are not flesh, they are not bone,
They see not with the human eye,

⟶

1 the lowest, gloomiest region of Hades, into which Zeus hurled the Titans and Giants; hell.

35   And from their iron lips is blown
A dreadful and monotonous cry;
And whoso of our mortal race
Should find that city unaware,
Lean Death would smite him face to face,
40   And blanch him with its venomed air:
Or caught by the terrific spell,
Each thread of memory snapt and cut,
His soul would shrivel and its shell
Go rattling like an empty nut.

45   It was not always so, but once,
In days that no man thinks upon,
Fair voices echoed from its stones,
The light above it leaped and shone:
Once there were multitudes of men,
50   That built that city in their pride,
Until its might was made, and then
They withered age by age and died.
But now of that prodigious race,
Three only in an iron tower,
55   Set like carved idols face to face,
Remain the masters of its power;
And at the city gate a fourth,
Gigantic and with dreadful eyes,
Sits looking toward the lightless north,
60   Beyond the reach of memories;
Fast rooted to the lurid floor,
A bulk that never moves a jot,
In his pale body dwells no more,
Or mind or soul, — an idiot!
65   But sometime in the end those three
Shall perish and their hands be still,
And with the master's touch shall flee
Their incommunicable skill.
A stillness absolute as death
70   Along the slacking wheels shall lie,
And, flagging at a single breath,

The fires that moulder out and die.
The roar shall vanish at its height,
And over that tremendous town
75   The silence of eternal night
Shall gather close and settle down.
All its grim grandeur, tower and hall,
Shall be abandoned utterly,
And into rust and dust shall fall
80   From century to century;
Nor ever living thing shall grow,
Nor trunk of tree, nor blade of grass;
No drop shall fall, no wind shall blow,
Nor sound of any foot shall pass:
85   Alone of its accursèd state,
One thing the hand of Time shall spare,
For the grim Idiot at the gate
Is deathless and eternal there.

(1899)

Duncan Campbell Scott (1862–1947)

One of the Confederation Poets, a group inspired by the success of Charles
G.D. Roberts to work toward a distinctly Canadian poetry, Duncan Campbell
Scott often substituted for the pastoral subjects that characterized the work of
his colleagues portraits of the indigenous peoples and of wilderness landscapes.
Born in Ottawa, Scott was a lifelong civil servant who rose to be deputy super-
intendent general in the Department of Indian Affairs. As a consequence of his
duties, which enabled him to travel throughout the Canadian North and West,
he came to believe that the Native peoples were doomed to extinction as sep-
arate peoples, a belief evident in a number of his poems. His experiences also
developed in him a deep feeling for the wilderness, which he described as a
replacement for the church of his youth. Scott was both lyrical and intellec-
tual. He declared in "An Autobiographical Note" that "Everything I write starts
with its rhythmical life..." and that "I value brain power at the bottom of
everything." As a lyric poet, he organized this "rhythmical life" through care-
fully developed metres, rhymes, and repetition; as an intellectual poet, he char-
acteristically exercised "brain power" by organizing poems according to dialectic
oppositions or paired terms.

The Forsaken

I

Once in the winter
Out on a lake
In the heart of the north-land,
Far from the Fort
5   And far from the hunters,
A Chippewa woman
With her sick baby,
Crouched in the last hours
Of a great storm.
10   Frozen and hungry,
She fished through the ice
With a line of the twisted
Bark of the cedar,
And a rabbit-bone hook
15   Polished and barbed;
Fished with the bare hook
All through the wild day,
Fished and caught nothing;
While the young chieftain
20   Tugged at her breasts,
Or slept in the lacings
Of the warm *tikanagan*.[1]
All the lake-surface
Streamed with the hissing
25   Of millions of iceflakes
Hurled by the wind;
Behind her the round
Of a lonely island
Roared like a fire
30   With the voice of the storm
In the deeps of the cedars.
Valiant, unshaken,
She took of her own flesh,

———→

1 cradle-board to which is fastened a moss-bag for carrying an infant.

Baited the fish-hook,
35 Drew in a gray-trout,
Drew in his fellows,
Heaped them beside her,
Dead in the snow.
Valiant, unshaken,
40 She faced the long distance,
Wolf-haunted and lonely,
Sure of her goal
And the life of her dear one:
Tramped for two days,
45 On the third in the morning,
Saw the strong bulk
Of the Fort by the river,
Saw the wood-smoke
Hang soft in the spruces,
50 Heard the keen yelp
Of the ravenous huskies
Fighting for whitefish:
Then she had rest.

II

Years and years after,
55 When she was old and withered,
When her son was an old man
And his children filled with vigour,
They came in their northern tour on the verge of winter,
To an island in a lonely lake.
60 There one night they camped, and on the morrow
Gathered their kettles and birch-bark
Their rabbit-skin robes and their mink-traps,
Launched their canoes and slunk away through the islands,
Left her alone forever,
65 Without a word of farewell,
Because she was old and useless,
Like a paddle broken and warped,
Or a pole that was splintered.

→

Then, without a sigh,
70 Valiant, unshaken,
She smoothed her dark locks under her kerchief,
Composed her shawl in state,
Then folded her hands rigid with sinews and corded with veins,
Folded them across her breasts spent with the nourishing of children,
75 Gazed at the sky past the tops of the cedars,
Saw two spangled nights arise out of the twilight,
Saw two days go by filled with the tranquil sunshine,
Saw, without pain, or dread, or even a moment of longing:
Then on the third great night there came thronging and thronging
80 Millions of snowflakes out of a windless cloud;
They covered her close with a beautiful crystal shroud,
Covered her deep and silent.
But in the frost of the dawn,
Up from the life below,
85 Rose a column of breath
Through a tiny cleft in the snow,
Fragile, delicately drawn,
Wavering with its own weakness,
In the wilderness a sign of the spirit,
90 Persisting still in the sight of the sun
Till day was done.
Then all light was gathered up by the hand of God and hid in His breast,
Then there was born a silence deeper than silence,
Then she had rest.

(1905)

Night Hymns on Lake Nipigon

Here in the midnight, where the dark mainland and island
Shadows mingle in shadow deeper, profounder,
Sing we the hymns of the churches, while the dead water
     Whispers before us.

5 Thunder is travelling slow on the path of the lightning;
One after one the stars and the beaming planets
Look serene in the lake from the edge of the storm-cloud,
     Then have they vanished.

While our canoe, that floats dumb in the bursting thunder,
10 Gathers her voice in the quiet and thrills and whispers,
Presses her prow in the star-gleam, and all her ripple
     Lapses in blackness.

Sing we the sacred ancient hymns of the churches,
Chanted first in old-world nooks of the desert,
15 While in the wild, pellucid Nipigon reaches
     Hunted the savage.

Now have the ages met in the Northern midnight,
And on the lonely, loon-haunted Nipigon reaches
Rises the hymn of triumph and courage and comfort,
20   Adeste Fideles.[1]

Tones that were fashioned when the faith brooded in darkness,
Joined with sonorous vowels in the noble Latin,
Now are married with the long-drawn Ojibwa,
     Uncouth and mournful.

25 Soft with the silver drip of the regular paddles
Falling in rhythm, timed with the liquid, plangent
Sounds from the blades where the whirlpools break and are carried
     Down into darkness;

Each long cadence, flying like a dove from her shelter
30 Deep in the shadow, wheels for a throbbing moment,
Poises in utterance, returning in circles of silver
     To nest in the silence.

1 "O Come All Ye Faithful."

All wild nature stirs with the infinite, tender
Plaint of a bygone age whose soul is eternal,
35   Bound in the lonely phrases that thrill and falter
        Back into quiet.

Back they falter as the deep storm overtakes them,
Whelms them in splendid hollows of booming thunder,
Wraps them in rain, that, sweeping, breaks and on-rushes
40   Ringing like cymbals.

(1905)

William Butler Yeats (1865–1939)

Born and raised in Dublin, Ireland, William Butler Yeats became one of the leaders in the Irish nationalist movement in the late nineteenth and early twentieth centuries, and was influential in the formation of the Irish Literary Society and the Irish National Theatre Company. Many of his poems and plays are based on Irish legends and folklore. Yeats rejected conventional religious beliefs and studied a variety of religious and philosophical systems, out of which he developed his own poetic mythology, published in *A Vision* (1925, revised in 1937). He believed that history was divided into 2000-year cycles. As he implied in "Leda and the Swan," the classical age had begun with the union of the god Zeus (who assumed the form of a swan) and a human being, Leda. The Christian age, which ended the classical, commenced with the union of the Holy Spirit (in the form of a dove) and the Virgin Mary. The period of the Byzantine Empire, between the fifth and fifteenth centuries, represented the Christian age's era of greatest artistic achievement, while the twentieth century marked the final phase of its destruction. Many of the ideas in his system are complex and obscure and are dismissed by some as muddle-headed and foolish; however, it provided him with a number of symbols that, in "The Second Coming," "Sailing to Byzantium," and "Among School Children," are used to present the individual's quest for meaning in the chaotic modern world. In such poems as "Easter 1916," Yeats commented on the tumultuous and often tragic conflicts between the Irish and the British. "Crazy Jane Talks with the Bishop" embodies his belief that great wisdom can be found in the words of old, common, or apparently crazy people.

Easter 1916[1]

I have met them at close of day
Coming with vivid faces
From counter or desk among grey
Eighteenth-century houses.
I have passed with a nod of the head
Or polite meaningless words,
Or have lingered awhile and said
Polite meaningless words,
And thought before I had done
Of a mocking tale or a gibe
To please a companion
Around the fire at the club,
Being certain that they and I
But lived where motley[2] is worn:
All changed, changed utterly:
A terrible beauty is born.

That woman's days were spent
In ignorant good-will,
Her nights in argument
Until her voice grew shrill.
What voice more sweet than hers
When, young and beautiful,
She rode to harriers?[3]
This man had kept a school
And rode our wingèd horse;[4]
This other his helper and friend
Was coming into his force;
He might have won fame in the end,
So sensitive his nature seemed,
So daring and sweet his thought.
This other man I had dreamed
A drunken, vainglorious lout.
He had done most bitter wrong
To some who are near my heart,
Yet I number him in the song;
He, too, has resigned his part

$\longrightarrow$

1 at Easter 1916, Irish nationalists unsuccessfully rebelled against the British government. Many nationalists were executed. 2 many-coloured cloth often used in the clothing of court jesters. 3 i.e., on a hunt with hounds. 4 Pegasus, the winged horse associated with poetry in Greek mythology.

In the casual comedy;
He, too, has been changed in his turn,
Transformed utterly:
40 A terrible beauty is born.

Hearts with one purpose alone
Through summer and winter seem
Enchanted to a stone
To trouble the living stream.
45 The horse that comes from the road,
The rider, the birds that range
From cloud to tumbling cloud,
Minute by minute they change;
A shadow of cloud on the stream
50 Changes minute by minute;
A horse-hoof slides on the brim,
And a horse plashes within it;
The long-legged moor-hens dive,
And hens to moor-cocks call;
55 Minute by minute they live:
The stone's in the midst of all.

Too long a sacrifice
Can make a stone of the heart.
O when may it suffice?
60 That is Heaven's part, our part
To murmur name upon name,
As a mother names her child
When sleep at last has come
On limbs that had run wild.
65 What is it but nightfall?
No, no, not night but death;
Was it needless death after all?
For England may keep faith
For all that is done and said.
70 We know their dream; enough
To know they dreamed and are dead;
And what if excess of love
Bewildered them till they died?
I write it out in a verse —
75 MacDonagh and MacBride

——————→

And Connolly and Pearse[5]
Now and in time to be,
Wherever green is worn,
Are changed, changed utterly:
80 A terrible beauty is born.

(1916)   (1921)

The Second Coming[1]

Turning and turning in the widening gyre[2]
The falcon cannot hear the falconer;
Things fall apart; the centre cannot hold;
Mere anarchy is loosed upon the world,
5 The blood-dimmed tide is loosed, and everywhere
The ceremony of innocence is drowned;
The best lack all conviction, while the worst
Are full of passionate intensity.

Surely some revelation is at hand;
10 Surely the Second Coming is at hand.
The Second Coming! Hardly are those words out
When a vast image out of *Spiritus Mundi*[3]
Troubles my sight; somewhere in sands of the desert
A shape with lion body and the head of a man,
15 A gaze blank and pitiless as the sun,
Is moving its slow thighs, while all about it
Reel shadows of the indignant desert birds.
The darkness drops again; but now I know
That twenty centuries of stony sleep
20 Were vexed to nightmare by a rocking cradle,
And what rough beast, its hour come round at last,
Slouches towards Bethlehem[4] to be born?

(1919)   (1920)

5 four Irish patriots who were executed by the British after the Easter uprising.
1 traditionally, the coming of Jesus Christ on the Day of Judgement. 2 spiral. 3 the Spirit of the Universe.
4 birthplace of Jesus Christ.

Leda and the Swan[1]

A sudden blow: the great wings beating still
Above the staggering girl, her thighs caressed
By the dark webs, her nape caught in his bill,
He holds her helpless breast upon his breast.

5   How can those terrified vague fingers push
The feathered glory from her loosening thighs?
And how can body, laid in that white rush,
But feel the strange heart beating where it lies?

A shudder in the loins engenders there
10 The broken wall, the burning roof and tower[2]
And Agamemnon dead.[3]
                    Being so caught up,
So mastered by the brute blood of the air,
Did she put on his knowledge with his power
Before the indifferent beak could let her drop?

(1923)   (1924)

Sailing to Byzantium[1]

I

That is no country for old men. The young
In one another's arms, birds in the trees
— Those dying generations — at their song,
The salmon-falls, the mackerel-crowded seas,
5   Fish, flesh, or fowl, commend all summer long
Whatever is begotten, born, and dies.
Caught in that sensual music all neglect
Monuments of unageing intellect.

---

1 Zeus, in the form of a swan, raped Leda, a Spartan Queen, who subsequently gave birth to Helen and
Clytemnestra. 2 Helen, the most beautiful woman in the world, married Menelaus, but Paris abducted her,
thus causing the war that ended in the destruction of Troy. 3 Agamemnon, the leader of the Greek forces
attacking Troy, was murdered by Clytemnestra, his wife, when he returned from the Trojan War.
1 Greek city on whose site was built the city of Constantinople (now known as Istanbul), noted for its
exceptional art.

II

An aged man is but a paltry thing,
A tattered coat upon a stick, unless
Soul clap its hands and sing, and louder sing
For every tatter in its mortal dress,
Nor is there singing school but studying
Monuments of its own magnificence;
And therefore I have sailed the seas and come
To the holy city of Byzantium.

III

O sages standing in God's holy fire
As in the gold mosaic of a wall,
Come from the holy fire, perne in a gyre,[2]
And be the singing-masters of my soul.
Consume my heart away; sick with desire
And fastened to a dying animal
It knows not what it is; and gather me
Into the artifice of eternity.

IV

Once out of nature I shall never take
My bodily form from any natural thing,
But such a form as Grecian goldsmiths make
Of hammered gold and gold enamelling
To keep a drowsy Emperor awake;
Or set upon a golden bough to sing
To lords and ladies of Byzantium
Of what is past, or passing, or to come.

(1926)   (1927)

Among School Children

I

I walk through the long schoolroom questioning;
A kind old nun in a white hood replies;

——→

2 spin in a spiral motion.

The children learn to cipher and to sing,
To study reading-books and histories,
5   To cut and sew, be neat in everything
In the best modern way — the children's eyes
In momentary wonder stare upon
A sixty-year-old smiling public man.

II

I dream of a Ledaean[1] body, bent
10   Above a sinking fire, a tale that she
Told of a harsh reproof, or trivial event
That changed some childish day to tragedy —
Told, and it seemed that our two natures blent
Into a sphere from youthful sympathy,
15   Or else, to alter Plato's parable,[2]
Into the yolk and white of the one shell.

III

And thinking of that fit of grief or rage
I look upon one child or t'other there
And wonder if she stood so at that age —
20   For even daughters of the swan can share
Something of every paddler's heritage —
And had that colour upon cheek or hair,
And thereupon my heart is driven wild:
She stands before me as a living child.

IV

25   Her present image floats into the mind —
Did Quattrocento[3] finger fashion it
Hollow of cheek as though it drank the wind
And took a mess of shadows for its meat?
And I though never of Ledaean kind
30   Had pretty plumage once — enough of that,
Better to smile on all that smile, and show
There is a comfortable kind of old scarecrow.

1 like Leda, a beautiful woman in Greek mythology. 2 in this legend, human beings originally had four legs,
four arms, and two faces. This body later split into two. The embrace of love was an attempt to become
reunified. 3 fifteenth century. The term usually refers to Italian painting of the period.

V

What youthful mother, a shape upon her lap
Honey of generation had betrayed,
35 And that must sleep, shriek, struggle to escape
As recollection or the drug decide,
Would think her son, did she but see that shape
With sixty or more winters on its head,
A compensation for the pang of his birth,
40 Or the uncertainty of his setting forth?

VI

Plato thought nature but a spume that plays
Upon a ghostly paradigm of things;
Solider Aristotle played the taws
Upon the bottom of a king of kings;
45 World-famous golden-thighed Pythagoras[4]
Fingered upon a fiddle-stick or strings
What a star sang and careless Muses heard:
Old clothes upon old sticks to scare a bird.

VII

Both nuns and mothers worship images,
50 But those the candles light are not as those
That animate a mother's reveries,
But keep a marble or a bronze repose.
And yet they too break hearts — O Presences
That passion, piety or affection knows,
55 And that all heavenly glory symbolise —
O self-born mockers of man's enterprise;

VIII

Labour is blossoming or dancing where
The body is not bruised to pleasure soul,
Nor beauty born out of its own despair,
60 Nor blear-eyed wisdom out of midnight oil.
O chestnut-tree, great-rooted blossomer,
Are you the leaf, the blossom or the bole?
O body swayed to music, O brightening glance,
How can we know the dancer from the dance?

(1926)   (1927)

4 Plato, Aristotle, and Pythagoras were ancient Greek philosophers.

Crazy Jane Talks with the Bishop

I met the Bishop on the road
And much said he and I.
"Those breasts are flat and fallen now,
Those veins must soon be dry;
5   Live in a heavenly mansion,
Not in some foul sty."

"Fair and foul are near of kin,
And fair needs foul," I cried.
"My friends are gone, but that's a truth
10   Nor grave nor bed denied,
Learned in bodily lowliness
And in the heart's pride.

"A woman can be proud and stiff
When on love intent;
15   But Love has pitched his mansion in
The place of excrement;
For nothing can be sole or whole
That has not been rent."

(1931)   (1932)

Robert Frost (1874–1963)

Though born in California, Robert Frost wrote most of his poetry about life in New England, where his family originated and where he moved at age eleven with his widowed mother. Frost had the ability, rare in modern times, to appeal to both sophisticated and unsophisticated audiences with the same poems, and he eventually became the most popular serious poet of his country. But success did not come easily. He wrote in obscurity until middle age, supporting his family mainly by farming and teaching, and received recognition in his own country only after his first two books, *A Boy's Will* (1913) and *North of Boston* (1914), had been published and praised in England.

Although Frost was learned and intellectual, and taught in various universities after 1915, he preferred to present himself as a rustic sage whose wisdom was derived from common sense and the everyday experiences he explored in his poetry. Despite its wide appeal, this public persona, together with Frost's reliance on traditional forms and his treatment of homely subjects, gives many of his best-known poems the deceptive appearance of slightness, but Frost confronts the darkness and philosophical uncertainty of modern life as honestly as any of his contemporaries, and his work is highly innovative in its use of vernacular speech and conversational rhythms.

After Apple-Picking

My long two-pointed ladder's sticking through a tree
Toward heaven still,
And there's a barrel that I didn't fill
Beside it, and there may be two or three
5   Apples I didn't pick upon some bough.
But I am done with apple-picking now.
Essence of winter sleep is on the night,
The scent of apples: I am drowsing off.
I cannot rub the strangeness from my sight
10   I got from looking through a pane of glass
I skimmed this morning from the drinking trough
And held against the world of hoary grass.
It melted, and I let it fall and break.
But I was well
15   Upon my way to sleep before it fell,
And I could tell
What form my dreaming was about to take.
Magnified apples appear and disappear,
Stem end and blossom end,
20   And every fleck of russet showing clear.
My instep arch not only keeps the ache,
It keeps the pressure of a ladder-round.
I feel the ladder sway as the boughs bend.
And I keep hearing from the cellar bin
25   The rumbling sound
Of load on load of apples coming in.
For I have had too much
Of apple-picking: I am overtired
Of the great harvest I myself desired.
30   There were ten thousand thousand fruit to touch,
Cherish in hand, lift down, and not let fall.
For all
That struck the earth,
No matter if not bruised or spiked with stubble,
35   Went surely to the cider-apple heap
As of no worth.
One can see what will trouble

⎯⎯⎯⟶

This sleep of mine, whatever sleep it is.
Were he not gone,
40   The woodchuck could say whether it's like his
Long sleep, as I describe its coming on,
Or just some human sleep.

(1914)

An Old Man's Winter Night

All out-of-doors looked darkly in at him
Through the thin frost, almost in separate stars,
That gathers on the pane in empty rooms.
What kept his eyes from giving back the gaze
5   Was the lamp tilted near them in his hand.
What kept him from remembering what it was
That brought him to that creaking room was age.
He stood with barrels round him — At a loss.
And having scared the cellar under him
10   In clomping here, he scared it once again
In clomping off; — and scared the outer night,
Which has its sounds, familiar, like the roar
Of trees and crack of branches, common things,
But nothing so like beating on a box.
15   A light he was to no one but himself
Where now he sat, concerned with he knew what,
A quiet light, and then not even that.
He consigned to the moon, such as she was,
So late-arising, to the broken moon
20   As better than the sun in any case
For such a charge, his snow upon the roof,
His icicles along the wall to keep;
And slept. The log that shifted with a jolt
Once in the stove, disturbed him and he shifted,
25   And eased his heavy breathing, but still slept.
One aged man — one man — can't keep a house,
A farm, a countryside, or if he can,
It's thus he does it of a winter night.

(1916)

Stopping by Woods on a Snowy Evening

Whose woods these are I think I know.
His house is in the village though;
He will not see me stopping here
To watch his woods fill up with snow.

5   My little horse must think it queer
To stop without a farmhouse near
Between the woods and frozen lake
The darkest evening of the year.

He gives his harness bells a shake
10   To ask if there is some mistake.
The only other sound's the sweep
Of easy wind and downy flake.

The woods are lovely, dark and deep,
But I have promises to keep,
15   And miles to go before I sleep,
And miles to go before I sleep.

(1923)

Acquainted with the Night

I have been one acquainted with the night.
I have walked out in rain — and back in rain.
I have outwalked the furthest city light.

I have looked down the saddest city lane.
5   I have passed by the watchman on his beat
And dropped my eyes, unwilling to explain.

I have stood still and stopped the sound of feet
When far away an interrupted cry
Came over houses from another street,

10   But not to call me back or say good-by;
     And further still at an unearthly height,
     One luminary clock against the sky

     Proclaimed the time was neither wrong nor right.
     I have been one acquainted with the night.

                                                        (1928)

Design

     I found a dimpled spider, fat and white,
     On a white heal-all,[1] holding up a moth
     Like a white piece of rigid satin cloth —
     Assorted characters of death and blight
5   Mixed ready to begin the morning right,
     Like the ingredients of a witches' broth —
     A snow-drop spider, a flower like a froth,
     And dead wings carried like a paper kite.

     What had that flower to do with being white,
10   The wayside blue and innocent heal-all?
     What brought the kindred spider to that height,
     Then steered the white moth thither in the night?
     What but design of darkness to appall? —
     If design govern in a thing so small.

                                                        (1936)

1 plant (*Prunella vulgaris*, also called woundwort), normally with blue flowers, thought to have healing power.

Wallace Stevens (1879–1955)

Born in Pennsylvania and educated at Harvard and the New York Law School, Wallace Stevens lived most of his adult life in Hartford, Connecticut, where he advanced to the rank of vice-president with the Hartford Accident and Indemnity Company. Although Stevens began writing poetry seriously when at university, he devoted much of his energy to law and business in the years that followed and was forty-four when his first collection of poems, *Harmonium* (1923), was published. From late middle age on, having become financially secure, Stevens devoted himself increasingly to his poetry. Although he is a philosophical poet, much concerned with ideas of order and the relationship between imagination and reality, Stevens is also a master at evoking complex sensuous experience; his poems are distinguished by the originality of their opulent, intricate images and their subtle, deftly controlled rhythms.

Thirteen Ways of Looking at a Blackbird

I

Among twenty snowy mountains,
The only moving thing
Was the eye of the blackbird.

II

I was of three minds,
Like a tree
In which there are three blackbirds.

III

The blackbird whirled in the autumn winds.
It was a small part of the pantomime.

IV

A man and a woman
Are one.
A man and a woman and a blackbird
Are one.

V

I do not know which to prefer,
The beauty of inflections
15   Or the beauty of innuendoes,
The blackbird whistling
Or just after.

VI

Icicles filled the long window
With barbaric glass.
20   The shadow of the blackbird
Crossed it, to and fro.
The mood
Traced in the shadow
An indecipherable cause.

VII

25   O thin men of Haddam,[1]
Why do you imagine golden birds?
Do you not see how the blackbird
Walks around the feet
Of the women about you?

VIII

30   I know noble accents
And lucid, inescapable rhythms;
But I know, too,
That the blackbird is involved
In what I know.

IX

35   When the blackbird flew out of sight,
It marked the edge
Of one of many circles.

1 town in Connecticut.

X

At the sight of blackbirds
Flying in a green light,
40   Even the bawds of euphony
Would cry out sharply.

XI

He rode over Connecticut
In a glass coach.
Once, a fear pierced him,
45   In that he mistook
The shadow of his equipage
For blackbirds.

XII

The river is moving.
The blackbird must be flying.

XIII

50   It was evening all afternoon.
It was snowing
And it was going to snow.
The blackbird sat
In the cedar-limbs.

(1931)

The Idea of Order at Key West

She sang beyond the genius of the sea.
The water never formed to mind or voice,
Like a body wholly body, fluttering
Its empty sleeves; and yet its mimic motion
5   Made constant cry, caused constantly a cry,
That was not ours although we understood,
Inhuman, of the veritable ocean.

The sea was not a mask. No more was she.
The song and water were not medleyed sound
10   Even if what she sang was what she heard,
Since what she sang was uttered word by word.
It may be that in all her phrases stirred
The grinding water and the gasping wind;
But it was she and not the sea we heard.
15   For she was the maker of the song she sang.
The ever-hooded, tragic-gestured sea
Was merely a place by which she walked to sing.
Whose spirit is this? we said, because we knew
It was the spirit that we sought and knew
20   That we should ask this often as she sang.

If it was only the dark voice of the sea
That rose, or even colored by many waves;
If it was only the outer voice of sky
And cloud, of the sunken coral water-walled,
25   However clear, it would have been deep air,
The heaving speech of air, a summer sound
Repeated in a summer without end
And sound alone. But it was more than that,
More even than her voice, and ours, among
30   The meaningless plungings of water and the wind,
Theatrical distances, bronze shadows heaped
On high horizons, mountainous atmospheres
Of sky and sea.
                It was her voice that made
The sky acutest at its vanishing.
35   She measured to the hour its solitude.
She was the single artificer of the world
In which she sang. And when she sang, the sea,
Whatever self it had, became the self
That was her song, for she was the maker. Then we,
40   As we beheld her striding there alone,
Knew that there never was a world for her
Except the one she sang and, singing, made.

Ramon Fernandez,[1] tell me, if you know,
Why, when the singing ended and we turned
45 Toward the town, tell why the glassy lights,
The lights in the fishing boats at anchor there,
As the night descended, tilting in the air,
Mastered the night and portioned out the sea,
Fixing emblazoned zones and fiery poles,
50 Arranging, deepening, enchanting night.
Oh! Blessed rage for order, pale Ramon,
The maker's rage to order words of the sea,
Words of the fragrant portals, dimly-starred,
And of ourselves and of our origins,
55 In ghostlier demarcations, keener sounds.

(1935)

E.J. Pratt (1882–1964)

Edwin John Pratt, son of a Methodist minister, was born in Western Bay, Newfoundland. After graduating from St. John's Methodist College and serving as both a teacher and a preacher in several outport villages, he attended Victoria College, University of Toronto, receiving his B.A. (1911), M.A. (1912), B.D. (1913), and Ph.D. (1917). Although ordained in 1913, Pratt never served as a minister. Instead, he became a member of the Victoria College English Department in 1920. He is best known for his lengthy narratives, such as *The Titanic* (1935), *Brébeuf and His Brethren* (1940), and *Towards the Last Spike* (1952), the latter two of which won Governor General's Awards. Pratt's concern for scientific and technological matters, ranging from evolution to communication, is evident throughout his work. His religious background and ethical ideas are embodied in biblical references and images of individuals sacrificing themselves for the common good or enduring inevitable suffering.

The Shark

He seemed to know the harbour,
So leisurely he swam;
His fin,
Like a piece of sheet-iron,
5 Three-cornered,
And with knife-edge,

---

1 Stevens said he simply made this name up with no actual person in mind.

Stirred not a bubble
As it moved
With its base-line on the water.

10   His body was tubular
And tapered
And smoke-blue,
And as he passed the wharf
He turned,
15   And snapped at a flat-fish
That was dead and floating.
And I saw the flash of a white throat,
And a double row of white teeth,
And eyes of metallic grey,
20   Hard and narrow and slit.

Then out of the harbour,
With that three-cornered fin
Shearing without a bubble the water
Lithely,
25   Leisurely,
He swam —
That strange fish,
Tubular, tapered, smoke-blue,
Part vulture, part wolf,
30   Part neither — for his blood was cold.

(1923)

From Stone to Steel

From stone to bronze, from bronze to steel
Along the road-dust of the sun,
Two revolutions of the wheel
From Java[1] to Geneva[2] run.

5   The snarl Neanderthal[3] is worn
Close to the smiling Aryan[4] lips,
The civil polish of the horn
Gleams from our praying finger tips.

The evolution of desire
10   Has but matured a toxic wine,
Drunk long before its heady fire
Reddened Euphrates or the Rhine.[5]

Between the temple and the cave
The boundary lies tissue-thin:
15   The yearlings still the altars crave
As satisfaction for a sin.

The road goes up, the road goes down —
Let Java or Geneva be —
But whether to the cross or crown,
20   The path lies through Gethsemane.[6]

(1932)

1 the site of the discovery in 1891 of the fossil remains of an early type of human, Pithecanthropus, or, as he was popularly called, "Java Ape Man." 2 a city long identified with advocating humane and reasonable conduct — the Geneva Convention of 1864 codified rules of war, for example — it was chosen as head-quarters for the League of Nations in 1919. 3 cave-dwelling early human of the Upper Pleistocene Age, whose remains were first located in sites in Europe. 4 even before Hitler assumed power in 1933, the term, originally describing a prehistoric group of peoples whose language was presumed to be the basis of most Indo-European languages, was being used to refer to non-Jews of European, especially Nordic, descent. 5 the Euphrates, a major river in southwest Asia, and the Rhine, the principal waterway of Europe, were influential in developing civilizations and were sites of numerous wars. 6 a garden outside the walls of Jerusalem, it was the site of what is known as the agony of Christ: the sorrowing Christ prayed that his coming trials might be removed, yet also resigned himself, saying that God's will, not his own, should prevail. Shortly afterward, Judas betrayed Christ in this garden.

The Truant

"What have you there?" the great Panjandrum[1] said
To the Master of the Revels who had led
A bucking truant with a stiff backbone
Close to the foot of the Almighty's throne.

5   "Right Reverend, most adored,
And forcibly acknowledged Lord
By the keen logic of your two-edged sword!
This creature has presumed to classify
Himself — a biped, rational, six feet high
10 And two feet wide; weighs fourteen stone;[2]
Is guilty of a multitude of sins.
He has abjured his choric origins,
And like an undomesticated slattern,
Walks with tangential step unknown
15 Within the weave of the atomic pattern.
He has developed concepts, grins
Obscenely at your Royal bulletins,
Possesses what he calls a will
Which challenges your power to kill."

20 "What is his pedigree?"

"The base is guaranteed, your Majesty —
Calcium, carbon, phosphorus, vapour
And other fundamentals spun
From the umbilicus of the sun,
25 And yet he says he will not caper
Around your throne, nor toe the rules
For the ballet of the fiery molecules."
"His concepts and denials — scrap them, burn them —
To the chemists with them promptly."
                          "Sire,
30 The stuff is not amenable to fire.
Nothing but their own kind can overturn them.

                            ⟶

1 coined by the English dramatist Samuel Foote (1720–77), this is a mock title for a pompous official of exaggerated importance or power. 2 British unit of weight equal to fourteen pounds or about six kilograms.

The chemists have sent back the same old story —
'With our extreme gelatinous apology,
We beg to inform your Imperial Majesty,
Unto whom be dominion and power and glory,
There still remains that strange precipitate
Which has the quality to resist
Our oldest and most trusted catalyst.
It is a substance we cannot cremate
By temperatures known to our Laboratory.'"

And the great Panjandrum's face grew dark —
"I'll put those chemists to their annual purge,
And I myself shall be the thaumaturge[3]
To find the nature of this fellow's spark.
Come, bring him nearer by yon halter rope:
I'll analyse him with the cosmoscope."

Pulled forward with his neck awry,
The little fellow six feet short,
Aware he was about to die,
Committed grave contempt of court
By answering with a flinchless stare
The Awful Presence seated there.

The ALL HIGH swore until his face was black.
He called him a coprophagite,[4]
A genus *homo*, egomaniac,
Third cousin to the family of worms,
A sporozoan[5] from the ooze of night,
Spawn of a spavined[6] troglodyte:[7]
He swore by all the catalogue of terms
Known since the slang of carboniferous[8] Time.
He said that he could trace him back
To pollywogs and earwigs in the slime.
And in his shrillest tenor he began
Reciting his indictment of the man,
Until he closed upon this capital crime —

⟶

3 worker of miracles or wonders. 4 one who eats dung. 5 class of parasitic protozoans. 6 suffering from spavin, a disease of horses in which the hock joint becomes inflamed; by extension, lame or broken down. 7 cave-dweller. 8 geological period, beginning about 315 million years ago, during which conditions produced a lush growth of vegetation, the remains of which formed the great coal beds.

"You are accused of singing out of key,
(A foul unmitigated dissonance)
Of shuffling in the measures of the dance,
Then walking out with that defiant, free
70 Toss of your head, banging the doors,
Leaving a stench upon the jacinth⁹ floors.
You have fallen like a curse
On the mechanics of my Universe.

"Herewith I measure out your penalty —
75 Hearken while you hear, look while you see:
I send you now upon your homeward route
Where you shall find
Humiliation for your pride of mind.
I shall make deaf the ear, and dim the eye,
80 Put palsy in your touch, make mute
Your speech, intoxicate your cells and dry
Your blood and marrow, shoot
Arthritic needles through your cartilage,
And having parched you with old age,
85 I'll pass you wormwise through the mire;
And when your rebel will
Is mouldered, all desire
Shrivelled, all your concepts broken,
Backward in dust I'll blow you till
90 You join my spiral festival of fire.
Go, Master of the Revels — I have spoken."

And the little genus *homo*, six feet high,
Standing erect, countered with this reply —
"You dumb insouciant invertebrate,
95 You rule a lower than a feudal state —
A realm of flunkey decimals that run,
Return; return and run; again return,
Each group around its little sun,
And every sun a satellite.
100 There they go by day and night,
Nothing to do but run and burn,
Taking turn and turn about,
Light-year in and light-year out,

⟶

9 reddish-orange gem.

Dancing, dancing in quadrillions,
105   Never leaving their pavilions.

"Your astronomical conceit
Of bulk and power is anserine.[10]
Your ignorance so thick,
You did not know your own arithmetic.
110   We flung the graphs about your flying feet;
We measured your diameter —
Merely a line
Of zeros prefaced by an integer.
Before we came
115   You had no name.
You did not know direction or your pace;
We taught you all you ever knew
Of motion, time and space.
We healed you of your vertigo
120   And put you in our kindergarten show,
Perambulated you through prisms, drew
Your mileage through the Milky Way,
Lassoed your comets when they ran astray,
Yoked Leo, Taurus, and your team of Bears[11]
125   To pull our kiddy cars of inverse squares.

"Boast not about your harmony,
Your perfect curves, your rings
Of *pure and endless light*[12] —'Twas we
Who pinned upon your Seraphim[13] their wings,
130   And when your brassy heavens rang
With joy that morning while the planets sang
Their choruses of archangelic lore,
'Twas we who ordered the notes upon their score
Out of our winds and strings.
135   Yes! all your shapely forms
Are ours — parabolas of silver light,
Those blueprints of your spiral stairs
From nadir depth to zenith height,
Coronas, rainbows after storms,

———→

10 goose-like; thus, stupid or foolish. 11 constellations: Leo, the lion; Taurus, the bull; and Ursa Major and Ursa Minor, the big bear and little bear, respectively. 12 phrase from the opening of "The World" (1650) by Henry Vaughan (1621–95):
     I saw eternity the other night
     Like a great ring of pure and endless light.
13 one of the highest orders of angels.

140 Auroras on your eastern tapestries
    And constellations over western seas.

    "And when, one day, grown conscious of your age,
    While pondering an eolith,[14]
    We turned a human page
145 And blotted out a cosmic myth
    With all its baby symbols to explain
    The sunlight in Apollo's eyes,[15]
    Our rising pulses and the birth of pain,
    Fear, and that fern-and-fungus breath
150 Stalking our nostrils to our caves of death —
    That day we learned how to anatomize
    Your body, calibrate your size
    And set a mirror up before your face
    To show you what you really were — a rain
155 Of dull Lucretian atoms[16] crowding space,
    A series of concentric waves which any fool
    Might make by dropping stones within a pool,
    Or an exploding bomb forever in flight
    Bursting like hell through Chaos and Old Night.[17]

160 "You oldest of the hierarchs
    Composed of electronic sparks,
    We grant you speed,
    We grant you power, and fire
    That ends in ash, but we concede
165 To you no pain nor joy nor love nor hate,
    No final tableau of desire,
    No causes won or lost, no free
    Adventure at the outposts — only
    The degradation of your energy[18]
170 When at some late
    Slow number of your dance your sergeant-major Fate

                                                    ⟶

14 roughly shaped tool from the earliest stone age. 15 Apollo, the Greek god of music, poetry, archery,
healing, and prophecy, was often identified with Helios, the sun god, and given the epithet Phoebus
("Shining One"). 16 in *De rerum natura* (*On the Nature of Things*), the Roman poet and philosopher
Lucretius (c. 96–55 B.C.) sought to provide a reasonable explanation for natural phenomena. He argued that,
since nothing can come from nothing, all being has its source in minuscule seeds of matter that rain down
from a void. 17 in *Paradise Lost* (I.541–43), Milton says of the fallen angels:
        ... the universal host up sent
        A shout that tore Hell's concave, and beyond
        Frighted the reign of Chaos and Old Night.
In Milton's schema, Chaos and Old Night represent the first materials of the cosmos. 18 entropy, one of the
concepts of thermodynamics, suggests that the universe must eventually lose all of its energy.

Will catch you blind and groping and will send
You reeling on that long and lonely
Lockstep of your wave-lengths towards your end.

175   "We who have met
With stubborn calm the dawn's hot fusillades;[19]
Who have seen the forehead sweat
Under the tug of pulleys on the joints,
Under the liquidating tally
180   Of the cat-and-truncheon bastinades;[20]
Who have taught our souls to rally
To mountain horns and the sea's rockets
When the needle ran demented through the points;
We who have learned to clench
185   Our fists and raise our lightless sockets
To morning skies after the midnight raids,
Yet cocked our ears to bugles on the barricades,
And in cathedral rubble found a way to quench
A dying thirst within a Galilean valley —[21]
190   No! by the Rood,[22] we will not join your ballet."

(1943)

William Carlos Williams   (1883–1963)

A medical doctor as well as a writer, William Carlos Williams spent most of his life in Rutherford, New Jersey, where he maintained a busy practice as a pediatrician. Williams worked in various genres, producing more than two dozen volumes of poetry, fiction, essays, plays, and autobiography, but he was most influential as a poet. While studying at the University of Pennsylvania, he developed a lasting friendship with Ezra Pound, and through Pound was influenced by imagism, an Anglo-American poetic movement stressing concentration, freedom in form and subject matter, and especially precise, concrete images. Working from imagism, Williams developed a distinctive style of free verse, characterized by careful observation, vivid images, and a reliance on the rhythms and diction of common American speech. Although initially overshadowed by other modernist poets, Williams's influence on American poets since World War II has equalled that of any of his contemporaries.

19 simultaneous discharge of firearms. 20 beatings with whips (cat-o'-nine-tails) and sticks or clubs (truncheons). 21 Galilee was a Roman province in northern Palestine during the time of Christ, who began his ministry there and was sometimes called the Galilean. 22 the cross upon which Christ died.

Tract

I will teach you my townspeople
how to perform a funeral —
for you have it over a troop
of artists —
5   unless one should scour the world —
you have the ground sense necessary.

See! the hearse leads.
I begin with a design for a hearse.
For Christ's sake not black —
10   nor white either — and not polished!
Let it be weathered — like a farm wagon —
with gilt wheels (this could be
applied fresh at small expense)
or no wheels at all:
15   a rough dray to drag over the ground.

Knock the glass out!
My God — glass, my townspeople!
For what purpose? Is it for the dead
to look out or for us to see
20   how well he is housed or to see
the flowers or the lack of them —
or what?
To keep the rain and snow from him?
He will have a heavier rain soon:
25   pebbles and dirt and what not.
Let there be no glass —
and no upholstery, phew!
and no little brass rollers
and small easy wheels on the bottom —
30   my townspeople what are you thinking of?

A rough plain hearse then
with gilt wheels and no top at all.
On this the coffin lies
by its own weight.

                          No wreaths please —
35   especially no hot-house flowers.
     Some common memento is better,
     something he prized and is known by:
     his old clothes — a few books perhaps —
     God knows what! You realize
40   how we are about these things,
     my townspeople —
     something will be found — anything —
     even flowers if he had come to that.
     So much for the hearse.

45   For heaven's sake though see to the driver!
     Take off the silk hat! In fact
     that's no place at all for him
     up there unceremoniously
     dragging our friend out to his own dignity!
50   Bring him down — bring him down!
     Low and inconspicuous! I'd not have him ride
     on the wagon at all — damn him —
     the undertaker's understrapper![1]
     Let him hold the reins
55   and walk at the side
     and inconspicuously too!

     Then briefly as to yourselves:
     Walk behind — as they do in France,
     seventh class, or if you ride
60   Hell take curtains! Go with some show
     of inconvenience; sit openly —
     to the weather as to grief.

     Or do you think you can shut grief in?
     What — from us? We who have perhaps
65   nothing to lose? Share with us
     share with us — it will be money
     in your pockets.
                          Go now
     I think you are ready.

                                                  (1917)

1 subordinate; underling.

———→

The Red Wheelbarrow

so much depends
upon

a red wheel
barrow

5   glazed with rain
water

beside the white
chickens.

(1923)

D.H. Lawrence (1885–1930)

The son of a miner, David Herbert Lawrence was born in Eastwood, Nottinghamshire, and was educated at Nottingham University, where he obtained a teacher's certificate in 1908. He gave up teaching in 1912 after falling in love with Frieda von Richthofen, the wife of one of his former professors. They went to Germany and, after her divorce, married in 1914. Lawrence returned to England during World War I, but he travelled extensively during the rest of his life, living for varying periods in Italy, Ceylon, Australia, the United States, Mexico, and France. Frequently ill, he died of tuberculosis in southern France. Lawrence is one of the twentieth century's greatest novelists, a rebel against conformity whose books were often attacked for their frank treatment of sexuality. His first published works, however, were poems printed in the *English Review* in 1909. Although not as obviously an innovator in his poetry, Lawrence rejected traditional forms, believing that each poem should find its own form. Lawrence celebrated the free expression of emotions as a natural part of human identity; he believed that modern civilization was artificial, that it had separated humanity from nature, and that it sought to repress natural and healthy feelings.

Snake

A snake came to my water-trough
On a hot, hot day, and I in pyjamas for the heat,
To drink there.

In the deep, strange-scented shade of the great dark carob-tree
5   I came down the steps with my pitcher
And must wait, must stand and wait, for there he was at the trough
       before me.

He reached down from a fissure in the earth-wall in the gloom
And trailed his yellow-brown slackness soft-bellied down, over the edge
       of the stone trough
And rested his throat upon the stone bottom,
10   And where the water had dripped from the tap, in a small clearness,
He sipped with his straight mouth,
Softly drank through his straight gums, into his slack long body,
Silently.

Someone was before me at my water-trough,
15   And I, like a second comer, waiting.

He lifted his head from his drinking, as cattle do,
And looked at me vaguely, as drinking cattle do,
And flickered his two-forked tongue from his lips, and mused a moment,
And stooped and drank a little more,
20   Being earth-brown, earth-golden from the burning bowels of the earth
On the day of Sicilian July, with Etna smoking.

The voice of my education said to me
He must be killed,
For in Sicily the black, black snakes are innocent, the gold are venomous.

25   And voices in me said, If you were a man
You would take a stick and break him now, and finish him off.

But must I confess how I liked him,
How glad I was he had come like a guest in quiet, to drink at my water-trough
And depart peaceful, pacified, and thankless,
30   Into the burning bowels of this earth?

Was it cowardice, that I dared not kill him?
Was it perversity, that I longed to talk to him?
Was it humility, to feel so honoured?
I felt so honoured.

35 And yet those voices:
If you were not afraid, you would kill him!

And truly I was afraid, I was most afraid,
But even so, honoured still more
That he should seek my hospitality
40 From out of the dark door of the secret earth.

He drank enough
And lifted his head, dreamily, as one who has drunken,
And flickered his tongue like a forked night on the air, so black,
Seeming to lick his lips,
45 And looked around like a god, unseeing, into the air,
And slowly turned his head,
And slowly, very slowly, as if thrice adream,
Proceeded to draw his slow length curving round
And climb again the broken bank of my wall-face.

50 And as he put his head into that dreadful hole,
And as he slowly drew up, snake-easing his shoulders, and entered farther,
A sort of horror, a sort of protest against his withdrawing into that horrid
    black hole,
Deliberately going into the blackness, and slowly drawing himself after,
Overcame me now his back was turned.

55 I looked round, I put down my pitcher,
I picked up a clumsy log
And threw it at the water-trough with a clatter.

I think it did not hit him,
But suddenly that part of him that was left behind convulsed
    in undignified haste,
60 Writhed like lightning, and was gone
Into the black hole, the earth-lipped fissure in the wall-front,
At which, in the intense still noon, I stared with fascination.

And immediately I regretted it.
I thought how paltry, how vulgar, what a mean act!
65   I despised myself and the voices of my accursed human education.

And I thought of the albatross,[1]
And I wished he would come back, my snake.

For he seemed to me again like a king,
Like a king in exile, uncrowned in the underworld,
70   Now due to be crowned again.

And so, I missed my chance with one of the lords
Of life.
And I have something to expiate;
A pettiness.

(1923)

Ezra Pound (1885–1972)

Ezra Pound was born in Idaho but grew up in Pennsylvania. He specialized in Romance languages and literature at the University of Pennsylvania and received an M.A. in 1906. Considering his native country intellectually oppressive, Pound lived most of the rest of his life in Europe. A leader in the modernist revolution in literature, Pound influenced and assisted dozens of modern writers, including James Joyce, W.B. Yeats, Ernest Hemingway, and T.S. Eliot, whose famous poem "The Waste Land" he edited. Early in his poetic career, he advocated the concentration, free forms, and precise, concrete images of the imagist movement, and while he soon moved away from imagism to write erudite, esoterically allusive poems that all but specialists find daunting, his early insistence on unforced rhythms and clear detail had a pervasive, lasting effect on twentieth-century poetry.

Critical opinion of Pound's own work is divided, partly because it varies in quality and is sometimes extremely difficult, and partly because it reflects his unpopular social and political views. Living in Italy between the world wars and increasingly convinced that art prospered in stable societies with strong leaders, Pound actively supported Italian dictator Benito Mussolini. He became stridently anti-Semitic and attacked the American political and economic system in both writing and radio broadcasts. Charged with treason at the end of World

---

1 see Coleridge's "The Rime of the Ancient Mariner" (page 116), in which the mariner wantonly slays an albatross, which is then hung around his neck as a symbol of his guilt.

War II, he was confined at Pisa and brought to the United States only after his mental condition had deteriorated to the point where he was judged unfit to stand trial. He was confined at St. Elizabeth's Hospital for the criminally insane in Washington until efforts by American writers led to his release in 1958, after which he lived the remainder of his life in Italy.

The River-Merchant's Wife: A Letter[1]

While my hair was still cut straight across my forehead
I played about the front gate, pulling flowers.
You came by on bamboo stilts, playing horse,
You walked about my seat, playing with blue plums.
5   And we went on living in the village of Chokan:[2]
Two small people, without dislike or suspicion.

At fourteen I married My Lord you.
I never laughed, being bashful.
Lowering my head, I looked at the wall.
10   Called to, a thousand times, I never looked back.

At fifteen I stopped scowling,
I desired my dust to be mingled with yours
Forever and forever and forever.
Why should I climb the look out?

15   At sixteen you departed,
You went into far Ku-to-yen,[3] by the river of swirling eddies,
And you have been gone five months.
The monkeys make sorrowful noise overhead.

You dragged your feet when you went out.
20   By the gate now, the moss is grown, the different mosses,
Too deep to clear them away!
The leaves fall early this autumn, in wind.
The paired butterflies are already yellow with August
Over the grass in the West garden;
25   They hurt me. I grow older.
If you are coming down through the narrows of the river Kiang,

———→

1 adapted from a translation of the Chinese poet Li Po (701?–62), called Rihaku in Japanese. 2 suburb of Nanjing, China. 3 island hundreds of miles up the Kiang River from Nanjing.

Please let me know beforehand,
And I will come out to meet you
> As far as Cho-fu-Sa.[4]

(1915)

In a Station of the Metro

The apparition of these faces in the crowd;
Petals on a wet, black bough.

(1916)

Ancient Music[1]

Winter is icummen in,
Lhude sing Goddamm,
Raineth drop and staineth slop,
And how the wind doth ramm!
>   Sing: Goddamm.

5

Skiddeth bus and sloppeth us,
An ague hath my ham.
Freezeth river, turneth liver,
>   Damn you, sing: Goddamm.

10

Goddamm, Goddamm, 'tis why I am, Goddamm.
>   So 'gainst the winter's balm.

Sing goddamm, damm, sing Goddamm,
Sing goddamm, sing goddamm, DAMM.

(1917)

---

4 beach on the Kiang River not far from Ku-to-yen.
1 parody of the medieval lyric "The Cuckoo Song" (see page 27).

T.S. Eliot (1888–1965)

Thomas Stearns Eliot grew up in St. Louis, Missouri, where his grandfather had founded Washington University. His parents were well-to-do; his mother wrote poetry and supported cultural activities. Eliot attended Harvard, from which he received an M.A., the Sorbonne in Paris, and Oxford. After 1914, he lived mainly in England and became a British subject in 1927. While he first made his living as a teacher, then from 1917 to 1925 as a banker, and later as an editor with the British publisher Faber and Faber, Eliot also devoted himself to writing criticism. In his essays, no less than in his poetry, he had an immense influence on the literature of his time.

The development of Eliot's poetry reflects his personal struggle to find meaning and order in an age that seemed to many to deny them. Such early poems as "The Love Song of J. Alfred Prufrock" and "The Waste Land" captured the mood of doubt, the loss of confidence in Western traditions and religion, that followed World War I. *The Four Quartets* and his verse plays, written after his conversion to Anglo-Catholicism in the late 1920s, reflect his personal solutions to this earlier doubt. Despite its changing perspective, however, most of Eliot's poetry, early and late, shows his concern with literary and religious tradition, which is reflected in a wealth of allusions; his interest in symbols, not only as literary devices but as manifestations of culture as well; and his facility for capturing speaking voices. Eliot's achievements were recognized with the Nobel Prize for literature in 1948.

The Love Song of J. Alfred Prufrock

S'io credesse che mia risposta fosse
A persona che mai tornasse al mondo,
Questa fiamma staria senza piu scosse.
Ma perciocche giammai di questo fondo
Non torno vivo alcun, s'i'odo il vero,
Senza tema d'infamia ti rispondo.[1]

Let us go then, you and I,
When the evening is spread out against the sky
Like a patient etherised upon a table;
Let us go, through certain half-deserted streets,
5   The muttering retreats

$\longrightarrow$

---

1 in Dante's *Inferno* XXXVII.61–66, Guido da Montefeltro answers Dante through the tongue of flame that imprisons him: "If I thought I were answering someone who could ever return to the world, this flame would be still; but since no one has returned alive from this depth, if what I hear is true, I respond without fear of ill repute."

Of restless nights in one-night cheap hotels
And sawdust restaurants with oyster-shells:
Streets that follow like a tedious argument
Of insidious intent
10   To lead you to an overwhelming question . . .
Oh, do not ask, "What is it?"
Let us go and make our visit.

In the room the women come and go
Talking of Michelangelo.

15   The yellow fog that rubs its back upon the window-panes,
The yellow smoke that rubs its muzzle on the window-panes
Licked its tongue into the corners of the evening,
Lingered upon the pools that stand in drains,
Let fall upon its back the soot that falls from chimneys,
20   Slipped by the terrace, made a sudden leap,
And seeing that it was a soft October night,
Curled once about the house, and fell asleep.

And indeed there will be time
For the yellow smoke that slides along the street,
25   Rubbing its back upon the window-panes;
There will be time, there will be time
To prepare a face to meet the faces that you meet;
There will be time to murder and create,
And time for all the works and days of hands
30   That lift and drop a question on your plate;
Time for you and time for me,
And time yet for a hundred indecisions,
And for a hundred visions and revisions,
Before the taking of a toast and tea.

35   In the room the women come and go
Talking of Michelangelo.

And indeed there will be time
To wonder, "Do I dare?" and, "Do I dare?"
Time to turn back and descend the stair,
40   With a bald spot in the middle of my hair —
[They will say: "How his hair is growing thin!"]

———→

My morning coat, my collar mounting firmly to the chin,
My necktie rich and modest, but asserted by a simple pin —
[They will say: "But how his arms and legs are thin!"]
45   Do I dare
Disturb the universe?
In a minute there is time
For decisions and revisions which a minute will reverse.

For I have known them all already, known them all —
50   Have known the evenings, mornings, afternoons,
I have measured out my life with coffee spoons;
I know the voices dying with a dying fall
Beneath the music from a farther room.
      So how should I presume?

55   And I have known the eyes already, known them all —
The eyes that fix you in a formulated phrase,
And when I am formulated, sprawling on a pin,
When I am pinned and wriggling on the wall,
Then how should I begin
60   To spit out all the butt-ends of my days and ways?
      And how should I presume?

And I have known the arms already, known them all —
Arms that are braceleted and white and bare
[But in the lamplight, downed with light brown hair!]
65   Is it perfume from a dress
That makes me so digress?
Arms that lie along a table, or wrap about a shawl.
      And should I then presume?
      And how should I begin?

. . . . .

70   Shall I say, I have gone at dusk through narrow streets
And watched the smoke that rises from the pipes
Of lonely men in shirt-sleeves, leaning out of windows?...

I should have been a pair of ragged claws
Scuttling across the floors of silent seas.

. . . . .

75   And the afternoon, the evening, sleeps so peacefully!
Smoothed by long fingers,
Asleep — tired — or it malingers,
Stretched on the floor, here beside you and me.
Should I, after tea and cakes and ices,
80   Have the strength to force the moment to its crisis?
But though I have wept and fasted, wept and prayed,
Though I have seen my head [grown slightly bald] brought in upon a platter,[2]
I am no prophet — and here's no great matter;
I have seen the moment of my greatness flicker,
85   And I have seen the eternal Footman hold my coat, and snicker,
And in short, I was afraid.

And would it have been worth it, after all,
After the cups, the marmalade, the tea,
Among the porcelain, among some talk of you and me,
90   Would it have been worth while,
To have bitten off the matter with a smile,
To have squeezed the universe into a ball
To roll it toward some overwhelming question,
To say: "I am Lazarus, come from the dead,[3]
95   Come back to tell you all, I shall tell you all" —
If one, settling a pillow by her head,
    Should say: "That is not what I meant at all.
    That is not it, at all."

And would it have been worth it, after all,
100   Would it have been worth while,
After the sunsets and the dooryards and the sprinkled streets,
After the novels, after the teacups, after the skirts that trail along the floor —
And this, and so much more? —
It is impossible to say just what I mean!
105   But as if a magic lantern threw the nerves in patterns on a screen:
Would it have been worth while
If one, settling a pillow or throwing off a shawl,
And turning toward the window, should say:
    "That is not it at all,
110   That is not what I meant, at all."

. . . . .

2 the head of John the Baptist was presented on a platter to Queen Herodias (see Matthew 14; Mark 6).
3 Christ raised Lazarus from the dead. See John 11.

No! I am not Prince Hamlet, nor was meant to be;
Am an attendant lord, one that will do
To swell a progress, start a scene or two,
Advise the prince; no doubt, an easy tool,
115   Deferential, glad to be of use,
Politic, cautious, and meticulous;
Full of high sentence, but a bit obtuse;
At times, indeed, almost ridiculous —
Almost, at times, the Fool.

120   I grow old . . . I grow old . . .
I shall wear the bottoms of my trousers rolled.

Shall I part my hair behind? Do I dare to eat a peach?
I shall wear white flannel trousers, and walk upon the beach.
I have heard the mermaids singing, each to each.

125   I do not think that they will sing to me.

I have seen them riding seaward on the waves
Combing the white hair of the waves blown back
When the wind blows the water white and black.

We have lingered in the chambers of the sea
130   By sea-girls wreathed with seaweed red and brown
Till human voices wake us, and we drown.

(1915)

The Hollow Men

Mistah Kurtz — he dead.[1]

A penny for the Old Guy[2]

I

We are the hollow men
We are the stuffed men
Leaning together
Headpiece filled with straw. Alas!
5 Our dried voices, when
We whisper together
Are quiet and meaningless
As wind in dry grass
Or rats' feet over broken glass
10 In our dry cellar

Shape without form, shade without colour,
Paralysed force, gesture without motion;

Those who have crossed
With direct eyes, to death's other Kingdom
15 Remember us — if at all — not as lost
Violent souls, but only
As the hollow men
The stuffed men.

II

Eyes I dare not meet in dreams
20 In death's dream kingdom
These do not appear:
There, the eyes are
Sunlight on a broken column
There, is a tree swinging
25 And voices are
In the wind's singing

$\longrightarrow$

1 in Joseph Conrad's *Heart of Darkness*, Kurtz's European cultural values fail him in the African jungle
and he dies insane. 2 refers to an English children's custom of begging on Guy Fawkes Day (November 5),
the anniversary of the execution of the leading conspirator in the plot to blow up the Houses of Parliament
in 1605.

More distant and more solemn
Than a fading star.

Let me be no nearer
30   In death's dream kingdom
Let me also wear
Such deliberate disguises
Rat's coat, crowskin, crossed staves
In a field
35   Behaving as the wind behaves
No nearer —

Not that final meeting
In the twilight kingdom

III

This is the dead land
40   This is cactus land
Here the stone images
Are raised, here they receive
The supplication of a dead man's hand
Under the twinkle of a fading star.

45   Is it like this
In death's other kingdom
Waking alone
At the hour when we are
Trembling with tenderness
50   Lips that would kiss
Form prayers to broken stone.

IV

The eyes are not here
There are no eyes here
In this valley of dying stars
55   In this hollow valley
This broken jaw of our lost kingdoms

In this last of meeting places
We grope together

———→

And avoid speech
60   Gathered on this beach of the tumid river

Sightless, unless
The eyes reappear
As the perpetual star
Multifoliate rose
65   Of death's twilight kingdom
The hope only
Of empty men.

V

Here we go round the prickly pear
Prickly pear prickly pear
70   *Here we go round the prickly pear*
At five o'clock in the morning.

Between the idea
And the reality
Between the motion
75   And the act
Falls the Shadow
                    For Thine is the Kingdom

Between the conception
And the creation
80   Between the emotion
And the response
Falls the Shadow
                    Life is very long

Between the desire
85   And the spasm
Between the potency
And the existence
Between the essence
And the descent
90   Falls the Shadow
                    For Thine is the Kingdom
For Thine is

                ⟶

Life is
For Thine is the

95   *This is the way the world ends*
This is the way the world ends
This is the way the world ends
Not with a bang but a whimper.

(1925)

Journey of the Magi [1]

"A cold coming we had of it,
Just the worst time of the year
For a journey, and such a long journey:
The ways deep and the weather sharp,
5   The very dead of winter."[2]
And the camels galled, sore-footed, refractory,
Lying down in the melting snow.
There were times we regretted
The summer palaces on slopes, the terraces,
10   And the silken girls bringing sherbet.
Then the camel men cursing and grumbling
And running away, and wanting their liquor and women,
And the night-fires going out, and the lack of shelters,
And the cities hostile and the towns unfriendly
15   And the villages dirty and charging high prices:
A hard time we had of it.
At the end we preferred to travel all night,
Sleeping in snatches,
With the voices singing in our ears, saying
20   That this was all folly.

Then at dawn we came down to a temperate valley,
Wet, below the snow line, smelling of vegetation;
With a running stream and a water-mill beating the darkness,
And three trees on the low sky,

———▶

1 the wise men who brought gifts to the infant Jesus (see Matthew 2).   2 adapted from a Christmas sermon
by Bishop Lancelot Andrewes (1555–1626), who helped prepare the 1611 King James version of the Bible.

25 And an old white horse galloped away in the meadow.
Then we came to a tavern with vine-leaves over the lintel,
Six hands at an open door dicing for pieces of silver,
And feet kicking the empty wine-skins.
But there was no information, and so we continued
30 And arrived at evening, not a moment too soon
Finding the place; it was (you may say) satisfactory.

    All this was a long time ago, I remember,
And I would do it again, but set down
This set down
35 This: were we led all that way for
Birth or Death? There was a Birth, certainly,
We had evidence and no doubt. I had seen birth and death,
But had thought they were different; this Birth was
Hard and bitter agony for us, like Death, our death.
40 We returned to our places, these Kingdoms,
But no longer at ease here, in the old dispensation,
With an alien people clutching their gods.
I should be glad of another death.

                             (1927)

Wilfred Owen (1893–1918)

Although his best poems were written in the year before his death in action during World War I, Wilfred Owen had decided to become a poet while a boy in Shropshire, England. He was critical of conventional religious beliefs before the war and had written many war poems before his 1917 meeting with Siegfried Sassoon; however, the meeting was the catalyst for the creation of the works for which he is now remembered, many of which were included in the libretto of composer Benjamin Britten's *War Requiem* (1962). In the Preface to his *Collected Poems*, Owen stated: "My subject is War, and the pity of War. The Poetry is in the pity." He achieves his startling, moving effects through the sharp contrasts of his language and the careful modulation of rhythms, rhyme schemes, and sound patterns. In "*Dulce et Decorum Est*," the Latin motto, with its conventional notions of glorious, patriotic death, is set against vivid, realistic details of a gas attack. "Anthem for Doomed Youth" juxtaposes the noises of war with the quietness of mourning. In "Strange Meeting," the speaker escapes from the terrors of war into a place marked by the muted sadness of lives ended before their time.

Anthem[1] for Doomed Youth

What passing-bells[2] for these who die as cattle?
   — Only the monstrous anger of the guns.
   Only the stuttering rifles' rapid rattle
Can patter out their hasty orisons.[3]
No mockeries now for them; no prayers nor bells;
   Nor any voice of mourning save the choirs, —
The shrill, demented choirs of wailing shells;
   And bugles calling for them from sad shires.[4]

What candles may be held to speed them all?
   Not in the hands of boys but in their eyes
Shall shine the holy glimmers of goodbyes.
   The pallor of girls' brows shall be their pall;
Their flowers the tenderness of patient minds,
And each slow dusk a drawing-down of blinds.

(1917)   (1920)

Dulce et Decorum Est[1]

Bent double, like old beggars under sacks,
Knock-kneed, coughing like hags, we cursed through sludge,
Till on the haunting flares we turned our backs
And towards our distant rest began to trudge.
Men marched asleep. Many had lost their boots
But limped on, blood-shod. All went lame; all blind;
Drunk with fatigue; deaf even to the hoots
Of tired, outstripped Five-Nines[2] that dropped behind.

Gas! GAS! Quick, boys! — An ecstasy of fumbling,
Fitting the clumsy helmets just in time;
But someone still was yelling out and stumbling,
And flound'ring like a man in fire or lime ...
Dim, through the misty panes and thick green light,
As under a green sea, I saw him drowning.

              ————>

---

1 song of praise. 2 church bells rung to announce a death. 3 prayers. 4 districts, counties.
1 "It is sweet and fitting [to die for one's country]" (Horace *Odes* III.2.13). 2 shells that are 5.9 inches
(or 150 mm) in diameter.

15 In all my dreams, before my helpless sight,
He plunges at me, guttering, choking, drowning.

If in some smothering dreams you too could pace
Behind the wagon that we flung him in,
And watch the white eyes writhing in his face,
20 His hanging face, like a devil's sick of sin;
If you could hear, at every jolt, the blood
Come gargling from the froth-corrupted lungs,
Obscene as cancer, bitter as the cud
Of vile, incurable sores on innocent tongues, —
25 My friend, you would not tell with such high zest
To children ardent for some desperate glory,
The old Lie: Dulce et decorum est
Pro patria mori.

(1917)   (1920)

Strange Meeting

It seemed that out of battle I escaped
Down some profound dull tunnel, long since scooped
Through granites which titanic wars had groined.

Yet also there encumbered sleepers groaned,
5 Too fast in thought or death to be bestirred.
Then, as I probed them, one sprang up, and stared
With piteous recognition in fixed eyes,
Lifting distressful hands, as if to bless.
And by his smile, I knew that sullen hall,
10 By his dead smile I knew we stood in Hell.

With a thousand pains that vision's face was grained;
Yet no blood reached there from the upper ground,
And no guns thumped, or down the flues made moan.
"Strange friend," I said, "here is no cause to mourn,"
15 "None," said that other, "save the undone years,
The hopelessness. Whatever hope is yours,
Was my life also; I went hunting wild
After the wildest beauty in the world,

Which lies not calm in eyes, or braided hair,
20 But mocks the steady running of the hour,
And if it grieves, grieves richlier than here.
For by my glee might many men have laughed,
And of my weeping something had been left,
Which must die now. I mean the truth untold,
25 The pity of war, the pity war distilled.
Now men will go content with what we spoiled,
Or, discontent, boil bloody, and be spilled.
They will be swift with swiftness of the tigress.
None will break ranks, though nations trek from progress.
30 Courage was mine, and I had mystery,
Wisdom was mine, and I had mastery:
To miss the march of this retreating world
Into vain citadels that are not walled.
Then, when much blood had clogged their chariot wheels,
35 I would go up and wash them from sweet wells,
Even with truths that lie too deep for taint.
I would have poured my spirit without stint
But not through wounds; not on the cess of war.
Foreheads of men have bled where no wounds were.

40 "I am the enemy you killed, my friend.
I knew you in this dark: for so you frowned
Yesterday through me as you jabbed and killed.
I parried; but my hands were loath and cold.
Let us sleep now. . . ."

(1918)   (1920)

E.E. Cummings (1894–1962)

Born in Cambridge, Massachusetts, and educated at Harvard, Edward Estlin
Cummings became one of the most unconventional of modern American poets.
Cummings was a successful painter and wrote both fiction and drama, but his
greatest artistic achievement was his poetry. Sometimes lyric, sometimes satir-
ical, Cummings's poetry celebrates spontaneous feeling, individualism, the love
of nature, and erotic love; it attacks institutions, formality, and stuffiness gener-
ally. He has sometimes been criticized for being exhibitionist and overly playful
in his manipulations of diction, syntax, stanzaic forms, and typography, but,
notwithstanding his eccentricities, Cummings was always a careful craftsman and

serious artist. His ardent rebellion against both poetic conventions and what he considered the complacent, middle-class narrowness of his country gave him considerable influence with poets after World War II.

in Just-   spring

in Just-
spring   when the world is mud-
luscious the little
lame balloonman

5   whistles   far   and wee

and eddieandbill come
running from marbles and
piracies and it's
spring

10   when the world is puddle-wonderful

the queer
old balloonman whistles
far   and   wee
and bettyandisbel come dancing

15   from hop-scotch and jump-rope and

it's
spring
and
    the

20   goat-footed

balloonMan   whistles
far
and
wee

(1923)

next to of course god america i

"next to of course god america i
love you land of the pilgrims' and so forth oh
say can you see by the dawn's early my
country 'tis of centuries come and go
and are no more what of it we should worry
in every language even deafanddumb
thy sons acclaim your glorious name by gorry
by jingo by gee by gosh by gum
why talk of beauty what could be more beaut-
iful than these heroic happy dead
who rushed like lions to the roaring slaughter
they did not stop to think they died instead
then shall the voice of liberty be mute?"

He spoke.   And drank rapidly a glass of water

(1926)

l(a

l(a

le
af
fa

ll

s)
one
l

iness

(1958)

F.R. Scott (1899–1985)

The son of Frederick George Scott (1861–1944), an Anglican clergyman and minor poet of the Confederation group, Francis Reginald Scott made remarkable contributions to Canadian life in several areas. Born in Quebec City, he was educated at Bishop's College, Oxford University, where he was a Rhodes Scholar, and McGill University, where he eventually became dean of the law school. As a social reformer, he was active in founding the Co-operative Commonwealth Federation, the forerunner of the New Democratic Party. As a lawyer, he defended civil liberties in several important court cases. As a professor of constitutional law, he promoted the cause of social justice and served as a member of the Royal Commission on Bilingualism and Biculturalism. As a poet and anthologist, he was a leader in the fight against romantic and traditional poetry as outmoded and insincere forms of verse. He began writing while still a student, but his first collection was not published until 1945. His *Collected Poems* (1981) won the Governor General's Award. Often sharply satirical, his poetry is notable for its precision and grace of expression, its unpretentious allusions, and its wit.

The Canadian Authors Meet[1]

Expansive puppets percolate self-unction
Beneath a portrait of the Prince of Wales.[2]
Miss Crotchet's muse has somehow failed to function,
Yet she's a poetess. Beaming, she sails

5 From group to chattering group, with such a dear
Victorian saintliness, as is her fashion,
Greeting the other unknowns with a cheer —
Virgins of sixty who still write of passion.

The air is heavy with Canadian topics,
10 And Carman, Lampman, Roberts, Campbell, Scott,
Are measured for their faith and philanthropics,
Their zeal for God and King, their earnest thought.

The cakes are sweet, but sweeter is the feeling
That one is mixing with the *literati*;[3]

---

1 an earlier version of this poem appeared in the *McGill Fortnightly Review* in April 1927, shortly after Scott had attended a meeting of the Canadian Authors' Association. Scott viewed the CAA as a group smugly content with the clichés and forms of the past and incapable of appreciating or promoting meaningful writing of the present. 2 Edward, Prince of Wales when the poem was written, became King Edward VIII on January 21, 1936, and abdicated on December 11, 1936, in order to marry an American divorcée, Wallis Warfield Simpson. 3 people of letters; the learned.

15   It warms the old, and melts the most congealing.
      Really, it is a most delightful party.

      Shall we go round the mulberry bush, or shall
      We gather at the river, or shall we
      Appoint a Poet Laureate this fall,
20   Or shall we have another cup of tea?

      O Canada, O Canada, Oh can
      A day go by without new authors springing
      To paint the native maple, and to plan
      More ways to set the selfsame welkin[4] ringing?

      (1927)   (1945)

Trans Canada

      Pulled from our ruts by the made-to-order gale
      We sprang upward into a wider prairie
      And dropped Regina below like a pile of bones.[1]

      Sky tumbled upon us in waterfalls,
5   But we were smarter than a Skeena[2] salmon
      And shot our silver body over the lip of air
      To rest in a pool of space
      On the top storey of our adventure.

      A solar peace
10   And a six-way choice.

      Clouds, now, are the solid substance,
      A floor of wool roughed by the wind
      Standing in waves that halt in their fall.
      A still of troughs.

15   The plane, our planet,
      Travels on roads that are not seen or laid
      But sound in instruments on pilots' ears,

————→

4 sky, or vault of heaven; a poetic archaism.
1 because of a huge pile of bones left after buffalo hunts, Regina was originally known as Pile of Bones Creek.
2 the Skeena River, which empties into the Pacific Ocean near Prince Rupert, British Columbia, has been an important salmon fishery for well over a hundred years.

While underneath
The sure wings
20 Are the everlasting arms of science.

Man, the lofty worm, tunnels his latest clay,
And bores his new career.

This frontier, too, is ours.
This everywhere whose life can only be led
25 At the pace of a rocket
Is common to man and man,
And every country below is an I land.

The sun sets on its top shelf,
And stars seem farther from our nearer grasp.

30 I have sat by night beside a cold lake
And touched things smoother than moonlight on still water,
But the moon on this cloud sea is not human,
And here is no shore, no intimacy,
Only the start of space, the road to suns.

(1945)

Laurentian Shield

Hidden in wonder and snow, or sudden with summer,
This land stares at the sun in a huge silence
Endlessly repeating something we cannot hear.
Inarticulate, arctic,
5 Not written on by history, empty as paper,
It leans away from the world with songs in its lakes
Older than love, and lost in the miles.

This waiting is wanting.
It will choose its language
10 When it has chosen its technic,
A tongue to shape the vowels of its productivity.
A language of flesh and of roses.[1]

---

1 line from Stephen Spender's "The Making of a Poem," an essay in which Spender discusses the landscape of an English mining region as a kind of language expressing human thoughts and wishes; Spender argues that humans aspire to "a language of flesh and roses."

Now there are pre-words,
Cabin syllables,
15   Nouns of settlement
Slowly forming, with steel syntax,
The long sentence of its exploitation.

The first cry was the hunter, hungry for fur,
And the digger for gold, nomad, no-man, a particle;
20   Then the bold commands of monopoly, big with machines,
Carving its kingdoms out of the public wealth;
And now the drone of the plane, scouting the ice,
Fills all the emptiness with neighbourhood
And links our future over the vanished pole.

25   But a deeper note is sounding, heard in the mines,
The scattered camps and the mills, a language of life,
And what will be written in the full culture of occupation
Will come, presently, tomorrow,
From millions whose hands can turn this rock into children.

(1954)

For Bryan Priestman

(Drowned while attempting to save a child.)

The child fell, turning slowly with arms outstretched like a doll,
One shrill cry dying under the arches,
And floated away, her time briefer than foam.

Nothing was changed on the summer's day. The birds sang,
5   The busy insects followed their fixed affairs.
Only a Professor of Chemistry, alone on the bridge,
Suddenly awoke from his reverie, into the intense moment,
Saw all the elements of his life compounded for testing,
And plunged with searching hands into his last experiment.
10   This was a formula he had carried from childhood,
That can work but once in the life of a man.
His were the labels of an old laboratory,
And the long glass tubes of the river.

(1954)

Earle Birney (1904–1995)

Born in Calgary, Birney grew up on a farm in the British Columbia interior and in Banff. He studied at British Columbia and Toronto before completing a Ph.D. on Chaucer's irony at the University of Toronto in 1938. He spent most of his academic career at the University of British Columbia. Twice winner of the Governor General's Award, for his first volume, *David and Other Poems* (1942), and for *Now Is Time* (1945), he also wrote two novels, the first of which, *Turvey* (1949), won the Leacock Medal for humour.

Literally and figuratively, Birney was a peripatetic poet. For much of his life he travelled throughout the world, writing poems about his observations. He also journeyed widely through poetic forms, producing everything from poems based on Anglo-Saxon metrics (see "Anglosaxon Street") to concrete poetry mobiles. Not surprisingly, journeys of various kinds are prominent thematic elements in much of his poetry. In fact, Birney saw life itself as a journey, and his poems are "signals out of the loneliness into which all of us are born and in which we die, affirmations of kinship with other wayfarers. . . ."

Vancouver Lights

About me the night   moonless   wimples[1] the mountains
wraps ocean   land   air   and mounting
sucks at the stars   The city   throbbing below
webs the sable peninsula   The golden
5   strands overleap the seajet   by bridge and buoy
vault the shears of the inlet   climb the woods
toward me   falter   and halt   Across to the firefly
haze of a ship on the gulf's erased horizon
roll the lambent spokes of a lighthouse

10   Through the feckless years we have come to the time
when to look on this quilt of lamps is a troubling delight
Welling from Europe's bog   through Africa flowing
and Asia   drowning the lonely lumes[2] on the oceans
tiding up over Halifax   now to this winking
15   outpost comes flooding the primal ink[3]

On this mountain's brutish forehead with terror of space
I stir   of the changeless night and the stark ranges
of nothing   pulsing down from beyond and between

→

1 veils. 2 lights. 3 in *The Cow Jumped Over the Moon* (1972), Birney explains that this stanza describes the spreading of blackouts during World War II.

the fragile planets   We are a spark beleaguered
20   by darkness   this twinkle we make in a corner of emptiness
how shall we utter our fear that the black Experimentress
will never in the range of her microscope find it?   Our Phoebus[4]
himself is a bubble that dries on Her slide   while the Nubian[5]
wears for an evening's whim a necklace of nebulae

25   Yet we must speak   we the unique glowworms
Out of the waters and rocks of our little world
we conjured these flames   hooped these sparks
by our will   From blankness and cold we fashioned stars
to our size   and signalled Aldebaran[6]
30   This must we say   whoever may be to hear us
if murk devour   and none weave again in gossamer:

                              These rays were ours
we made and unmade them   Not the shudder of continents
doused us   the moon's passion   nor crash of comets
35   In the fathomless heat of our dwarfdom   our dream's combustion
we contrived the power   the blast that snuffed us
No one bound Prometheus   Himself he chained
and consumed his own bright liver[7]   O stranger
Plutonian[8]   descendant   or beast in the stretching night —
40   there was light

(1941)   (1942)

Anglosaxon Street

Dawndrizzle ended   dampness steams from
blotching brick and   blank plasterwaste
Faded housepatterns   hoary and finicky
unfold stuttering   stick like a phonograph

5   Here is a ghetto   gotten for goyim[1]
O with care denuded   of nigger and kike

                    ⟶

---

4 Phoebus Apollo, the sun. 5 black native from Nubia, in northeastern Africa. 6 the brightest star in the
constellation Taurus. 7 Prometheus stole fire for mankind, and Zeus punished him by chaining him to a
rock, where every day an eagle ate his liver, which was renewed each night. 8 pertaining to Pluto, god of the
dead, or to the dark lower world where the souls of the dead lived.
1 Gentiles; non-Jews.

No coonsmell rankles   reeks only cellarrot
attar of carexhaust   catcorpse and cookinggrease
Imperial hearts   heave in this haven
10   Cracks across windows   are welded with slogans
There'll Always Be An England   enhances geraniums
and V's for Victory   vanquish the housefly

Ho! with climbing sun   march the bleached beldames
festooned with shopping bags   farded[2] flatarched
15   bigthewed Saxonwives[3]   stepping over buttrivers
waddling back wienerladen   to suckle smallfry

Hoy! with sunslope   shrieking over hydrants
flood from learninghall   the lean fingerlings
Nordic nobblecheeked[4]   not all clean of nose
20   leaping Commandowise   into leprous lanes

What! after whistleblow!   spewed from wheelboat
after daylong doughtiness   dire handplay
in sewertrench or sandpit   come Saxonthegns[5]
Junebrown Jutekings   jawslack for meat

25   Sit after supper   on smeared doorsteps
not humbly swearing   hatedeeds on Huns[6]
profiteers politicians   pacifists Jews

Then by twobit magic   to muse in movie
unlock picturehoard   or lope to alehall
30   soaking bleakly   in beer skittleless

Home again to hotbox   and humid husbandhood
in slumbertrough adding   sleepily to Anglekin
Alongside the lanenooks   carling[7] and leman[8]
caterwaul and clip   careless of Saxonry
35   with moonglow and haste   and a higher heartbeat

Slumbers now slumtrack   unstinks cooling
waiting brief for milkmaid   mornstar and worldrise

(*Toronto 1942*)   (1966)

2 painted, here with cosmetics. 3 the Saxons were one of three Germanic tribes, the others — mentioned
later in the poem — being the Jutes and the Angles, who conquered Britain in the fifth century. 4 ulcerous
or pimpled. 5 a thegn was a freeman who held land by virtue of military service. 6 fierce Asiatic tribe of
nomads who conquered much of eastern and central Europe; a derogatory appellation for Germans during
the two world wars. 7 woman. 8 lover.

Bushed

He invented a rainbow but lightning struck it
shattered it into the lake-lap of a mountain
so big his mind slowed when he looked at it

Yet he built a shack on the shore
5   learned to roast porcupine belly and
wore the quills on his hatband

At first he was out with the dawn
whether it yellowed bright as wood-columbine
or was only a fuzzed moth in a flannel of storm
10   But he found the mountain was clearly alive
sent messages whizzing down every hot morning
boomed proclamations at noon and spread out
a white guard of goat
before falling asleep on its feet at sundown

15   When he tried his eyes on the lake   ospreys
would fall like valkyries[1]
choosing the cut-throat[2]
He took then to waiting
till the night smoke rose from the boil of the sunset

20   But the moon carved unknown totems
out of the lakeshore
owls in the beardusky woods derided him
moosehorned cedars circled his swamps and tossed
their antlers up to the stars
25   then he knew   though the mountain slept   the winds
were shaping its peak to an arrowhead
poised

And now he could only
bar himself in and wait
30   for the great flint to come singing into his heart

(*Wreck Beach 1951*)   (1952)

---

1 in Norse mythology, the Valkyries (Choosers of the Slain) were handmaidens of Odin who hovered over battlefields in order to choose the heroes killed in battle and escort them to Valhalla. 2 this pun points to both the slain warriors awaiting the Valkyries and a kind of large trout found in the Rocky Mountain region.

The Bear on the Delhi Road

Unreal   tall as a myth
by the road the Himalayan bear
is beating the brilliant air
with his crooked arms
5   About him two men   bare
spindly as locusts   leap

One pulls on a ring
in the great soft nose   His mate
flicks   flicks with a stick
10   up at the rolling eyes

They have not led him here
down from the fabulous hills
to this bald alien plain
and the clamorous world   to kill
15   but simply to teach him to dance

They are peaceful both   these spare
men of Kashmir   and the bear
alive is their living   too
If   far on the Delhi way
20   around him galvanic they dance
it is merely to wear   wear
from his shaggy body the tranced
wish forever to stay
only an ambling bear
25   four-footed in berries

It is no more joyous for them
in this hot dust to prance
out of reach of the praying claws
sharpened to paw for ants
30   in the shadows of deodars[1]
It is not easy to free
myth from reality

⟶

---

1 the deodar, or "tree of the gods," is a cedar native to the Western Himalayas.

or rear this fellow up
to lurch   lurch with them
35   in the tranced dancing of men

(*Srinagar 1958/Île des Porquerolles 1959*)   (1962)

W.H. Auden (1907–1973)

Though born in Britain and educated at Oxford, Wystan Hugh Auden lived in
the United States much of the time after 1939 and became an American citizen
in 1946. He began writing poetry in school, revealed a remarkable talent for han-
dling various styles, and established himself as a leader among the younger
poets in Britain while he was still in his twenties. Early in his career, Auden was
influenced by Marxism and was much concerned with satirizing the British
middle class. Later, however, while still showing an ironic bent, his work became
more generally philosophical as it explored the need for meaning in modern life.
Typically less personal and more analytical than most modern poets, Auden
demonstrated an unsurpassed gift for capturing the political and intellectual
temper of the times in which he lived.

     Primarily a poet, Auden also produced a body of non-poetic work, including
travel literature, philosophical writings, plays, and criticism, that is impressive
both in its extent and its variety.

The Unknown Citizen

(*To JS/07/M/378*
This Marble Monument
Is Erected by the State)

He was found by the Bureau of Statistics to be
One against whom there was no official complaint,
And all the reports on his conduct agree
That, in the modern sense of an old-fashioned word, he was a saint,
5   For in everything he did he served the Greater Community.
Except for the War till the day he retired
He worked in a factory and never got fired,
But satisfied his employers, Fudge Motors Inc.
Yet he wasn't a scab or odd in his views,
10   For his Union reports that he paid his dues,

→

(Our report on his Union shows it was sound)
And our Social Psychology workers found
That he was popular with his mates and liked a drink.
The Press are convinced that he bought a paper every day
15   And that his reactions to advertisements were normal in every way.
Policies taken out in his name prove that he was fully insured,
And his Health-card shows he was once in hospital but left it cured.
Both Producers Research and High-Grade Living declare
He was fully sensible to the advantages of the Instalment Plan
20   And had everything necessary to the Modern Man,
A phonograph, a radio, a car and a frigidaire.
Our researchers into Public Opinion are content
That he held the proper opinions for the time of year;
When there was peace, he was for peace; when there was war, he went.
25   He was married and added five children to the population,
Which our Eugenist says was the right number for a parent of his generation,
And our teachers report that he never interfered with their education.
Was he free? Was he happy? The question is absurd:
Had anything been wrong, we should certainly have heard.

(1939)

In Memory of W.B. Yeats

(D. Jan. 1939)

I

He disappeared in the dead of winter:
The brooks were frozen, the airports almost deserted,
And snow disfigured the public statues;
The mercury sank in the mouth of the dying day.
5   What instruments we have agree
The day of his death was a dark cold day.

Far from his illness
The wolves ran on through the evergreen forests,
The peasant river was untempted by the fashionable quays;
10   By mourning tongues
The death of the poet was kept from his poems.

But for him it was his last afternoon as himself,
An afternoon of nurses and rumours;
The provinces of his body revolted,
15   The squares of his mind were empty,
Silence invaded the suburbs,
The current of his feeling failed; he became his admirers.

Now he is scattered among a hundred cities
And wholly given over to unfamiliar affections,
20   To find his happiness in another kind of wood
And be punished under a foreign code of conscience.
The words of a dead man
Are modified in the guts of the living.

But in the importance and noise of to-morrow
25   When the brokers are roaring like beasts on the floor of the Bourse,[1]
And the poor have the sufferings to which they are fairly accustomed,
And each in the cell of himself is almost convinced of his freedom,
A few thousand will think of this day
As one thinks of a day when one did something slightly unusual.
30   What instruments we have agree
The day of his death was a dark cold day.

II

You were silly like us; your gift survived it all:
The parish of rich women, physical decay,
Yourself. Mad Ireland hurt you into poetry.
35   Now Ireland has her madness and her weather still,
For poetry makes nothing happen: it survives
In the valley of its making where executives
Would never want to tamper, flows on south
From ranches of isolation and the busy griefs,
40   Raw towns that we believe and die in; it survives,
A way of happening, a mouth.

III

Earth, receive an honoured guest:
William Yeats is laid to rest.
Let the Irish vessel lie
45   Emptied of its poetry.[2]

1 French Stock Exchange. 2 in the original version written in 1939, Auden included three more stanzas here
in which Time, while indifferent to other gifts and virtues, is said to pardon the failings of those who write well.

In the nightmare of the dark
All the dogs of Europe bark,
And the living nations wait,
Each sequestered in its hate;

50 Intellectual disgrace
Stares from every human face,
And the seas of pity lie
Locked and frozen in each eye.

Follow, poet, follow right
55 To the bottom of the night,
With your unconstraining voice
Still persuade us to rejoice;

With the farming of a verse
Make a vineyard of the curse,
60 Sing of human unsuccess
In a rapture of distress;

In the deserts of the heart
Let the healing fountain start,
In the prison of his days
65 Teach the free man how to praise.

(1939)   (1966)

Musée des Beaux Arts [1]

About suffering they were never wrong,
The Old Masters: how well they understood
Its human position; how it takes place
While someone else is eating or opening a window or just walking dully along;
5 How, when the aged are reverently, passionately waiting
For the miraculous birth, there always must be
Children who did not specially want it to happen, skating
On a pond at the edge of the wood:

1 refers to the Museum of Fine Arts in Brussels, Belgium, where *The Fall of Icarus*, a painting by Flemish painter Pieter Brueghel the Elder (c. 1525–69), still hangs.

They never forgot
10   That even the dreadful martyrdom must run its course
Anyhow in a corner, some untidy spot
Where the dogs go on with their doggy life and the torturer's horse
Scratches its innocent behind on a tree.

In Brueghel's *Icarus*,[2] for instance: how everything turns away
15   Quite leisurely from the disaster; the ploughman may
Have heard the splash, the forsaken cry,
But for him it was not an important failure; the sun shone
As it had to on the white legs disappearing into the green
Water; and the expensive delicate ship that must have seen
20   Something amazing, a boy falling out of the sky,
Had somewhere to get to and sailed calmly on.

(1940)

Theodore Roethke   (1908–1963)

Theodore Roethke's family operated greenhouses in Saginaw, Michigan, and, growing up surrounded by plants, he developed the almost mystical sympathy with primitive life that characterized his early nature lyrics. He received an M.A. from the University of Michigan, did graduate work at Harvard, and devoted his working life to college teaching as well as writing poetry.

During much of his adult life, Roethke suffered from alcoholism and mental illness, which caused him to experience alternating bouts of manic energy and depression. He managed to turn these problems to poetic advantage, however, by exploring his changing mental states as poetic journeys through interior psychic landscapes.

Root Cellar

Nothing would sleep in that cellar, dank as a ditch,
Bulbs broke out of boxes hunting for chinks in the dark,
Shoots dangled and drooped,
Lolling obscenely from mildewed crates,
5   Hung down long yellow evil necks, like tropical snakes.

———→

2 in Greek myth, the skilled craftsman Daedalus made wings of wax and feathers in order to escape with Icarus, his son, from the Cretan labyrinth, which he himself had designed. When Icarus flew too near the sun, the wax melted and he fell into the sea.

And what a congress of stinks! —
Roots ripe as old bait,
Pulpy stems, rank, silo-rich,
Leaf-mold, manure, lime, piled against slippery planks.
10 Nothing would give up life:
Even the dirt kept breathing a small breath.

(1948)

My Papa's Waltz

The whiskey on your breath
Could make a small boy dizzy;
But I hung on like death:
Such waltzing was not easy.

5 We romped until the pans
Slid from the kitchen shelf;
My mother's countenance
Could not unfrown itself.

The hand that held my wrist
10 Was battered on one knuckle;
At every step you missed
My right ear scraped a buckle.

You beat time on my head
With a palm caked hard by dirt,
15 Then waltzed me off to bed
Still clinging to your shirt.

(1948)

The Waking

I wake to sleep, and take my waking slow.
I feel my fate in what I cannot fear.
I learn by going where I have to go.

We think by feeling. What is there to know?
5   I hear my being dance from ear to ear.
I wake to sleep, and take my waking slow.

Of those so close beside me, which are you?
God bless the Ground! I shall walk softly there,
And learn by going where I have to go.

10   Light takes the Tree; but who can tell us how?
The lowly worm climbs up a winding stair;
I wake to sleep, and take my waking slow.

Great Nature has another thing to do
To you and me; so take the lively air,
15   And, lovely, learn by going where to go.

This shaking keeps me steady. I should know.
What falls away is always. And is near.
I wake to sleep, and take my waking slow.
I learn by going where I have to go.

(1953)

A.M. Klein   (1909–1972)

Abraham Moses Klein was born in Ratno, Ukraine, and came to Montreal with his parents in 1910. After receiving a B.A. from McGill University in 1930, he studied law at the Université de Montréal and was admitted to the bar in 1933: A mental breakdown and several suicide attempts forced his retirement in 1956. Klein became reclusive and completely abandoned all writing, but he had already made a permanent literary contribution as one of the leading figures in the development of modern poetry in Canada.

Jewish themes dominate Klein's writing: his first book, *Hath Not a Jew...* (1940), celebrates the rich heritage and customs of the Jewish people, and much of his later work treats Jewish suffering. *The Rocking Chair* (1948), winner of the Governor General's Award for poetry, contained poems about Quebec, as well as his finest work, "Portrait of the Poet as Landscape." He returned to Jewish themes in his complex visionary novel, *The Second Scroll* (1951). Klein's poetry is both intellectual and witty; it is characterized by learned allusions, metaphors, puns, archaisms, and words derived from several languages.

Heirloom

My father bequeathed me no wide estates;
No keys and ledgers were my heritage;
Only some holy books with *yahrzeit* dates[1]
Writ mournfully upon a blank front page —

5   Books of the Baal Shem Tov,[2] and of his wonders;
Pamphlets upon the devil and his crew;
Prayers against road demons, witches, thunders;
And sundry other tomes for a good Jew.

Beautiful: though no pictures on them, save
10   The scorpion crawling on a printed track;
The Virgin floating on a scriptural wave,
Square letters twinkling in the Zodiac.[3]

The snuff left on this page, now brown and old,
The tallow stains of midnight liturgy —
15   These are my coat of arms, and these unfold
My noble lineage, my proud ancestry!

And my tears, too, have stained this heirloomed ground,
When reading in these treatises some weird
Miracle, I turned a leaf and found
20   A white hair fallen from my father's beard.

(1940)

1 anniversary dates of the death of ancestors. 2 the eighteenth-century rabbi who founded Hasidism, a
Jewish movement that emphasizes communion with God through joyful prayer, encourages religious expres-
sion in song and dance, and values the experience of the natural world and a simple delight in service to
God more than the legal dialectic of traditional study of the Torah. 3 in a letter to A.J.M. Smith dated
January 21, 1943, Klein explained that "Hebrew prayer books are never illustrated. The only drawings that
appear in the liturgy are the signs of the Zodiac illustrating the prayers for rain and fertility."

Portrait of the Poet as Landscape

i

Not an editorial-writer, bereaved with bartlett,[1]
mourns him, the shelved Lycidas.[2]
No actress squeezes a glycerine[3] tear for him.
The radio broadcast lets his passing pass.
5 And with the police, no record. Nobody, it appears,
either under his real name or his alias,
missed him enough to report.

It is possible that he is dead, and not discovered.
It is possible that he can be found some place
10 in a narrow closet, like the corpse in a detective story,
standing, his eyes staring, and ready to fall on his face.
It is also possible that he is alive
and amnesiac, or mad, or in retired disgrace,
or beyond recognition lost in love.

15 We are sure only that from our real society
he has disappeared; he simply does not count,
except in the pullulation[4] of vital statistics —
somebody's vote, perhaps, an anonymous taunt
of the Gallup poll, a dot in a government table —
20 but not felt, and certainly far from eminent —
in a shouting mob, somebody's sigh.

O, he who unrolled our culture from his scroll —
the prince's quote, the rostrum-rounding roar —
who under one name made articulate
25 heaven, and under another the seven-circled air,[5]
is, if he is at all, a number, an x,
a Mr. Smith in a hotel register, —
incognito, lost, lacunal.[6]

1 *Familiar Quotations*, first published in 1855 by John Bartlett and frequently updated. 2 "Lycidas" (1638),
a pastoral elegy by John Milton, mourns the drowning of Edward King, a young poet (see page 54).
3 used to simulate tears on stage. 4 teeming; rapid sprouting or breeding. 5 before Nicolaus Copernicus
(1473–1543), people believed that the earth was the fixed centre of the universe and that it was surrounded
by seven concentric circles. 6 a lacuna is a blank space or missing portion.

ii

The truth is he's not dead, but only ignored —
30   like the mirroring lenses forgotten on a brow
that shine with the guilt of their unnoticed world.
The truth is he lives among neighbours, who, though they will allow
him a passable fellow, think him eccentric, not solid,
a type that one can forgive, and for that matter, forgo.

35   Himself he has his moods, just like a poet.
Sometimes, depressed to nadir,[7] he will think all lost,
will see himself as throwback, relict,[8] freak,
his mother's miscarriage, his great-grandfather's ghost,
and he will curse his quintuplet senses, and their tutors
40   in whom he put, as he should not have put, his trust.

Then he will remember his travels over that body —
the torso verb, the beautiful face of the noun,
and all those shaped and warm auxiliaries!
A first love it was, the recognition of his own.
45   Dear limbs adverbial, complexion of adjective,
dimple and dip of conjugation!

And then remember how this made a change in him
affecting for always the glow and growth of his being;
how suddenly was aware of the air, like shaken tinfoil,[9]
50   of the patents of nature, the shock of belated seeing,
the loneliness peering from the eyes of crowds;
the integers of thought; the cube-roots of feeling.

Thus, zoomed to zenith, sometimes he hopes again,
and sees himself as a character, with a rehearsed role:
55   the Count of Monte Cristo,[10] come for his revenges;
the unsuspecting heir, with papers; the risen soul;
or the chloroformed prince awakening from his flowers;
or — deflated again — the convict on parole.

7 the lowest point; the point opposite the zenith. 8 plant or animal surviving from a previous age. 9 see line
2 of "God's Grandeur," by Gerard Manley Hopkins (page 214). 10 in *The Count of Monte Cristo* (1844–45),
by Alexandre Dumas *père* (1802–70), Edmond Dantes elaborately plots the ruin of those whose false accusa-
tions led to his prolonged imprisonment.

iii

He is alone; yet not completely alone.
60 Pins on a map of a colour similar to his,
each city has one, sometimes more than one;
here, caretakers of art, in colleges;
in offices, there, with arm-bands, and green-shaded;
and there, pounding their catalogued beats in libraries,—

65 everywhere menial, a shadow's shadow.
And always for their egos — their outmoded art.
Thus, having lost the bevel[11] in the ear,
they know neither up nor down, mistake the part
for the whole, curl themselves in a comma,
70 talk technics, make a colon their eyes. They distort —
such is the pain of their frustration — truth
to something convolute and cerebral.
How they do fear the slap of the flat of the platitude!
Now Pavlov's victims[12] their mouths water at bell,
75 the platter empty.
                    See they set twenty-one jewels
into their watches; the time they do not tell!

Some, patagonian[13] in their own esteem,
and longing for the multiplying word,
join party and wear pins, now have a message,
80 an ear, and the convention-hall's regard.
Upon the knees of ventriloquists, they own,
of their dandled[14] brightness, only the paint and board.

And some go mystical, and some go mad.
One stares at a mirror all day long, as if
85 to recognize himself; another courts
angels,— for here he does not fear rebuff;
and a third, alone, and sick with sex, and rapt,
doodles him symbols convex and concave.

11 instrument for determining angles; thus, the sense of balance. 12 Ivan Petrovich Pavlov (1849–1936), a
Russian physiologist, studied conditioned reflexes by ringing a bell when he provided food to dogs. Later,
even if he did not serve them food, the dogs salivated when he rang the bell. 13 the natives of Patagonia, at
the extreme southern tip of South America, were reputed to be the tallest people in the world; figuratively,
patagonian means gigantic. 14 to be moved up and down on one's knee, as with a child.

O schizoid solitudes! O purities
90   curdling upon themselves! Who live for themselves,
or for each other, but for nobody else;
desire affection, private and public loves;
are friendly, and then quarrel and surmise
the secret perversions of each other's lives.

iv

95   He suspects that something has happened, a law
been passed, a nightmare ordered. Set apart,
he finds himself, with special haircut and dress,
as on a reservation. Introvert.
He does not understand this; sad conjecture
100   muscles and palls thrombotic on his heart.

He thinks an impostor, having studied his personal biography,
his gestures, his moods, now has come forward to pose
in the shivering vacuums his absence leaves.
Wigged with his laurel, that other, and faked with his face,
105   he pats the heads of his children, pecks his wife,
and is at home, and slippered, in his house.

So he guesses at the impertinent silhouette
that talks to his phone-piece and slits open his mail.
Is it the local tycoon who for a hobby
110   plays poet, he so epical in steel?
The orator, making a pause? Or is that man
he who blows his flash of brass in the jittering hall?

Or is he cuckolded by the troubadour
rich and successful out of celluloid?
115   Or by the don who unrhymes atoms? Or
the chemist death built up? Pride, lost impostor'd pride,
it is another, another, whoever he is,
who rides where he should ride.

v

Fame, the adrenalin:[15] to be talked about;
120   to be a verb; to be introduced as *The*:
to smile with endorsement from slick paper; make
caprices anecdotal; to nod to the world; to see
one's name like a song upon the marquees played;
to be forgotten with embarrassment; to be —
125   to be.

It has its attractions, but is not the thing;
nor is it the ape mimesis[16] who speaks from the tree
ancestral; nor the merkin[17] joy . . .
Rather it is stark infelicity
130   which stirs him from his sleep, undressed, asleep
to walk upon roofs and window-sills and defy
the gape of gravity.

vi

Therefore he seeds illusions. Look, he is
the nth Adam taking a green inventory
135   in world[18] but scarcely uttered, naming, praising,
the flowering fiats in the meadow, the
syllabled fur, stars aspirate, the pollen
whose sweet collusion sounds eternally.
For to praise

140   the world — he, solitary man — is breath
to him. Until it has been praised, that part
has not been. Item by exciting item —
air to his lungs, and pressured blood to his heart —
they are pulsated, and breathed, until they map,
145   not the world's, but his own body's chart!

And now in imagination he has climbed
another planet, the better to look
with single camera view upon this earth —
its total scope, and each afflated[19] tick,
150   its talk, its trick, its tracklessness — and this,
this, he would like to write down in a book!

15 Milton's "Lycidas" also argues about a poet's motivation, first declaring that "Fame is the spur" (line 70) and then rejecting this notion. 16 imitation. 17 false hairpiece for the female genitalia. 18 in Genesis 2:19–20, Adam names the animals. 19 inspired.

To find a new function for the *déclassé*[20] craft
archaic like the fletcher's;[21] to make a new thing;
to say the word that will become sixth sense;
155   perhaps by necessity and indirection bring
new forms to life, anonymously, new creeds —
O, somehow pay back the daily larcenies of the lung!

These are not mean ambitions. It is already something
merely to entertain them. Meanwhile, he
160   makes of his status as zero a rich garland,
a halo of his anonymity,
and lives alone, and in his secret shines
like phosphorus. At the bottom of the sea.

(1948)

Dorothy Livesay (1909–1996)

Dorothy Livesay's poetry developed through a number of distinct phases. Born in Winnipeg, Livesay began her career while an undergraduate at the University of Toronto. Thematically, her first book, *Green Pitcher* (1928), displayed her sensitivity to nature and its relationship to people; technically, it showed the influence of the imagists. After studying at the Sorbonne and returning to Toronto for a degree in social work, she joined the Communist Party and was active as an organizer. Her poetry during the Depression and war years was dominated by political issues and her concern for workers' rights. Two collections of her leftist poetry won the Governor General's Award — *Day and Night* (1944) and *Poems for People* (1947). Livesay served as a teacher in Zambia (1960–63) and earned her M.Ed. at the University of British Columbia in 1964. After this, her career entered a new phase. With the publication of *The Unquiet Bed* (1967), she established herself as a lyric poet capable of giving fresh, sensitive, and forceful expression to issues of female identity and sexuality.

Bartok[1] and the Geranium

She lifts her green umbrellas
Towards the pane
Seeking her fill of sunlight

———▸

20 outmoded. 21 arrow-maker's.
1 Béla Bartók (1881–1945), a Hungarian composer of intense, passionate music, exerted a profound influence on modern music through his efforts to free himself from strict tonality and the bar-measure system.

Or of rain;
5   Whatever falls
She has no commentary
Accepts, extends,
Blows out her furbelows,[2]
Her bustling boughs;

10   And all the while he whirls
Explodes in space,
Never content with this small room:
Not even can he be
Confined to sky
15   But must speed high and higher still
From galaxy to galaxy,
Wrench from the stars their momentary notes
Steal music from the moon.

She's daylight
20   He is dark
She's heaven-held breath
He storms and crackles
Spits with hell's own spark.

Yet in this room, this moment now
25   These together breathe and be:
She, essence of serenity,
He in a mad intensity
Soars beyond sight
Then hurls, lost Lucifer,
30   From heaven's height.

And when he's done, he's out:
She leans a lip against the glass
And preens herself in light.

(1955)

2 ornamental pleats or flounces.

The Three Emilys[1]

These women crying in my head
Walk alone, uncomforted:
The Emilys, these three
Cry to be set free —
5   And others whom I will not name
Each different, each the same.

Yet they had liberty!
Their kingdom was the sky:
They batted clouds with easy hand,
10   Found a mountain for their stand;
From wandering lonely they could catch
The inner magic of a heath —
A lake their palette, any tree
Their brush could be.

15   And still they cry to me
As in reproach —
I, born to hear their inner storm
Of separate man in woman's form,
I yet possess another kingdom, barred
20   To them, these three, this Emily.[2]
I move as mother in a frame,
My arteries
Flow the immemorial way
Towards the child, the man;
25   And only for brief span
Am I an Emily on mountain snows
And one of these.

And so the whole that I possess
Is still much less —
30   They move triumphant through my head:
I am the one
Uncomforted.

(1953)   (1972)

1 a note identifying the three as Emily Brontë, Emily Dickinson, and Emily Carr appeared with first publica-
tion of this poem in *The Canadian Forum* (September 1953). Emily Brontë (1818–48) was a British poet and
author of the novel *Wuthering Heights* (1848); Emily Dickinson (1830–86) was an American poet (see pages
208–212); Emily Carr (1871–1945) was a Canadian painter and author. 2 none of the three Emilys married
or gave birth, whereas Livesay married and raised two children.

Irving Layton (b. 1912)

Born in Romania, Layton (originally Lazarovitch) came to Montreal as an infant. He was educated at Macdonald College and McGill University, taught parochial school in Montreal, and eventually became an English professor at York University. A prolific writer, he published his first book in 1945. *A Red Carpet for the Sun* (1959) won the Governor General's Award. Layton is probably as well known for his controversial attacks on those who disagree with him or criticize him as he is for his poetry. The guardians of official morality, intellectuals, women resistant to his charms, and Christians—all of whom he has grouped among the forces of repression—have felt his deliberately outrageous assaults. In spite of the provocations and bombast in his public statements, his poetry is not always acerbic: it can express tenderness, pathos, humour, and complex ideas, often in elegantly memorable language. Furthermore, Layton has a lofty vision of his calling, which he expresses in terms of his Jewish heritage. He believes that the true poet is, like the Hebrew prophets, one who knows truth, one whose work is of extreme importance: "Poetry, by giving dignity and utterance to our distress, enables us to hope, makes compassion reasonable."

The Birth of Tragedy [1]

And me happiest when I compose poems.
     Love, power, the huzza of battle
     are something, are much;
yet a poem includes them like a pool
5   water and reflection.
In me, nature's divided things —
     tree, mould on tree —
     have their fruition;
I am their core. Let them swap,
10 bandy, like a flame swerve
I am their mouth; as a mouth I serve.

And I observe how the sensual moths
     big with odour and sunshine
     dart into the perilous shrubbery;
15 or drop their visiting shadows
     upon the garden I one year made

———→

1 in *The Birth of Tragedy* (1872), the German philosopher Friedrich Nietzsche (1844–1900) sought to explain the origins of Greek tragedy in a fusion of opposite tendencies. One, the Apollonian, stood for order and idealism; the other, the Dionysian, represented energy and actual experience.

of flowering stone to be a footstool
      for the perfect gods:
      who, friends to the ascending orders,
20 sustain all passionate meditations
and call down pardons
for the insurgent blood.

A quiet madman, never far from tears,
      I lie like a slain thing
25   under the green air the trees
inhabit, or rest upon a chair
      towards which the inflammable air
tumbles on many robins' wings;
      noting how seasonably
30   leaf and blossom uncurl
and living things arrange their death,
while someone from afar off
blows birthday candles for the world.

(1954)

Keine Lazarovitch 1870–1959

When I saw my mother's head on the cold pillow,
Her white waterfalling hair in the cheeks' hollows,
I thought, quietly circling my grief, of how
She had loved God but cursed extravagantly his creatures.

5 For her final mouth was not water but a curse,
A small black hole, a black rent in the universe,
Which damned the green earth, stars and trees in its stillness
And the inescapable lousiness of growing old.

And I record she was comfortless, vituperative,
10 Ignorant, glad, and much else besides; I believe
She endlessly praised her black eyebrows, their thick weave,
Till plagiarizing Death leaned down and took them for his mould.

And spoiled a dignity I shall not again find,
And the fury of her stubborn limited mind;

———→

15 Now none will shake her amber beads and call God blind,
Or wear them upon a breast so radiantly.

O fierce she was, mean and unaccommodating;
But I think now of the toss of her gold earrings,
Their proud carnal assertion, and her youngest sings
20 While all the rivers of her red veins move into the sea.

(1961)

Douglas LePan (b. 1914)

Winner of the Governor General's Award for both poetry and fiction, Douglas LePan has been a professor and a member of the diplomatic service. Born in Toronto, he was educated at the University of Toronto and Oxford. His first published volume, *The Wounded Prince* (1948), contains some of his best-known and most important work, including "A Country without a Mythology." A significant contribution to the tradition that stretches at least as far back as Charles G.D. Roberts and the Confederation Poets — the attempt to create a distinctly Canadian poetry through treatment of the Canadian landscape — this poem contains sharply rendered scenes of external nature. It is not, however, simply another romantic landscape poem: its concern with myth transforms it into a compelling mental landscape and gives it an ironic edge as a comment on the traditions and possibilities of Canadian poetry.

A Country without a Mythology

No monuments or landmarks guide the stranger
Going among this savage people, masks
Taciturn or babbling out an alien jargon
And moody as barbaric skies are moody.

5   Berries must be his food. Hurriedly
He shakes the bushes, plucks pickerel from the river,
Forgetting every grace and ceremony,
Feeds like an Indian, and is on his way.

And yet, for all his haste, time is worth nothing.
10 The abbey clock, the dial in the garden,
Fade like saint's days and festivals.
Months, years, are here unbroken virgin forests.

There is no law — even no atmosphere
To smooth the anger of the flagrant sun.
15   November skies sting sting like icicles.
The land is open to all violent weathers.

Passion is not more quick. Lightnings in August
Stagger, rocks split, tongues in the forest hiss,
As fire drinks up the lovely sea-dream coolness.
20   This is the land the passionate man must travel.

Sometimes — perhaps at the tentative fall of twilight —
A belief will settle that waiting around the bend
Are sanctities of childhood, that melting birds
Will sing him into a limpid gracious Presence.

25   The hills will fall in folds, the wilderness
Will be a garment innocent and lustrous
To wear upon a birthday, under a light
That curls and smiles, a golden-haired Archangel.

And now the channel opens. But nothing alters.
30   Mile after mile of tangled struggling roots,
Wild-rice, stumps, weeds, that clutch at the canoe,
Wild birds hysterical in tangled trees.

And not a sign, no emblem in the sky
Or boughs to friend him as he goes; for who
35   Will stop where, clumsily constructed, daubed
With war-paint, teeters some lust-red manitou?[1]

(1948)

Dylan Thomas   (1914–1953)

Gifted with a richly expressive voice, Dylan Thomas attracted many who had never previously felt the beauty and emotional power of poetry. At the same time, he often repelled those who met him because of his excessive drinking and blunt, irreverent wit. Born in Swansea, Wales, Thomas earned fame with his first collection, *Eighteen Poems* (1934). Later collections, such as *The Map of*

1 the spirit worshipped as a force of nature by Algonquin Indians.

Love (1939) and *Deaths and Entrances* (1946), consolidated his reputation as the leading lyric poet of his generation. Thomas, who worked at the beginning of his career as a script-writer and broadcaster for the BBC, was also an accomplished prose writer, his best-known works being the novel *Portrait of the Artist as a Young Dog* (1940), the radio drama *Under Milk Wood* (1954), and his reminiscence, *A Child's Christmas in Wales* (1954). Much of his popularity, however, came because of performances — readings of poems by himself and others, phonograph recordings, and three American tours. His readings stressed the musical and oral qualities of the poetry. His own poems are distinctive in employing a profusion of sonorous images, for, as he once said, "A poem by myself *needs* a host of images, because its centre is a host of images." Although his sequences of images can sometimes seem an incoherent, surrealistic jumble, his best work unifies the abundant imagery through theme. His major themes are childhood experience, the cycle of nature, religious sensibility, sex, and death.

And Death Shall Have No Dominion[1]

And death shall have no dominion.
Dead men naked they shall be one
With the man in the wind and the west moon;
When their bones are picked clean and the clean bones gone,
5 They shall have stars at elbow and foot;
Though they go mad they shall be sane,
Though they sink through the sea they shall rise again;
Though lovers be lost love shall not;
And death shall have no dominion.

10 And death shall have no dominion.
Under the windings of the sea
They lying long shall not die windily;
Twisting on racks when sinews give way,
Strapped to a wheel, yet they shall not break;
15 Faith in their hands shall snap in two,
And the unicorn evils run them through;
Split all ends up they shan't crack;
And death shall have no dominion.

And death shall have no dominion.
20 No more may gulls cry at their ears
Or waves break loud on the seashores;

———→

1 an echo of Romans 6:9: "Knowing that Christ being raised from the dead dieth no more; death hath no more dominion over him."

Where blew a flower may a flower no more
Lift its head to the blows of the rain;
Though they be mad and dead as nails,
25   Heads of the characters hammer through daisies;
Break in the sun till the sun breaks down,
And death shall have no dominion.

(1934)

The Force That Through the Green Fuse Drives the Flower

The force that through the green fuse drives the flower
Drives my green age; that blasts the roots of trees
Is my destroyer.
And I am dumb to tell the crooked rose
5   My youth is bent by the same wintry fever.

The force that drives the water through the rocks
Drives my red blood; that dries the mouthing streams
Turns mine to wax.
And I am dumb to mouth unto my veins
10   How at the mountain spring the same mouth sucks.

The hand that whirls the water in the pool
Stirs the quicksand; that ropes the blowing wind
Hauls my shroud sail.
And I am dumb to tell the hanging man
15   How of my clay is made the hangman's lime.

The lips of time leech to the fountain head;
Love drips and gathers, but the fallen blood
Shall calm her sores.
And I am dumb to tell a weather's wind
20   How time has ticked a heaven round the stars.

And I am dumb to tell the lover's tomb
How at my sheet goes the same crooked worm.

(1934)

Fern Hill [1]

Now as I was young and easy under the apple boughs
About the lilting house and happy as the grass was green,
   The night above the dingle [2] starry,
    Time let me hail and climb
5   Golden in the heydays of his eyes,
And honoured among wagons I was prince of the apple towns
And once below a time I lordly had the trees and leaves
    Trail with daisies and barley
   Down the rivers of the windfall [3] light.

10 And as I was green and carefree, famous among the barns
About the happy yard and singing as the farm was home,
   In the sun that is young once only,
    Time let me play and be
    Golden in the mercy of his means,
15 And green and golden I was huntsman and herdsman, the calves
Sang to my horn, the foxes on the hills barked clear and cold,
    And the sabbath rang slowly
   In the pebbles of the holy streams.

All the sun long it was running, it was lovely, the hay
20 Fields high as the house, the tunes from the chimneys, it was air
   And playing, lovely and watery
    And fire green as grass.
   And nightly under the simple stars
As I rode to sleep the owls were bearing the farm away,
25 All the moon long I heard, blessed among stables, the nightjars [4]
   Flying with the ricks, [5] and the horses
    Flashing into the dark.

And then to awake, and the farm, like a wanderer white
With the dew, come back, the cock on his shoulder: it was all
30   Shining, it was Adam and maiden,
    The sky gathered again
   And the sun grew round that very day.

$$\longrightarrow$$

---

1 the Welsh farm of Ann Jones, the aunt with whom Thomas spent holidays away from Swansea. 2 deep
dell or hollow, usually wooded. 3 a transferred epithet: windfall apples are those blown down by the wind.
4 common nocturnal bird. 5 stacks of hay.

So it must have been after the birth of the simple light
In the first, spinning place, the spellbound horses walking warm
35   Out of the whinnying green stable
          On to the fields of praise.

And honoured among foxes and pheasants by the gay house
Under the new made clouds and happy as the heart was long,
     In the sun born over and over,
40   I ran my heedless ways,
     My wishes raced through the house high hay
And nothing I cared, at my sky blue trades, that time allows
In all his tuneful turning so few and such morning songs
     Before the children green and golden
45   Follow him out of grace,

Nothing I cared, in the lamb white days, that time would take me
Up to the swallow thronged loft by the shadow of my hand,
     In the moon that is always rising,
          Nor that riding to sleep
50   I should hear him fly with the high fields
And wake to the farm forever fled from the childless land.
Oh as I was young and easy in the mercy of his means,
     Time held me green and dying
     Though I sang in my chains like the sea.

(1946)

Do Not Go Gentle into That Good Night[1]

Do not go gentle into that good night,
Old age should burn and rave at close of day;
Rage, rage against the dying of the light.

Though wise men at their end know dark is right,
5 Because their words had forked no lightning they
Do not go gentle into that good night.

Good men, the last wave by, crying how bright
Their frail deeds might have danced in a green bay,
Rage, rage against the dying of the light.

1 written in 1951 and addressed to his dying father.

10 Wild men who caught and sang the sun in flight,
And learn, too late, they grieved it on its way,
Do not go gentle into that good night.

Grave men, near death, who see with blinding sight
Blind eyes could blaze like meteors and be gay,
15 Rage, rage against the dying of the light.

And you, my father, there on the sad height,
Curse, bless, me now with your fierce tears, I pray.
Do not go gentle into that good night.
Rage, rage against the dying of the light.

(1952)

P.K. Page (b. 1916)

Patricia Kathleen Page was born in Swanage, England, but came to Red Deer, Alberta, when she was two. She began her career as a poet in Montreal, where she was associated with the founders of *Preview*, a literary journal that championed formally sophisticated and intellectually demanding poetry. Her first collection, published in 1946, showed concern with both social issues and psychology. Page is also a graphic artist, and the abundant imagery and profusion of metaphors in her poetry are signs of her intensely visual sensibility. Nevertheless, Page tries to present more than surface appearance. In doing so, especially in her later work, she has been influenced by Sufism. Thus in her poetry, Page is a mystic, seeking, with what she calls her "two-dimensional consciousness," a glimpse of the three-dimensional unity beyond mundane appearances.

The Stenographers

After the brief bivouac of Sunday,
their eyes, in the forced march of Monday to Saturday,
hoist the white flag, flutter in the snow-storm of paper,
haul it down and crack in the mid-sun of temper.

5 In the pause between the first draft and the carbon
they glimpse the smooth hours when they were children —

———→

the ride in the ice-cart, the ice-man's name,
the end of the route and the long walk home;

remember the sea where floats at high tide
10   were sea marrows growing on the scatter-green vine
or spools of grey toffee, or wasps' nests on water;
remember the sand and the leaves of the country.

Bell rings and they go and the voice draws their pencil
like a sled across snow; when its runners are frozen
15   rope snaps and the voice then is pulling no burden
but runs like a dog on the winter of paper.

Their climates are winter and summer — no wind
for the kites of their hearts — no wind for a flight;
a breeze at the most, to tumble them over
20   and leave them like rubbish — the boy-friends of blood.

In the inch of the noon as they move they are stagnant.
The terrible calm of the noon is their anguish;
the lip of the counter, the shapes of the straws
like icicles breaking their tongues, are invaders.

25   Their beds are their oceans — salt water of weeping
the waves that they know — the tide before sleep;
and fighting to drown they assemble their sheep
in columns and watch them leap desks for their fences
and stare at them with their own mirror-worn faces.

30   In the felt of the morning the calico-minded,
sufficiently starched, insert papers, hit keys,
efficient and sure as their adding machines;
yet they weep in the vault, they are taut as net curtains
stretched upon frames. In their eyes I have seen
35   the pin men of madness in marathon trim
race round the track of the stadium pupil.

(1946)

Stories of Snow

Those in the vegetable rain retain
an area behind their sprouting eyes
held soft and rounded with the dream of snow
precious and reminiscent as those globes —
5 souvenir of some never-nether land —
which hold their snow-storms circular, complete,
high in a tall and teakwood cabinet.

In countries where the leaves are large as hands
where flowers protrude their fleshy chins
10 and call their colours,
an imaginary snow-storm sometimes falls
among the lilies.
And in the early morning one will waken
to think the glowing linen of his pillow
15 a northern drift, will find himself mistaken
and lie back weeping.
And there the story shifts from head to head,
of how in Holland, from their feather beds
hunters arise and part the flakes and go
20 forth to the frozen lakes in search of swans —
the snow-light falling white along their guns,
their breath in plumes.
While tethered in the wind like sleeping gulls
ice-boats wait the raising of their wings
25 to skim the electric ice at such a speed
they leap jet strips of naked water,
and how these flying, sailing hunters feel
air in their mouths as terrible as ether.
And on the story runs that even drinks
30 in that white landscape dare to be no colour;
how flasked and water clear, the liquor slips
silver against the hunters' moving hips.
And of the swan in death these dreamers tell
of its last flight and how it falls, a plummet,
35 pierced by the freezing bullet
and how three feathers, loosened by the shot,
descend like snow upon it.
While hunters plunge their fingers in its down
deep as a drift, and dive their hands

———→

40   up to the neck of the wrist
in that warm metamorphosis of snow
as gentle as the sort that woodsmen know
who, lost in the white circle, fall at last
and dream their way to death.

45   And stories of this kind are often told
in countries where great flowers bar the roads
with reds and blues which seal the route to snow —
as if, in telling, raconteurs unlock
the colour with its complement and go
50   through to the area behind the eyes
where silent, unrefractive whiteness lies.

(1946)

The Landlady

Through sepia air the boarders come and go,
impersonal as trains. Pass silently
the craving silence swallowing her speech;
click doors like shutters on her camera eye.

5   Because of her their lives become exact:
their entrances and exits are designed;
phone calls are cryptic. Oh, her ticklish ears
advance and fall back stunned.

Nothing is unprepared. They hold the walls
10   about them as they weep or laugh. Each face
is dialled to zero publicly. She peers
stippled with curious flesh;

pads on the patient landing like a pulse,
unlocks their keyholes with the wire of sight,
15   searches their rooms for clues when they are out,
pricks when they come home late.

Wonders when they are quiet, jumps when they move,
dreams that they dope or drink, trembles to know
the traffic of their brains, jaywalks their street
20   in clumsy shoes.

Yet knows them better than their closest friends:
their cupboards and the secrets of their drawers,
their books, their private mail, their photographs
are theirs and hers.

25   Knows when they wash, how frequently their clothes
go to the cleaners, what they like to eat,
their curvature of health, but even so
is not content.

And like a lover must know all, all, all.
30   Prays she may catch them unprepared at last
and palm the dreadful riddle of their skulls —
hoping the worst.

(1974)

Al Purdy   (1918–2000)

Born in Wooler, Ontario, Alfred Purdy left school after Grade 10, riding freight
trains to Vancouver, where he worked in a mattress factory and at other manual
labour. Purdy published his first book in 1944 and won the Governor General's
Award for *The Cariboo Horses* (1965). Much of his early poetry relies upon his
experiences as a labourer and uses the voice of a "common person." Combining
colloquial expressions, vulgarity, and poetic sentimentality, this conversational
voice is frequently an effective vehicle for philosophic thought and social crit-
icism because it casts ideas into unexpected forms. Purdy has travelled widely
and written about his travels throughout Canada, including the Arctic, and
such places as Cuba, Mexico, South America, Greece, and Japan. Nevertheless,
he is quintessentially the poet of a single place, the area around his home of
Ameliasburg, Ontario. Purdy conveys his love of Canada, of ordinary working
people, and of tradition in these poems, which mingle past and present and
thereby transform the area into a mythic landscape.

The Country North of Belleville

Bush land scrub land —
        Cashel Township and Wollaston
Elzevir McClure and Dungannon
green lands of Weslemkoon Lake
5   where a man might have some

———→

```
              opinion of what beauty
        is and none deny him
                          for miles —


        Yet this is the country of defeat
10      where Sisyphus¹ rolls a big stone
        year after year up the ancient hills
        picnicking glaciers have left strewn
        with centuries' rubble
                              backbreaking days
15                              in the sun and rain
        when realization seeps slow in the mind
        without grandeur or self deception in
                              noble struggle
        of being a fool —


20      A country of quiescence and still distance
        lean land
                          not like the fat south
        with inches of black soil on
                          earth's round belly —
25      And where the farms are
                          it's as if a man stuck
        both thumbs in the stony earth and pulled


                          it apart
                          to make room
30      enough between the trees
        for a wife
                          and maybe some cows and
                          room for some
        of the more easily kept illusions —
35      And where the farms have gone back
        to forest
                          are only soft outlines
                          shadowy differences —


        Old fences drift vaguely among the trees
40                          a pile of moss-covered stones
```

1 king of Corinth whose punishment in Hades was to roll a heavy stone up a hill, only to have it roll down again when it neared the top.

gathered for some ghost purpose
has lost meaning under the meaningless sky
       — they are like cities under water
and the undulating green waves of time
45   are laid on them —

This is the country of our defeat
          and yet
during the fall plowing a man
might stop and stand in a brown valley of the furrows
50   and shade his eyes to watch for the same
           red patch mixed with gold
           that appears on the same
           spot in the hills
           year after year
55   and grow old
plowing and plowing a ten-acre field until
the convolutions run parallel with his own brain —

And this is a country where the young
           leave quickly
60   unwilling to know what their fathers know
or think the words their mothers do not say —

Herschel Monteagle and Faraday
lakeland rockland and hill country
a little adjacent to where the world is
65   a little north of where the cities are and
sometime
we may go back there
              to the country of our defeat
Wollaston Elzevir and Dungannon
70   and Weslemkoon lake land
where the high townships of Cashel
            McClure and Marmora once were —
But it's been a long time since
and we must enquire the way
75   of strangers —

(1965)   (1972)

Trees at the Arctic Circle
(Salix Cordifolia — Ground Willow)

They are 18 inches long
or even less
crawling under rocks
grovelling among the lichens
5 bending and curling to escape
making themselves small
finding new ways to hide
Coward trees
I am angry to see them
10 like this
not proud of what they are
bowing to weather instead
careful of themselves
worried about the sky
15 afraid of exposing their limbs
like a Victorian married couple

I call to mind great Douglas Firs
I see tall maples waving green
and oaks like gods in autumn gold
the whole horizon jungle dark
20 and I crouched under that continual night
But these
even the dwarf shrubs of Ontario
mock them
Coward trees

25 And yet — and yet —
their seed pods glow
like delicate grey earrings
their leaves are veined and intricate
like tiny parkas
30 They have about three months
to ensure the species does not die
and that's how they spend their time
unbothered by any human opinion
just digging in here and now

——→

35   sending their roots down down down
      And you know it occurs to me
              about 2 feet under
      those roots must touch permafrost
      ice that remains ice forever
40   and they use it for their nourishment
      use death to remain alive

      I see that I've been carried away
      in my scorn of the dwarf trees
      most foolish in my judgements
45   To take away the dignity
              of any living thing
      even tho it cannot understand
              the scornful words
      is to make life itself trivial
50   and yourself the Pontifex Maximus[1]
              of nullity
      I have been stupid in a poem
      I will not alter the poem
      but let the stupidity remain permanent
55   as the trees are
      in a poem
      the dwarf trees of Baffin Island

      Pangnirtung   (1967)

Lament for the Dorsets

(Eskimos extinct in the 14th century A.D.*)*[1]

      Animal bones and some mossy tent rings
      scrapers and spearheads   carved ivory swans
      all that remains of the Dorset giants
      who drove the Vikings back to their long ships
5   talked to spirits of earth and water

                          ⟶

---

1 highest priest of the Roman religion and chief administrator of religious affairs.
1 in about A.D. 1000, the Dorset people were displaced from most of the Arctic regions by Thule Inuit
from Alaska, but they continued to live in northern Quebec and Labrador until about A.D. 1500, when
they disappeared.

— a picture of terrifying old men
so large they broke the backs of bears
so small they lurk behind bone rafters
in the brain of modern hunters
10   among good thoughts and warm things
and come out at night
to spit on the stars

The big men with clever fingers
who had no dogs and hauled their sleds
15   over the frozen northern oceans
awkward giants
               killers of seal
they couldn't compete with little men
who came from the west with dogs
20   Or else in a warm climatic cycle
the seals went back to cold waters
and the puzzled Dorsets scratched their heads
with hairy thumbs around 1350 A.D.
— couldn't figure it out
25   went around saying to each other
plaintively
        "What's wrong? What happened?
        Where are the seals gone?"
And died

30   Twentieth-century people
apartment dwellers
executives of neon death
warmakers with things that explode
— they have never imagined us in their future
35   how could we imagine them in the past
squatting among the moving glaciers
six hundred years ago
with glowing lamps?
As remote or nearly
40   as the trilobites and swamps
when coal became
or the last great reptile hissed
at a mammal the size of a mouse
that squeaked and fled

             →

45 Did they ever realize at all
    what was happening to them?
    Some old hunter with one lame leg
    a bear had chewed
    sitting in a caribou-skin tent
50 — the last Dorset?
    Let's say his name was Kudluk
    and watch him sitting there
    carving 2-inch ivory swans
    for a dead grand-daughter
55 taking them out of his mind
    the places in his mind
    where pictures are
    He selects a sharp stone tool
    to gouge a parallel pattern of lines
60 on both sides of the swan
    holding it with his left hand
    bearing down and transmitting
    his body's weight
    from brain to arm and right hand
65 and one of his thoughts
    turns to ivory
    The carving is laid aside
    in beginning darkness
    at the end of hunger
70 and after a while wind
    blows down the tent and snow
    begins to cover him

    After 600 years
    the ivory thought
75 is still warm

                                    (1968)

Wilderness Gothic

Across Roblin Lake, two shores away,
they are sheathing the church spire
with new metal. Someone hangs in the sky

                    ⟶

over there from a piece of rope,
5   hammering and fitting God's belly-scratcher,
working his way up along the spire
until there's nothing left to nail on —
Perhaps the workman's faith reaches beyond:
touches intangibles, wrestles with Jacob,[1]
10 replacing rotten timber with pine thews,
pounds hard in the blue cave of the sky,
contends heroically with difficult problems of
gravity, sky navigation and mythopeia,
his volunteer time and labour donated to God,
15 minus sick benefits of course on a non-union job —

Fields around are yellowing into harvest,
nestling and fingerling are sky and water borne,
death is yodelling quiet in green woodlots,
and bodies of three young birds have disappeared
20 in the sub-surface of the new county highway —

That picture is incomplete, part left out
that might alter the whole Dürer[2] landscape:
gothic ancestors peer from medieval sky,
dour faces trapped in photograph albums escaping
25 to clop down iron roads with matched greys:
work-sodden wives groping inside their flesh
for what keeps moving and changing and flashing
beyond and past the long frozen Victorian day.
A sign of fire and brimstone? A two-headed calf
30 born in the barn last night? A sharp female agony?
An age and a faith moving into transition,
the dinner cold and new-baked bread a failure,
deep woods shiver and water drops hang pendant,
double yolked eggs and the house creaks a little —
35 Something is about to happen. Leaves are still.
Two shores away, a man hammering in the sky.
Perhaps he will fall.

(1968)

1 Jacob wrestled with an angel, refusing to release him until the angel gave him a blessing;
see Genesis 32:24–29. 2 landscapes in many paintings and engravings by German artist Albrecht Dürer
(1471–1528) are elaborate, often gloomy combinations of realistic details and visionary symbolism.

Oodgeroo Noonuccal
(Kath Walker) (1920-1993)

The first prominent Aboriginal poet and protest writer in Australia, Kath Walker, who used her Aboriginal name, Oodgeroo Noonuccal, was born on Stradbroke Island, off the Queensland coast near Brisbane. At the age of thirteen, she began work as a domestic servant. When she was sixteen, she encountered a powerful example of official discrimination: because she was part Aboriginal, she was denied admission to nursing studies. A leading advocate of Aboriginal rights, she was involved in the campaign that led to the 1967 repeal of constitutional discrimination against Aborigines. The title of her first volume of poetry, *We Are Going* (1964), she has said, was "a warning to the white people: we can go out of existence, or with proper help we could also go on and live in this world in peace and harmony...." She has also said that her poems are "sloganistic, civil rightish, plain and simple." At their best, however, they are powerfully emotional presentations of the culture and history of the Aborigines; they clearly portray the abuses whites have inflicted, the dignity of Aborigines, and the value of an ancient way of life lived close to the land.

We Are Going

For Grannie Coolwell

They came in to the little town
A semi-naked band subdued and silent,
All that remained of their tribe.
They came here to the place of their old bora ground[1]
5 Where now the many white men hurry about like ants.
Notice of estate agent reads: "Rubbish May Be Tipped Here."
Now it half covers the traces of the old bora ring.
They sit and are confused, they cannot say their thoughts:
"We are as strangers here now, but the white tribe are the strangers.
10 We belong here, we are of the old ways.
We are the corroboree[2] and the bora ground,
We are the old sacred ceremonies, the laws of the elders.
We are the wonder tales of Dream Time,[3] the tribal legends told.
We are the past, the hunts and the laughing games, the wandering camp fires.

1 the term *bora* is applied both to the most solemn of Aboriginal rites, in which a young boy is admitted to the rights of manhood, and to the site of the ceremony. The bora ground is usually called a bora ring because it is most often a circular earthen bank or an area marked off by a ring of stones. 2 Aboriginal dance ceremony, sometimes sacred and sometimes secular, involving singing and rhythmical musical accompaniment. 3 the time of mythic events; the time of the first ancestors or the time, beyond living memory, in which the physical, spiritual, and moral world was developed.

15   We are the lightning-bolt over Gaphembah Hill[4]
Quick and terrible,
And the Thunderer[5] after him, that loud fellow.
We are the quiet daybreak paling the dark lagoon.
We are the shadow-ghosts creeping back as the camp fires burn low.
20   We are nature and the past, all the old ways
Gone now and scattered.
The scrubs are gone, the hunting and the laughter.
The eagle is gone, the emu[6] and the kangaroo are gone from this place.
The bora ring is gone.
25   The corroboree is gone.
And we are going."

(1964)

Philip Larkin   (1922–1985)

Born at Coventry and educated at Oxford, Larkin led a quiet and unremarkable life. He worked as a librarian in several places, completing his career as head librarian at the University of Hull, a post he took up in 1955. His first poetry collection was *The North Ship* (1945), but it was *The Less Deceived* (1955) that established him as one of the most popular British poets of the postwar era. Larkin was opposed to what he considered the overly complex techniques of modernist and academic poetry, such as that written by Eliot and Pound. Instead, he favoured carefully crafted works that speak directly to people who may not have a specialized understanding of literature and literary tradition. Poetry should be, he said, "emotional in nature and theatrical in operation, a skilled re-creation of emotion in other people." Therefore, like Thomas Hardy, whose poems obviously influenced him, he used traditional forms and techniques, employed the language of ordinary people, and used his own experiences, rather than other poetry or works of art, as the basis for most of his poems. Larkin's range was narrow, but people responded favourably because his poetry was both witty and accessible.

4 on Stradbroke Island, behind Myora Springs and near Moongalba, where the author, also known as Oodgeroo Noonuccal Moongalba, lives. 5 thunder; Aboriginal beliefs tend to be localized, rather than universal among the various tribes, and mythic figures, such as Thunderer, are often attached to specific sites or regions. 6 large, flightless bird that can run at a speed of approximately 50 kilometres per hour.

Next, Please

Always too eager for the future, we
Pick up bad habits of expectancy.
Something is always approaching; every day
Till then we say,

5   Watching from a bluff the tiny, clear,
Sparkling armada¹ of promises draw near.
How slow they are! And how much time they waste,
Refusing to make haste!

Yet still they leave us holding wretched stalks
10   Of disappointment, for, though nothing balks,
Each big approach, leaning with brasswork prinked,²
Each rope distinct,

Flagged, and the figurehead with golden tits
Arching our way, it never anchors; it's
15   No sooner present than it turns to past.
Right to the last

We think each one will heave to and unload
All good into our lives, all we are owed
For waiting so devoutly and so long.
20   But we are wrong:

Only one ship is seeking us, a black-
Sailed unfamiliar, towing at her back
A huge and birdless silence. In her wake
No waters breed or break.

(1955)

1 large fleet. 2 spruced up, shined.

Church Going

Once I am sure there's nothing going on
I step inside, letting the door thud shut.
Another church: matting, seats, and stone,
And little books; sprawlings of flowers, cut
5   For Sunday, brownish now; some brass and stuff
Up at the holy end; the small neat organ;
And a tense, musty, unignorable silence,
Brewed God knows how long. Hatless, I take off
My cycle-clips in awkward reverence,

10   Move forward, run my hand around the font.
From where I stand, the roof looks almost new —
Cleaned, or restored? Someone would know: I don't.
Mounting the lectern, I peruse a few
Hectoring large-scale verses, and pronounce
15   'Here endeth' much more loudly than I'd meant.
The echoes snigger briefly. Back at the door
I sign the book, donate an Irish sixpence,
Reflect the place was not worth stopping for.

Yet stop I did: in fact I often do,
20   And always end much at a loss like this,
Wondering what to look for; wondering, too,
When churches fall completely out of use
What we shall turn them into, if we shall keep
A few cathedrals chronically on show,
25   Their parchment, plate and pyx[1] in locked cases,
And let the rest rent-free to rain and sheep.
Shall we avoid them as unlucky places?

Or, after dark, will dubious women come
To make their children touch a particular stone;
30   Pick simples[2] for a cancer; or on some
Advised night see walking a dead one?
Power of some sort or other will go on
In games, in riddles, seemingly at random;

—→

1 vessel in which the consecrated Host is reserved. 2 herbs or plants used for medicinal purposes.

But superstition, like belief, must die,
35 And what remains when disbelief has gone?
Grass, weedy pavement, brambles, buttress, sky,

A shape less recognisable each week,
A purpose more obscure. I wonder who
Will be the last, the very last, to seek
40 This place for what it was; one of the crew
That tap and jot and know what rood-lofts[3] were?
Some ruin-bibber,[4] randy for antique,
Or Christmas-addict, counting on a whiff
Of gowns-and-bands and organ-pipes and myrrh?
45 Or will he be my representative,

Bored, uninformed, knowing the ghostly silt
Dispersed, yet tending to this cross of ground
Through suburb scrub because it held unspilt
So long and equably what since is found
50 Only in separation — marriage, and birth,
And death, and thoughts of these — for which was built
This special shell? For, though I've no idea
What this accoutred frowsty[5] barn is worth,
It pleases me to stand in silence here;

55 A serious house on serious earth it is,
In whose blent air all our compulsions meet,
Are recognised, and robed as destinies.
And that much never can be obsolete,
Since someone will forever be surprising
60 A hunger in himself to be more serious,
And gravitating with it to this ground,
Which, he once heard, was proper to grow wise in,
If only that so many dead lie round.

(1955)

3 loft or gallery over a rood-screen, a screen with a cross on top separating the nave from the choir or chancel. 4 a bibber is one who drinks frequently; hence, a ruin-bibber frequents ruins or antiquities. 5 musty, or stale-smelling.

Toads

Why should I let the toad *work*
    Squat on my life?
Can't I use my wit as a pitchfork
    And drive the brute off?

5   Six days of the week it soils
    With its sickening poison —
Just for paying a few bills!
    That's out of proportion.

Lots of folk live on their wits:
10   Lecturers, lispers,
Losels, loblolly-men,[1] louts —
    They don't end as paupers;

Lots of folk live up lanes
    With fires in a bucket,
15 Eat windfalls and tinned sardines —
    They seem to like it.

Their nippers[2] have got bare feet,
    Their unspeakable wives
Are skinny as whippets[3] — and yet
20   No one actually *starves*.

Ah, were I courageous enough
    To shout *Stuff your pension!*
But I know, all too well, that's the stuff
    That dreams are made on:

25 For something sufficiently toad-like
    Squats in me, too;
Its hunkers are heavy as hard luck,
    And cold as snow,

1 losels are worthless persons, scoundrels, or rakes; loblolly-men are bumpkins or rustics. 2 children.
3 short-haired dogs, resembling but smaller than greyhounds, that are bred for speed.

And will never allow me to blarney
30   My way to getting
The fame and the girl and the money
     All at one sitting.

I don't say, one bodies the other
     One's spiritual truth;
35 But I do say it's hard to lose either,
     When you have both.

(1955)

Phyllis Webb   (b. 1927)

Born in Victoria, B.C., Phyllis Webb received her B.A. from the University of British Columbia and studied briefly at McGill. She has taught at UBC and the University of Victoria and was writer in residence at the University of Alberta. She has also been a producer for the Canadian Broadcasting Corporation. Her first book of poetry was *Trio* (1954), which also featured the work of two other poets. *The Vision Tree: Selected Poems* (1982) won the Governor General's Award. An intellectual with an often bleak vision of the world, Webb develops ideas carefully through complex structures and careful arrangements of sounds, creating what she calls "the dance of the intellect in the syllables."

Marvell's Garden [1]

Marvell's garden, that place of solitude,
is not where I'd choose to live
yet is the fixed sundial
that turns me round
5 unwillingly
in a hot glade
as closer, closer I come to contradiction
to the shade green within the green shade. [2]

1 see Andrew Marvell's "The Garden" (page 65), in which a garden symbolizes the solitary contemplative life. 2 in "The Garden," Marvell speaks of "a green thought in a green shade" (line 48). Green symbolizes a cool detachment from human concerns.

The garden where Marvell scorned love's solicitude —
10   that dream — and played instead an arcane solitaire,
shuffling his thoughts like shadowy chance
across the shrubs of ecstasy,
and cast the myths away to flowering hours[3]
as yes, his mind, that sea,[4] caught at green
15   thoughts shadowing a green infinity.

And yet Marvell's garden was not Plato's[5]
garden — and yet — he did care more for the form
of things than for the thing itself —
ideas and visions,
20   resemblances and echoes,
things seeming and being
not quite what they were.

That was his garden, a kind of attitude
struck out of an earth too carefully attended,
25   wanting to be left alone.
And I don't blame him for that.
God knows, too many fences fence us out
and his garden closed in on Paradise.[6]

On Paradise! When I think of his hymning
30   Puritans in the Bermudas, the bright oranges
lighting up that night![7] When I recall
his rustling tinsel hopes
beneath the cold decree of steel,
Oh, I have wept for some new convulsion
35   to tear together this world and his.[8]

3 the fourth stanza of "The Garden" recounts the stories of Daphne and Syrinx, maidens who escaped seduction when they were transformed into, respectively, a laurel and a reed. 4 Marvell's poem (lines 43–44) refers to the mind as an ocean because, like the ocean, which was thought to contain a form of everything on land, the mind contains a resemblance of everything on earth. 5 Plato argued that any earthly thing was but a pale reflection or shadow of the ideal form or idea of that thing. 6 Marvell compared his garden, a solitary place — and thus free from sexual passion — to Eden before the creation of Eve: "Two paradises 'twere in one, / To live in paradise alone" (lines 63–64). 7 in "Bermudas" (1681), Marvell wrote of Puritans seeking refuge from English bishops in a land "far kinder than our own." In praising God, who gave the Puritans such a beautiful refuge, he says God "hangs in shades the orange bright, / Like golden lamps in a green night." 8 in "The Definition of Love" (1681), a poem about a lover's despair because he can never consummate his love, Marvell speaks of "feeble hope," which "vainly flapped its tinsel wing." Fate's "decrees of steel" separate the lovers as if they were the poles of the earth. He declares that they will remain apart "Unless the giddy heaven fall, / And earth some new convulsion tear," joining the lovers by flattening the globe.

But then I saw his luminous plumèd Wings
prepared for flight,
and then I heard him singing glory
in a green tree,
40 and then I caught the vest he'd laid aside
all blest with fire.[9]

And I have gone walking slowly in
his garden of necessity
leaving brothers, lovers, Christ
45 outside my walls
where they have wept without
and I within.

(1956)

Treblinka[1] Gas Chamber

Klostermayer ordered another count of the children.
Then their stars were snipped off and thrown into
the center of the courtyard. It looked like a field of
buttercups.
    — Joseph Hyams, *A Field of Buttercups*

fallingstars
            "a field of
                    buttercups"

                yellow stars
5   of David
                                falling
the prisoners   ⟶

---

9 in the seventh stanza of "The Garden," Marvell speaks of his soul casting off "the body's vest" to fly like a
bird into the trees.
1 extermination camp in Poland where the Nazis gassed thousands of Jews during World War II.

                    the children
                              falling

10   in heaps
                         on one another
                                        they go down
      Thanatos[2]
                  showers
15   his dirty breath
                                    they must breathe
                                                him in
                         they see stars
                                    behind their
20   eyes
      David's
            "a field of
                        buttercups"

            a metaphor
25   where all that's
                                    left lies down

                                                            (1980)

Adrienne Rich   (b. 1929)

Adrienne Rich grew up in Baltimore, Maryland, where she began writing poetry
as a girl. While formal and restrained compared with her later work, her first
book, *A Change of World* (1951), showed remarkable maturity of thought and
technique for a 22-year-old and won the Yale Series of Younger Poets award.
Only after marrying early and having three sons in quick succession did Rich
begin breaking away from stereotypical female roles. Beginning with her third
book, *Snapshots of a Daughter-in-Law* (1963), her forms are freer, her voice is
more personal, and her growing resentment of the limitations she sees imposed
on her in a male-dominated society is made plain. Beginning with her opposi-
tion to the Vietnam War in the 1960s, Rich — guided always by a strong fem-
inist commitment — has become increasingly involved in various liberal political
movements. In 1986, she became professor of English and feminist studies at
Stanford University.

2 the ancient Greek personification of Death.

Aunt Jennifer's Tigers

Aunt Jennifer's tigers prance across a screen,
Bright topaz denizens of a world of green.
They do not fear the men beneath the tree;
They pace in sleek chivalric certainty.

5   Aunt Jennifer's fingers fluttering through her wool
Find even the ivory needle hard to pull.
The massive weight of Uncle's wedding band
Sits heavily upon Aunt Jennifer's hand.

When Aunt is dead, her terrified hands will lie
10   Still ringed with ordeals she was mastered by.
The tigers in the panel that she made
Will go on prancing, proud and unafraid.

(1951)

Diving into the Wreck

First having read the book of myths,
and loaded the camera,
and checked the edge of the knife-blade,
I put on
5   the body-armor of black rubber
the absurd flippers
the grave and awkward mask.
I am having to do this
not like Cousteau[1] with his
10   assiduous team
aboard the sun-flooded schooner
but here alone.
There is a ladder.
The ladder is always there
15   hanging innocently
close to the side of the schooner.
We know what it is for,
we who have used it.

⟶

---

1 Jacques Cousteau (1910–97), French author, filmmaker, and underwater explorer.

Otherwise
20   it's a piece of maritime floss
some sundry equipment.

I go down.
Rung after rung and still
the oxygen immerses me
25   the blue light
the clear atoms
of our human air.
I go down.
My flippers cripple me,
30   I crawl like an insect down the ladder
and there is no one
to tell me when the ocean
will begin.

First the air is blue and then
35   it is bluer and then green and then
black I am blacking out and yet
my mask is powerful
it pumps my blood with power
the sea is another story
40   the sea is not a question of power
I have to learn alone
to turn my body without force
in the deep element.

And now: it is easy to forget
45   what I came for
among so many who have always
lived here
swaying their crenellated fans
between the reefs
50   and besides
you breathe differently down here.

I came to explore the wreck.
The words are purposes.
The words are maps.

⟶

55   I came to see the damage that was done
and the treasures that prevail.
I stroke the beam of my lamp
slowly along the flank
of something more permanent
60   than fish or weed.

the thing I came for:
the wreck and not the story of the wreck
the thing itself and not the myth
the drowned face always staring
65   toward the sun
the evidence of damage
worn by salt and sway into this threadbare beauty
the ribs of the disaster
curving their assertion
70   among the tentative haunters.

This is the place.
And I am here, the mermaid whose dark hair
streams black, the merman in his armored body
We circle silently
75   about the wreck
we dive into the hold.
I am she: I am he

whose drowned face sleeps with open eyes
whose breasts still bear the stress
80   whose silver, copper, vermeil cargo lies
obscurely inside barrels
half-wedged and left to rot
we are the half-destroyed instruments
that once held to a course
85   the water-eaten log
the fouled compass

We are, I am, you are
by cowardice or courage
the one who find our way
—→

90   back to this scene
      carrying a knife, a camera
      a book of myths
      in which
      our names do not appear.

                                                                              (1973)

What Kind of Times Are These[1]

There's a place between two stands of trees where the grass grows uphill
and the old revolutionary road breaks off into shadows
near a meeting-house abandoned by the persecuted
who disappeared into those shadows.

5   I've walked there picking mushrooms at the edge of dread, but don't be fooled,
     this isn't a Russian poem, this is not somewhere else but here,
     our country moving closer to its own truth and dread,[2]
     its own ways of making people disappear.

     I won't tell you where the place is, the dark mesh of the woods
10   meeting the unmarked strip of light —
     ghost-ridden crossroads, leafmold paradise:
     I know already who wants to buy it, sell it, make it disappear.

     And I won't tell you where it is, so why do I tell you
     anything? Because you still listen, because in times like these
15   to have you listen at all, it's necessary
     to talk about trees.

     (1991)   (1995)

1 in her note to this poem, Rich says, "The title is from Bertolt Brecht's poem 'An Die Nachgeborenen'
('For Those Born Later'): *What kind of times are these / When it's almost a crime to talk about trees / Because it
means keeping still about so many evil deeds?*" 2 Rich explains that this line "echoes Osip Mandelstam's 1921
poem that begins *I was washing outside in the darkness* and ends *The earth's moving closer to truth and to dread....*
Mandelstam was forbidden to publish, then exiled and sentenced to five years of hard labor for a poem
caricaturing Stalin; he died in a transit camp in 1938."

In Those Years

In those years, people will say, we lost track
of the meaning of *we*, of *you*
we found ourselves
reduced to *I*
5   and the whole thing became
silly, ironic, terrible:
we were trying to live a personal life
and, yes, that was the only life
we could bear witness to

10   But the great dark birds of history screamed and plunged
into our personal weather
They were headed somewhere else but their beaks and pinions drove
along the shore, through the rags of fog
where we stood, saying *I*

(1991)   (1995)

Derek Walcott   (b. 1930)

Recipient of the Nobel Prize for literature in 1992, Derek Walcott was born in
Castries on the Caribbean island of St. Lucia. He proved to be a precocious
writer, publishing his first collection of poems when he was only eighteen
and seeing his first play produced when he was just twenty. After he gradu-
ated from the University College of the West Indies, Jamaica, in 1953, Walcott
moved to Trinidad, where he worked full-time as a writer, art critic, and
theatre director. He took up a position as a professor of creative writing at
Boston University in 1981. In poems characterized by wit, passion, and learn-
ing, Walcott presents the Caribbean as a region in which the landscape and
the memories it triggers keep alive a history of oppression. At the same time,
as a person whose education has taught him to value European culture and
whose own ancestry is racially mixed (see the final note to "A Far Cry from
Africa"), he expresses deeply divided feelings about the conflicts between
colonialists and native populations.

A Far Cry from Africa

A wind is ruffling the tawny pelt
Of Africa. Kikuyu,[1] quick as flies,
Batten upon the bloodstreams of the veldt.[2]
Corpses are scattered through a paradise.
5 Only the worm, colonel of carrion, cries:
"Waste no compassion on these separate dead!"
Statistics justify and scholars seize
The salients of colonial policy.
What is that to the white child hacked in bed?
10 To savages, expendable as Jews?

Threshed out by beaters,[3] the long rushes break
In a white dust of ibises[4] whose cries
Have wheeled since civilization's dawn
From the parched river or beast-teeming plain.
15 The violence of beast on beast is read
As natural law, but upright man
Seeks his divinity by inflicting pain.
Delirious as these worried beasts, his wars
Dance to the tightened carcass of a drum,
20 While he calls courage still that native dread
Of the white peace contracted by the dead.

Again brutish necessity wipes its hands
Upon the napkin of a dirty cause, again
A waste of our compassion, as with Spain,[5]
25 The gorilla wrestles with the superman.
I who am poisoned with the blood of both,[6]
Where shall I turn, divided to the vein?

1 tribe from the highlands of south-central Kenya whose members formed the Mau Mau, a secret revolution-
ary organization that employed terrorist activities in order to drive out British colonialists. 2 open country
covered with grass and bushes, but having few trees. 3 natives hired to drive game birds and animals from
cover. 4 wading birds notable for their long, downward-curving bills. 5 in the Spanish Civil War
(1936–39), the Loyalists, supported by liberal intellectuals and Soviet Communists, were defeated by the
insurgents of Generalissmo Francisco Franco (1892–1975), who were supported by Nazi Germany and
Fascist Italy. 6 Walcott is of mixed ancestry: both of his grandfathers were white, and both of his grand-
mothers were black.

I who have cursed
The drunken officer of British rule, how choose
30   Between this Africa and the English tongue I love?
Betray them both, or give back what they give?
How can I face such slaughter and be cool?
How can I turn from Africa and live?

(1962)

Ruins of a Great House[1]

though our longest sun sets at right declensions and
makes but winter arches, it cannot be long before we
lie down in darkness, and have our light in ashes...
                    — Browne, *Urn Burial*[2]

Stones only, the disjecta membra[3] of this Great House,
Whose moth-like girls are mixed with candledust,
Remain to file the lizard's dragonish claws.
The mouths of those gate cherubs shriek with stain;
5   Axle and coach wheel silted under the muck
Of cattle droppings.
                    Three crows flap for the trees
And settle, creaking the eucalyptus boughs.
A smell of dead limes quickens in the nose
The leprosy of empire.
                    "Farewell, green fields,
10   Farewell, ye happy groves!"
Marble like Greece, like Faulkner's[4] South in stone,
Deciduous beauty prospered and is gone,
But where the lawn breaks in a rash of trees
A spade below dead leaves will ring the bone
15   Of some dead animal or human thing
Fallen from evil days, from evil times.

1 the main house on a plantation, usually the residence of the owner or manager. 2 *Hydriotaphia, Urne-Buriall* (1658) is a meditation on death and burial practices that Sir Thomas Browne (1605–82), an English physician, wrote after viewing old funeral urns excavated in Norwich. 3 scattered limbs or parts; from "disjecti membra poetae," "the scattered limbs of the poet" (*Satires* of Horace). 4 William Faulkner (1897–1962), an American novelist and winner of the Nobel Prize for literature (1949), wrote about the collapse of the aristocratic South and the guilt its slave-holding culture bequeathed to future generations.

It seems that the original crops were limes
Grown in the silt that clogs the river's skirt;
The imperious rakes are gone, their bright girls gone,
20 The river flows, obliterating hurt.
I climbed a wall with the grille ironwork
Of exiled craftsmen protecting that great house
From guilt, perhaps, but not from the worm's rent
Nor from the padded cavalry of the mouse.
25 And when a wind shook in the limes I heard
What Kipling[5] heard, the death of a great empire, the abuse
Of ignorance by Bible and by sword.

A green lawn, broken by low walls of stone,
Dipped to the rivulet, and pacing, I thought next
30 Of men like Hawkins, Walter Raleigh, Drake,[6]
Ancestral murderers and poets, more perplexed
In memory now by every ulcerous crime.
The world's green age then was a rotting lime
Whose stench became the charnel galleon's text.
35 The rot remains with us, the men are gone.
But, as dead ash is lifted in a wind
That fans the blackening ember of the mind,
My eyes burned from the ashen prose of Donne.[7]

Ablaze with rage I thought,
40 Some slave is rotting in this manorial lake,
But still the coal of my compassion fought
That Albion too was once
A colony like ours, "part of the continent, piece of the main,"
Nook-shotten, rook o'erblown, deranged
45 By foaming channels and the vain expense
Of bitter faction.

All in compassion ends
So differently from what the heart arranged:
"as well as if a manor of thy friend's . . ."

(1962)

---

5 Rudyard Kipling (1865–1936), an Indian-born English author, was famous for the imperialistic sentiments
he expressed in many of his works. 6 Sir John Hawkins (1532–95), Sir Walter Raleigh (1552–1618), and
Sir Francis Drake (c. 1540–96) were English explorers and adventurers, who sailed to the West Indies.
7 John Donne (1572–1631), English metaphysical poet and clergyman; phrases from a famous passage in
"Meditation XVII" of his *Devotions upon Emergent Occasions* (1624) are quoted, somewhat incorrectly, in
lines 43 and 48: "No man is an island, entire of itself; every man is a piece of the continent, a part of the
main. If a clod be washed away by the sea, Europe is the less, as well as if a promontory were, as well as if a
manor of thy friend's or thine own were."

The Virgins[1]

Down the dead streets of sun-stoned Frederiksted,[2]
the first freeport[3] to die for tourism,
strolling at funeral pace, I am reminded
of life not lost to the American dream;
5   but my small-islander's[4] simplicities
can't better our new empire's civilized
exchange of cameras, watches, perfumes, brandies
for the good life, so cheaply underpriced
that only the crime rate is on the rise
10   in streets blighted with sun, stone arches
and plazas blown dry by the hysteria
of rumour. A condominium drowns
in vacancy; its bargains are dusted,
but only a jewelled housefly drones
15   over the bargains. The roulettes spin
rustily to the wind; the vigorous trade[5]
that every morning would begin afresh
by revving up green water round the pierhead
heading for where the banks of silver thresh.

(1976)

Ted Hughes (1930–1998)

Born in the small Yorkshire town of Mytholmroyd, Hughes received B.A. and M.A. degrees from Cambridge. His first wife was the American poet Sylvia Plath. Hughes, who was appointed England's Poet Laureate in 1984, achieved critical respect with his very first volume of poems, *The Hawk in the Rain* (1957), which introduced one of his dominant subjects, animal life. Although some critics contend that Hughes celebrates raw power and brutality in his animal poems, even accusing him of presenting the figure of a fascist in "Hawk Roosting," Hughes contends that he is presenting "Nature thinking. Simply Nature." Hughes says: "What excites my imagination is the war between vitality and death, and my poems may be said to celebrate the exploits of the warriors of either side." For him, animals combine "the arrogance of blood and bone" with "an energy too strong for death." Hughes compares his poetic technique to that of a composer. He says that he turns each of his combatants "into a bit of music" and then resolves "the whole uproar into as formal and balanced a figure of melody and rhythm as I can."

1 the Virgin Islands lie east of Puerto Rico in the Caribbean. 2 the largest port in St. Croix, the American Virgin Islands. 3 port that does not charge customs taxes. 4 St. Lucia, Walcott's birthplace, is smaller than St. Croix. 5 trade winds, nearly constant easterly winds that dominate in tropical regions.

Pike

Pike, three inches long, perfect
Pike in all parts, green tigering the gold.
Killers from the egg: the malevolent aged grin.
They dance on the surface among the flies.

5 Or move, stunned by their own grandeur,
Over a bed of emerald, silhouette
Of submarine delicacy and horror.
A hundred feet long in their world.

In ponds, under the heat-struck lily pads —
10 Gloom of their stillness:
Logged on last year's black leaves, watching upwards.
Or hung in an amber cavern of weeds

The jaws' hooked clamp and fangs
Not to be changed at this date;
15 A life subdued to its instrument;
The gills kneading quietly, and the pectorals.

Three we kept behind glass,
Jungled in weed: three inches, four,
And four and a half: fed fry to them —
20 Suddenly there were two. Finally one.

With a sag belly and the grin it was born with.
And indeed they spare nobody.
Two, six pounds each, over two feet long,
High and dry and dead in the willow-herb —

25 One jammed past its gills down the other's gullet:
The outside eye stared: as a vice locks —
The same iron in this eye
Though its film shrank in death.

A pond I fished, fifty yards across,
30 Whose lilies and muscular tench[1]

$\longrightarrow$

1 fresh-water fish that inhabits still, deep waters.

Had outlasted every visible stone
Of the monastery that planted them —

Stilled legendary depth:
It was as deep as England. It held
35 Pike too immense to stir, so immense and old
That past nightfall I dared not cast

But silently cast and fished
With the hair frozen on my head
For what might move, for what eye might move.
40 The still splashes on the dark pond,

Owls hushing the floating woods
Frail on my ear against the dream
Darkness beneath night's darkness had freed,
That rose slowly towards me, watching.

(1960)

Hawk Roosting

I sit in the top of the wood, my eyes closed.
Inaction, no falsifying dream
Between my hooked head and hooked feet:
Or in sleep rehearse perfect kills and eat.

5 The convenience of the high trees!
The air's buoyancy and the sun's ray
Are of advantage to me;
And the earth's face upward for my inspection.

My feet are locked upon the rough bark.
10 It took the whole of Creation
To produce my foot, my each feather:
Now I hold Creation in my foot

Or fly up, and revolve it all slowly —
I kill where I please because it is all mine.
15 There is no sophistry in my body:
My manners are tearing off heads —

The allotment of death.
For the one path of my flight is direct
Through the bones of the living.
20   No arguments assert my right:

The sun is behind me.
Nothing has changed since I began.
My eye has permitted no change.
I am going to keep things like this.

(1960)

Sylvia Plath (1932–1963)

The daughter of German and Austrian parents who taught at Boston University, Sylvia Plath was both precocious and ambitious. She excelled at school and college, began writing as a child, and was publishing in popular magazines while still in her teens. She was also manic-depressive and suffered emotionally from the pressure she felt to succeed at everything. Married to English poet Ted Hughes and living in England with her two young children, she committed suicide at age thirty.

Plath's early poems are deftly controlled but fairly conventional, and it is mainly to her later work, most of which appeared in book form only after her death, that she owes her reputation. In her later poems, Plath turned inward to confront the darker side of her psyche — her anger at her parents, her resentment at the cost to her art of motherhood, her sense of evil in modern society, and her obsession with self-destruction as a means of escape — in powerful, highly original, intensely disturbing poems.

Daddy[1]

You do not do, you do not do
Any more, black shoe
In which I have lived like a foot
For thirty years, poor and white,
5   Barely daring to breathe or Achoo.

Daddy, I have had to kill you.
You died before I had time —

———→

1 Plath's father was of German descent but came to America from Poland at age fifteen. He was an expert on bees and taught at Boston University until his early death in 1940.

Marble-heavy, a bag full of God,
Ghastly statue with one gray toe[2]
10   Big as a Frisco seal

And a head in the freakish Atlantic
Where it pours bean green over blue
In the waters off beautiful Nauset.
I used to pray to recover you.
15   Ach, du.[3]

In the German tongue, in the Polish town
Scraped flat by the roller
Of wars, wars, wars.
But the name of the town is common.
20   My Polack friend

Says there are a dozen or two.
So I never could tell where you
Put your foot, your root,
I never could talk to you.
25   The tongue stuck in my jaw.

It stuck in a barb wire snare.
Ich, ich, ich, ich,[4]
I could hardly speak.
I thought every German was you.
30   And the language obscene

An engine, an engine
Chuffing me off like a Jew.
A Jew to Dachau, Auschwitz, Belsen.[5]
I began to talk like a Jew.
35   I think I may well be a Jew.

The snows of the Tyrol, the clear beer of Vienna
Are not very pure or true.
With my gipsy ancestress and my weird luck
And my Taroc pack and my Taroc pack
40   I may be a bit of a Jew.

2 Plath's father died of blood poisoning when his diabetes led to gangrene in a toe. 3 Ah, you (German).
4 I, I, I, I (German). 5 Nazi concentration camps.

I have always been scared of *you*,
With your Luftwaffe, your gobbledygoo.
And your neat mustache
And your Aryan eye, bright blue.
45 Panzer-man, panzer-man, O You —

Not God but a swastika
So black no sky could squeak through.
Every woman adores a Fascist,
The boot in the face, the brute
50 Brute heart of a brute like you.

You stand at the blackboard, daddy,
In the picture I have of you,
A cleft in your chin instead of your foot
But no less a devil for that, no not
55 Any less the black man who

Bit my pretty red heart in two.
I was ten when they buried you.
At twenty I tried to die
And get back, back, back to you.
60 I thought even the bones would do.

But they pulled me out of the sack,
And they stuck me together with glue.
And then I knew what to do.
I made a model of you,
65 A man in black with a Meinkampf[6] look

And a love of the rack and the screw.
And I said I do, I do.
So daddy, I'm finally through.
The black telephone's off at the root,
70 The voices just can't worm through.

---

6 before coming to power, Adolf Hitler (1889–1945) outlined his plans for world domination in *Mein Kampf*,
"my struggle" in German.

If I've killed one man, I've killed two —
The vampire who said he was you
And drank my blood for a year,
Seven years, if you want to know.
75 Daddy, you can lie back now.

There's a stake in your fat black heart
And the villagers never liked you.
They are dancing and stamping on you.
They always *knew* it was you.
80 Daddy, daddy, you bastard, I'm through.

(1965)

Mirror

I am silver and exact. I have no preconceptions.
Whatever I see I swallow immediately
Just as it is, unmisted by love or dislike.
I am not cruel, only truthful —
5 The eye of a little god, four-cornered.
Most of the time I meditate on the opposite wall.
It is pink, with speckles. I have looked at it so long
I think it is a part of my heart. But it flickers.
Faces and darkness separate us over and over.

10 Now I am a lake. A woman bends over me,
Searching my reaches for what she really is.
Then she turns to those liars, the candles or the moon.
I see her back, and reflect it faithfully.
She rewards me with tears and an agitation of hands.
15 I am important to her. She comes and goes.
Each morning it is her face that replaces the darkness.
In me she has drowned a young girl, and in me an old woman
Rises toward her day after day, like a terrible fish.

(1961)   (1971)

Lady Lazarus [1]

I have done it again.
One year in every ten
I manage it —

A sort of walking miracle, my skin
5   Bright as a Nazi lampshade,
My right foot

A paperweight,
My face a featureless, fine
Jew linen.

10   Peel off the napkin
O my enemy.
Do I terrify?—

The nose, the eye pits, the full set of teeth?
The sour breath
15   Will vanish in a day.

Soon, soon the flesh
The grave cave ate will be
At home on me

And I a smiling woman.
20   I am only thirty.
And like the cat I have nine times to die.

This is Number Three.
What a trash
To annihilate each decade.

25   What a million filaments.
The peanut-crunching crowd
Shoves in to see

Them unwrap me hand and foot —
The big strip tease.
30   Gentlemen, ladies

1 Lazarus was brought back from death by Jesus (John 11).

These are my hands
My knees.
I may be skin and bone,

Nevertheless, I am the same, identical woman.
35   The first time it happened I was ten.
It was an accident.

The second time I meant
To last it out and not come back at all.
I rocked shut

40   As a seashell.
They had to call and call
And pick the worms off me like sticky pearls.

Dying
Is an art, like everything else.
45   I do it exceptionally well.

I do it so it feels like hell.
I do it so it feels real.
I guess you could say I've a call.

It's easy enough to do it in a cell.
50   It's easy enough to do it and stay put.
It's the theatrical

Comeback in broad day
To the same place, the same face, the same brute
Amused shout:

55   "A miracle!"
That knocks me out.
There is a charge

For the eyeing of my scars, there is a charge
For the hearing of my heart —
60   It really goes.

And there is a charge, a very large charge
For a word or a touch
Or a bit of blood

Or a piece of my hair or my clothes.
So, so, Herr Doktor.
So, Herr Enemy.

I am your opus,
I am your valuable,
The pure gold baby

That melts to a shriek.
I turn and burn.
Do not think I underestimate your great concern.

Ash, ash —
You poke and stir.
Flesh, bone, there is nothing there —

A cake of soap,
A wedding ring,
A gold filling.

Herr God, Herr Lucifer
Beware
Beware.

Out of the ash
I rise with my red hair
And I eat men like air.

(1965)

Wole Soyinka (b. 1934)

A poet, playwright, novelist, essayist, filmmaker, and academic, Wole Soyinka won the Nobel Prize for literature in 1986, becoming the first African to do so. Born in Abeokuta, Nigeria, Soyinka was educated at the University College, Ibadan, and at Leeds University, where he took a degree in English. A passionate defender of human freedom, Soyinka has had several brushes with Nigerian authorities. During the Nigerian Civil War, he was imprisoned by the military government, an experience that produced some of his most powerful prose and poetry. After he protested the cancellation of election results in 1993, the government seized his passport. Soyinka was forced to live in exile, travelling on a U.N. passport. Nevertheless, the Nigerian government charged him with treason in March 1997, claiming that he and other dissidents were instrumental in a series of bombings of army installations. In 1999, the year after the charges were dropped, Soyinka visited Nigeria. He also published *The Burden of Memory, the Muse of Forgiveness*, about African crimes against humanity and the problems of reconciliation.

Although he can write biting satire, such as "Telephone Conversation," Soyinka tends to be a profound and complex writer, drawing on sources as disparate as Yoruba culture, the Bible, and Greek mythology. He can evoke a sense of the African landscape as a physical and psychological setting, but his dominant concerns are universal: a respect for life and a desire for a society in which individuals can live in dignity and freedom.

Telephone Conversation

The price seemed reasonable, location
Indifferent. The landlady swore she lived
Off premises. Nothing remained
But self-confession. "Madam," I warned,
5 "I hate a wasted journey — I am African."
Silence. Silenced transmission of
Pressurized good-breeding. Voice, when it came,
Lipstick coated, long gold-rolled
Cigarette-holder pipped. Caught I was, foully.
10 "HOW DARK?"... I had not misheard..."ARE YOU LIGHT
OR VERY DARK?" Button B. Button A.[1] Stench
Of rancid breath of public hide-and-speak.

———▶

---

1 at the time the poem was written, on coin-operated telephones in England the caller pressed Button A to make a connection and Button B to cancel the call and to retrieve coins if the number was busy or if no one answered.

Red booth. Red pillar-box.[2] Red double-tiered
Omnibus squelching tar. It *was* real! Shamed
15 By ill-mannered silence, surrender
Pushed dumbfoundment to beg simplification.
Considerate she was, varying the emphasis —
"ARE YOU DARK? OR VERY LIGHT?" Revelation came.
"You mean — like plain or milk chocolate?"
20 Her assent was clinical, crushing in its light
Impersonality. Rapidly, wave-length adjusted,
I chose. "West African sepia"— and as afterthought,
"Down in my passport." Silence for spectroscopic[3]
Flight of fancy, till truthfulness clanged her accent
25 Hard on the mouthpiece. "WHAT'S THAT?" conceding
"DON'T KNOW WHAT THAT IS." "Like brunette."
"THAT'S DARK, ISN'T IT?" "Not altogether.
Facially, I am brunette, but madam, you should see
The rest of me. Palm of my hand, soles of my feet
30 Are a peroxide blonde. Friction, caused —
Foolishly madam — by sitting down, has turned
My bottom raven black — One moment madam!"— sensing
Her receiver rearing on the thunderclap
About my ears — "Madam," I pleaded, "wouldn't you rather
35 See for yourself?"

(1960)

I Think It Rains

I think it rains
That tongues may loosen from the parch
Uncleave roof-tops of the mouth, hang
Heavy with knowledge

5 I saw it raise
The sudden cloud, from ashes. Settling
They joined in a ring of grey; within,
The circling spirit

2 cylindrical postal box. 3 a spectroscope is an instrument that enables analysis of a range of colours.

Oh it must rain
10   These closures on the mind, binding us
In strange despairs, teaching
Purity of sadness

And how it beats
Skeined transparencies on wings
15   Of our desires, searing dark longings
In cruel baptisms

Rain-reeds, practised in
The grace of yielding, yet unbending
From afar, this your conjugation with my earth
20   Bares crouching rocks.

(1967)

Procession I: Hanging Day

Hanging day. A hollow earth
Echoes footsteps of the grave procession
Walls in sunspots
Lean to shadows of the shortening morn

5   Behind, an eyepatch lushly blue.
The wall of prayer[1] has taken refuge
In a peace of blindness, closed
Its grey recessive deeps. Fretful limbs

And glances that would sometimes
10   Conjure up a drawbridge
Raised but never lowered between
Their gathering and my sway

Withdraw, as all the living world
Belie their absence in a feel of eyes
15   Barred and secret in the empty home
Of shuttered windows. I know the heart
Has journeyed far from present

1 prison wall where the inmates prayed and sang hymns.

Tread. Drop. Dread Drop. Dead

What may I tell you? What reveal?
20 I who before them peered unseen
Who stood one-legged on the untrodden
Verge — lest I should not return.

That I received them? That I
Wheeled above and flew beneath them
25 And brought them on their way
And came to mine, even to the edge
Of the unspeakable encirclement?
What may I tell you of the five
Bell-ringers on the ropes to chimes
30 Of silence?
What tell you of rigors of the law?
From watchtowers on stunted walls,
Raised to stay a siege of darkness
What whisper to their football thunders
35 Vanishing to shrouds of sunlight?

Let no man speak of justice, guilt.
Far away, blood-stained in their
Tens of thousands, hands that damned
These wretches to the pit triumph
40 But here, alone the solitary deed.

(1972)

Alden Nowlan (1933–1983)

Although he had a limited formal education — he left school after Grade 5 —
Nowlan became one of the leading literary figures in Atlantic Canada. Born in
Windsor, Nova Scotia, he held various jobs as a manual labourer until he moved
to New Brunswick to work as a journalist. He began his literary career as a
poet, publishing his first collection in 1958. *Bread, Wine and Salt* (1967) won the
Governor General's Award. Later, he turned his hand to other genres, produc-
ing plays, stories, and a novel. Although he is a regionalist, painting relatively real-
istic pictures of nature and society in Atlantic Canada, Nowlan infuses his poems
with universal significance. He can also, like a backwoods storyteller, be by

turns sentimental and ironic. "The Bull Moose," his most famous poem, shows his characteristic attitudes; he evokes sympathy for victims and imbues even mundane events with religious or spiritual importance.

The Bull Moose

Down from the purple mist of trees on the mountain,
lurching through forests of white spruce and cedar,
stumbling through tamarack swamps,
came the bull moose
5 to be stopped at last by a pole-fenced pasture.

Too tired to turn or, perhaps, aware
there was no place left to go, he stood with the cattle.
They, scenting the musk of death, seeing his great head
like the ritual mask of a blood god, moved to the other end
10 of the field, and waited.

The neighbours heard of it, and by afternoon
cars lined the road. The children teased him
with alder switches and he gazed at them
like an old, tolerant collie. The women asked
15 if he could have escaped from a Fair.

The oldest man in the parish remembered seeing
a gelded moose yoked with an ox for plowing.
The young men snickered and tried to pour beer
down his throat, while their girlfriends took their pictures.

20 And the bull moose let them stroke his tick-ravaged flanks,
let them pry open his jaws with bottles, let a giggling girl
plant a little purple cap
of thistles on his head.

When the wardens came, everyone agreed it was a shame
25 to shoot anything so shaggy and cuddlesome.
He looked like the kind of pet
women put to bed with their sons.

So they held their fire. But just as the sun dropped in the river
the bull moose gathered his strength
30   like a scaffolded king, straightened and lifted his horns
so that even the wardens backed away as they raised their rifles.
When he roared, people ran to their cars. All the young men
leaned on their automobile horns as he toppled.

(1962)

Leonard Cohen (b. 1934)

Born into a wealthy Montreal family, Cohen received a B.A. from McGill University in 1955. Since then, he has moved freely between literature and popular culture, becoming an internationally successful poet and singer, and a controversial experimental novelist. He won, but refused to accept, the Governor General's Award for *Selected Poems* (1968). Cohen has received three Juno Awards for his recordings, and in 1993 he was honoured for his lifetime achievement with a Governor General's Performing Arts Award.

In much of Cohen's work, traditional poetic elements contrast with the contemporary subject matter. That is to say, their lush imagery and abundant musical qualities mark his poems as conventionally romantic and deliberately "poetic" works. However, their bleakness and shocking assaults on conventional moral assumptions make them thoroughly modern. Cohen frequently combines images from classical mythology or religion (drawing on both his own Jewish heritage and that of the dominant Catholic culture of Quebec) with images of sex, suffering, violence, and death. In this way he attempts to create an informal mythology to replace what he considers the worn-out myths of the past. The exact meaning of Cohen's poems is often elusive, but one figure is central. The "saint" renounces the ordinary world, enduring consequent suffering and even destruction of the self in order to achieve the purity necessary to attain a higher state. In Cohen's mythic world, the only winners are beautiful losers.

A Kite Is a Victim

A kite is a victim you are sure of.
You love it because it pulls
gentle enough to call you master,
strong enough to call you fool;
5   because it lives
like a trained falcon
in the high sweet air,
and you can always haul it down
to tame it in your drawer.

10   A kite is a fish you have already caught
in a pool where no fish come,
so you play him carefully and long,
and hope he won't give up,
or the wind die down.

15   A kite is the last poem you've written,
so you give it to the wind,
but you don't let it go
until someone finds you
something else to do.

20   A kite is a contract of glory
that must be made with the sun,
so you make friends with the field
the river and the wind,
then you pray the whole cold night before,
25   under the travelling cordless moon,
to make you worthy and lyric and pure.

(1961)

For E.J.P.[1]

I once believed a single line
     in a Chinese poem could change
       forever how blossoms fell
and that the moon itself climbed on
5   the grief of concise weeping men
       to journey over cups of wine
I thought invasions were begun for crows
     to pick at a skeleton
       dynasties sown and spent

⟶

1 E.J. Pratt (see page 250).

10   to serve the language of a fine lament
          I thought governors ended their lives
                as sweetly drunken monks
     telling time by rain and candles
          instructed by an insect's pilgrimage
15   across the page — all this
     so one might send an exile's perfect letter
     to an ancient home-town friend

     I chose a lonely country
          broke from love
20   scorned the fraternity of war
     I polished my tongue against the pumice moon
          floated my soul in cherry wine
                a perfumed barge for Lords of Memory
     to languish on to drink to whisper out
25   their store of strength
                as if beyond the mist along the shore
     their girls their power still obeyed
          like clocks wound for a thousand years
     I waited until my tongue was sore

30   Brown petals wind like fire around my poems
          I aimed them at the stars but
                like rainbows they were bent
     before they sawed the world in half
          Who can trace the canyoned paths
35   cattle have carved out of time
     wandering from meadowlands to feasts
          Layer after layer of autumn leaves
                are swept away
     Something forgets us perfectly

                                        (1964)

Suzanne Takes You Down

Suzanne takes you down
to her place near the river,
you can hear the boats go by
you can stay the night beside her.

                    ⟶

5 And you know that she's half crazy
but that's why you want to be there
and she feeds you tea and oranges
that come all the way from China.
Just when you mean to tell her
10 that you have no gifts to give her,
she gets you on her wave-length
and she lets the river answer
that you've always been her lover.
    And you want to travel with her,
15 you want to travel blind
    and you know that she can trust you
    because you've touched her perfect body
    with your mind.

Jesus was a sailor
20 when he walked upon the water
and he spent a long time watching
from a lonely wooden tower
and when he knew for certain
only drowning men could see him
25 he said All men will be sailors then
until the sea shall free them,
but he himself was broken
long before the sky would open,
forsaken, almost human,
30 he sank beneath your wisdom like a stone.
    And you want to travel with him,
    you want to travel blind
    and you think maybe you'll trust him
    because he touched your perfect body
35 with his mind.

Suzanne takes your hand
and she leads you to the river,
she is wearing rags and feathers
from Salvation Army counters.
40 The sun pours down like honey
on our lady of the harbour
as she shows you where to look
among the garbage and the flowers,
there are heroes in the seaweed

$\longrightarrow$

45   there are children in the morning,
they are leaning out for love
they will lean that way forever
while Suzanne she holds the mirror.
    And you want to travel with her
50   and you want to travel blind
and you're sure that she can find you
because she's touched her perfect body
with her mind.

(1966)

Closing Time

So we're drinking and we're dancing
and the band is really happening
and the Johnny Walker[1] wisdom running high
And my very sweet companion
5   she's the Angel of Compassion
and she's rubbing half the world against her thigh
Every drinker, every dancer
lifts a happy face to thank her
and the fiddler fiddles something so sublime
10   All the women tear their blouses off
and the men they dance on the polka-dots
and it's partner found and it's partner lost
and it's hell to pay when the fiddler stops
It's closing time

15   We're lonely, we're romantic
and the cider's laced with acid[2]
and the Holy Spirit's crying, "Where's the beef?"[3]
And the moon is swimming naked
and the summer night is fragrant
20   with a mighty expectation of relief
So we struggle and we stagger
down the snakes and up the ladder

$\longrightarrow$

1 brand of Scotch whisky. 2 lysergic acid diethylamide (LSD), a hallucinogenic drug. 3 slogan made
popular by commercials for a hamburger chain.

to the tower where the blessed hours chime
And I swear it happened just like this:
25 a sigh, a cry, a hungry kiss
the Gates of Love they budged an inch
I can't say much has happened since
but closing time

I loved you for your beauty
30 but that doesn't make a fool of me —
you were in it for your beauty too
I loved you for your body
there's a voice that sounds like G-d to me
declaring that your body's really you
35 I loved you when our love was blessed
and I love you now there's nothing left
but sorrow and a sense of overtime
And I miss you since our place got wrecked
I just don't care what happens next
40 looks like freedom but it feels like death
it's something in between, I guess
it's closing time

And I miss you since the place got wrecked
by the winds of change and the weeds of sex
45 looks like freedom but it feels like death
it's something in between, I guess
it's closing time

We're drinking and we're dancing
but there's nothing really happening
50 the place is dead as Heaven on a Saturday night
And my very close companion
gets me fumbling, gets me laughing
she's a hundred but she's wearing something tight
And I lift my glass to the Awful Truth
55 which you can't reveal to the Ears of Youth
except to say it isn't worth a dime
And the whole damn place goes crazy twice
and it's once for the Devil and it's once for Christ
but the Boss don't like these dizzy heights —
60 we're busted in the blinding lights
of closing time.

(1992)

Seamus Heaney (b. 1939)

Winner of the 1995 Nobel Prize for literature, Seamus Heaney has been praised for his evocative language and for the integrity of his treatment of the troubles in Northern Ireland. Born in County Derry in Northern Ireland, he graduated from Queen's University, Belfast, in 1961 and obtained a teacher's diploma the next year. He has held a number of teaching appointments, including positions at his alma mater and at Harvard University. He published his first full-length collection, *Death of a Naturalist*, to critical acclaim in 1966. A Roman Catholic increasingly upset by the conflict in Northern Ireland, Heaney moved to the Irish Republic in 1972 in order, he said, "to put the practice of poetry more deliberately at the centre of my life." Ireland—its traditions, its rural landscape, and its political and religious difficulties—is at the centre of Heaney's poetry, but he also explores universal themes, such as the role of the poet and the nature of art. A poet whose unobtrusive craftsmanship produces works that are immediately accessible but also deeply moving and memorable, he has described poetry "as a point of entry into the buried life of the feelings or as a point of exit for it."

Death of a Naturalist

All year the flax-dam festered in the heart
Of the townland; green and heavy headed
Flax had rotted there, weighted down by huge sods.
Daily it sweltered in the punishing sun.
5 Bubbles gargled delicately, bluebottles
Wove a strong gauze of sound around the smell.
There were dragon-flies, spotted butterflies,
But best of all was the warm thick slobber
Of frogspawn that grew like clotted water
10 In the shade of the banks. Here, every spring
I would fill jampotfuls of the jellied
Specks to range on window-sills at home,
On shelves at school, and wait and watch until
The fattening dots burst into nimble-
15 Swimming tadpoles. Miss Walls would tell us how
The daddy frog was called a bullfrog
And how he croaked and how the mammy frog
Laid hundreds of little eggs and this was
Frogspawn. You could tell the weather by frogs too
20 For they were yellow in the sun and brown
In rain.

Then one hot day when fields were rank
With cowdung in the grass the angry frogs
Invaded the flax-dam; I ducked through hedges
25 To a coarse croaking that I had not heard
Before. The air was thick with a bass chorus.
Right down the dam gross-bellied frogs were cocked
On sods; their loose necks pulsed like sails. Some hopped:
The slap and plop were obscene threats. Some sat
30 Poised like mud grenades, their blunt heads farting.
I sickened, turned, and ran. The great slime kings
Were gathered there for vengeance and I knew
That if I dipped my hand the spawn would clutch it.

(1966)

The Singer's House

When they said *Carrickfergus*[1] I could hear
the frosty echo of saltminers' picks.
I imagined it, chambered and glinting,
a township built of light.

5 What do we say any more
to conjure the salt of our earth?
So much comes and is gone
that should be crystal and kept

and amicable weathers
10 that bring up the grain of things,
their tang of season and store,
are all the packing we'll get.

So I say to myself *Gweebarra*[2]
and its music hits off the place
15 like water hitting off granite.
I see the glittering sound

1 Northern Irish salt-mining area and seaport, the subject of a popular Irish folksong. 2 the bay in County
Donegal in the Irish Republic.

framed in your window,
knives and forks set on oilcloth,
and the seals' heads, suddenly outlined,
20   scanning everything.

People here used to believe
that drowned souls lived in the seals.
At spring tides they might change shape.
They loved music and swam in for a singer

25   who might stand at the end of summer
in the mouth of a whitewashed turf-shed,
his shoulder to the jamb, his song
a rowboat far out in evening.

When I came here first you were always singing,
30   a hint of the clip of the pick
in your winnowing climb and attack.
Raise it again, man. We still believe what we hear.

(1979)

The Harvest Bow

As you plaited the harvest bow
You implicated the mellowed silence in you
In wheat that does not rust
But brightens as it tightens twist by twist
5   Into a knowable corona,
A throwaway love-knot of straw.

Hands that aged round ashplants and cane sticks
And lapped the spurs on a lifetime of game cocks
Harked to their gift and worked with fine intent
10   Until your fingers moved somnambulant:
I tell and finger it like braille,
Gleaning the unsaid off the palpable,

And if I spy into its golden loops
I see us walk between the railway slopes
15 Into an evening of long grass and midges,
Blue smoke straight up, old beds and ploughs in hedges,
An auction notice on an outhouse wall —
You with a harvest bow in your lapel,

Me with the fishing rod, already homesick
20 For the big lift of these evenings, as your stick
Whacking the tips off weeds and bushes
Beats out of time, and beats, but flushes
Nothing: that original townland
Still tongue-tied in the straw tied by your hand.

25 *The end of art is peace*
Could be the motto of this frail device
That I have pinned up on our deal dresser —
Like a drawn snare
Slipped lately by the spirit of the corn
30 Yet burnished by its passage, and still warm.

(1979)

Casualty [1]

I

He would drink by himself
And raise a weathered thumb
Towards the high shelf,
Calling another rum
5 And blackcurrant, without
Having to raise his voice,
Or order a quick stout
By a lifting of the eyes
And a discreet dumb-show

——→

1 Heaney has identified the subject of this poem as Louis O'Neill, who frequented a pub owned by Heaney's father-in-law in County Tyrone. An alcoholic, O'Neill defied a curfew imposed by Catholics who were mourning the thirteen men shot dead by British soldiers on "Bloody Sunday," January 30, 1972. The men were killed after violence erupted during an illegal march organized by the Derry Civil Rights Association. As Heaney noted, O'Neill was killed by a bomb "planted by his own people."

10   Of pulling off the top;
      At closing time would go
      In waders and peaked cap
      Into the showery dark,
      A dole-kept[2] breadwinner
15   But a natural for work.
      I loved his whole manner,
      Sure-footed but too sly,
      His deadpan sidling tact,
      His fisherman's quick eye
20   And turned observant back.

      Incomprehensible
      To him, my other life.
      Sometimes, on his high stool,
      Too busy with his knife
25   At a tobacco plug
      And not meeting my eye,
      In the pause after a slug
      He mentioned poetry.
      We would be on our own
30   And, always politic
      And shy of condescension,
      I would manage by some trick
      To switch the talk to eels
      Or lore of the horse and cart
35   Or the Provisionals.[3]

      But my tentative art
      His turned back watches too:
      He was blown to bits
      Out drinking in a curfew
40   Others obeyed, three nights
      After they shot dead
      The thirteen men in Derry.
      PARAS THIRTEEN, the walls said,

                    ⟶

2 one who lives on social assistance payments "doled out" by the government. 3 the Provisional Irish
Republican Army, a militant group that split off from the IRA in December 1969 when the IRA decided to
give at least token recognition to three parliaments: Westminster, Dublin, and Stormont.

BOGSIDE NIL.[4] That Wednesday
45   Everybody held
His breath and trembled.

II

It was a day of cold
Raw silence, wind-blown
Surplice and soutane:[5]
50   Rained-on, flower-laden
Coffin after coffin
Seemed to float from the door
Of the packed cathedral
Like blossoms on slow water.
55   The common funeral
Unrolled its swaddling band,
Lapping, tightening
Till we were braced and bound
Like brothers in a ring.

60   But he would not be held
At home by his own crowd
Whatever threats were phoned,
Whatever black flags waved.
I see him as he turned
65   In that bombed offending place,
Remorse fused with terror
In his still knowable face,
His cornered outfaced stare
Blinding in the flash.

70   He had gone miles away
For he drank like a fish
Nightly, naturally
Swimming towards the lure
Of warm lit-up places,
75   The blurred mesh and murmur

→

---

4 the slogan on the wall is like a football score. Paras are the members of the First Parachute Regiment, who had killed the thirteen men on Bloody Sunday; Bogside is the working-class Catholic district in which the killings occurred. 5 a soutane, or cassock, is a long, loose-fitting garment worn by priests, altar boys, and choristers; a surplice is a loose-fitting, wide-sleeved white vestment worn over the soutane.

Drifting among glasses
In the gregarious smoke.
How culpable was he
That last night when he broke
80 Our tribe's complicity?
"Now you're supposed to be
An educated man,"
I hear him say. "Puzzle me
The right answer to that one."

III

85 I missed his funeral,
Those quiet walkers
And sideways talkers
Shoaling out of his lane
To the respectable
90 Purring of the hearse...
They move in equal pace
With the habitual
Slow consolation
Of a dawdling engine,
95 The line lifted, hand
Over fist, cold sunshine
On the water, the land
Banked under fog: that morning
I was taken in his boat,
100 The screw purling,[6] turning
Indolent fathoms white,
I tasted freedom with him.
To get out early, haul
Steadily off the bottom,
105 Dispraise the catch, and smile
As you find a rhythm
Working you, slow mile by mile,
Into your proper haunt
Somewhere, well out, beyond...

110 Dawn-sniffing revenant,[7]
Plodder through midnight rain,
Question me again.

(1979)

6 the boat's propeller, or screw, is making a murmuring sound. 7 one who returns, such as a ghost or spirit after death.

Margaret Atwood (b. 1939)

Internationally successful as both a poet and a novelist, Margaret Atwood was born in Ottawa and educated at the University of Toronto and Radcliffe College, Harvard. She has worked as a book editor, has taught English at several universities, and has been a university writer in residence. Her first book was a thin volume of poems, *Double Persephone* (1961). Her second collection, *The Circle Game* (1966), won the Governor General's Award. Her novels include *Surfacing* (1972) and *The Handmaid's Tale* (1985), winner of the Governor General's Award for fiction. *Survival* (1972) is a controversial study of Canadian literature in which she expands upon Northrop Frye's analysis of the "garrison mentality" and argues that Canadian literature is dominated by images of victims. In her own poetry, she often explores victimization and liberation, dissecting the personal, psychological, cultural, political, and sexual ideas or myths confining the individual. This exploration frequently challenges both conventional perceptions of reality and conventional logic. Although she has said that sound and phrasing are important elements in her poetry, Atwood does not indulge in verbal pyrotechnics. Typically, her narrators employ startlingly provocative and often violent images, but they make thematic pronouncements in a flat, unemotional voice. In this way, she conveys both the violence of the modern world and the alienation of its victims.

Progressive Insanities of a Pioneer

i

He stood, a point
on a sheet of green paper
proclaiming himself the centre,

with no walls, no borders
5   anywhere; the sky no height
above him, totally un-
enclosed
and shouted:
Let me out!

ii

10 He dug the soil in rows,
imposed himself with shovels
He asserted
into the furrows, I
am not random.

———>

15 The ground
replied with aphorisms:

a tree-sprout, a nameless
weed, words
he couldn't understand.

iii

20 The house pitched
the plot staked
in the middle of nowhere.

At night the mind
inside, in the middle
25 of nowhere.

The idea of an animal
patters across the roof.

In the darkness the fields
defend themselves with fences
30 in vain:
          everything
          is getting in.

iv

By daylight he resisted.
He said, disgusted
35 with the swamp's clamourings and the outbursts
of rocks,
          This is not order
          but the absence
          of order.

40 He was wrong, the unanswering
forest implied:

          It was
          an ordered absence

v

For many years
45   he fished for a great vision,
dangling the hooks of sown
roots under the surface
of the shallow earth.

It was like
50   enticing whales with a bent
pin. Besides he thought

in that country
only the worms were biting.

vi

If he had known unstructured
55   space is a deluge
and stocked his log house-
boat with all the animals

even the wolves,

he might have floated.

60   But obstinate he
stated, The land is solid
and stamped,

watching his foot sink
down through stone
65   up to the knee.

vii

Things
refused to name themselves; refused
to let him name them.

The wolves hunted
70   outside.

On his beaches, his clearings,
by the surf of under-
growth breaking
at his feet, he foresaw
75   disintegration
        and in the end
through eyes
made ragged by his
effort, the tension
80   between subject and object,

the green
vision, the unnamed
whale invaded.

(1968)

The Animals in That Country

In that country the animals
have the faces of people:

the ceremonial
cats possessing the streets

5   the fox run
politely to earth, the huntsmen
standing around him, fixed
in their tapestry of manners

the bull, embroidered
10   with blood and given
an elegant death, trumpets, his name
stamped on him, heraldic brand
because

(when he rolled
15   on the sand, sword in his heart, the teeth
in his blue mouth were human)

he is really a man

even the wolves, holding resonant
conversations in their
20   forests thickened with legend.

In this country the animals
have the faces of
animals.

Their eyes
25   flash once in car headlights
and are gone.

Their deaths are not elegant.

They have the faces of
no-one.

(1968)

Further Arrivals[1]

After we had crossed the long illness
that was the ocean, we sailed up-river

On the first island
the immigrants threw off their clothes
5   and danced like sandflies

We left behind one by one
the cities rotting with cholera,
one by one our civilized
distinctions

10   and entered a large darkness.

1 the speaker in this poem is Susanna Moodie (1803–85), a pioneer settler and author. Atwood based events in this and the other poems in *The Journals of Susanna Moodie* (1970) on Mrs. Moodie's accounts of her life in *Roughing It in the Bush* (1852) and *Life in the Clearings* (1853).

It was our own
ignorance we entered.

I have not come out yet

My brain gropes nervous
15 tentacles in the night, sends out
fears hairy as bears,
demands lamps; or waiting

for my shadowy husband, hears
malice in the trees' whispers.

20 I need wolf's eyes to see
the truth.

I refuse to look in a mirror.

Whether the wilderness is
real or not
25 depends on who lives there.

(1970)

you fit into me

you fit into me
like a hook into an eye

a fish hook
an open eye

(1973)

Siren Song[1]

This is the song everyone
would like to learn: the song
that is irresistible:

the song that forces men
5   to leap overboard in squadrons
even though they see the beached skulls

the song nobody knows
because anyone who has heard it
is dead, and the others can't remember.

10   Shall I tell you the secret
and if I do, will you get me
out of this bird suit?

I don't enjoy it here
squatting on this island
15   looking picturesque and mythical

with these two feathery maniacs,
I don't enjoy singing
this trio, fatal and valuable.

I will tell the secret to you,
20   to you, only to you.
Come closer. This song

is a cry for help: Help me!
Only you, only you can,
you are unique

25   at last. Alas
it is a boring song
but it works every time.

(1974)

---

1 in Greek mythology, the three sirens, who were half woman and half bird, lured sailors to destruction with enchanting songs.

Variations on the Word *Love*

This is a word we use to plug
holes with. It's the right size for those warm
blanks in speech, for those red heart-
shaped vacancies on the page that look nothing
5   like real hearts. Add lace
and you can sell
it. We insert it also in the one empty
space on the printed form
that comes with no instructions. There are whole
10   magazines with not much in them
but the word *love*, you can
rub it all over your body and you
can cook with it too. How do we know
it isn't what goes on at the cool
15   debaucheries of slugs under damp
pieces of cardboard? As for the weed-
seedlings nosing their tough snouts up
among the lettuces, they shout it.
Love! Love! sing the soldiers, raising
20   their glittering knives in salute.

Then there's the two
of us. This word
is far too short for us, it has only
four letters, too sparse
25   to fill those deep bare
vacuums between the stars
that press on us with their deafness.
It's not love we don't wish
to fall into, but that fear.
30   This word is not enough but it will
have to do. It's a single
vowel in this metallic
silence, a mouth that says
O again and again in wonder
35   and pain, a breath, a finger-
grip on a cliffside. You can
hold on or let go.

(1981)

A Women's Issue

The woman in the spiked device
that locks around the waist and between
the legs, with holes in it like a tea strainer
is Exhibit A.

5 The woman in black with a net window
to see through and a four-inch
wooden peg jammed up
between her legs so she can't be raped
is Exhibit B.

10 Exhibit C is the young girl
dragged into the bush by the midwives
and made to sing while they scrape the flesh
from between her legs, then tie her thighs
till she scabs over and is called healed.

15 Now she can be married.
For each childbirth they'll cut her
open, then sew her up.
Men like tight women.
The ones that die are carefully buried.

20 The next exhibit lies flat on her back
while eighty men a night
move through her, ten an hour.
She looks at the ceiling, listens
to the door open and close.
25 A bell keeps ringing.
Nobody knows how she got here.

You'll notice that what they have in common
is between the legs. Is this
why wars are fought?
30 Enemy territory, no man's
land, to be entered furtively,
fenced, owned but never surely,
scene of these desperate forays
at midnight, captures

35   and sticky murders, doctors' rubber gloves
greasy with blood, flesh made inert, the surge
of your own uneasy power.

This is no museum.
Who invented the word *love*?

(1981)

Helen of Troy[1] Does Counter Dancing

The world is full of women
who'd tell me I should be ashamed of myself
if they had the chance. Quit dancing.
Get some self-respect
5   and a day job.
Right. And minimum wage,
and varicose veins, just standing
in one place for eight hours
behind a glass counter
10   bundled up to the neck, instead of
naked as a meat sandwich.
Selling gloves, or something.
Instead of what I do sell.
You have to have talent
15   to peddle a thing so nebulous
and without material form.
Exploited, they'd say. Yes, any way
you cut it, but I've a choice
of how, and I'll take the money.

20   I do give value.
Like preachers, I sell vision,
like perfume ads, desire
or its facsimile. Like jokes
or war, it's all in the timing.

—————→

1 according to Greek legend, Helen was the most beautiful woman in the world and the cause of the Trojan War. Her mother was Leda, and her father was Zeus, who assumed the form of a swan and raped Leda. Helen, who had many suitors, married Menelaus, but Paris seduced her and carried her off to Troy. Menelaus and her Greek suitors then waged war on Troy to recover her. (See also Yeats's "Leda and the Swan," page 261.)

25 I sell men back their worst suspicions:
that everything's for sale,
and piecemeal. They gaze at me and see
a chain-saw murder just before it happens,
when thigh, ass, inkblot, crevice, tit, and nipple
30 are still connected.
Such hatred leaps in them,
my beery worshippers! That, or a bleary
hopeless love. Seeing the rows of heads
and upturned eyes, imploring
35 but ready to snap at my ankles,
I understand floods and earthquakes, and the urge
to step on ants. I keep the beat,
and dance for them because
they can't. The music smells like foxes,
40 crisp as heated metal
searing the nostrils
or humid as August, hazy and languorous
as a looted city the day after,
when all the rape's been done
45 already, and the killing,
and the survivors wander around
looking for garbage
to eat, and there's only a bleak exhaustion.

Speaking of which, it's the smiling
50 tires me out the most.
This, and the pretence
that I can't hear them.
And I can't, because I'm after all
a foreigner to them.
55 The speech here is all warty gutturals,
obvious as a slab of ham,
but I come from the province of the gods
where meanings are lilting and oblique.
I don't let on to everyone,
60 but lean close, and I'll whisper:
My mother was raped by a holy swan.
You believe that? You can take me out to dinner.
That's what we tell all the husbands.
There sure are a lot of dangerous birds around.

65   Not that anyone here
     but you would understand.
     The rest of them would like to watch me
     and feel nothing. Reduce me to components
     as in a clock factory or abattoir.
70   Crush out the mystery.
     Wall me up alive
     in my own body.
     They'd like to see through me,
     but nothing is more opaque
75   than absolute transparency.
     Look — my feet don't hit the marble!
     Like breath or a balloon, I'm rising,
     I hover six inches in the air
     in my blazing swan-egg of light.
80   You think I'm not a goddess?
     Try me.
     This is a torch song.[2]
     Touch me and you'll burn.

                                                        (1995)

Tom Dawe   (b. 1940)

Born in Long Pond, Manuels, Conception Bay, Tom Dawe graduated from
Memorial University, St. John's, Newfoundland. After teaching for seven years
at outport schools, he became a member of Memorial's English Department in
1969. Dawe's first collection of poems was *Connections* (1972), which also con-
tains work by Tom Moore. *Hemlock Cove and After* (1975) was the first book
devoted solely to his own poems. Dawe has been active in promoting
Newfoundland literature, being one of the founding members of Breakwater
Books and a founding editor of *TickleAce*. A respected painter as well as a poet,
Dawe brings a sharp visual sense to his writing, often capturing outport scenes
in crisp, imagistic phrases.

---

2 song concerned with failure in love.

The Bear

Once in a long gone night
before any people came
and the island's trees
were spears of ice
5   against the frosty stars
he came ashore
and used the land
as a stepping stone
in miles of polar ice.
10   His great tracks
in a long cryptic chain
from shore to shore
were there for days and nights
before another snowfall
15   filled them in
and trees waved in resonance
as a rising surf
rolled the ice offshore.

Years later when a few people lived here
20   there was once
a long winter famine
with the fish all gone
and a grave-digger worked hard
getting below the snow and earth
25   on energy from his last meal
of potato peels.
One day in this starvation spell
he came back again
walking out of a blizzard
30   like some misty giant
from the children's books
walking towards the village guns
and bringing the famine to an end.

In another age
35   when only the old remembered
the hungry times
he came ashore one day
→

from the loose ice-pans
unlocking from the shoreline
40   in the south-west wind.
Some people saw him
and watched him cross the beach
on his way past flakes and stages
and low root-cellars.
45   Others came with spears and guns
and tracked him to the tree-line.

Later, in a sea-port town
they charged people ten cents
to look at him
50   propped up with ropes
against the wall of a merchant's shed.

Years later with the island abandoned
two boys returned one spring
to fish for salmon
55   in the land of their ancestors
and in a night
with pebbles rolling
in the land-wash moonlight
the bear returned
60   brushing by their tent
on his way down the river bank.

Next morning they found his body
stiff under fly-buzzing
on the warm beach stones.
65   They saw the swollen head
that had starved for some time
with a tin-can stuck
on the gangrene tongue.

Tonight in the glow from televisions
70   descendants of the island people
half-listen to somebody
reading late news
linked across a nation
and near the end

—————▶

75 just before the Late Show
they hear of another large bear
roaming dangerously close
to some town dump
where concerned officials
80 are on the way
with a sleeping-drug
on the tips of gun-powered needles.
They will do their best
to fly him far back somewhere
85 from any civilized community.

(1975)

The Naked Man

In a wet August day
with salt wind on the berry leaves,
he loomed in the close fog
across the cape
5 and bog meadows slanting down
to the ocean's roar.
Around him, dim cattle stood
still as rock piles
in the driftwood light.
10 Above him gulls screamed
down the dark tide
and gannets darted
in the herring shine.

I asked him to come with me
15 down through wet marshes
where the pond was hidden
but he had fences to mend
and cattle to tend
and a sure way for me
20 to find the pond myself.
His face was granite smiling
and offering warm pipes
and chairs by a cracking stove
and brown china mugs

$\longrightarrow$

25   where kitchen-saints smiled down
      through kettle steam.

      Later, in the half-gone morning,
      I found his marker to the pond:
      "the naked man"
30   of weathered, wind-honed stones
      and snakes of juniper stumps,
      a clumsy rock man
      leaning back from the sea wind.

      Still later, returning in twilight,
35   I crept by the man of stones
      silently watching me
      returning to my road-sign world
      with small trout in a plastic bag,
      silently watching me
40   wander on wet, pathless moss,
      groping in metamorphic shadows
      in bog-sucking footsteps
      away from those cryptic rocks,
      me, the most naked man of all.

      (1978)   (1981)

Gwendolyn MacEwen   (1941–1987)

Born in Toronto, Gwendolyn MacEwen grew up there and in Winnipeg. She dis-
covered her calling as a writer early: at the age of seventeen she published her
first poem, and she left school the next year to pursue her career. In addition to
poetry, MacEwen wrote two novels, a collection of short stories, two children's
books, and a number of radio plays and documentaries. Her books of poetry
include *A Breakfast for Barbarians* (1966), *The Shadow-Maker* (1969), winner
of the Governor General's Award, and *The T.E. Lawrence Poems* (1982). MacEwen
said of her work: "I write basically to communicate joy, mystery, passion...
not the joy that naïvely exists without knowledge of pain, but that joy which
arises out of and conquers pain. I want to construct a myth." MacEwen con-
structs her myth, which celebrates the triumph of the human spirit, with mate-
rials borrowed from a variety of traditions. Lush, even exotic, imagery establishes
the dualities that are central to her mythic vision. Throughout her poetry, she
explores meaningful relationships between spiritual and physical worlds, arche-
typal and mundane experience, waking and dreaming consciousness, past and
present times, painful and joyful events, and male and female lives.

A Breakfast for Barbarians

my friends, my sweet barbarians,
there is that hunger which is not for food —
but an eye at the navel turns the appetite
round
5 with visions of some fabulous sandwich,
the brain's golden breakfast
          eaten with beasts
          with books on plates

let us make an anthology of recipes,
10 let us edit for breakfast
our most unspeakable appetites —
let us pool spoons, knives
and all cutlery in a cosmic cuisine,
let us answer hunger
15 with boiled chimera[1]
and apocalyptic tea,
an arcane salad of spiced bibles,
tossed dictionaries —
          (O my barbarians
20   we will consume our mysteries)

and can we, can we slake the gaping eye of our desires?
we will sit around our hewn wood table
until our hair is long and our eyes are feeble,
eating, my people, O my insatiates,
25 eating until we are no more able
to jack up the jaws any longer —

to no more complain of the soul's vulgar cavities,
to gaze at each other over the rust-heap of cutlery,
drinking a coffee that takes an eternity —
30 till, bursting, bleary,
we laugh, barbarians, and rock the universe —
and exclaim to each other over the table

                  ⟶

1 in Greek mythology, a fire-breathing monster with a lion's head, a goat's body, and a serpent's tail; also used figuratively to indicate an absurdly fanciful or impossible idea.

over the table of bones and scrap metal
over the gigantic junk-heaped table:

35   by God that was a meal

(1966)

Dark Pines under Water

This land like a mirror turns you inward
And you become a forest in a furtive lake;
The dark pines of your mind reach downward,
You dream in the green of your time,
5   Your memory is a row of sinking pines.

Explorer, you tell yourself this is not what you came for
Although it is good here, and green;
You had meant to move with a kind of largeness,
You had planned a heavy grace, an anguished dream.

10   But the dark pines of your mind dip deeper
And you are sinking, sinking, sleeper
In an elementary world;
There is something down there and you want it told.

(1969)

Suniti Namjoshi (b. 1941)

Born in Bombay, Namjoshi worked as an officer in the Indian Administrative Service before coming to Canada to pursue a Ph.D. at McGill University. After teaching for several years in Toronto, she took up an academic post in Devon, England, where she now lives. Namjoshi has had a peripatetic career, but she locates her cultural and artistic roots in India. For instance, she notes that she derives her interest in fables, evident in such volumes as *Feminist Fables* (1981) and *The Blue Donkey Fables* (1988), from India's heritage of myth-making and storytelling. At once mythical and autobiographical, Namjoshi's work examines the matrices of desire that determine her diasporic, feminist, and lesbian perspectives. Although issues of gender and sexuality dominate much of her work, Namjoshi is pursuing an interest in cultural formation and artistic collaboration in her latest book, *Building Babel* (1996), which has an electronic component that allows readers to contribute to the architectural blueprint of a structured but everchanging culture.

Look, Medusa![1]

Medusa living on a remote shore
troubled no one: fish swam, birds flew, and the sea
did not turn to glass. All was as before.
A few broken statues lay untidily
5   on the lonely beach, but other than these
there was nothing wrong with that peaceful scene.
And so, when the hero Perseus[2] came to seize
the Gorgon's head, he thought he might have been
mistaken. He watched for a while, but she turned
10   nothing to stone. The waves roared as waves will,
till at last the hidden hero burned
to be seen by her whom he had come to kill.
"Look, Medusa, I am Perseus!" he cried,
thus gaining recognition before he died.

(1988)

Poem Against Poets

I fall upon the thorns of life,
            I weep, I bleed,[1]
but to what purpose?
            There was once a poet
5   who thought she was a nightingale,[2]
            and another
who thought she was a rose —
            charming perhaps,
able certainly, having found at least
10   a way to cope.
Would the nightingale's entrails

———▶

1 in Greek legend, a Gorgon whose hair was composed of snakes and whose face could turn the viewer to
stone. 2 semi-divine hero who managed to behead Medusa by looking at her reflection in his shield.
1 see line 54 of Percy Bysshe Shelley's "Ode to the West Wind" (page 141). 2 like the rose in line 7, a con-
ventional Romantic poetic symbol. Namjoshi told the editors of this anthology that she did not have any
actual women poets in mind in these examples but that she referred to female poets "simply because of the
reference to Philomel, and also, I suppose, because I tend to make the heroes (and anti-heroes) female
whenever possible."

have been more powerful
(as emblematic objects)
        laid out on the floor
15 of a room that you came to, and then
            withdrew from,
startled and amazed?
        Oh the rose is bloodless,
she is white with pain;
20   and Philomel[3] wails
in the woods again.
        But there are the other
more ordinary animals.
        They are not literary.
25   They own their pain.

(1988)

Michael Ondaatje (b. 1943)

Born in Colombo, Ceylon (now Sri Lanka), Ondaatje moved to England when he was eleven and came to Canada in 1962. He received a B.A. from the University of Toronto and an M.A. from Queen's University. He currently teaches at York University. Ondaatje began his career as a poet, publishing his first book in 1967. He has also produced novels, films, criticism, and anthologies. Two of his poetry collections have won the Governor General's Award: *The Collected Works of Billy the Kid* (1970), in which he combined poetry and prose, and *There's a Trick with a Knife I'm Learning to Do: Poems 1973–1978* (1979). He also received the Governor General's Award and the Booker Prize for his novel *The English Patient* (1992). His complex novel about civil unrest in Sri Lanka, *Anil's Ghost* (2000), was co-winner of the Giller Prize. Ondaatje most frequently explores the tensions between the subjective inner vision and the supposedly objective and logical realm of outward reality. Dissatisfied with traditional classifications and methods, he challenges both conventional perceptions and literary forms by mixing prose and poetry, fact and fiction, realism and surrealism, lyricism and violence.

---

3 in Greek mythology, Philomel, or Philomela, avenges her violation by her brother-in-law, Tereus, and then turns herself into a tongueless swallow and her sister, Procne, into a nightingale. The later, more influential Latin version of the story reverses the sisters' roles.

Elizabeth¹

Catch, my Uncle Jack² said
and oh I caught this huge apple
red as Mrs Kelly's³ bum.
It's red as Mrs Kelly's bum, I said
5   and Daddy⁴ roared
and swung me on his stomach with a heave.
Then I hid the apple in my room
till it shrunk like a face
growing eyes and teeth ribs.

10   Then Daddy took me to the zoo
he knew the man there
they put a snake around my neck
and it crawled down the front of my dress.
I felt its flicking tongue
15   dripping onto me like a shower.
Daddy laughed and said Smart Snake
and Mrs Kelly with us scowled.

In the pond where they kept the goldfish
Philip⁵ and I broke the ice with spades
20   and tried to spear the fishes;
we killed one and Philip ate it,
then he kissed me
with raw saltless fish in his mouth.

My sister Mary's got bad teeth
25   and said I was lucky, then she said
I had big teeth, but Philip said I was pretty.
He had big hands that smelled.

I would speak of Tom,⁶ soft laughing,
who danced in the mornings round the sundial

→

1 the speaker is Elizabeth I (1533–1603). 2 fictitious character, probably not an actual uncle but a man given that title because of familiarity with the child. 3 fictitious character, probably a nurse. 4 Elizabeth's father, Henry VIII (1491–1547). 5 Philip II of Spain (1527–98) married Elizabeth's sister, Mary Tudor (1515–58), in 1554. After Mary's death, he unsuccessfully sought to marry Elizabeth. 6 Lord Thomas Seymour of Sudeley (c. 1508–49) was executed for intriguing against his brother, Edward, Duke of Somerset, Lord Protector of the Realm. He vainly sought the hand of Elizabeth, having treated her with marked indelicacy when she stayed at his house.

30 teaching me the steps from France, turning
    with the rhythm of the sun on the warped branches,
    who'd hold my breast and watch it move like a snail
    leaving his quick urgent love in my palm.
    And I kept his love in my palm till it blistered.

35 When they axed his shoulders and neck
    the blood moved like a branch into the crowd.
    And he staggered with his hanging shoulder
    cursing their thrilled cry, wheeling,
    waltzing in the French style to his knees
40 holding his head with the ground,
    blood settling on his clothes like a blush;
    this way
    when they aimed the thud into his back.

    And I find cool entertainment now
45 with white young Essex,[7] and my nimble rhymes.[8]

                                                    (1967)

Letters & Other Worlds

"for there was no more darkness for him and, no doubt
like Adam before the fall, he could see in the dark"[1]

        My father's body was a globe of fear
        His body was a town we never knew
        He hid that he had been where we were going
        His letters were a room he seldom lived in
5   In them the logic of his love could grow

        My father's body was a town of fear
        He was the only witness to its fear dance
        He hid where he had been that we might lose him
        His letters were a room his body scared

---

7 Robert Devereux (1566–1601), the second Earl of Essex and one of Elizabeth's confidants, was
executed for attempting to raise a rebellion. 8 Elizabeth wrote lyric poetry.
1 from "*Descendit ad infernos*" (He Descends to the Underworld), a chapter for Alfred Jarry's *La dragonne*
(1943), quoted in Roger Shattuck's *The Banquet Years: The Arts in France, 1885–1918* (1955). The clause
immediately preceding the section Ondaatje quotes is "But soon he could drink no more."

10 He came to death with his mind drowning.
On the last day he enclosed himself
in a room with two bottles of gin, later
fell the length of his body
so that brain blood moved
15 to new compartments
that never knew the wash of fluid
and he died in minutes of a new equilibrium.

His early life was a terrifying comedy
and my mother divorced him again and again.
20 He would rush into tunnels magnetized
by the white eye of trains
and once, gaining instant fame,
managed to stop a Perahara² in Ceylon
— the whole procession of elephants dancers
25 local dignitaries — by falling
dead drunk onto the street.

As a semi-official, and semi-white at that,
the act was seen as a crucial
turning point in the Home Rule Movement
30 and led to Ceylon's independence in 1948.

(My mother had done her share too —
her driving so bad
she was stoned by villagers
whenever her car was recognized)

35 For 14 years of marriage
each of them claimed he or she
was the injured party.
Once on the Colombo docks
saying goodbye to a recently married couple
40 my father, jealous
at my mother's articulate emotion,
dove into the waters of the harbour
and swam after the ship waving farewell.
My mother pretending no affiliation
45 mingled with the crowd back to the hotel.

2 Sinhalese for *procession*; a *perahara* was most frequently associated with a religious celebration or marriage.

Once again he made the papers
though this time my mother
with a note to the editor
corrected the report — saying he was drunk
50   rather than broken hearted at the parting of friends.
The married couple received both editions
of The Ceylon Times when their ship reached Aden.[3]

And then in his last years
he was the silent drinker,
55   the man who once a week
disappeared into his room with bottles
and stayed there until he was drunk
and until he was sober.

There speeches, head dreams, apologies,
60   the gentle letters, were composed.
With the clarity of architects
he would write of the row of blue flowers
his new wife had planted,
the plans for electricity in the house,
65   how my half-sister fell near a snake
and it had awakened and not touched her.
Letters in a clear hand of the most complete empathy
his heart widening and widening and widening
to all manner of change in his children and friends
70   while he himself edged
into the terrible acute hatred
of his own privacy
till he balanced and fell
the length of his body
75   the blood screaming in
the empty reservoir of bones
the blood searching in his head without metaphor

(1973)

.

3 the capital of the British colony of Aden and later the capital of the People's Democratic Republic of
Yemen; port of call on voyages through the Suez Canal.

The Cinnamon Peeler[1]

If I were a cinnamon peeler
I would ride your bed
and leave the yellow bark dust
on your pillow.

5   Your breasts and shoulders would reek
you could never walk through markets
without the profession of my fingers
floating over you. The blind would
stumble certain of whom they approached
10   though you might bathe
under rain gutters, monsoon.

Here on the upper thigh
at this smooth pasture
neighbour to your hair
15   or the crease
that cuts your back. This ankle.
You will be known among strangers
as the cinnamon peeler's wife.

I could hardly glance at you
20   before marriage
never touch you
— your keen nosed mother, your rough brothers.
I buried my hands
in saffron, disguised them
25   over smoking tar,
helped the honey gatherers...

        . . . . .

When we swam once
I touched you in water
and our bodies remained free,
30   you could hold me and be blind of smell.
You climbed the bank and said

1 one who peels from the cinnamon tree the bark whose inner layer provides the aromatic spice.

        this is how you touch other women
the grass cutter's wife, the lime burner's daughter.
And you searched your arms
35   for the missing perfume
            and knew

        what good is it
to be the lime burner's daughter
left with no trace
40   as if not spoken to in the act of love
as if wounded without the pleasure of a scar.

You touched
your belly to my hands
in the dry air and said
45   I am the cinnamon
peeler's wife. Smell me.

                              (1982)

To a Sad Daughter

All night long the hockey pictures
gaze down at you
sleeping in your tracksuit.
Belligerent goalies are your ideal.

5   Threats of being traded
cuts and wounds
— all this pleases you.
O my god! you say at breakfast
reading the sports page over the Alpen[1]
10   as another player breaks his ankle
or assaults the coach.

When I thought of daughters
I wasn't expecting this
but I like this more.

       →

---

1 a brand of breakfast cereal.

15 I like all your faults
even your purple moods
when you retreat from everyone
to sit in bed under a quilt.
And when I say "like"
20 I mean of course "love"
but that embarrasses you.
You who feel superior to black and white movies
(coaxed for hours to see *Casablanca*)[2]
though you were moved
25 by *Creature from the Black Lagoon*.[3]

One day I'll come swimming
beside your ship or someone will
and if you hear the siren[4]
listen to it. For if you close your ears
30 only nothing happens. You will never change.

I don't care if you risk
your life to angry goalies
creatures with webbed feet.
You can enter their caves and castles
35 their glass laboratories. Just
don't be fooled by anyone but yourself.

This is the first lecture I've given you.
You're "sweet sixteen" you said.
I'd rather be your closest friend
40 than your father. I'm not good at advice
you know that, but ride
the ceremonies
until they grow dark.

Sometimes you are so busy
45 discovering your friends
I ache with a loss
— but that is greed.

———————→

2 celebrated 1942 film starring Humphrey Bogart and Ingrid Bergman. 3 1954 monster film starring Richard
Carlson. 4 sirens were mythical creatures, half-woman and half-bird, who used their sweet song to lure
sailors. In the *Odyssey*, Odysseus (Ulysses) escaped by stopping the ears of the members of his crew with wax
and then lashing himself to the ship's mast.

And sometimes I've gone
into my purple world
50   and lost you.

One afternoon I stepped
into your room. You were sitting
at the desk where I now write this.
Forsythia outside the window
55   and sun spilled over you
like a thick yellow miracle
as if another planet
was coaxing you out of the house
— all those possible worlds! —
60   and you, meanwhile, busy with mathematics.

I cannot look at forsythia now
without loss, or joy for you.
You step delicately
into the wild world
65   and your real prize will be
the frantic search.
Want everything. If you break
break going out not in.
How you live your life I don't care
70   but I'll sell my arms for you,
hold your secrets forever.

If I speak of death
which you fear now, greatly,
it is without answers,
75   except that each
one we know is
in our blood.
Don't recall graves.
Memory is permanent.
80   Remember the afternoon's
yellow suburban annunciation.
Your goalie
in his frightening mask
dreams perhaps
85   of gentleness.

(1984)

Leona Gom (b. 1946)

Born in the Peace River district of Alberta, Gom lived for twenty years on an isolated farm. She received a B.Ed. and M.A. from the University of Alberta, where she taught for two years before taking up posts in English and creative writing at U.B.C. and at Douglas/Kwantlen College (Surrey, B.C.), where she was editor of the literary magazine *Event* for almost a decade. Gom has published five novels, the first of which, *Housebroken* (1986), won the Ethel Wilson Fiction Prize. The third of her six books of poetry, *Land of the Peace* (1980), won the Canadian Authors' Association Award for Best Book of Poetry. Gom's poetry is particularly notable for her ability to invest commonplace details and events with both emotion and broad significance.

Metamorphosis

Something is happening
to this girl.

She stands on one leg
on the third block
5   of her hopscotch game,
lifts herself forward
to the next double squares,
and, as she jumps,
something changes.

10   Her straight child's body
curls slowly in the air,
the legs that assert themselves
apart on the squares
curve in calf and thigh,
15   angles become arches;
her arms pumping slowly
to her sides adjust
to a new centre of gravity,
the beginnings of breasts
20   push at her sweater,
her braids have come undone
and her hair flies loose around her.

Behind her
the schoolhouse blurs,
25   becomes insubstantial
and meaningless,
and the boys in the playground
move toward her,
something sure and sinister
30   in their languid circling.

Slowly she picks up the beanbag.
When she straightens,
her face gathers
the bewildered awareness
35   of the body's betrayal,
the unfamiliar feel
of the child's toy
in her woman's hand.

(1980)

Marlene Nourbese Philip (b. 1947)

Born in Moriah, Tobago, Philip spent much of her youth in Trinidad. After a residence in Jamaica, she received her B.Sc. in economics from the University of the West Indies. Moving to Canada, she earned both an M.A. in political science and an LL.B. at the University of Western Ontario. Philip then practised law for seven years, writing the entire time. Since 1982, she has devoted herself to writing professionally, and has also been a part-time academic. Philip published her first collection of poetry, *Thorns*, in 1980, and her second, *Salmon Courage*, in 1983. In 1988, she won the *Casa del las Americas* prize for the manuscript version of *She Tries Her Tongue; Her Silence Softly Breaks* (1989). Exploring the same cultural grounds as her previous collections, Philip's third book comprises grouped series of poetic utterances, grammar lessons, multiple choice questions, aphorisms, fictional excerpts, bibilical allusions, and linguistic violence. In her essay, "Managing the Unmanagable" (1990), Philip suggests that such formal and linguistic experimentation is necessary for a historically colonized voice to emerge authentically from within the confines of the colonizer's language. By juxtaposing Western and African mythology, standard and demotic English, and male and female sexuality, Philip repeatedly attempts to subvert the hegemonic, white, male construction of history and to give voice to the "mother-tongue," the racial consciousness connecting the diasporic poet to her African ancestors. A relentlessly political artist, Philip is a founding member of Vision 21, a collective dedicated to fighting racism in the arts.

Blackman Dead

The magnum pistol barked
its last command
broke his chest —
red words of silence erupt
5   silken ribbons of death
wreathe the sullen Sunday morning madness.

A magnum pistol broke the secret
Sunday morning pact,
red roads of silence
10   lead us
nowhere

but to bury him
bury him
in a plain pine coffin
15   and repeat after me
how bad he was because,
because he was
just another immigrant
I say repeat
20   after me
how he deserved to die
because he didn't learn our ways
the ways of death
repeat
25   after me blackman dead, blackman dead
blackman dead.

as we dress dong
in we tree piece suit

———→

we disco dress
30   an' we fancy wheels —
dere is a magnum fe each one a we.

Listen me, listen me,
dey say every man palace is 'is 'ome
dat no man is
35   one hisland honto 'imself
dat if yuh mark one crass
pon yuh door
in blood
all we fus born is safe,

40   I say repeat
after me
how he deserved to die
because he didn't learn our ways
the ways of death
45   repeat
after me
blackman dead, blackman dead
blackman dead.

Toronto has no silk cotton trees
50   strong enough to bear
one blackman's neck
the only crosses that burn
are those upon our souls
and the lynch mobs meet
55   at Winstons[1]....

Blackman dead, blackman dead,
blood seeps beneath
the subterfuged lie
living as men
60   how can we die as niggers,
red roads of silence
lead us where
no birds sing

⟶

1 an upscale restaurant, now defunct.

blackman dead
65   blackman dead
black roses for blackman dead.

(1980)

Meditations on the Declension of Beauty by the Girl with the Flying Cheek-bones

If not   If not   If
Not
If not in yours
                    In whose
5   In whose language
Am I
If not in yours
                    In whose
In whose language
10   Am I   I am
                        If not in yours
In whose
            Am I
(if not in yours)
15   I am yours
In whose language
                    Am I not
Am I not   I am yours
If not in yours
If not in yours
20   In whose
In whose language
                    Am I...

Girl with the flying cheek-bones:
She is
25   I am
Woman with the behind that drives men mad
And if not in yours

$\longrightarrow$

Where is the woman with a nose broad
As her strength
30   If not in yours
In whose language
Is the man with the full-moon lips
Carrying the midnight of colour
Split by the stars — a smile
35   If not in yours
        In whose

In whose language
        Am I
        Am I not
40   Am I   I am yours
        Am I not   I am yours

        Am I   I am
If not in yours
        In whose
45   In whose language
        Am I
If not in yours
        Beautiful

                            (1989)

Dionne Brand (b. 1953)

Born in Guayguayare, Trinidad, Dionne Brand moved to Toronto in 1970 to study at the University of Toronto, where she earned an honours degree in English and drama, and an M.A. in the philosophy of education. She published her first volume of poetry, 'Fore Day Morning, in 1978. Chronicles of the Hostile Sun (1984) records her experiences in Grenada in the months leading up to the American invasion in October 1983. One of the major concerns of No Language Is Neutral (1990) is the living presence of the past. In Land to Light On (1997), winner of the Governor General's Literary Award, Brand mingles prose and poetry to investigate her status as an outsider. A vocal feminist and advocate for black rights, Brand frequently attacks imperialism and patriarchy in her poetry. Impassioned and allusive, these poems focus on the abuses suffered and the heroism displayed by both blacks and women.

Blues Spiritual for Mammy Prater

On looking at "the photograph of Mammy Prater an ex-slave,
115 years old when her photograph was taken"

she waited for her century to turn
she waited until she was one hundred and fifteen
years old to take a photograph
to take a photograph and to put those eyes in it
5   she waited until the technique of photography was
suitably developed
to make sure the picture would be clear
to make sure no crude daguerreotype[1] would lose
her image
10 would lose her lines and most of all her eyes
and her hands
she knew the patience of one hundred and fifteen years
she knew that if she had the patience,
to avoid killing a white man
15 that I would see this photograph
she waited until it suited her
to take this photograph and to put those eyes in it.

in the hundred and fifteen years which it took her to
wait for this photograph she perfected this pose
20 she sculpted it over a shoulder of pain,
a thing like despair which she never called
this name for she would not have lasted
the fields, the ones she ploughed
on the days that she was a mule, left
25 their etching on the gait of her legs
deliberately and unintentionally
she waited, not always silently, not always patiently,
for this self portrait
by the time she sat in her black dress, white collar,
30 white handkerchief, her feet had turned to marble,
her heart burnished red,
and her eyes.

1 picture produced by a method invented in 1839 by Louis Daguerre (1789–1851); the image was taken upon a silver-coated copper plate sensitized by iodine and was developed by being treated with vapour of mercury.

she waited one hundred and fifteen years
until the science of photography passed tin and
35   talbotype[2] for a surface sensitive enough
to hold her eyes
she took care not to lose the signs
to write in those eyes what her fingers could not script
a pact of blood across a century, a decade and more
40   she knew then that it would be me who would find
her will, her meticulous account, her eyes,
her days when waiting for this photograph
was all that kept her sane
she planned it down to the day,
45   the light,
the superfluous photographer
her breasts,
her hands
this moment of
50   my turning the leaves of a book,
noticing, her eyes.

(1990)

Louise Bernice Halfe (b.1953)

Also known as Sky Dancer, Halfe was born in Two Hill, Alberta, and raised on the Saddle Lake Indian Reserve. Interested in improving the social and psychological conditions of Native Canadians, Halfe earned a bachelor of social work from the University of Regina and a certificate in drugs and alcohol counselling from from the Nechi Institute (St. Albert, Alberta). Though she had been keeping a journal since high school, it was during a six-year residency in Saskatchewan that Halfe first collected her journal writings into a book of poetry, *Bear Bones & Feathers* (1994). Shortlisted for both the Spirit of Saskatchewan Award and the Gerald Lambert Award, this collection won the Milton Acorn People's Poetry Award in 1996. Her second collection, *Blue Marrow* (1998), which was nominated for the Governor General's Award for Poetry, combines prose, poetry, and journal entries to express the polyphonic voices of her Native ancestors and their spiritual inheritors. The poems reprinted below show a distinctive feature of Halfe's talent: her ability to use dialect and humour for pointed social comment.

2 a tintype, also known as a ferrotype, is a photograph taken as a positive image on a sheet of coated tin or iron; the talbotype (originally called the callotype) was named after its inventor, William Henry Fox Talbot (1800–77), who, in 1841, patented a process for producing photographic images on paper sensitized with iodide of silver.

My Ledders

dear pope
i no, i no, you tired of my ledders
i couldn't let dis one go
i dought you could do somedin 'bout it.
5 years ago you stopped *nōkhom* and *nimosōm*[1]
from prayin in da sweatlodge and sundance,
drummin, singin and dancin.
you even stopped dem from Indian speakin
and storydellin.
10 well you must have some kind of bower
cuz da govment sure listen.

well, pope
last night on DV
i watched some whitemen
15 sweat in da lodge, and at
dinner dime on da radio
i heard dat man dell us
dat some darafist was havin a retreat
and to register.
20 what dat mean, i not sure
anyway he is buildin' a sweatlodge.
i never hear anybody before on da radio
dell da whole world dat.
i sure surprise and kinda made me mad.

25 i wonder if you could dell da govment
to make dem laws dat stop dat
whiteman from dakin our *isistāwina*[2]
cuz i dell you pope
i don't dink you like it
30 if i dook you
gold cup and wine
pass it 'round our circles
cuz i don't have you drainin
from doze schools.

———→

1 my grandmother and my grandfather. 2 a word that can have deep, sacred implications, but essentially meaning customs, rites, or beliefs.

35 i haven't married you jeesuz
    and i don't kneel to him,
    cuz he ain't my god.

    dese men, pope, don't know what
    tobacco mean, what suffer mean,
40 alls dey no is you jeesuz die for dem
    dey don't no what fastin' mean
    dey jist dake and gobble our *mātotsān*[3]
    as if dey own it.
    dey don't no what it mean to dake
45 from da earth and give somedin' back
    i so dired of all dis *kimoti*,[4] pope
    deach your children.
    eat your jeesuz body.
    drink his blood.
50 dell dem to go back to dere own deachings,
    pope.

                                    (1994)

Body Politics

Mama said,

Real woman
don't steal
from the sky and wear clouds
5   on their eyelids.

Real woman
eat rabbit well-done
not left half-raw
on their mouth.

10 Real woman
have lots of meat
on their bones.
They're not starving,

                →

3 sweat lodges. 4 theft.

hobbled horses
15 with bony, grinding hips.

Real woman caress
with featherstone hands
not with falcon fingernails
that have never worked.

20 When she was finished talking
she clicked her teeth
lifted her arse
and farted
at the passing
25 city women.

(1994)

Erin Mouré (b. 1955)

A supervisor for VIA Rail, Erin Mouré is notable as one of the few working-class female poets to have earned critical respect in Canada. Born and educated in Calgary, she published her first book, *Empire, York Street,* in 1979. In 1982 she won the DuMaurier Award for Poetry. The railroad, current events, and social issues figure prominently in her poems, which often develop themes of social and political criticism. Whether looking at the way popular culture and economic forces shape individual lives, especially those of women, or portraying universal experiences such as love and loneliness, Mouré typically moves from physical perception and emotion to an attempt at intellectual comprehension.

Miss Chatelaine[1]

In the movie, the horse almost dies.
A classic for children, where the small girl pushes a thin
knife into the horse's side.
Later I am sitting in brightness with the women
5 I went to high school with in Calgary,
fifteen years later we are all feminist, talking of the girl
in the film.

———→

1 *Miss Chatelaine* (now published as *Flare*) was a magazine of fashion, beauty, and lifestyles for young Canadian women.

The horse who has some parasite & is afraid of the storm,
& the girl who goes out to save him.
10   We are in a baggage car on VIA Rail around a huge table,
its varnish light & cold,
as if inside the board rooms of the corporation;
the baggage door is open
to the smell of dark prairie,
15   we are fifteen years older, serious
about women, these images:
the girl running at night between the house & the barn,
& the noise of the horse's fear mixed in with the rain.

Finally there are no men between us.
20   Finally none of us are passing or failing according to
Miss Chatelaine.
I wish I could tell you how much I love you,
my friends with your odd looks, our odd looks,
our nervousness with each other,
25   the girl crying out as she runs in the darkness,
our decoration we wore, so many years ago, high school
boys watching from another table.

Finally I can love you.
Wherever you have gone to, in your secret marriages.
30   When the knife goes so deeply into the horse's side, a
few seconds & the rush of air.
In the morning, the rain is over.
The space between the house & barn is just a space again.
Finally I can meet with you & talk this over.
35   Finally I can see us meeting, & our true tenderness, emerge.

(1988)

The Producers

What the producers do to meat, you pay for in your cells.
It is your cells I have come to speak about.
Only a certain thickness separates me from the air in this room.
Density. Its whirligig[1] spinning
5   to the tune of bouzouki[2] music.
My body the street fair offers you the altered clothing of the cells.
It offers you the chance to read a novel by a famous woman
in which other women reproduce, & their
value is this:
10   reproduction.

It is because of this I have come to speak to you:
because it is possible that
the meaning of a woman is the meaning of a single cell.

A certain thickness prevents me from saying what I might say.
15   The difference between a human cell & the atoms in this table.
I lean my head against the wood.
Where are you, I want to speak to you.
What the producers do to lettuce, you pay for in your cells.
Everything they do, you will pay for.
20   Your cells will not recognize what they are to become.
It is on behalf of your cells.
I speak to you without election because the cells know nothing
of democracy.
They think not of the good of the whole, but of themselves.
25   They think of their thin unguarded border.
The illusion of wholeness captivates us, as a kind of slavery.
I asked a woman with cancer, who told me.
Now she has died because some cells wanted to go
someplace else.
30   Before she died, she thought about the producers
of x-rays,
& how we once believed we could see thru anything,
we humans.

(1988)

---

1 spinning toy, such as a top. 2 fretted musical instrument, something like a mandolin, having three or
four courses of double metal strings and traditionally used in Greece to play music for dancing and social
entertainment.

Marilyn Dumont (b. 1955)

Born in Olds, Alberta, Dumont received a B.A. from the University of Alberta and an M.F.A. from the University of British Columbia. A descendent of the legendary Gabriel Dumont, who led Métis military forces during the Northwest Resistance of 1885, Dumont has long been a Native educator and rights activist. Her first collection of poetry, *A Really Good Brown Girl* (1996), winner of the Gerald Lampert Award, examines the manifest ways that western hegemonic society, or "White Noise," distorts and does violence to Native and Métis notions of self and culture. In particular, these poems show the debilitating self-consciousness that develops because white society constantly sits in judgement of people outside of the pale of the main culture. By juxtaposing images of her Cree/Métis heritage with images showing the dominant culture debasing or suppressing that heritage, especially its verbal heritage, these poems are also self-conscious in a more positive way. Dumont's poems, that is, do more than protest victimization: they express consciousness of an identity formed by both oppression and by traditions and family relationships of which the oppressors lack understanding; they thus celebrate the vitality and persistence of the outsider. See the interview with Dumont, pages 417–421.

Letter to Sir John A. Macdonald[1]

Dear John: I'm still here and halfbreed,
after all these years
you're dead, funny thing,
that railway you wanted so badly,
5   there was talk a year ago
of shutting it down
and part of it was shut down,
the dayliner at least,
"from sea to shining sea,"
10   and you know, John,
after all that shuffling us around to suit the settlers,
we're still here and Métis.

We're still here
after Meech Lake[2] and

    ⟶

---

1 Sir John Alexander Macdonald (1815–1891), the first prime minister of Canada (1867–1873, 1878–1891), promoted construction of the transcontinental railway, using it before it was even completed to send troops to suppress Louis Riel's last rebellion (see note 4). 2 a proposed amendment to the Constitution Act, agreed to in principle by Prime Minister Brian Mulroney and ten provincial premiers in meetings at Meech Lake, Quebec, on April 30, 1987. The final proposal was issued in Ottawa on June 3, 1987. Because it would have granted Quebec designation as a "distinct society," objectors, notably Manitoba MLA Elijah Harper, an Ojibway Cree, successfully campaigned against ratification of the Meech Lake Accord.

15   one no-good-for-nothin-Indian
     holdin-up-the-train,
     stalling the "Cabin syllables / Nouns of settlement,
     /… steel syntax [and] / The long sentence of its exploitation"[3]
     and John, that goddamned railroad never made this a great nation,
20   cause the railway shut down
     and this country is still quarreling over unity,
     and Riel[4] is dead
     but he just keeps coming back
     in all the Bill Wilsons[5] yet to speak out of turn or favour
25   because you know as well as I
     that we were railroaded
     by some steel tracks that didn't last
     and some settlers who wouldn't settle
     and it's funny we're still here and callin ourselves halfbreed.

                                                                    (1996)

The Devil's Language

1.   I have since reconsidered Eliot[1]
     and the Great White way of writing English
     standard that is
     the great white way
5   has measured, judged and assessed me   all my life
     by its
     lily white words
     its picket fence sentences
     and manicured paragraphs
10   one wrong sound and you're shelved in the Native Literature section
     resistance writing
     a mad Indian
     unpredictable

                    ──────▶

3 F.R. Scott, "Laurentian Shield" [Dumont's note]. 4 Louis Riel (1844–1885), leader of Métis uprisings over
land rights in the Red River valley (1869) and in Saskatchewan (1884–85). Despite legends of his madness
and his official execution for treason, Riel embodies for many native and other Canadians a national revolu-
tionary ideal. 5 Wilson (Hemas Ka-lee-lee-kla), member of the Cape Mudge Indian Band of Comox, B.C.,
became an important national representative for Native rights, especially through his involvement in the
Assembly of First Nations.
1 T.S. Eliot (1888–1965), influential American-born English poet, dramatist and critic (see pages 267–276),
wrote learned, allusive poetry. He expressed his reverence for tradition in his essay "Tradition and the
Individual Talent" (1922), which envisions literary history as shaped by the unique talents of great poets, the
examples of whom are white males.

on the war path
15   native ethnic protest
the Great White way could silence us all
if we let it
it's had its hand over my mouth since my first day of school
since Dick and Jane, ABC's and fingernail checks
20   syntactic laws: use the wrong order or
register and you're a dumb Indian
dumb, drunk or violent
my father doesn't read or write
the King's English says he's
25   dumb but he speaks Cree
how many of you speak Cree?
correct Cree not correct English
grammatically correct Cree
is there one?

30   2. is there a Received Pronunciation of Cree, is there
a Modern Cree Usage?
the Chief's Cree not the King's English

as if violating God the Father and standard English
is like talking back(wards)

35   as if speaking the devil's language is
talking back
back(words)
back to your mother's sound, your mother's tongue, your mother's language
back to that clearing in the bush
40   in the tall black spruce

3. near the sound of horses and wind
where you sat on her knee in a canvas tent
and she fed you bannock and tea
and syllables
45   that echo in your mind now, now
that you can't make the sound
of that voice that rocks you and sings you to sleep
in the devil's language.

(1996)

INTERVIEW
with Marilyn Dumont

Q. *Why are you a poet?*

A. I guess because I'm obsessed with words. I guess I was always looking for the exact word, which led me to metaphor and simile, because I could never find the exact word.

Q. *When did you first become aware of your interest in language and thus in poetry?*

A. I probably became aware at university in the 80s when I was taking some poetry courses. It seemed to me that poetry had an ineffable quality to it. I liked the different levels that poetry worked on. I liked that it was also philosophy and music and — I don't really want to say theology — perhaps spirituality, too.

Q. *Poetry doesn't make the bestseller lists, so it is not reaching massive audiences. What is the role or function of poetry today? Why should students care about it?*

A. I think it's our conscience, and I think that is why students should care about it. A lot of poets ask questions that, maybe because of our societal norms or taboos, we are not supposed to ask. For me, that is what is important. Poets have been the ones who have resisted conformity, and lots of poets have been revolutionaries. That's why it's important.

Q. *Your poems play with various line lengths. How do you decide on the length of lines in a poem?*

A. To me a line is like breath. It's the length of my breath when I conceive it. To me it's how much verbal impact, intensity, power you need to deliver this particular message. Most of the time I try to work towards my poems being music so that when people hear them, first of all, as with music, they're engaged by a sound or rhythm that piques their interest, and then they give over to content. It has a lot to do with sound and rhythm. In working with words and line lengths, I go by the sound and by how the sound relates to all the other lines. For example, I think about whether I want contrast or symmetry between the lines. It's like creating a musical score. I've always envied musicians. I've never been able to be a musician, so in a way, poetry is a way of expressing my musical side.

Q. *In your poem "For Bruce: The Night We Sat Studying Cree," one not included in this anthology, you say that "Cree Language Structures and Common Errors in English book-end / my life." To what extent do you feel caught between two cultures, a double outsider?*

A. That question is hard for me to answer. I guess I just feel that I've been between all my life. Sometimes I wish I could identify with being treaty or status or just one thing, but I realize that my life is in the middle. That's the way I have been looking at the world ever since I can remember. I think that it has actually given me strength as a writer, as a poet.

Q. *Were you able to borrow from both traditions?*

A. Yes, I borrow from both, but because I stand on the outside of both, I can criticize both of them. It gives me a sense of distance or dissonance. By that I mean that, if you're always on the outside, there's always a sense of bitterness. You know you're not inside the circle; you're outside, and that's where you'll always be.

Q. *What prompted you to address a "Letter to Sir John A. Macdonald"?*

A. Part of it was tongue in cheek because of my heritage. Gabriel Dumont is a third great-uncle. Writing that poem was a way of speaking of that hegemony, that oppression in history, of the Métis people. It was a way of talking back to that hegemony, to say, "I am still here; we are still here," even though we were seen as being "the other," and the other was always seen as being a problem. It was sarcasm. Being sarcastic is an angry way of being funny. Sarcasm comes from a place where one feels powerless, and is a way of biting back.

Q. *So it is an expression of power within powerlessness, an ironic state itself?*

A. Yes.

Q. *Do you think that your protests and your revelations of differences of view in such poems as "The Devil's Language" will change anything?*

A. Native people have come up to me and said that they are glad that I said that. I think that the situation is that I give them permission to at least have those feelings and to express that resentment, those feelings of hostility, that they might have but weren't able to articulate. It may also be that they sense that I am pointing to language — or any kind of rule — as a way of assimilating people. I think that it may have made a difference, but maybe not as much as I wanted it to. Poets aren't read a heck of a lot, but I still write, hoping that somebody will read and be affected by my poems.

Q. *You (or the persona through whom you speak in your poems) are obviously self-conscious, intensely aware of yourself as an object of observation and judgement because of your racial background. you are also self-conscious in a second, more positive sense, in that you are intensely aware of who you are and what you feel as both a member of a racial group and as a woman. Is poetry a way of insisting on a complex identity as both a victim of history and an aggressive racial other?*

A. I never quite thought of it in those terms, but you really hit the nail on the head when you said the word *judgement* because that has been a large part of my life. This was internalized racism that was passed on to me by my parents, who got it from their parents, and on and on and on. We felt that we always had to prove that we were good enough. That whole sense of judgement was always there and I was aware of it. There is that sense of self-awareness.

Q. *Is there also a sense in which you are trying to show that this self-aware person has not been victimized or trodden down?*

A. Yes, again, it's a way of feeling a sense of power.

Q. *Are you thumbing your nose at the official culture?*

A. Oh, yeah; in fact, any culture that has colonized any other culture; it's not just white.

Q. *What is "the Great White way of writing" that you reject in the opening lines of "The Devil's Language"?*

A. The Great White way of writing is the perpetuation of the sexist, racist, and classist underpinnings in the subtext of the English language. Languages are not just neutral forms of communication. All languages are ways of perceiving the world and one's place in it. Languages inhabit and define ways of being in the world, and "the Great White way of writing" is one way of seeing the world. Because Canada's aboriginal people were colonized by the British and the French, those languages have imposed their belief systems on all of us, but particularly aboriginal people in Canada.

Q. *How are you resisting that way in your writing?*

A. I am resisting through the content, rather than the form. I have tried to subvert the socio-political forces that labeled me woman, aboriginal, and poor. Of course, the most pernicious force of all is one's own internalized sexism, racism, and classism. In my writing, I try to raise the awareness of these issues in all of us, myself included.

Q. *At the end of "The Devil's Language," you move in tone from what we might call the stridency of protest to a romantic nostalgia, looking back in lyrical tenderness on memories of a Cree mother and her child, who when grown, lovingly remembers the native language that she herself cannot speak. How does this change in tone and rhythm illustrate your opposition to "the Great White way"?*

A. In one sense I am feeling angry at and resistant to the English language, but at the same time I feel sorrow and loss, and probably in some ways, a sense of resignation that I'm going to have to live with my feelings because the English language is not going to go away, nor are the accessories that go along with it — values, for example. I'm part of that now.

Q. *What, specifically, are you rejecting?*

A. The sense that certain people are better because they are more powerful. Again, going back to the judgement thing, I was aware early on that my parents felt very uncomfortable in certain situations because their English was different from, say, the English that a doctor may have spoken, the English that a school principal may have spoken, or the English that a priest may have spoken. I was always aware of that discomfort and the apology that they spoke Cree. Ideas of hierarchy are inherent in language. English has gendered pronouns (he and she), but Cree has animate and inanimate words: to me that's a good illustration of a difference in world view. I always felt at a loss in not being able to speak Cree. One of the forces that stopped me from acquiring the Cree language was that people thought that it was primitive, that it wasn't of any use in this day and age, that its ideas of animate and inanimate were heathen. I want people to acknowledge difference without believing that one way is inferior just because it's different; I want people to consider that Aboriginal language is as important, as powerful, as the English language. The English language is being used worldwide because of political reasons; it's a weapon.

Q. *If you could preserve only one of your poems, which would it be?*

A. "The Devil's Language." I think that in ten or twenty years it's still going to make an impact on people. In fact, I know a lot of Asian students respond to this poem in classes, and maybe it's because of their multi-linguistic backgrounds. They know what I'm talking about. I think the kind of linguistic issues to which I refer are still going to be around.

Robert Crawford (b. 1959)

A scholar, an editor, and a poet, Robert Crawford was born in 1959 at Bellshill, near Glasgow. After receiving an M.A from Glasgow University, he studied at Oxford University, earning the degree of D.Phil. He is now Professor of Modern Scottish Literature at the University of St Andrews. As an academic, Crawford has explored, in such books as *Devolving English Literature* (1992) and *The Scottish Invention of English Literature* (1998), the attempts of Scottish writers to maintain their distinctive culture in spite of the dominance of English political and cultural institutions. As co-editor of the international poetry magazine *Verses* and of *The Penguin Book of Poetry since 1945 from Britain and Ireland* (1998), he has been instrumental in bringing the work of younger poets to critical attention. Crawford himself has published four collections of poetry: *A Scottish Assembly* (1990), *Talkies* (1992), *Masculinity* (1996), and *Spirit Machines* (1999). This poetry is regional in the best sense of the term, displaying a profound understanding of the ways in which history, social conditions, and rugged landscape have affected the character of the Scottish people. Although they are always evident, even if it is just in the mention of setting, the regional concerns are not always foremost; Crawford also explores deeply personal issues, such as the emotions that arise in modern relationships. In all of his poems, however, Crawford tends to make his points more through implication, through wit and verbal restraint, than through overt pronouncements of ideas.

Anne of Green Gables[1]

Short moneyless summers at West Kilbride[2] you sat out
On the back steps with a view of the outside toilet
Reading the Anne books, one after the datestamped next,

Anne of Windy Willows, Anne of Avonlea,
5   *Anne of the Island, Anne's House of Dreams.*
No books were ever as good as these

From West Kilbride Public Library
That always had to go back.
When we got married, one by one

10   You bought the whole set, reading them through. At first
I was jealous when you sat not speaking,
Then put the books away on your own shelf.

"'How white the moonlight is tonight,' said Anne
Blythe to herself." [3] At first
15   I was jealous. Not now.

(1992)

Mary Shelley on Broughty Ferry Beach[1]

One small boat tugs the enormous corpse inshore
Towards waiting locals. A lad opens up its mouth
And wades inside, clutching a flensing tool
For blubber. Piece by hacked-off piece

1 Anne Shirley, the central character of *Anne of Green Gables* (1908), by Lucy Maud Montgomery
(1874–1942), is an orphan who displays a romantic love of nature and beauty. She is adopted by an elderly
brother and sister, who live on a Prince Edward Island farm called Green Gables. Her story continues in a
number of sequels, including *Anne of Windy Poplars* (1936), which was released in the United Kingdom as
Anne of Windy Willows, Anne of Avonlea (1909), *Anne of the Island* (1915), *Anne's House of Dreams* (1917).
In this last title, she marries her one-time school rival, Gilbert Blythe. 2 coastal town in Ayrshire, southwest
of Glasgow. 3 first part of the opening sentence of *Anne of Ingleside* (1939).
1 Broughty Ferry is a Scottish coastal town just east of Dundee on the Firth of Tay. Mary Shelley
(1797–1851), author of *Frankenstein* (1818), a novel about a scientist who creates a monster from parts of
corpses, stayed in Dundee with the Baxters, friends of her father, in 1812-13, returning a few times later
about 1814.

5   Men deconstruct the outcast zeppelin body,
    Carting lumps back to beachfront cottages —
    Sturdy food and good oil for the winter.
    Harpoons glint in the candlelight.

    Safe home, the men of Broughty Ferry take
10 Their sweet uncorseted wives to bed, or croon
    Shanties to bairns beside toys made of teeth.
    The Tay flows quiet. Dundee's lights wink their yellow.

    A sad girl walks from the beach, carefully picking
    Her steps as she sneaks past a leftover eye
15 Flung on the sand, and other small last bits
    Of monster littering the promenade.

                                              (1992)

George Elliot Clarke (b. 1960)

Born in Windsor Plains, Nova Scotia, Clarke was raised in Halifax. Clarke, who holds a Ph.D. from Queen's University, taught English and Canadian studies at Duke University and was the third Seagram Visiting Chair of Canadian Studies at McGill (1998-99). Now a professor at the University of Toronto, he has published numerous critical articles in creative and scholarly journals. He has also edited *Fire on the Water: An Anthology of Black Nova Scotian Writing* (1991-92) and *Eyeing the North Star: Directions in African-Canadian Literature* (1997). Clarke's first published collection, *Saltwater Spirituals and Deeper Blues* (1983), nominated for the Bliss Carman Award for poetry, explores the aesthetic and spiritual concerns of Nova Scotia's black citizens. In *Whylah Falls* (1990), winner of the Archibald Lampman Award for poetry, Clarke attempts to "remap" Nova Scotia by tracing the spiritual geography of the black community, one that has often been exiled from Canadian historical and political writing. In *Lush Dreams, Blue Exile: Fugitive Poems, 1978-1993* (1994), Clarke coined the term "Africadian" to describe his community. Throughout his poetry and other writings, he has sought make readers aware of the unique Africadian perspective on aesthetic and political values.

Salvation Army Blues

Seeking after hard things —
muscular work or sweat-swagger action —
I rip wispy, Help Wanted ads,
dream of water-coloured sailors
5   pulling apart insect wings of maps,
stagger down saxophone blues avenues
where blackbirds cry for crumbs.
I yearn to be Ulyssean[1], to roam
foaming oceans or wrest
10   a wage from tough, mad adventure.
    For now, I labour language,
earn a cigarette
for a poem, a coffee
for a straight answer,
15   and stumble, punch-drunk,
down these drawn-and-quartered streets,
tense hands manacled
to snarling pockets.

(1983)

Blank Sonnet

The air smells of rhubarb, occasional
Roses, or first birth of blossoms, a fresh,
Undulant hurt, so body snaps and curls
Like flower. I step through snow as thin as script,
5   Watch white stars spin dizzy as drunks, and yearn
To sleep beneath a patchwork quilt of rum.
I want the slow, sure collapse of language
Washed out by alcohol. Lovely Shelley,[1]
I have no use for measured, cadenced verse
10   If you won't read. Icarus-like,[2] I'll fall
Against this page of snow, tumble blackly
Across vision to drown in the white sea
That closes every poem — the white reverse
That cancels the blackness of each image.

(1990)

---

1 Ulysses, the Roman name for Odysseus, was a Trojan war hero and legendary wanderer.
1 Shelley Clemence, a female resident of the fictional Whylah Falls, is the beloved of the narrator, known as
X. 2 in Greek mythology, Icarus, son of Daedalus, escaped from Crete on wings his father had made for him.
He flew so close to the sun, however, that the wax holding together the wings melted, and he fell into the
Aegean Sea.

Evelyn Lau   (b. 1971)

A teenage prostitute and drug abuser, Evelyn Lau became the youngest person ever nominated for the Governor General's Award for poetry. Born in Vancouver, Lau was unable to tolerate the strict routine her parents imposed on her, especially because they forbade her to do any kind of writing. At the age of fourteen, she therefore ran away. Although she felt hurt and confused — she even attempted suicide — her sordid experiences had one positive value: they provided the dramatic material that enabled her to fulfil her dream of becoming a writer. *Runaway: Diary of a Street Kid* (1989), an autobiography seething with rage, made her a literary celebrity, especially after the CBC turned it into a movie. Lau has since published three collections of poetry, a volume of short stories, and a novel. Lau's work is autobiographical and emotional, but she says, "When I'm translating personal experiences onto the page, there is very much a writerly presence at work, so that it's not just spilling my guts." Lau portrays a night-time world of illicit sex and drugs that most readers have never experienced, but she suggests that the desperate role-playing, constant deceptions, and chronic sensual excesses that characterize that world are really expresions of a universal longing for acceptance and love.

What We Do in the Name of Money

heavy feet on the back stairs announce
300 lbs. of stock promoter
you wonder what it's like to drive across town at midnight
for a blow job[1]
5   guess it's no different than going out for a hamburger

every time you see a father now
in real life or on TV
you see you're young enough to be their daughter
instead you've become the girl they visit
10   on nights like these
you caress their faces differently
than a daughter's hands
it changes the way you watch happy families in the sitcoms

1 slang term for oral sex.

tug the sash of your silk robe tighter
15   walk fast to the door
his mouth opens as if to swallow you
like the boxes of shortbread cookies he consumes
in his unconfessed loneliness
you know him well, 2 years and enough conversations
20   but tonight the history doesn't show
you light his cigarettes, put on coffee
exaggerate the slavery he hands you with the folded bills

the robe falls like water down a rock
he sprawls on your bed
25   the fan in the bathroom whirs for the next hour
the apartment lights burn your brain into white metal
your thighs straddle his shoulders like run-on sentences
his hands clench the edges of the comforter
brown and defenseless
30   he raises them to cover his face
his mindless words are lost to you, the expletives
forced out between lubricated lips
your bed is awash with his sweat
you will wrap yourself in its smell for days
35   its acridity relieved by cologne

memo: don't brush your teeth for 15 minutes afterwards
when you should be licking your lips
he watches you now with that cool reservation
only guilt can bring
40   on the slow painful descent down the back stairs
he puckers his lips
whistles at the sightless constellations.

(1990)

Nineteen

the men file home with flowers in their hands
rubbery petals scent the rain, it is late
the hours pass in dreams, you wake
after the shade of night is tugged down
5   the men walk past in white trenchcoats, asking directions.
it is February and the flowers in the grocery stores
are dying in their white pails, the grocer is bending down
and picking them up, taking them inside,
taking them away.

10   the men say they love you, your hair
falls over their alcoholic faces in slick blue curls
you kiss them randomly. oh, the men:
precious as ivory,
dead flowers uprooted in their hands.
15   all you have to show for them is a few roses,
a smattering of pills in the green glass ashtray,
but he calls you Baby Girl and you watch porn movies together
on the white leather sectional, pop antibiotics and drink scotch
when there's nothing else around.
20   you know he's your last chance.

he keeps pictures of you in his drawer
your artificial hair whipping against the camera
your model's pout damp with hunger
your eyes like tombstones, black and white.
25   upstairs the beds are quiet.
at three AM you smash the twisted iron gate and run to the cab
to a driver who assaults you with hard hands
you say nothing, tell no one

is it not enough that you got away?
30   four AM and you sit in the hallway listening to the rain
emptying out through the drains in the balcony
a stench in the bathroom
knees drawn up in that classic position, you're alive
which should be enough for anybody, but already
35   you've begun to stop wanting
and more and more men in their ivory skins pass you
in the increasing night, carrying away flowers til all is dark.

(1992)

WRITING ESSAYS ABOUT LITERATURE

PUTTING THE JOB IN PERSPECTIVE

Writing well on any academic subject is demanding work, and writing about literature is among the most demanding kinds of academic writing. It helps to remember, however, that confronting the task seriously will improve not only the way you express what you think but your ability to think, as well. Mastering the critical and interpretive essays required in English courses will prepare you to handle other writing jobs with comparative ease. Whether you are committed to specializing in English or interested mainly in doing as well as you can in a required English course before going on to other areas of study, the advice that follows will help you make your choices sensibly and get the most from the work you do.

Writing about literature often starts with a feeling — you either like something or not — or an intuition about how a piece of writing works. In expressing these inklings in writing, you clarify them for yourself, identify the assumptions behind them, and learn how well they are grounded in the work you are considering. In the process, you not only come to understand better how literature works, but you also discover a good deal about how you think. Writing about literature is challenging for the same reasons it is rewarding because it requires you to confront yourself as well as what you read.

When you explore literature in essays, you will rarely be looking for answers that are absolutely right or wrong. Depending on the approach taken and the questions asked, a wide variety of conclusions can be drawn about an individual work of literature, and because of the personal element in responses, even writers approaching questions in similar ways will often come up with quite different answers. Think of your essays about literature as part of an ongoing search for understanding, a process that begins when an author, poet, or playwright confronts his or her perceptions about the world in writing and that continues as long as somebody is reading and writing about the original creation. Remembering that you are taking part in a continuing dialogue rather than solving a problem with a single, predetermined answer will help you resist obvious conclusions and make your confrontation with a demanding subject less intimidating.

But again, "less intimidating" does not mean easy. The lack of pat answers, though reassuring in some ways, is no excuse for either slack thinking or sloppy writing. On the contrary, because your essays will be judged more by the quality of thought and expression they demonstrate than by how close they come to some established position, care is especially important. Originality is a start, but your original perceptions have to be supported scrupulously with evidence from the work in question; you must impress your audience by convincing it.

PREPARING TO WRITE

An essay about a literary work should say something illuminating about it, and an illumination depends on focus as well as initial brilliance. Thoughtful insights take time to develop, and an essential step in writing about literature involves clarifying for yourself what it is you want to say. Only when you are sure of your message can you decide how best to present it clearly and convincingly to your readers. The work cannot be rushed at this stage, so it is essential to leave yourself adequate time, not only to draft and revise, but to think, to plan, and to criticize your own ideas, as well.

PROCESS IN SUMMARY

Preparing to Write

Step 1: Prepare for writing assignments in advance by reading all assigned texts in a course as early as possible and by including speculation about potential lines of argument in your notes.

Step 2: Once you receive a writing assignment, evaluate it carefully to determine special requirements and anticipate problems.

Step 3: Choose a subject that interests you.

Step 4: Choose a topic you can handle well in the time available.

Step 5: If you are confused about any aspect of an assignment or if you anticipate deviating in any way from the directions, check with your instructor.

Step 6: Review the primary works you are writing about carefully, taking notes and identifying key passages as you read.

Step 7: Read whatever background material you consider necessary.

Drafting

Step 1: Begin generating ideas in writing while you still have more time than you need to complete your essay.

Step 2: Focus your ideas into a manageable thesis and state this thesis clearly in a single sentence.

Step 3: Prepare a simple, tentative outline. Do not spend a lot of time on this outline because it will probably have to be modified later. Repeat Step 2 if necessary.

Step 4: Working from your outline and keeping your thesis statement clearly in mind, complete a rough draft of the entire essay without stopping to revise.

(continued)

Revising and Editing

Step 1:   Review your essay to identify any parts that do not relate clearly to your thesis; cut or adapt these as necessary.

Step 2:   Add support at any point where your conclusions seem to need it.

Step 3:   Revise your opening to ensure that the main points of your essay are clear and supply any additional information your reader may need to follow your approach.

Step 4:   When you are satisfied with the content of your essay, continue revising it for clarity and style until you are satisfied that it is the best you can make it or until the deadline requires you to commit yourself to a final version.

Step 5:   When you are rested and free from distractions, proofread your essay carefully, making neat changes on the manuscript where necessary.

Reading with Awareness

The most fundamental preparation for writing about literature is reading. Read the piece you intend to write about, and then reread it. Read not just superficially to get a basic idea of what the piece says, but carefully, with an awareness of implications beneath the surface and of how the way it is written determines the way it affects you. Taking English courses and studying what others write about literature will teach you the kinds of things to look for, but you will need more. Serious reading, like serious writing, takes practice and cannot be rushed: putting off thinking about literature in general until you are required to write about a particular piece is like putting off training for a race until just before you have to run it. Developing the habit of reading seriously will put you far ahead of students who read only when forced to by an assignment, and it will also yield a great deal of satisfaction in itself.

Taking Notes

While reading thoughtfully is essential, it is not enough. You will find that your reading translates more readily into essays if you record your responses. Take notes as you read, perhaps on the text itself if it is your own copy and an inexpensive one. Marking particularly interesting passages will be a great help when you come back later to sort out evidence for an idea you are developing in an essay. When taking notes in class, record not only what your instructor says but the ideas that occur to you as well. If what is said about one work suggests comparison with another, take note of the possibility. Remark contradictions and unanswered questions. Your dissenting opinions, which you might well forget if you neglected to write them down at the time, will often provide the foundation for your most original essays and may in the long run prove to be the most valuable material you record in class.

An excellent practice for bridging the gap between the sketchy notes you write in class and fully developed essays is to extend your notes in a journal. Rather than reviewing class notes only when you are preparing for an exam, take time between classes to review and expand on the ideas your notes record. Consider which of your ideas may yield topics for essays, and test the manageability of these topics by sketching outlines. Elaborate in a paragraph or two on ideas you have had time to record in only a sentence. If you have recorded questions in your notes, attempt to answer them yourself in writing. The best time to develop your notes into something more useful occurs when the ideas they record are still fresh in your mind. While keeping a literary journal is not so different from taking notes, it allows you time to develop your ideas more thoughtfully and provides practice that will help you become more comfortable with critical writing.

Evaluating Assignments

Before attempting a writing assignment, you must first determine exactly what it requires and whether you can carry out any approach you are considering in the time available. The time you invest in evaluating assignments is rarely wasted. However eager you may be to get started, be cautious; enthusiasm is great, but you will win few races by sprinting off in the wrong direction.

Be especially careful when choosing topics from a list, a point at which the work of a few minutes can make the difference between success and failure. While you can assume that your instructor considers all suggested topics suitable for some students in your class, you cannot assume that all the topics will be suitable for all the students. Resist the temptation to commit yourself to the first topic that catches your interest. Evaluate all your options, eliminating the obvious impossibilities first. It will usually be clear that some works and some approaches are too difficult for you to manage. Personal taste is also an important consideration: until you gain more experience as a critic, you will rarely write successful essays about literary works you dislike. Once you have narrowed the choice to a few possibilities, sketch brief outlines to give yourself a better idea of where you might go with each topic. Determine whether you can meet all the requirements in each case. For example, even though you admire a certain poem, you may not be capable of handling a topic that requires you to produce a successful essay about how that poem's metrical patterns reinforce its meaning. While there can be long-term benefits in taking the extra time required to prepare for specialized topics, be sure you can manage the workload. Be wary of ambitious failures.

Once you find an assignment you think you can handle well, consider its wording carefully. Are you sure what all the terms mean? If not, ask your instructor to explain. Is there anything about the approach you are considering that seems at odds with the assignment as stated? Perhaps, for example, an assignment asks you to compare characterization in two stories, only one of which particularly impresses you. It may be permissible to concentrate on the one you like while using the other to illuminate by contrast what you admire in your favourite, but, then again, your instructor may want a more balanced comparison. Find out before you devote a lot of time to a questionable approach. Similarly, even though you plan no deviations from the stated requirements, you may find an assignment ambiguous in some respect. If you are told to compare two poems, for example, does this mean you are obligated to consider all aspects of the two poems? Or will you be permitted to devote most of your comparison to some aspect that seems especially revealing? While the more focused approach may seem more interesting to you, your instructor may have left the comparison general to test your understanding of a variety of elements in the poems. Any number of misunderstandings can occur, and you will be wise to anticipate them while you still have plenty of time to adapt.

Think early. Check early. Doing so can save you time, effort, and disappointment.

Research

In a very limited sense, any essay you write on a literary subject will involve research: you will have to read the works you intend to write about very carefully, probably a number of times, and even with an assignment that does not formally require research, you will often read other works by the same writer and explore his or her personal and historical background.

In a formal research paper, however, you will also be expected to find and evaluate what others have written about your subject. In this case, finding and properly acknowledging your debt to secondary material — writings about literature rather than the literature itself — will be a major part of your job. A detailed explanation of research methods and the format for acknowledging sources is beyond the scope of this chapter, but most college-level writing textbooks cover such material thoroughly. If you plan to take more than a few English courses, *The MLA Handbook for Writers of Research Papers*, which provides an exhaustive guide to the standard format used in English essays, is a good investment. Here it will suffice to provide a few general hints that can save you a lot of time and trouble.

Many students get into difficulty by confusing random sampling with research. They find the call number of a book on their topic, go to the specified shelf in the library, pull out several books on the same general subject, and consider their search complete. The one advantage of this approach — speed — cannot compensate for the problems it will almost certainly create. Books chosen at random rarely provide more than brief, general comment on an essay topic; what relevant comment they do include is often slanted according to their focal concerns. In addition, books stay on library shelves long after what they say has been qualified by later observations, and the material you find in a random selection will certainly not be the most recent available. This is not to say that books are of no value; the point is that books must be chosen carefully and supplemented by reference to up-to-date articles from scholarly journals.

The annotated bibliographies and the periodical indexes available in reference libraries will allow you to find material relevant to your topic quickly, and they will also give you an overview of the kinds of approaches to the work in question that others have found useful. But, as valuable as they are in saving you the trouble of reviewing irrelevant or barely relevant material, these resources will not solve all your problems. Often, they will list far more apparently relevant resources than you have time to consult. How are you to choose? In some cases your instructor will make suggestions, but such advice may still leave you guessing about which comments are most important and influential. One of the easiest ways into ongoing critical debates is to look first at the most recent writings you can find on your topic, taking careful note of the earlier works these cite. When two or three recent sources refer to an older one, it will usually be worth your while to check what it says directly. No method of sampling is a substitute for an exhaustive review of criticism, but methods that allow you to make an informed selection should be sufficient for most of your essays. They will certainly serve you better than random choice.

Seeking out the most pertinent material is not the only challenge in research, however. When you set out to research critical comment, remember that you are in at least as much danger from what you find as from what you miss. Discovering a source that carries on your line of argument so well that it leaves you little to add will take the satisfaction out of your work as well as the challenge, and you will learn little from basing your essay on such a source. Moreover, depending heavily on a source increases the chances of unintentional plagiarism — not making it entirely clear which ideas are really yours and which are borrowed. Thus, finding a published essay that covers much of what you intend to say about a topic is a good reason to consider changing topics or at least modifying your approach.

Much more serious than occasional reliance on secondary sources for ideas is developing a habit of dependency. It is all too easy to drift into a pattern of reviewing criticism before you begin to form your own ideas, thereby allowing others to shape your views. Always keep in mind when dealing with critical opinions that they are just that — opinions. Be impressed if you like, but never be intimidated. Even the best critics are human and therefore fallible. They are influenced by the prevailing critical assumptions of their times and often by specific theoretical affiliations. You have every right to disagree with published critics or, for that matter, with your instructors, provided you state your case clearly and support it conscientiously with references to the text in question. Consider other views carefully and with the respect any honest effort to advance understanding deserves, but then, when writing your essays, think for yourself.

STARTING TO WRITE

In contrast with the many difficulties involved in completing a good critical essay on time, putting off getting started is one of the easiest things you will ever do — easy and risky. It is human nature to put off the more difficult of competing tasks until the straightforward ones are out of the way, but with writing, the difficult jobs are precisely the ones to start first. Start early. Leave yourself time to explore blind alleys and, when you feel you are getting nowhere, to allow your subconscious mind to work on the problem while you are consciously engaged with other concerns. You will almost always find that ten hours invested in a writing project over a week will yield better results than a single ten-hour stretch of writing immediately before the deadline for submission.

Writer's Block

Unfortunately, even when you are well aware of the advantages of an early start, you may be held up by a psychological quirk commonly referred to as "writer's block."

Writer's block usually sets in at the earliest stages of a project, making it impossible to begin writing at all or, at best, to carry on past the first page or two. Because fear of failure is part of the cause, writer's block often strikes when you can least afford it — when you are involved in an especially important project or working under pressure. If you have never experienced writer's block, you may find the idea amusing, but sooner or later it affects most writers, and when it does, it can be both unpleasant and costly. Moreover, the anxiety created by one experience can lead to others, creating a steadily worsening problem. It makes sense, therefore, to prepare for writer's block before it strikes by experimenting with methods of resistance in order to determine which work best for you.

The methods described below are primarily intended to help you generate and shape ideas, but because they also encourage you to start writing early, not just when you have time to complete a project but when you have time to waste, they help eliminate writer's block as well. So, even if you find it fairly easy to think of things to say without writing, writing will usually help, and it will certainly make your work no harder.

Questions

Perhaps the most straightforward way to clarify what you think about a subject is to ask yourself questions about it. In order to avoid writer's block, not to mention loss and confusion, keep a record of your questions and answers in writing.

Beginning with very general questions, such as why you like or dislike something, progress gradually to questions that are more specific, quickly abandoning lines of inquiry that lead away from manageable topics. If you need help devising questions, you will find the lists included in writing textbooks many and varied, and most of them will work adequately up to a point. Watch for that point. At first, any question that forces you to examine your ideas will be better than none, but the further you carry on with a ready-made list, the more likely the questions are to limit your answers. As soon as a suggested line of inquiry begins to get in the way of your developing ideas, abandon it and strike off on your own. Such lists are generally more useful for getting started than for leading you to conclusions.

Be wary also of lists of questions not designed for students of literature. For example, lists are often based on the journalistic standard: Who? What? Where? When? Why? How? While such lists encourage thoroughness in getting at the facts of a situation, an essay about literature is, of course, far more subtle than a news story. Normally, your readers will be familiar with the facts of the works you are discussing and will not require a review. Thus you will be wise to pass quickly over the Who? What? Where? and When? and concentrate on questions concerned with Why? and How? More often than not, you will begin forming a useful argument only when you begin addressing these last two.

Interaction

If asking and answering questions by yourself seems lonely work, you may prefer to involve others. Approaches vary according to circumstances and temperament.

One common method of generating ideas, sometimes called brainstorming, involves gathering a group together, with tape recorder running or one member taking notes, and throwing out ideas. The exchange is kept as informal as possible to avoid inhibiting creativity. This sort of exercise works better in developing advertising slogans than critical essays, and a lot of what results will be useless, but finding and rejecting inappropriate approaches to a subject will often help you progress toward forming better ones. At least such an exchange of ideas will get you started.

If you lack the informed group required for brainstorming, you can sometimes develop ideas and free yourself from writer's block by talking to a single listener. Even if this person knows little about your subject, his or her responses can help you decide where your views lack clarity or need support. Remember, however, that in the end it should be you who judges and refines the ideas: using another person as a sounding board for your own ideas is not the same thing as allowing another person to tell you what to think. For the sake of honesty and your development as a critical thinker, avoid working with someone whose superior knowledge of your subject may make it hard to rely on your own judgement.

Free Writing

One of the most reliable ways of breaking writer's block is called "free writing." Free writing is a way of freeing yourself from worry about imperfections in expression that can inhibit the flow of ideas early in a project. It involves committing yourself to writing for a predetermined period of time. You simply sit down in a place where you will not be interrupted and, keeping your subject in mind, write until the time is up. Resist pausing for reflection or stopping to revise. At best, you will be well into a rough draft by the time you finish. At worst, what you produce will be only vaguely relevant to your subject, but, even if the written result is of little value, you will still have broken your writer's block and moved closer to understanding what you want to say. You can always begin a second session of free writing by reacting to the shortcomings of your first.

FOCUSING

Once you put your early inhibitions behind you and begin accumulating ideas, you will soon find yourself with more than you can hope to bring together in a paper. This is the time to turn your attention from generating ideas to pruning and focusing. Handling the focusing stage of a writing project well can save you a great deal of time later on, but it takes discipline. Piling up ideas becomes so easy once you get started that it is tempting to carry on too long, deluding yourself that you are accomplishing something when in fact you are rambling out of control. While writing anything is better than writing nothing at the start of the writing process, this does not remain true throughout. Avoid the common mistake of trying to substitute quantity for quality.

You can approach the job of focusing from two general directions — working from a thesis or toward one. If you are lucky, you will discover one particularly interesting line of argument early along. Stating your main ideas as a proposition to be proved — a proposition often referred to as a "thesis" and commonly announced near the beginning of an essay in a sentence termed a "thesis statement" — will provide you with a guide as you write, a premise to refer to as you choose which of your secondary ideas to expand, which to subordinate, and which to cut. If no clear thesis has emerged by the time you are ready to start focusing, you can develop one by grouping the most promising ideas and then pruning obvious loose ends. The more loose ends you cut, the more clearly you will see the best potential lines of argument. By the time you have narrowed the possibilities to two or three, you will not only be in a good position to choose the best, but you will also have developed a general idea of how best to support the one you choose.

Be certain, however, that you do not stop before the job is done. Just as it is important to begin focusing before you are overwhelmed with an unmanageable accumulation of ideas, it is also vital to carry on to the desired end — a single, supportable thesis:

> **Not** "Although Andrew Marvell's 'To His Coy Mistress' is manipulative to some extent in taking advantage of flattery, sophistry, and shocking images of mutability, it sometimes reveals a genuine regard for the object of passion and leaves the reader wondering how fully the object of Marvell's affection — or lust — would be capable of appreciating what is going on in the poem."

> **But** "In 'To His Coy Mistress,' Andrew Marvell is addressing a well-educated woman whose intelligence he respects."

> **Or** "Andrew Marvell's most compelling means of seduction in 'To His Coy Mistress' is neither flattery nor shock, but logic."

The first statement above has more than its share of interesting ideas, but it would likely yield either two or three papers tacked loosely together or, worse still, a muddled blend. Parting with ideas can be hard, but attempting to fit more notions into an essay than you can explain and support adequately will be much harder. Saving a few minutes by rushing the focusing stage can cost you many hours later on.

Outlines

Quite a few writing textbooks advise preparing a detailed outline before attempting the first draft, a practice that is usually less effective for critical arguments than expository essays. In essays devoted mainly to reviewing large amounts of factual information, information that is readily gathered and organized in advance of writing, a detailed outline will prove an invaluable tool, one that can greatly speed the process of writing and revision. In more speculative essays, however, the kind of essays commonly written about literature, the difficulty of deciding what you are going to say, and in what order, without a certain amount of groping on paper will often make a detailed outline harder to produce than a draft.

Therefore, using outlines for essays on literature requires flexibility. If planning is one of your strengths, beginning your writing with an outline will definitely speed the work that follows. But if you find preparing outlines more difficult than diving in and writing a draft without one, you will be wise not to spend too much time struggling to follow advice that is more appropriate for some types of writers and for some types of writing than others. Do what works for you.

Tree-Diagramming

If you like working from an outline yet find outlines difficult to organize while you are still generating ideas, try "tree-diagramming," a method that can help you form an outline in something the same way free writing helps you progress toward a first draft. Place a word or phrase representing your central idea in the middle of a large sheet of paper and work outward, connecting related ideas through a series of branches. Though the result of this exercise will rarely resemble a tree, it will provide you with an overview of relationships, revealing both dead ends and useful lines of inquiry quickly. (See Figures 1 and 2.)

WRITING AND REVISING

If you start early and use your time efficiently, you should have developed and focused your ideas several days before your essay is due. At this point, you will have at least a general idea of how your essay will be organized to support your thesis, and you will probably have done some drafting. The next step, completing your first draft, should be fairly straightforward if you resist the temptation to stop and polish style.

Once you have a completed draft that makes sense and includes all your main points, distance yourself from what you have written by leaving it alone

Figure 1   Writer's Block: First Tree Diagram

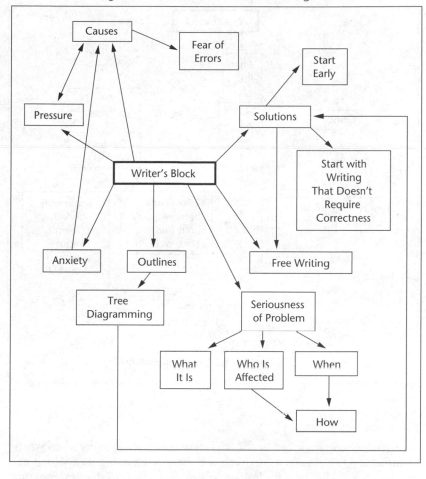

for a day or two. Then, coming back to the project relatively fresh, you will be able to decide more quickly and reliably whether what you have written needs cutting, expansion, or restructuring. After you are satisfied with the form and the essential content, it will be time for polishing style and fine-tuning your argument.

Remember: an essay you write over a week or ten days will almost always be better than one you produce in a single marathon effort, even though you invest the same number of hours in total.

Audience

As you revise your essay, you will have two main concerns — making your argument clear and forceful, and maintaining one consistent appropriate

Figure 2   Writer's Block: Second Tree Diagram

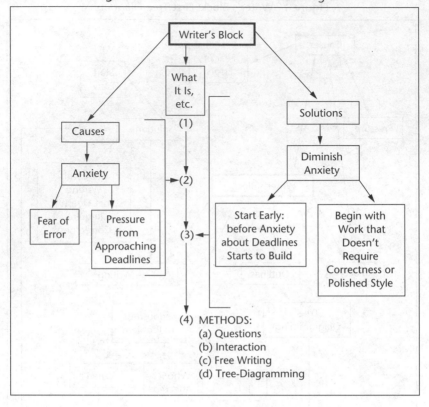

style throughout. Style can be the trickier of the two, especially when you try to affect it. Do not assume an overly sophisticated, erudite style which may not be appropriate even for literary critics. You will find that an unnatural style will be very difficult to maintain for an entire essay. A much easier and more reliable approach is to let your audience and your relationship with it control your style automatically, as they would your voice if you were speaking.

What audience do you write for? The answer is less obvious than you might think. While you probably want most to impress the instructor who will eventually give your work a grade, you may well find that writing with another audience in mind makes this easier. Consider the unnaturalness of explicating literature for someone who knows a great deal more about it than you and who has probably encountered views similar to yours many times before. Will this situation inspire you with confidence? Or is it more likely to make you adopt an apologetic tone and be slightly dismissive about your ideas? How do you feel about writing for someone who can be expected to note technical errors and lower your grade in consequence? Will this audience encourage a confident, forceful style? Hardly.

It makes more sense to write for an audience you can persuade and enlighten, one at about your own level of ability. An audience made up of the better students in your class is a sensible choice. You know this audience well, you can assume it will be familiar with the works you are considering, and you can be confident that it will find your insights fresh and interesting. Writing for an audience of equals will also make it easier for you to adopt a natural, unpretentious style — your own.

In addition to helping you find an appropriate style, writing for an audience of equals will also help you decide what needs to be explained and what does not. For example, since your audience has read and understood the surface meaning of the works you are writing about, you will not need to summarize plot or review other obvious facts. When you need to make specific references to plot or character in support of your developing argument, you will keep these references brief — reminders, rather than revelations. On the other hand, you cannot assume that your audience has seen reasoning similar to yours before, and you should therefore make your line of thinking and the connections between evidence and the conclusions you draw from it more explicit than you might if you were writing exclusively for your instructor.

Openings

Inexperienced writers often get into trouble by working on the assumption that the parts of an essay should be finished one at a time from first to last. This assumption is wrong on two counts. First, if you have the time, it is almost always easier to improve all the parts of an essay at about the same rate as you work through a series of drafts. Second, when lack of time makes a series of drafts impossible and you have to finish sections in sequence, it is usually easier to write the rest of the essay before you put the finishing touches on the opening.

If you are like most student writers, you have more difficulty with openings than with any other part of your essays. Your opening paragraphs may be wordy, vague, and repetitive, even though they receive more attention line for line than other sections. The problem is poor timing. While good essays generally require several drafts, inexperienced writers working under pressure hope to arrive at a final version in as few drafts as possible. In this hope, they attempt to produce a final, polished version when they have only an incomplete or very rough draft to revise, and they naturally start with the opening, struggling to introduce what they will say before they are sure of precisely what this will be. The time-consuming tinkering with wording and groping for ideas that ensue can take more time than revising the whole essay less meticulously. Even worse, having put so much effort into the opening, they are reluctant to make necessary changes once they finish the rest of the essay. The result: a vague, inflated introduction followed by a hastily composed argument that had to be dashed off because of all the time wasted in introducing it. There is nothing wrong with including an opening paragraph containing a clear thesis statement in your first draft; in fact it helps to keep your argument on topic. But, having done that, you will usually find it easiest to leave the opening rough until the rest of your essay is polished to its conclusion.

At this point, you will have a much more certain idea of what you want to introduce in the opening, and you will find writing it much easier in consequence.

Keep in mind as you complete your opening that it should actually accomplish something — excite your reader's interest, persuade your reader of the value of your approach, prepare your reader to grasp what follows. You can achieve these aims only when you yourself fully understand where your essay is going.

Revising for Correctness

While your first concerns throughout most of the writing process should be to make sense and express yourself in an appropriate, consistent style, you cannot afford to ignore correctness — following the accepted conventions of grammar, punctuation, and spelling. While correctness cannot in itself guarantee success, carelessness or incompetence in handling basic writing will certainly ensure failure.

Fortunately, whether they believe it or not, most students who are penalized for errors know enough about grammar and punctuation to write correctly. Attitude more than ignorance is the cause. If you tend to make a lot of mistakes, do not let discouragement or frustration exaggerate your weakness. Convincing yourself that you lack the ability to write correctly is simply an excuse for not investing the time and the work required to master correctness. Seriously confronted, the job of revising for correctness will become easier and less time-consuming with practice.

TEN COMMON MISTAKES TO AVOID IN WRITING ABOUT LITERATURE

Occasionally, even when you start early and work conscientiously, you will still get into difficulty in writing an essay about literature. More often than not this stems from one of the common errors below. While being on guard against these mistakes cannot guarantee success, it will greatly increase your chances.

1. Taking On Unrealistically Ambitious Projects
Be realistic in choosing topics. Avoid topics that will take more space, time, specialized knowledge, or research than you can put into them. If you are not sure whether your plans are manageable, check with your instructor.

2. Plagiarizing by Mistake
Be careful not to drift into plagiarism by keeping sloppy records of your research. Record complete information for references immediately upon

(continued)

encountering a source you may want to refer to later. When taking notes, make a clear distinction between recorded information, para-phrases, and quotations.

3. Retaining Irrelevant Material from Early Drafts

If sections of an essay seem loosely connected with each other or with the controlling thesis, try to put the essay in order by supplying clear transitions showing the reader how each part relates to the whole. If you find it difficult to justify a section, cut or shorten it. The ideas that could produce two or three good essays will usually make one bad one.

4. Attempting to Polish Style Too Early

Do not attempt to perfect style while you are still unsure of what you want to say. Be especially wary of polishing openings before you have a clear idea of what will follow.

5. Writing about Yourself Rather than Your Topic

Concentrate on your topic rather than your feelings, doubts, or difficulties as you write. Avoid such redundant insertions as "it seems to me that" and "I think that"; your reader will know you are doing the thinking that goes into your essay without constantly being reminded.

6. Summarizing Plot and Explaining the Obvious

Avoid boring your reader by summarizing what happens in literary works and reviewing obvious facts at length. Assume an audience of intelligent readers familiar with the works you are analyzing and supply only the information this audience will need to evaluate your argument.

Do not be influenced by the summaries provided in various publications termed "notes." These summaries do not constitute serious criticism and should not be imitated.

7. Confusing Verb Tenses

Keep the sequences of verb tenses within long sentences as simple as possible, and avoid shifting tenses unnecessarily. Using the conventional present tense to describe characters, circumstances, and events in literary works will help greatly.

8. Inflating Style

Inflated style is no substitute for good ideas. Impress your readers with the clarity and sense of your thinking rather than the sophistication of your presentation. Strive to write in your own voice; keep your sentence structure as straightforward as you can without being choppy and repetitive;

(continued)

use only those literary terms that you understand. If you work with a thesaurus, use it to find the most accurate and readily understood terms available rather than as a shortcut to pretentiousness and obscurity.

9. Failing to Follow Conventions of Manuscript Form

Follow the accepted conventions for presenting your work on the page and acknowledging sources. It helps to remember that these conventions are not merely decorative; rather, they are an essential code for communicating information efficiently and accurately.

10. Proofreading Inattentively

Proofread when you are rested, preferably after a good night's sleep, rather than immediately after you finish an essay. Proofread in a place free from distractions, and give the job the full attention it requires. The half hour or so you take to proofread an essay properly will often have more effect on the grade than any other half hour of work you invest in the project.

Time is the key factor. To write correctly you must know your limitations and allow yourself time to compensate for them. If you find yourself penalized for errors regularly, understand why. Is it carelessness in the final stages of writing? Or do you lack the background in the basics of writing? If you know what you are doing but make careless mistakes, you need merely improve your proofreading skills and find an appropriate proofreading time, which is to say a time when you will not be too tired to concentrate or likely to be distracted. If your problem is more serious and you are uncertain of what is correct in some cases, budget the extra time you will need to check. Checking your own work is a good way to learn, and you will probably find once you confront the problem of errors that you know more than you think you do. Like most students who are penalized for errors, you probably make the same types of errors again and again, although you handle most elements correctly. Take note of the types of things that go wrong and concentrate on these. Make a checklist of things to watch for. Review the relevant rules as you approach the final stages of writing. Ignorance, in this case, is no excuse: all the information you need about grammar and punctuation can be found easily in writing handbooks, and spelling can, of course, be checked in a dictionary — provided you allow yourself time to do the work.

Once you are satisfied that your own writing is correct, turn your attention to another aspect of your essay that requires care. Most instructors consider the format and accuracy of quotations and references to be just as important as the correctness of your own writing, so check these carefully before submitting your essay. Have you provided all the requirements, such as a title and title page, that are mentioned in the assignment? Are all your quotations recorded exactly? Have you consistently followed the correct format in supplying notes and bibliographical references? Taking care with such details shows that you are serious about your work; allowing even a few mistakes can call the accuracy of all your work into question.

One further word of warning, however: remember that timing is just as important as taking time in correcting your essays. It is as serious a mistake to let your concern with correctness preoccupy you during the earlier stages of writing as it is to neglect correctness later on. Worrying about errors early along will distract you from the important work of forming ideas, and it may also encourage you to adopt an overly cautious style aimed more at avoiding errors than communicating. So leave the job of checking for correctness till the end of your project, and then take it seriously.

*****

While you cannot avoid the basic fact that writing well about literature involves hard work, you can, by following the advice supplied here, avoid wasting the work you do and ensure that your hard work yields the good results it deserves. But be sceptical: this advice is a basis, not a formula, for success. Keep in mind that writing is a personal endeavour and that no one method will work best for every person and every occasion. Treat this and all advice on writing critically, measuring its usefulness against your experience of what works best for you as you continue to grow as a writer.

GLOSSARY OF LITERARY TERMS

accent The stress that makes a syllable more emphatic or prominent in pronunciation than neighbouring syllables.

act A main division of a drama.

action What happens in a drama; the physical activity represented on the stage, but also the mental activity stimulated in a reader or audience.

alliteration The repetition of consonant sounds, particularly at the beginning of words close to one another.

allusion A reference to characters, places, events, or objects from history, religion, mythology, or literature, which the reader is supposed to recognize and connect to the subject of the work in which the allusion appears.

ambiguity The presence of multiple meanings in a word or phrase, whether intentional or accidental.

amphibrach (amphibrachic) A poetic foot of three syllables, only the middle one being accented. See FOOT and Table 1, "The Metrical Feet," in the Introduction to Poetry.

amphimacer (amphimacric) A poetic foot of three syllables, the first and last being accented; also called a cretic. See FOOT and Table 1, "The Metrical Feet," in the Introduction to Poetry.

anapest (anapestic) A poetic foot of three syllables, only the last being accented. See FOOT and Table 1, "The Metrical Feet," in the Introduction to Poetry.

antagonist Any character who opposes another; most often applied to one opposing the main character (the protagonist).

apostrophe An address to an absent or dead person, to an object, or to an abstraction.

archetype A character type, symbol, plot, or theme that appears frequently in works of literature and therefore seems to have universal meaning.

aside Words delivered by one character to another or to the audience, and understood not to be heard by other characters on the stage.

assonance Repetition of similar vowel sounds.

ballad A form of narrative poetry used continuously since medieval times, consisting of four-line stanzas usually alternating iambic tetrameter and iambic trimeter and rhyming *abcb*, often characterized by repetition and repeated refrains. Ballads are usually classed as either popular or literary ballads. Popular ballads were transmitted orally and were frequently intended to be sung; they

446

originated with anonymous authors among the folk, or common people of rural society. Literary ballads are conscious imitations of these popular ballads and are intended to be read or recited, not sung. Because they are often composed by individuals familiar with literary traditions, however, they may employ complex symbolism lacking in the popular ballads.

blank verse Lines of unrhymed iambic pentameter.

blocking The planning of movement on the stage for a production of a drama.

caesura A pause within a poetic line, created by punctuation, by the phrasing of ideas, or by the manipulation of metre.

carpe diem A Latin phrase, meaning "seize the day," often used to describe poems that urge the enjoyment of the moment because time is fleeting.

character A person in a work of literature or one of the *dramatis personae* of a play; also the moral, psychological, and intellectual traits of such a person. A *round* character possesses the complexities, contradictions, and subtle depths of personality associated with actual human beings. A *flat* character, in contrast, seems relatively two dimensional: the character is presented briefly and has little depth of personality. Both kinds may be *dynamic*— a character who changes, for better or worse, during the course of a literary work — or *static*, a character who undergoes no development.

characterization The techniques used to depict the traits of a character in a literary work. See CHARACTER.

chorus In ancient Greek drama, a group of characters who comment in unison upon and sometimes take part in the action of a drama.

classic A work considered to be the best of its class.

classical literature The literature of ancient Greece and Rome.

classicism The application of artistic principles supposedly derived from the classical literatures of Greece and Rome, including formal control, proportion, simplicity, unity, and rationality. Classicism emerged on the Continent and in England among the humanists of the fifteenth and sixteenth centuries. See NEOCLASSICISM.

climax The crucial or high point of tension, understanding, or recognition in a plot and the turning point of the action.

closed couplet See COUPLET.

comedy A literary mode, especially in drama, that ends happily, with the resolution of difficulties, the restoration of fortunes, and the unity of the community, often symbolized by one or more marriages. Comedy can celebrate or satirize the values of a society or individual, but it affirms life through its presentation of good fortune, positive pleasures, meaningful societal values, and individuals as significant parts of society.

complication The problem near the beginning of a story or drama that causes the conflict.

conceit An elaborate or extended comparison, whether simile or metaphor; known as Petrarchan conceits (after Petrarch, the poet who popularized them in his sonnets) when they are conventional, as with the comparison of a lover to a ship, and as metaphysical conceits (after the metaphysical poets of the seventeenth century) when they are elaborate or ingenious comparisons of things not traditionally linked, as with the comparison of separated lovers to a compass.

conflict The opposition of forces within a character, or the struggles either between characters (protagonists) and other characters (antagonists) or between characters and natural or supernatural forces.

connotation The implications of a word; that is, the feelings, ideas, or associations suggested by a word in addition to its denotation, or dictionary meaning.

consonance Repetition of consonants within or at the end of words.

contextual symbol See SYMBOL.

convention A technique or feature included frequently in specific types of literature or in literature from a particular historical period. The Petrarchan conceit is a conventional feature in some Renaissance poetry; the use of heroic couplets is a conventional technique in eighteenth-century poetry.

conventional symbol See SYMBOL.

couplet Two adjacent lines of poetry that rhyme; called a closed couplet when the pair is end-stopped by significant punctuation and contains a complete thought; called a heroic couplet when the rhymed lines are in iambic pentameter.

cretic See AMPHIMACER.

dactyl (dactylic) A poetic foot of three syllables, only the first being accented. See FOOT and Table 1, "The Metrical Feet," in the Introduction to Poetry.

dactylic rhyme See RHYME.

denotation The dictionary meaning of a word, which depends significantly on context, without reference to its implications and associations.

dénouement See RESOLUTION.

deus ex machina Literally, "the god out of the machine"; the descent of a god, represented by an actor lowered to the main level of the stage in a mechanical device, to intercede and conclude an ancient Greek drama; by extension, any contrived and improbable ending.

dialogue The direct presentation of the spoken words of characters in a story or play.

diction The choice of types of words, specific words, and levels of language. Levels may be formal (lofty language such as that used in epics and in the speeches of nobles in Shakespearean drama), informal (the speech and idiom of daily life), or colloquial (the speech and idioms of particular social classes or groups, such as the Cockneys in England).

dimeter A term of poetic measurement indicating a line containing two feet. See FOOT, METRE, and Table 2, "Line Lengths," in the Introduction to Poetry.

double rhyme See RHYME.

dramatic monologue A form of poetry in which a character speaks to a definite but silent listener and thereby reveals his or her own character.

dramatis personae Literally, "the characters of the drama"; a descriptive list of characters prefixed to a drama; see CHARACTER.

dynamic character See CHARACTER.

elegy In classical Greece, a poem on any serious theme that was written in a couplet form known as elegiac metre; since the Renaissance, used to refer to a lyric that laments a death.

end rhyme See RHYME.

end-stopped line A line terminated with a relatively strong pause, usually indicated by the presence of a comma, semicolon, dash, or period; the opposite of enjambment.

enjambment The running over of meaning from one line to another unhindered by punctuation or syntactical pauses; the opposite of an end-stopped line.

epic A long narrative poem recounting in elevated language the deeds of heroes; settings are vast, sometimes extending beyond earth, and episodes may involve the gods or other supernatural beings.

epilogue The concluding, summarizing section of a drama in which all the strands of the plot are drawn together; sometimes the epilogue is an actual addition.

epiphany A religious term meaning a "manifestation" or "showing forth"; western Christianity celebrates the Feast of the Epiphany on January 6 to mark Christ's manifestation of divinity to the Magi; James Joyce applied the term to short fiction to describe the moment when events show forth their meaning, bringing illumination or revelation to a character.

exeunt The plural form of the Latin "*exit*"; literally, "they go out"; a stage direction signalling the exit of all characters in a scene; sometimes expressed as "*exeunt omnes*" ("all go out"); when names or categories follow the term, as in "*exeunt* Lords," only the named group leaves the stage.

exposition The presentation, usually at or near the beginning of a narrative or drama, of necessary background information about characters and situations.

expressionism An early-twentieth-century artistic movement that emphasized the inner world of emotions and thought and projected this inner world through distortions of real-world objects; unlike impressionism, expressionist literature and drama distorts and abstracts the external world, creating works that are symbolic, anti-realistic, and often nightmarish in vision; in prose, stream of consciousness narration is one of its major techniques.

eye rhyme See RHYME.

feminine rhyme See RHYME.

figurative language Language that uses figures of speech (such as metaphors or similes) so that it means more than the simple denotation of the words and, therefore, must be understood in more than a literal way.

flashback An interruption of the chronological sequence of events to present an event that occurred at an earlier time.

flat character See CHARACTER.

foot The basic metrical unit in poetry, consisting of one or more syllables, usually with one stressed or accented; a basic pattern of stressed and unstressed syllables commonly identified by names derived from Greek poetics, the most common being the iamb, the trochee, the dactyl, the anapest, and the spondee. See METRE and Glossary entries for each kind, or see Table 1, "The Metrical Feet," in the Introduction to Poetry for a list.

foreshadowing The presentation of incidents, characters, or objects that hint at important events that will occur later.

free verse Poetry that is free of regular rhythm, rhyme pattern, and verse form; often called *vers libre*.

Freytag's Pyramid A structural diagram, resembling a pyramid in shape, devised by the nineteenth-century German playwright and critic Gustav Freytag to illustrate the rising and falling action of a five-act drama:

3. Climax
2. Rising Action   4. Falling Action
1. Exposition   5. Resolution

genre A classification of literature into separate kinds, such as drama, poetry, and prose fiction; a major literary form that sometimes contains other related forms, which are known as subgenres.

heptameter A term of poetic measurement indicating a line containing seven feet. See FOOT, METRE, and Table 2, "Line Lengths," in the Introduction to Poetry.

heroic couplet See COUPLET.

heroic quatrain See QUATRAIN.

hexameter A term of poetic measurement indicating a line containing six feet. See FOOT, METRE, and Table 2, "Line Lengths," in the Introduction to Poetry.

hyperbole A figure of speech depending on exaggeration, the overstatement of the literal situation, to achieve dramatic or comic effects.

iamb (iambic) A poetic foot of two syllables, the second being accented. See FOOT and Table 1, "The Metrical Feet," in the Introduction to Poetry.

image See IMAGERY.

imagery At its most basic, the verbal creation of images, or pictures, in the imagination; also applied to verbal appeals to any of the senses.

imperfect rhyme See RHYME.

internal rhyme See RHYME.

irony A figure of speech that creates a discrepancy between appearance and reality, expectation and result, or surface meaning and implied meaning; traditionally categorized as verbal irony (a reversal of denotative meaning in which the thing stated is not the thing meant), dramatic irony (in which the discrepancy is between what a character believes or says and the truth possessed by the reader or audience), and situational irony (in which the result of a situation is the reverse of what a character expects).

Italian sonnet See SONNET AND SONNET, PETRARCHAN.

leitmotif A recurring word, phrase, situation, or theme running through a literary work. Also see MOTIF.

line length See Table 2, "Line Lengths," in the Introduction to Poetry for a list; consult this Glossary for descriptions of individual kinds.

lyric A form of poetry that is relatively short and that emphasizes emotions, moods, and thoughts, rather than story.

masculine rhyme See RHYME.

metaphor A figure of speech that makes a comparison by equating things, as in "His heart is a stone."

metaphysical conceit See CONCEIT.

metaphysical poets Seventeenth-century poets who linked physical with metaphysical or spiritual elements in their poetry.

metonymy A figure of speech that substitutes one idea or object for a related one, such as saying "the Crown" when referring to the monarchy or the government.

metre A measure of the feet in a line of poetry, and thus a term expressing the number of feet in a line and the pattern of the predominant feet in that line; the rhythmic pattern of a line. See Table 1, "The Metrical Feet," in the Introduction to Poetry.

Miltonic sonnet See SONNET, MILTONIC.

modernism An artistic movement of the early twentieth century that deliberately broke from the reliance on established forms and insisted that individual consciousness, not something objective or external, was the source of truth; modernist literature may be structurally fragmented; its themes tend to emphasize the philosophy of existentialism, the alienation of the individual, and the despair inherent in modern life.

monometer A term of poetic measurement indicating a line containing one foot. See FOOT, METRE, and Table 2, "Line Lengths," in the Introduction to Poetry.

mood A general emotional atmosphere created by the characters and setting and by the language chosen to present these.

motif An image, character, object, setting, situation, or theme recurring in many works. Also see LEITMOTIF.

motivation The psychological reason behind a character's words or actions.

myth A traditional story embodying ideas or beliefs of a people; also a story setting forth the ideas or beliefs of an individual writer.

narration The recounting, in summarized form, of events and conversations.

narrative poem A poem that tells a story.

narrator The person telling a story, either a fictional character or the implied author of the work; see POINT OF VIEW.

naturalism A literary movement based on philosophical determinism, the belief that the lives of ordinary people are determined by biological, economic, and social factors; naturalists tend to use the techniques of realism in order to present a tragic vision of the fate of individuals crushed by forces they cannot control.

near rhyme See RHYME.

neoclassicism The principles of those writers who emerged with the restoration of Charles II to the throne of England in 1660 and who sought to restore classical restraint in all areas of life. The literature of the Neoclassical Period, which extends until about the 1798 publication of Wordsworth and Coleridge's *Lyrical Ballads*, was highly formal (frequently being based on the heroic couplet), praised reason over emotion, and often used satire and irony to criticize deviations from decorum and propriety. See CLASSICISM.

oblique rhyme See RHYME.

octameter A term of poetic measurement indicating a line containing eight feet. See FOOT, METRE, and Table 2, "Line Lengths," in the Introduction to Poetry.

octave An eight-line stanza in any metre or any rhyme scheme; any eight-line unit of poetry, rhymed or unrhymed; the initial eight lines of a sonnet united by the rhyme scheme.

ode A long, often elaborate, lyric poem that uses a dignified tone and style in treating a lofty or serious theme; regular forms not frequently used in English include the Greek Pindaric ode, which was divided into three repeated types of stanzas (strophe, antistrophe, and epode), each with its own metrical pattern, and the Horatian ode, which retained a single pattern throughout every stanza.

off rhyme See RHYME.

onomatopoeia Words that imitate the sounds that they describe.

oxymoron An ironic figure of speech containing an overt contradiction, as in the word *oxymoron* itself, which means "sharp stupidity" in Greek, or in such phrases as "fearful joy" or "paper coin"; see IRONY and PARADOX.

paradox An apparent contradiction that, upon deeper analysis, contains a degree of truth.

parody A humorous imitation that mocks a given literary work by exaggerating or distorting some of its salient features.

pentameter A term of poetic measurement indicating a line containing five feet. See FOOT, METRE, and Table 2, "Line Lengths," in the Introduction to Poetry.

persona Literally, the mask; the speaking personality through which the author delivers the words in a poem or other literary work; the fictional "I" who acts as the actual author's mouthpiece in a literary work.

personification The attribution of human traits to inanimate objects or abstract concepts.

Petrarchan conceit See CONCEIT.

Petrarchan sonnet See SONNET and SONNET, PETRARCHAN.

plot The arrangement of actions in a drama or story, often in a sequence according to cause and effect.

point of view The angle of vision or perspective from which a story is told. The point of view may be first person (in which the narrator is a character within the story), third person (a character or an implied author outside the story), or, very rarely, second person (in which the narrator, as in "choose-your-adventure" books, addresses the reader as "you"). Narrative point of view also involves questions of knowledge and reliability. Narrators may be omniscient, knowing both external events and internal thoughts and motivations, or they may be limited to some degree, knowing only some external details. Reliable narrators (a category that includes omniscient narrators) tell the truth completely. Unreliable narrators have personal limitations, such as youth or lack of education, that make them misunderstand what they narrate.

prologue The preface or introduction to a play, often containing a plot summary.

protagonist The main character of a drama or story.

pyrrhic A poetic foot of two syllables, neither of which is accented. See FOOT and Table 1, "The Metrical Feet," in the Introduction to Poetry.

quatrain A four-line stanza in any metre or any rhyme scheme, except the heroic quatrain, which is in iambic pentameter and rhymes *abab*; any four-line unit of poetry, rhymed or unrhymed; four lines of a sonnet united by the rhyme scheme.

quintet A five-line stanza in any metre or any rhyme scheme; any five-line unit of poetry, rhymed or unrhymed.

realism The attempt to represent accurately the actual world; a literary movement that developed in reaction to the artificialities of romantic literature and melodramatic drama and that tended to focus on the lives of ordinary people, to use the language of daily speech, and to develop themes that offered social criticism and explored the problems of mundane life.

resolution A portion of a story or drama occurring after the climax that reveals the consequences of the plot and resolves conflicts.

rhyme (rime) The repetition of identical or similar final sounds in words, particularly at the end of lines of poetry. Single, or masculine, rhymes repeat only the last syllable of the words; double, or feminine, rhymes (also sometimes called trochaic rhymes) repeat identical sounds in both an accented syllable and the following unaccented syllable; triple, or dactylic, rhymes repeat identical sounds in an accented syllable and the two following unaccented syllables. End rhyme occurs when the rhyming words are at the end of their respective lines; internal rhyme occurs when one or both of the rhyming words are within a line. Most rhyme involves the exact repetition of sounds; near rhyme (also known as slant, off, imperfect, or oblique rhyme) depends upon the approximation, rather than duplication, of sounds: it repeats either the final consonant (but not the preceding vowels) or the vowels (but not the following consonants) of the words. Eye, or sight, rhyme depends on the similar spelling of words, not their pronunciation, as in *gone* and *lone*.

rhythm The flow of stressed and unstressed syllables; the patterned repetition of beats.

rising action The progression of events and development of the conflict of a story or play up to the point of the climax.

romanticism A literary movement that began in England sometime around the 1798 publication of Wordsworth and Coleridge's *Lyrical Ballads* and was a reaction to the restraint and order of neoclassicism. The Romantics praised emotion over reason and celebrated the imagination; their literature used a diction that was less formal and elevated than that of the classicists (see CLASSICISM), employed themes based on the supernatural, nature and nature's influence on human beings, and the power of the liberated imagination. "Romantic" and "romanticism" are applied to works that exhibit emotional and imaginative exuberance or that use such themes, whether or not written during the Romantic period.

round character See CHARACTER.

satire A literary form that uses wit and humour to ridicule persons, things, and ideas, frequently with the declared purpose of effecting a reformation of vices or follies.

scansion The analysis and marking of the metres and feet in a poem; see METRE and FOOT; see also Table 1, "The Metrical Feet," and Table 2, "Line Lengths," in the Introduction to Poetry.

septet A seven-line stanza in any metre or any rhyme scheme; any seven-line unit of poetry, rhymed or unrhymed.

sestet A six-line stanza in any metre or any rhyme scheme; any six-line unit of poetry, rhymed or unrhymed; the final six lines of a Petrarchan sonnet, which are united by the rhyme scheme.

setting Emotional, physical, temporal, and cultural context in which the action of the story or play takes place.

Shakespearean sonnet See SONNET and SONNET, ENGLISH.

sight rhyme See RHYME.

simile A figure of speech making a direct comparison between things by using *like* or *as* or similar words, as in "His heart is like a stone."

single rhyme See RHYME.

slant rhyme See RHYME.

soliloquy The thoughts and impulses of a character, voiced aloud on stage and shared with the audience.

sonnet A lyric form of fourteen lines, traditionally of iambic pentameter and following one of several established rhyme schemes; see SONNET, ENGLISH; SONNET, MILTONIC; SONNET, PETRARCHAN.

sonnet, English Also called the Shakespearean sonnet; a sonnet consisting of three quatrains and a couplet, rhyming *abab cdcd efef gg*; when the quatrains employ linked rhyme (*abab bcbc cdcd ee*), known as the Spenserian sonnet.

sonnet, Miltonic A variation of the Petrarchan sonnet that eliminates the pause at the end of the octave; thus, the *volta*, when it occurs, usually appears in the middle of the ninth line.

sonnet, Petrarchan Also called the Italian sonnet: the first eight lines (the octave) state a problem, and the final six lines (the sestet) frequently begin with a *volta*, or turn, such as *but*, *yet*, or *however*, and resolve or comment on the problem; originally limited to five rhymes, with the rhyme scheme of the octave usually being *abba abba* (thus dividing into two quatrains), and the rhyme scheme of the sestet varying, but generally being either *cde cde* (thus dividing into two tercets, or three-line units) or *cdcdcd*.

Spenserian sonnet See SONNET, ENGLISH.

spondee (spondaic) A poetic foot of two syllables, both of which are accented. See FOOT and Table 1, "The Metrical Feet," in the Introduction to Poetry.

stanza A division of a poem into a group of lines; traditionally, a grouping of lines according to rhyme scheme, number of lines, or metrical pattern that frequently is repeated in each stanza; a unit of two or more lines that are grouped together visually in any poem by being separated from preceding and following lines. See Table 3, "Names of Stanzas and Line Groupings," and Table 4, "Notable Fixed and Complex Forms," in the Introduction to Poetry.

static character See CHARACTER.

stream of consciousness A narrative presenting the flow of thoughts and emotions of a character.

structure The arrangement of elements within a work; the organization of and relationship between parts of a work; the plan, design, or form of a work.

style A writer's selection and arrangement of words.

suspense The anxiety created by a situation in which the outcome is uncertain.

symbol A figure of speech that links a person, place, object, or action to a meaning that is not necessarily inherent in it; a word so charged with implication that it means itself and also suggests additional meanings, which are the product of convention (the culture traditionally associates a particular image with a particular meaning) or of context (the placement of the image in a work and the details and emphases within that work add suggestiveness to the image, making it symbolic).

synecdoche A figure of speech in which a part stands for the whole or the whole stands for the part, as when the term "hands" signifies "sailors."

tercet A three-line stanza in any metre or any rhyme scheme, but usually called a triplet when all three lines rhyme; any three-line unit of poetry, rhymed or unrhymed; three lines united by the rhyme scheme in the sestet of a Petrarchan sonnet.

tetrameter A term of poetic measurement indicating a line containing four feet. See FOOT, METRE, and Table 2, "Line Lengths," in the Introduction to Poetry.

theme The central idea or meaning of a work; a generalization, or statement of underlying ideas, suggested by the concrete details of language, character, setting, and action in a work.

tone The speaker's attitude toward the subject matter or audience, as revealed by the choice of language and the rhythms of speech.

tragedy A literary work, especially a drama, presenting the failure and downfall of a character. Tragedy is a serious form demonstrating moral choice, error of judgement, and, in many cases, heroic death, as well as the enlightened understanding resulting from such considerations. Tragedy tends to deal with right and wrong, life and death, and the remorselessness of the universe in relationship to the puniness of human beings.

trimeter A term of poetic measurement indicating a line containing three feet. See FOOT, METRE, and Table 2, "Line Lengths," in the Introduction to Poetry.

triple rhyme See RHYME.

triplet A tercet; usually applied to one in which all three lines rhyme.

trochaic rhyme See RHYME.

trochee (trochaic) A poetic foot of two syllables, the first being accented. See FOOT and Table 1, "The Metrical Feet," in the Introduction to Poetry.

understatement A figure of speech, the opposite of exaggeration, that intensifies meaning ironically by deliberately minimizing, or underemphasizing, the importance of ideas, emotions, and situations.

unity The cohesiveness of a literary work in which all the parts and elements harmonize.

vers libre See FREE VERSE.

volta The turn of thought in a poem, especially after the octave of a Petrarchan sonnet.

zeugma A device in which one word is grammatically linked to two words (usually a verb to two objects or two subjects), with the linkage being logically appropriate in a different way for each word, as in Pope's "Or stain her honour, or her new Brocade."

CREDITS

Anonymous Medieval Lyrics "Western Wind" from *Early English Lyrics*, 1967, published by October House.

Anonymous Medieval Popular Ballads "Sir Patrick Spens" from *The Oxford Book of Ballads*, edited by Arthur Quiller-Couch (London: Oxford University Press, 1910).

Arnold, Matthew "Dover Beach" from *Arnold: Poetical Works*, edited by C.B. Tinker and H.F. Lowry (Oxford: Oxford University Press, 1950).

Atwood, Margaret "Progressive Insanities of a Pioneer," "The Animals in That Country," "Further Arrivals," "Variations on the Word *Love*," and "A Women's Issue" from *Selected Poems 1966–1984*. Copyright © 1990 by Margaret Atwood. Reprinted with the permission of Oxford University Press Canada. "you fit into me" from *Power Politics*, copyright © 1996 by Margaret Atwood. Reprinted by permission of House of Anansi Press. "Siren Song" from *You Are Happy* (Toronto: Oxford University Press, 1974). Reprinted with the permission of Oxford University Press Canada. "Helen of Troy Does Counter Dancing" from *Morning in the Burned House*.

Auden, W.H. "The Unknown Citizen," "In Memory of W.B. Yeats" and "Musée des Beaux Arts" from *Collected Poems of W.H. Auden*, edited by Edward Mendelson (London: Faber and Faber, 1976). Reprinted by permission of Faber and Faber Limited.

Birney, Earle "Vancouver Lights," "Anglosaxon Street," "Bushed," and "The Bear on the Delhi Road" from *Collected Poems of Earle Birney*. Used by permission of the Canadian Publishers, McClelland & Stewart, Toronto.

Blake, William Songs of Innocence: "The Lamb," "The Little Black Boy," "The Chimney Sweeper (1789)," "Holy Thursday (1789)," and "Nurse's Song (1789)"; and Songs of Experience: "The Tyger," "The Chimney Sweeper (1794)," "Holy Thursday (1794)," "Nurse's Song (1794)," "The Sick Rose," and "London" from *The Complete Poetry and Prose of William Blake*, revised edition, edited by David V. Erdman (New York: Doubleday, 1962).

Bradstreet, Anne "To my Dear and loving Husband," and "Upon the burning of our house, July 10, 1666" from *Poems of Anne Bradstreet*, edited by Robert Hutchinson (New York: Dover Publications, 1969).

Brand, Dionne "Blues Spiritual for Mammy Prater" copyright © 1990 by Dionne Brand from *No Language Is Neutral*. Reprinted by permission of Coach House Press.

Browning, Elizabeth Barrett "*From* Sonnets from the Portuguese: XLIII (How do I love thee?)," "Hiram Powers's Greek Slave," and "A Musical Instrument" from *The Complete Works of Elizabeth Barrett Browning* (New York: T.Y. Crowell, 1900).

Browning, Robert "My Last Duchess," "The Bishop Orders His Tomb at Saint Praxed's Church," and "'Childe Roland to the Dark Tower Came'" from *Robert Browning: The Poems, vol. 1*, edited by J. Pettigrew (New Haven: Yale University Press, 1981).

Byron, George Gordon, Lord "She Walks in Beauty" and "On This Day I Complete My Thirty-Sixth Year" from *The Poetical Works of Byron*, edited by Robert F. Gleckner (Boston: Houghton Mifflin, 1975).

Clarke, George Elliot "Salvation Army Blues" from *Lush Dreams, Blue Exile: Fugitive Poems, 1978–1993* (Lawrencetown Beach, NS: Pottersfield Press, 1994). "Blank Sonnet" from *Whylah Falls* (Vancouver, BC: Polestar Book Publishers, 1990).

Cohen, Leonard "A Kite Is a Victim," "For E.J.P.," "Suzanne Takes You Down," and "Closing Time" from *Stranger Music: Selected Poems and Songs* (Toronto: McClelland & Stewart, 1993). Used by permission of the Canadian Publishers, McClelland & Stewart, Toronto. "A Kite Is a Victim" originally published in *The Spice-Box of Earth*, 1961.

Coleridge, Samuel Taylor "Kubla Khan" and "The Rime of the Ancient Mariner" from *Coleridge: The Complete Poetical Works, Volume 1*, edited by Ernest Hartley Coleridge (Oxford: Oxford University Press, 1912).

Crawford, Robert "Anne of Green Gables" and "Mary Shelley on the Broughty Ferry Beach" from *Talkies* (London: Chatto and Windus, 1992). Used by permission of The Random House Group Limited.

Cummings, E.E. "in Just- spring" copyright 1923, 1951, © 1991 by the Trustees for the E.E. Cummings Trust. Copyright © 1976 by George James Firmage. "next to of course god america i" copyright 1926, 1954, © 1991 by the Trustees for the E.E. Cummings Trust. Copyright © 1985 by George James Firmage from *Complete Poems: 1904–1962*, edited by George J. Firmage. Reprinted by permission of Liveright Publishing Corporation. "1(a" Copyright © 1958, 1986, 1991 by the Trustees for the E.E. Cummings Trust.

Dawe, Tom "The Bear" from *Hemlock Cove and After* (Portugal Cove, NF: Breakwater Books, 1975). Reprinted with the permission of Breakwater Books, St. John's. "The Naked Man" from *Island Spell* (St. John's, NF: Harry Cuff Publications, 1981). Reprinted by permission of the author.

Dickinson, Emily "I'm Nobody! Who are you?," "The Soul selects her own Society —," "A Bird came down the Walk —," "I heard a Fly buzz — when I died —" and "I started Early — Took my Dog —" from *The Poems of Emily Dickinson*, edited by Thomas H. Johnson. (Cambridge, MA: The Belknap Press of Harvard University Press, Copyright © 1951, 1955, 1979, 1983 by the President and Fellows of Harvard College.) Reprinted by permission of the publishers and the Trustees of Amherst College.

Donne, John "Song (Go, and catch a falling star)," "The Bait," "A Valediction: Forbidding Mourning," "The Canonization," "The Flea," "Holy Sonnet X (Death be not proud)," and "Holy Sonnet XIV (Batter my heart)" from *John Donne: The Complete English Poems*, edited by A.J. Smith (Harmondsworth: Penguin, 1971).

Dumont, Marilyn "Letter to Sir John A. Macdonald" and "The Devil's Language" from *A Really Good Brown Girl* (London, ON: Brick Books, 1996).

Eliot, T.S. "The Love Song of J. Alfred Prufrock," "The Hollow Men," and "Journey of the Magi" from *Collected Poems 1909–1962* (London: Faber and Faber, 1964). Reprinted by permission of Faber and Faber Limited.

Frost, Robert "After Apple-Picking," "An Old Man's Winter Night," "Stopping by Woods on a Snowy Evening," "Acquainted with the Night," and "Design" from *The Poetry*

(London: Faber and Faber, 1971). Republished in *Collected Poems*, edited by Ted Hughes (London and Boston: Faber and Faber, 1981).

Pope, Alexander   "The Rape of the Lock; An Heroi-Comical Poem" from *The Rape of the Lock and Other Poems*, edited by Geoffrey Tillotson (London: Methuen, 1962).

Pound, Ezra   "The River-Merchant's Wife: A Letter," "In a Station of the Metro," and "Ancient Music" from *Personae*. Copyright © 1926 by Ezra Pound. Reprinted by permission of New Directions Publishing Corporation.

Pratt, E.J.   "The Shark," "From Stone to Steel," and "The Truant" from *E.J. Pratt: Complete Poems*, edited by Sandra Djwa and R.G. Moyles. Copyright © 1989 by University of Toronto Press. Reprinted by permission of University of Toronto Press Incorporated.

Purdy, Al   "The Country North of Belleville," "Lament for the Dorsets," and "Wilderness Gothic" from *Being Alive: Poems 1958–1978*, McClelland & Stewart, Toronto. "Trees at the Arctic Circle" from *North of Summer: Poems from Baffin Island* (Toronto: McClelland & Stewart, 1967). Reprinted by permission.

Rich, Adrienne   "Aunt Jennifer's Tigers" and "Diving into the Wreck" from *The Fact of a Doorframe: Poems Selected and New, 1950–1984*. Copyright © 1984. Copyright © 1975, 1978 by W.W. Norton & Company, Inc. Copyright © 1981 by Adrienne Rich. "What Kind of Times Are These" and "In Those Years" from *Dark Fields of the Republic: Poems 1991–1995*. Copyright © 1995 by Adrienne Rich. Reprinted by permission of W.W. Norton & Company, Inc.

Roberts, Sir Charles G.D.   "Tantramar Revisited," "The Potato Harvest," "The Winter Fields," and "The Herring Weir" from *The Collected Poems of Sir Charles G.D. Roberts* (Wolfville, NS: The Wombat Press, 1985). Copyright © by Mary Pacey and Lady Joan Roberts. Reprinted by permission of The Wombat Press.

Roethke, Theodore   "Root Cellar" by Theodore Roethke first appeared in *Poetry*, copyright © 1943. Reprinted by permission of Doubleday Broadway Publishing Group. "My Papa's Waltz" from *The Collected Poems of Theodore Roethke*, copyright 1942 by Hearst Magazines, Inc. Reprinted by permission of Doubleday Broadway Publishing Group. "The Waking" from *The Waking Poems: 1933–53* (New York: Doubleday, 1954). Used by permission of Doubleday, a division of Bantam Doubleday Dell Publishing Group, Inc.

Rossetti, Christina   "Song (When I am dead)," "The World," and "Goblin Market" from *The Poetical Works of Christina Georgina Rossetti*, edited by William Michael Rossetti (London: Macmillan, 1908).

Scott, Duncan Campbell   "The Forsaken" and "Night Hymns on Lake Nipigon" from *The Poems of Duncan Campbell Scott* (Toronto: McClelland & Stewart, 1926). Used by permission of John G. Aylen, Ottawa, Canada.

Scott, F.R.   "The Canadian Authors Meet," "Trans Canada," "Laurentian Shield," and "For Bryan Priestman" from *The Collected Poems of F.R. Scott*, edited by John Newlove. Reprinted with the permission of William Toye, Literary Executor for the Estate of F.R. Scott.

Shelley, Percy Bysshe   "Ozymandias," "Ode to the West Wind," and "To a Skylark" from *The Poetical Works of Percy Bysshe Shelley* (London: Macmillan, 1899).

INDEX OF AUTHORS

INDEX OF TITLES
AND FIRST LINES